When the Second Vatican Council issued its Declaration on Religious Liberty, all eyes turned to Spain. Looking toward Spain was natural and right, for only in Spain has the classic Roman plan for the "true" religion been fulfilled.

The long, bizarre history of Spanish Protestantism began, the author explains, in the sixteenth century as a spontaneous response to the waves of Humanism then sweeping the Continent. But heresy could not prevail against an Establishment fixed in the Roman tradition; by the late 1500's the pioneering Erasmists were dead or in exile and the Protestants physically and morally crushed.

Wiped free of Jewry by the work of the Inquisition in the previous century, of *moriscos* in the next, Spanish society became hermetically Catholic. Indeed, after the three great religious persecutions, the Faith became a racial faith like ancient Israel's: above and beyond its spiritual content, Spanish Catholicism conferred *nationhood*.

The political criterion endured. In 1939, at the end of the Civil War, a medieval religious state in fascist trappings came into being. In the eyes of the nascent Church-State, Protestantism stood equated with moral degeneracy and political subversion. As such, all its "external manifestations" were banned. Five thousand native heretics were given a choice between the practice of a "private" religion under the joint control of Madrid and Rome, or prosecution for attempting to dismember the "Catholic unity" of the nation. In spite of jail sentences and fines, of spiritual and emotional torment. the *evangélicos* grew by six hundred per cent in twenty-five years.

Madrid and the Vatican have yet to speak publicly on the resolution of the thorniest religious question in the West. Long before the Ecumenical Council was over, Spain had been called the test case of the Universal Church. Today it is far m⌐ ⌐⌐⌐ that: it is the last—and decisive—crisis ⌐ ⌐⌐d-ern world.

THE THIRTY THOUSAND

THE
THIRTY
THOUSAND

Modern Spain and Protestantism

CARMEN IRIZARRY

Harcourt, Brace & World, Inc., New York

3627

Copyright © 1966 by Carmen Irizarry

First edition

Library of Congress Catalog Card Number: 66-22276

Printed in the United States of America

For
José Cardona
and
Alberto Araujo,
who honor
Spain,
Protestantism
and
Christianity

CARRANZA

All of Spain, your Excellency, is bristling with suspicion and fear; every Spaniard is a voluntary spy, exacerbated, sick with religion. It is difficult to talk of one of the mysteries of the faith without having someone run to the Holy Office in case one of the phrases might have been heretical. Spain is like a fortress under siege where everyone is fearful lest he drop the password before the enemy.

ZUÑIGA

That is so, Fray Bartolomé; it is just as you have said. Spain is the City of God, and she is surrounded by a thousand dangers and ambushes; many attackers are indeed trying to discover the password so they may lower the drawbridge.

—Joaquín Calvo Sotelo, *The Process of Archbishop Carranza* (1964)

CONTENTS

CONTENTS

LIST OF ILLUSTRATIONS

(Between pages 210 and 211)

I

The City of God

1

It began with Erasmus of Rotterdam.

"People will argue," writes historian Marcelino Menéndez Pelayo, "that Erasmus, Ulrich of Hutten, Melanchthon and Joseph Camerarius were Humanists; and I will answer that rather than Humanists they were Germans, or as they were called in Italy, Barbarians." [1]

From Barbarians such as these came the disease of heterodoxy, the "Lutheran leprosy" which spread throughout Spain, when, at the apogee of her power, her domains extended east to America, west to Sicily and Naples, and north to Flanders. Having expanded her frontiers to include a sizable portion of Europe, sixteenth-century Spain was about to see her erudite, classically perfumed faith tainted by heresy from the pragmatic North.

And the man behind the first stirrings of rebellion was none other than Desiderius Erasmus—the Dutch Humanist whose half-smile, at once mocking and wise, was caught forever by Holbein's hand. Menéndez Pelayo's own portrait of the Dutchman is painted in stronger colors. This ethnic Barbarian, he reminds us, "laid the Reformation's egg":

he lived and died a *doctrinaire* Catholic (to use modern phraseology), weak and accommodating, ready to compromise . . . patriarch of

---

[1] Marcelino Menéndez Pelayo, *Historia de los heterodoxos españoles* (Madrid: Biblioteca de Autores Cristianos, 1956), I, 742.

that legion which, since the 16th century, has been parceling out its approval here and there, bent on the senseless mission of reconciling Christ and Satan, of winning over enemies by the dastardly sacrifice of a portion of the truth.[2]

I

In sixteenth-century Spain the "dastardly sacrifice" seemed not only feasible, but indeed convenient. The new, enlightened concept of Christianity embodied in Humanism had found a warm response in the bosom of Spanish society. Erasmus' books circulated throughout the country, passing from hand to hand among clergy and laity alike. "A singular crisis!" exclaims Menéndez Pelayo:

cloistered nuns peruse the *Misoganus* and *Poenitens* colloquies, which would seek to dissuade [people] from entering the religious life; ladies of the Spanish aristocracy take delight in the *Praise of Folly;* the Inquisition, headed by Don Alonso Manrique, forbids all writings against whom?—against Erasmus; the Emperor's secretaries and the Archbishop of Seville are Erasmists, and Erasmists fill the Cathedrals. . . .[3]

Marcel Bataillon, in his monumental study *Erasmo y España,* defines the situation more succinctly. "Erasmus," he writes, "earned in Spain a body of enthusiastic readers of the most cultured class; thereafter his fame went forth from mouth to mouth through certain easily framed formulas on the primacy of love . . . and the excessive burdens and ecclesiastical tyrannies that smother true Christianity." The French historian points out that the *Cortes* which had assembled in Valladolid in 1523 had asked Charles V to strive for peace in his dealings with the Christian princes and wage war only on the infidels. Further, "the *Cortes* were above all concerned with the abuses deriving from the sale of bulls for the Crusade; no less than six articles were devoted to this point among the delegates' petitions." [4]

[2] *Ibid.,* p. 772.
[3] *Ibid.,* p. 803.
[4] Marcel Bataillon, *Erasmo y España: estudios sobre la historia espiritual*

4

THE CITY OF GOD

The intellectual climate was no less promising. If Erasmus was Dutch, Humanism was international, and a vital part of the intellectual life of Spain. Greek and Latin letters flourished in centers of learning across the land. At the University of Alcalá de Henares a team of scholars unsurpassed anywhere in the West had produced the Polyglot Bible. Spanish theologians and scientists opened new paths in the study of God and Man. The country seemed in full command of her resources, eager and unafraid before the winds of change blowing from Germany and Flanders.

But as Bataillon wryly puts it, "Every time that Spain, eager for spiritual renovation, opens herself to foreign influence, this *unconquerable* land delegates one or several of her sons to say 'no' to the invader." [5] In this case the nay-sayer, indeed the proto-defender, was Diego López Zúñiga [5a] (Menéndez Pelayo spells it "Stúñiga"), a scholar from Alcalá. The year 1520 saw the publication of his *Annotationes* against Erasmus' translation of the New Testament: the Spaniard found fault with the Rotterdamer's Hebrew and Latin, denounced his theology, and accused him, among other things, of Arianism. Having fired the first salvo, Zúñiga hurled himself into battle and, in succeeding years, brought out diatribes against the *Enchiridion,* the *Compendium of True Theology, In Praise of Folly,* and several other works of Erasmus.

When Menéndez Pelayo sums up Zúñiga's objections to the Flemish Humanist, it looks like a forecast of the coming storm:

His accusations [against Erasmus] are as one might imagine: that he maligns friars, bishops and clerics; that he calls the Pope the "Vicar of Peter" and not the "Vicar of God"; that he impugns fasting and the celibacy of the clergy; that he applies the words *"Tu es Petrus"* ["Thou art Peter"] to the whole body of the Church and *"Pasce oves meas"* ["Tend my sheep"] to any one bishop ("which tastes of Lutheranism and Wycliffism," adds Zúñiga); that he has little respect for the cult of saints; that he belittles the authority of St. Jerome, etc.

---

del siglo XVI, translated by Antonio Alatorre (Mexico City: Fondo de Cultura Económica, 1950), I, 183.
[5] *Ibid.,* p. 107.
[5a] Not to be confused with Gaspar de Zúñiga, Archbishop of Santiago, the presiding judge at the trial of Archbishop Carranza.

Stúñiga offered this work as a "specimen" of a longer study in which he proposed to show that Erasmus was not only Lutheran, but the prince and head of Lutherans.[6]

In Rome, where Zúñiga lived, another Spaniard took up the cry against Erasmus. He was Sancho Carranza, whose brother Bartolomé was to be one of the most tragic figures in the Spanish Reformation. Erasmus, who had replied to Zúñiga's charges, also answered Carranza's and the latter gave up the debate—"not because Erasmus' arguments could have convinced anybody," says Menéndez Pelayo, "but because [Carranza] held him in sincere esteem." [7] Passing over the first part of this statement, it is well to consider the second. History texts and reference works in English often dwell on the Humanist's correspondence with friends in France, Italy and England, and overlook the warmth and depth of his contacts in Spain. "I've heard it said," Erasmus writes to Juan Vergara in 1527, "that Sancho is now well disposed towards me, having forgotten the old quarrel; if it were so, give him my regards." [8]

An even deeper friendship linked Erasmus to Vergara, a Professor of Philosophy at Alcalá who had been secretary to Cardinal Cisneros, and who later held the same post in the service of Cisneros' successor, Fonseca. The Dutch Humanist, in fact, seems to have known most of the Vergara family; not only did he correspond with Juan—whom he had met in Flanders—but with his brother Francisco, whose proficiency in Greek he greatly admired, and with Bernardino Tovar, identified as a maternal uncle by Menéndez Pelayo, and as a third brother by Bataillon.

By the 1520's Erasmists worked freely within and without the Establishment. Their company included Vergara; Luis Vives in faraway Bruges; Abbot Pedro de Lerma, former Canon at Burgos and Dean of Theology at the University of Paris; the Benedictine Alonso Virués, preacher to Charles V; theologian Luis Núñez Coronel, who had met Vives at the Sorbonne and through him

[6] Menéndez Pelayo, *op. cit.,* I, 783.
[7] *Ibid.,* p. 787.
[8] *Ibid.*

came in contact with Erasmus; Cardinal Fonseca; and Inquisitor Manrique. "It is impossible to understand the strong current of religious liberty which crosses the Spain of Charles V and Philip II," writes Bataillon, "without measuring the Erasmist wave that swept over the country between 1527 and 1533." [9]

With the two greatest Erasmists, Alfonso de Valdés—secretary to the Emperor—and his brother Juan, the abortive Reformation was to begin. But there was no sign of rebellion as yet. What Bataillon calls the "irenic dream" was still alive: Erasmists, as Erasmus himself, saw no conflict between their doctrines and the peace and unity of the Church.

The Church was, of course, of another mind. Members of the religious orders, stung by Erasmus' attacks on the monastic life, had long been clamoring against him. Their cry was taken up by the English Ambassador to Spain, Edward Lee, who, as Menéndez Pelayo points out, "was as much of a theologian as his King Henry VIII and a great enemy of Erasmus." [10] Lee produced an anti-Erasmist tract, read it to the resentful monks, and roused them to action. Soon the Franciscans of Salamanca were airing their charges openly from the pulpit. Though the Dominicans remained divided in their allegiances, one of their number, Pedro de Vitoria, also took up the cry. He called the Dutch Humanist an enemy of the Church and declared that Manrique's order banning all works against Erasmus was unjust and intolerable.

Manrique gave in and ordered the friars to enumerate their charges and submit them for examination. It was Lent, 1527. The monks—from seven different orders, and led by the Franciscans —set to work feverishly. In Bataillon's words, it was "a veritable hunt for the heretical across the works of Erasmus"; so great was the friars' activity that Lenten penitents were turned away from the confessional with the admonition that more important work was at hand. [11]

In March of that year, at a meeting of the monastic orders in Valladolid which coincided with the *Cortes,* the monks submitted

[9] Bataillon, *op. cit.,* I, 365.
[10] Menéndez Pelayo, *op. cit.,* I, 805.
[11] Bataillon, *op. cit.,* I, 276.

their articles to a theological Junta. Erasmus of Rotterdam stood charged on twenty-one counts:

1. That he denied the consubstantiality of the Word, as Arians did.

2. That he denied the divinity of the Son, or at least explained it in an Arian sense.

3. That he had stated that neither in Scripture nor in the Fathers—and especially not in Saint Hilary's *De Trinite*—is the name of God clearly applied to the Holy Ghost.

4. That he had misgivings on the Inquisition and did not sanction the temporal punishment of heretics.

5. That he denied the efficacy of baptism and that he himself was an Anabaptist.

6. That he believed oral confession to be a modern practice, born of secret counsel taken with bishops.

7. That he had erroneous doctrines on the sacrament of the Eucharist.

8. That he attributed priestly authority to the laity and impugned the primacy of the Pope.

9. That he defended divorce.

10. That he attacked the authority of Holy Scripture by describing some of the apostles as ignorant or absent-minded.

11. That he referred to all disputes between Lutherans and Catholics, mockingly, as "scholastic doings."

12. That he spoke of the Fathers, especially St. Jerome, with little respect.

13. That he was irreverent towards the cult of the Virgin Mary.

14. That he belittled the authority of the Pope and of the General Councils of the Church.

15. That he deemed ecclesiastical ceremonies, fasts and abstinences Judaic practices.

16. That he preferred marriage to virginity.

17. That he condemned scholastic theology absolutely.

18. That he thought indulgences, pilgrimages and the veneration of saints, relics and images were useless and vain.

19. That he doubted the Church's right to hold temporal goods.

20. That he had doubts on the doctrine of free will.

21. That he had doubts on the doctrine of hell.[12]

Twenty-nine theologians from the three great universities—Salamanca, Valladolid, Alcalá—began their deliberations immediately. But the debate was so intense that by May they hadn't got beyond the first two articles. The summer dragged on. In the middle of August, pleading the danger presented by an outbreak of the plague in Valladolid, Manrique saw fit to adjourn the Junta indefinitely. After six months' discussion, the theologians hadn't come to a single conclusion.

Erasmists exulted in their equivocal victory and clung to the hope of peaceful reform. But the year 1529 is singled out by Bataillon as "the turning point. Erasmists maneuvered deftly, openly, faithful to their ideal of spiritual renovation without rebellion . . . but the wheel of fortune was turning." [13]

Upon Fonseca's death in 1534, Vergara and Tovar were denounced to the Inquisition; both served long prison sentences before their innocence was established. After the death of Manrique in 1538 anti-Erasmists grew more powerful. Pedro de Lerma fled back to Paris. Vives did not suffer, for he was already at Bruges, far from the Spanish turmoil and safe from his personal furies; but Virués chose to remain in Spain and was subjected to four years of harassment which he spent, in his own words, "doing nothing but denying accusations, declarations, replies, refutations, libels and texts of all kinds in which I was accused of heresy, blasphemy, error, anathema and schism." [14]

The date of this declaration—part of Virués' *Philippicae Disputationes* against Lutheranism—is 1541. The sixteenth century was reaching its halfway mark and Spain was fast approaching that holy vendetta which was to win her forever the title of "Catholic."

Three and a half centuries later, Marcelino Menéndez Pelayo was to look over the period in both horror and disgust. To read

[12] Menéndez Pelayo, *op. cit.*, I, 809–10.
[13] Bataillon, *op. cit.*, I, 423.
[14] Quoted in Menéndez Pelayo, *op. cit.*, I, 826.

his *Historia de los heterodoxos* is to thread one's way through paroxysms of piety woven into the most thorough, exacting and professional labor of historiography that Spanish letters had yet seen. The work, completed in 1882, is a study of *all* religious dissent in the history of Spain. Its range alone is spectacular: it begins with the heresies of the early centuries (Priscillianism, Arianism) and of Visigothic times, goes on to the religious practices of Moors and Jews with their inherent lese majesty in the 1500's; the rise of *alumbrados, moriscos* and *judaizantes* in the seventeenth century; Voltairianism and Jansenism in the eighteenth; and the patchwork of liberalism, Krausism, covert Evangelism and other "subversive" ideologies of the nineteenth.

The original edition of the *Heterodoxos* ran to thirteen volumes. Today the work remains a milestone in Spanish scholarship and, far from being superseded by Bataillon's superior work, is the basic text for any study of the Spanish Reformation. It is also a sad monument to the genius of a man who, like all traditionalists before and after, derives his keenest intellectual *frisson* from submission to the authority of the Teaching Church.

On that sole authority Menéndez Pelayo builds his chronicle of the sixteenth century. For him, as for many Spaniards and like-minded Catholics today, the only Reformation to be countenanced in the Church was a Reformation in *discipline,* not in *dogma.* And this, the historian makes clear, had already been effected by Cardinal Cisneros' strict measures regularizing the internal life and organization of the religious orders.

From a distance of almost one century and many degrees of geographical and intellectual latitude, Bataillon takes Menéndez Pelayo to task for this simplification:

We are treading the wrong path if we are prone to believe that, thanks to [Cisneros], the problems which drowned Europe in blood and fire did not come up in Spain; [or] if we are prone to make Cisneros a mitered, almost crowned Savonarola who did away with all abuses in the Spanish Church and thus robbed the Reformation of its purpose. The concept of the Reformation as a simple rebellion against "abuses" is a poor one indeed.[15]

[15] Bataillon, *op. cit.,* I, 2.

10

It is, unfortunately, the only one admissible in the orthodox camp and the only one that guides the great scholar through the six chapters of the *Historia* that cover this harrowing period.

II

"A land fecund in heretics, illuminati, fanatics and extravagant personages of all kinds, as well as saints and holy men." [16] So reads Menéndez Pelayo's description of Cuenca, whose brooding, medieval capital was the birthplace of Alfonso and Juan de Valdés.

The historian calls Alfonso an "Erasmist" and his brother Juan a "Protestant," but the distinction is academic. Both came early under the influence of Erasmist ideas; both drew strength and inspiration abroad; both left a legacy whose doctrinal and literary merit stands firm to this day.

They were the sons of Don Fernando de Valdés, hereditary *regidor,* or Alderman, of the City of Cuenca. Of Alfonso there is first news in 1520, when he writes to a friend, the Italian Humanist Pietro Martire d'Angheria, during the course of a trip to Flanders and Germany in the Emperor's retinue.

By the early 1520's Alfonso had been appointed Charles' secretary. In this capacity he attended both the imperial coronation at Aix and the Diet of Worms, where Luther was to stand firm in heresy. Menéndez Pelayo underscores the Spaniard's shock at Luther's conduct and quotes him as saying: "How bold are the wicked!" [17] But it is interesting to note how Edward Boehmer, in his *Spanish Reformers of the Two Centuries,* describes Valdés' reaction to the same event:

He saw, in the burning of Luther's books . . . at Worms, "not the end, but the beginning of a tragedy." It then appeared to him as impudent upon the part of the monk of Wittenberg, to declare the Pope

[16] Menéndez Pelayo, *op. cit.,* II, 66. The word "fanatic" is applied almost exclusively to Protestants throughout the book.
[17] Menéndez Pelayo, *op. cit.,* I, 830.

to be a heretic and schismatic; but he nevertheless found it deplorable that the Pope showed repugnance to the convocation of a General Council. . . .[18]

Each writer illumines one half of the struggle which was only beginning in a soul exposed to heresy. For exposure was then, as it still is, the fountainhead of all sin. Like the Erasmists of his time and, to a certain extent, like Carranza a few years later, Alfonso de Valdés was led astray by direct contact with the "tainted" ideas of the spiritual revolution. But while Carranza—the tragic heir of Erasmists' "irenic dream"—died protesting his loyalty to Rome, Alfonso and Juan de Valdés were to go further than any Spaniards yet in formulating a doctrine which veered sharply from the clerical, dogmatic ethos of Catholicism.

Alfonso's first relations with Erasmus (much of their voluminous correspondence is still extant) probably date back to the 1520's; by 1525, Maximilian Transylvanus, Vice-Chancellor at Flanders, congratulates Alfonso for having undertaken "the defense and sponsorship of the Rotterdamer's affairs." [19]

Equally significant was Valdés' contact with the Protestant turmoil that was sweeping Northern Europe. As Charles' secretary, he was present not only at Worms but also at the Diet of Augsburg, directly after which he met with Melanchthon in an effort to conciliate the religious dispute. Menéndez Pelayo labels both men as "weak and accommodating." Boehmer takes another tack:

> The intercourse of these two mild and moderate men was a very friendly one, and with the Sovereign, Valdés successfully set off the conciliatory and reasonable tone of the Protestants, and smoothed the way to a public reading of their Confession in the presence of the Emperor and the powers of the realm.[20]

In effect, Valdés was instrumental in the presentation of the Lutheran articles of faith to an increasingly confused Charles.

[18] Edward Boehmer, *Spanish Reformers of Two Centuries; Their Lives and Writings, According to the Late Benjamin B. Wiffen's Plans and With the Use of His Materials* (Strassburg: Karl Trübner; London, Trübner & Co., 1874), I, 65.

[19] Menéndez Pelayo, *op. cit.,* I, 835.

[20] Boehmer, *op. cit.,* I, 66.

By the time of the Augsburg confession, Alfonso's heterodoxy was a fact: his conscience, in sharp contrast to the Emperor's, had been shaped in the diplomatic give-and-take of his calling. Unlike his brother Juan, whose mystical bent took him deeper into theology, Alfonso's spirituality was born of a political vision in which the Church stood revealed as a temporal power sickened by greed, luxury and authoritarianism. Whatever spell the air of his native Cuenca cast over his spirit, he was to make his name as the most articulate spokesman of Charles' case against Rome.

That case, whose antecedents lay in the complex relations between the Papal States and the Holy Roman Empire, had been climaxed by the formation of the Clementine Alliance in 1526. By virtue of this pact Pope Clement VII had joined forces with Florence, Venice and Milan in an effort to drive the Spaniards from their Italian possessions. Every pious Spanish historian goes out of his way to point out that the differences between Spain and Rome were political, not religious; and Charles' subsequent reconciliation with the Pope and his ultimate loyalty to Catholicism over the Protestant question certainly support this contention. But while hostilities raged imperial prudence was thrown to the winds, and in the 1520's a sullen clamor for the "reform" of the Church rose from Charles' household in a series of letters addressed to the Pontiff and the College of Cardinals.

Boehmer calls them *The Imperial Apologetics Against the Pope,* and cites Latin editions in 1526, 1527 and 1528, one in German in 1529, and one in Spanish in 1604. The letters, drafted and possibly worked over by Valdés, are distinctly subversive in both content and tone. "It goes without saying," Menéndez Pelayo points out, "that to incite the Cardinals to hold a council, if necessary against the Pope's will, was already schismatic and seditious." [21] Not only did Charles so incite the prelates, but his first communication ends on a note of warning:

And if your most reverent paternities should refuse to grant our request, We, *according to our imperial dignity,* shall have recourse to the proper remedies, so that we should not appear remiss before the

[21] Menéndez Pelayo, *op. cit.,* I, 834.

13

glory of Christ, or our own justice, or the health, peace and tranquility of the republic.[22]

The political differences ripened into war, and in February, 1527, Charles' forces, led by the Duke of Bourbon, attacked the Eternal City. There followed seven days of carnage, rape and pillage which were to shock even the battle-scarred burghers of Renaissance Europe. The sack of Rome became grist for the political and theological mills, "and all good people, even in Spain, censured the Emperor's conduct." [23]

Wishing to justify his action, the Emperor's aides gave out word that Rome's destruction had been ordained by Providence. As Menéndez Pelayo puts it:

There was only one way to rationalize the deed, or to make it less hateful, [and that was] to look on the sack of Rome as a just punishment from God for the frivolities, stupidities and vices of the Roman court and of the ecclesiastics.[24]

The idea took hold and prompted Valdés, not the least of its supporters, to write the first serious anti-Roman tract in Spanish history: *The Dialogue of the Things that Happened in Rome,* also known as *The Dialogue of Lactantius and the Archdeacon.* Boehmer lists one English edition of 1590 whose title reads:

The sacke / of Roome, / Exsequuted by the Emperour Charles / armie euen at the Natiutie of this Spanish / kinge Philip, / notablie described in a / Spanish Dialogue, with all the Horrible / accidents of this Sacke, and abhomina- / ble sinnes, superstitions & diseases / of that Cittie, which prouoked / these iust iudgements / of God. Translated latelie into the English / toungue, neuer fitter to bee read nor / deeplier considered, then euen / now at this present / time.

Lactantius, one of the two protagonists, is a gentleman from the Emperor's court who, in the Plaza of Valladolid, comes across an Archdeacon on his way back from Rome in soldier's uniform.

[22] *Ibid.,* pp. 834–35. Italics his.
[23] *Ibid.,* p. 845.
[24] *Ibid.*

They enter St. Francis' Church and there discuss the Roman catastrophe.

Lactantius thinks and talks like Valdés and admires Erasmus; his interlocutor—a finely drawn portrait of the pious pharisee—is a Cathedral dignitary who keeps religious laws to the letter although, as he says with surprising candor, "That other business with women . . . in the end, we're all men and God is merciful." [25]

The *Dialogue* is a review of all Erasmist charges against the Church: lust for power, worldliness, greed, traffic in indulgences, superstitious worship of relics, reliance on food laws, slavish devotion to ritual, etc. Coming as it did in the middle of the Erasmist uproar, it did not go unnoticed by the orthodox. Juan Alemán (or Jean Lallemand), another secretary to the Emperor, promptly denounced Valdés as a Lutheran before the Papal Nuncio, Baldassare Castiglione. The Nuncio in turn asked Charles to collect all copies of the book and have them burned.

Charles, in whose household heresy was becoming a veritable nuisance, stood by Alfonso; he made clear that although he had not read the *Dialogue* he esteemed Valdés as a good Christian. An appeal by Valdés' enemies to Inquisitor Manrique of the

---

[25] *Ibid.*, p. 847. Menéndez Pelayo invites the "curious" reader to consult the *Dialogue* (Alfonso de Valdés, *Diálogo de las cosas ocurridas en Roma* [Madrid: Ediciones de "La lectura," 1928], pp. 139–40) for more of the Archdeacon's thoughts on the subject. The passage he refers to is grimly humorous:

THE ARCHDEACON

Look, sir . . . ; if I were to marry, I should have to live with my wife, be she good or bad, ugly or beautiful, all the days of my life or of hers; but if the [woman] I have does not satisfy me tonight, I shall leave her tomorrow. Besides, if I do not want to take a woman for my own, all the beautiful women in the world are mine, or at least [all those] in the place where I live. You support them and we enjoy them.

LACTANTIUS

But the soul?

THE ARCHDEACON

Let that be, God is merciful. . . .

15

Erasmist persuasion also came to naught. The *Dialogue* was submitted to the scrutiny of the Archbishops of Seville and Santiago and cleared of all charges of heresy, but Castiglione persisted in his attack and as a last and most significant charge declared Valdés to be of Jewish blood.

Barely a year after the publication of the *Dialogue of the Things that Happened in Rome,* the mettlesome secretary was back in the fray with a new book, *The Dialogue of Mercury and Charon,* a work at once more fanciful and bold, full of barbs at the Simon-pure, complacent Christianity of the times. It is written in two parts. One takes place by the Stygian lagoon, the other on a mountain through which the souls of the blessed must pass on their way to heaven. In one passage the god Mercury, surveying the life of Christians, finds that some

put their trust in dresses,[26] others in a variety of foods, others in beads, . . . others in building churches and monasteries . . . others in disciplining themselves, others in fasting . . . and in all of them he found barely a spark of charity. . . . In eating he found them very superstitious; in sinning, expansive and generous. . . .[27]

Among the souls of the damned are a famous preacher, the counsellor to a king, a duke, a bishop, a cardinal, a tyrannical monarch (inspired, says Menéndez Pelayo, by Francis I), a scholastic theologian who juggles outrageous syllogisms, and a monumental hypocrite who "never slept in bed, even when sick; never wore a shirt, walked in his bare feet, disciplined himself three times a week, in more than thirty years never tasted meat." [28]

[26] The phrase probably does not refer to religious habits but to the superstition, common in Spain and Latin America to this day, of wearing a saint's "color" in supplication or thanksgiving. In modern Madrid the stores which supply material for these devotional garments (now worn only by women) are on the periphery of the Plaza Mayor, their windows covered with rectangles of colored cardboard bearing the names of the different mediators: St. Francis, St. Rita, La Paloma (The Virgin of the Dove), Medinaceli (the miracle-working effigy of Jesus), Lourdes, St. Teresa, etc.
[27] Quoted in Menéndez Pelayo, *op. cit.,* I, 885. Menéndez Pelayo attributes the *Dialogue* to Juan de Valdés; modern research has proved it was written by Alfonso.
[28] *Ibid.,* p. 887.

Menéndez Pelayo leaves it up to the reader to decide "if . . . Charles V's secretary was a more or less covert Protestant or a lukewarm Catholic." He himself finds Valdés, "a fanatical Erasmist" who, like Erasmus, "had notions on discipline and even on dogma which were incompatible with orthodoxy . . . and [who] did everything possible to rouse nations against Rome." [29] Alfonso died of the plague in Vienna in 1532, still in the service of his emperor.

The date of Juan de Valdés' birth is not known, and some authorities (notably Usoz, Wiffen and Boehmer) believe he and Alfonso were twins. His early life, like his brother's, is shrouded in obscurity, but it is not unreasonable to assume that he studied at Alcalá. It was Alfonso who put him in contact with Erasmus: in 1528 the Rotterdamer writes Juan encouraging him to continue his studies, and congratulating him for "embellishing his intellect, which was made for virtue, with all manner of ornaments." [30]

None of the nineteenth-century scholars had any knowledge of Juan de Valdés' first book, *The Dialogue of the Christian Doctrine,* discovered by Bataillon in Lisbon's National Library in the 1920's. Lacking this text, Menéndez Pelayo comes to the conclusion that it was in Italy that Valdés first came in contact with Lutheranism and began to work out his heretical teachings. In point of fact, the *Dialogue,* written in Spain around 1529, contains the heart and substance of Juan's "Protestantism."

A study of the book, which Bataillon calls "the first essay of one of the most authentic religious geniuses of the century," [31] sheds much light on Valdés' subsequent move to more tolerant Italy. Its four protagonists—the Archbishop of Granada (through whose mouth Valdés speaks), Antronio, Eusebio and a priest— come together to discuss the basic precepts of Christianity. And the discussion is rife with Erasmism:

ARCHBISHOP: [as for the sin of idolatry] it is necessary to know that there are two kinds: one external, one internal. External idolatry con-

[29] *Ibid.,* p. 859.
[30] *Ibid.,* p. 881.
[31] Bataillon, *op. cit.,* I, 421.

sists in the adoration of a piece of wood, a stone, an animal or some such things; . . . and it proceeds from interior idolatry, which occurs when man, through fear of punishment, or for his own advantage, leaves off external adoration of those things, but, interiorly, places his love and trust upon them.

ANTRONIO: . . . Let us see; what devotions do you think Christian children should be taught when they are old enough to know and understand things?

ARCHBISHOP: . . . it would be well to make them consider the devotion of loving God above all things and their neighbors as themselves, and to make them grow fond and enamored of the law of God, and [to have them] resolve to do good unto others whenever possible, and abstain from harming anybody.[32]

The counsel on "devotions" would have been enough to brand Valdés a heretic in a land where the religious spirit has ever burgeoned amid rite-laden Masses, processions, veneration of relics, coronations of statues, novenas, etc. Although, as Bataillon makes clear, the murmurs against Valdés never ripened into open persecution, the Reformer moved to Italy in 1530 and never again returned to his native land. He settled in Naples, where he produced a number of religious tracts. There too he wrote his secular masterpiece, *The Dialogue of the Language,* on which his Spanish fame, ever clouded by the rigors of censorship, was to rest in years to come.

Menéndez Pelayo calls the *Diálogo de la lengua* a "golden book." In so doing he honors that side of his scholarship which remains unclouded by prejudice: his deep, profoundly Spanish respect for literature. In reading the *Heterodoxos* one is reminded time and again that it is the work of a man nourished in the Latin tradition and rooted in the conviction that Greco-Roman civilization is, and will always be, superior to any "Barbaric" system from the North.[33] But so deep is Menéndez Pelayo's respect for classical letters and learning, that it translates into gallantry when

[32] Juan de Valdés, *Diálogo de la doctrina cristiana, nuevamente compuesto por un religioso* (Madrid: Librería Nacional Y Extranjera, 1929), pp. 28–29, 97.
[33] See Appendix, pp. 349–50.

18

an accomplished heretic is on the carpet: let a wayward soul write clear, graceful Latin, and the Spanish scholar will salute his achievement ungrudgingly. This is the case with Alfonso de Valdés' *Lactantius and the Archdeacon* ("a treasure of the language"), with Vergara's writings (though not with Erasmus', whose style is weighed and found wanting), with Juan de Enzinas' and Servet's.

Had Nebrija not written his *Grammar,* says Menéndez Pelayo, "we would have no qualms in calling the heretic from Cuenca the father of Spanish philology." [34] A study of Valdés' book is enough to warrant this statement. Witty, graceful, laced with delicious *coplas* and aphorisms, it is a triumph both in form and content. Between one verbal thrust and another, the four speakers—Marcio, Valdés, Coriolano and Pacheco—discuss the origins of the Spanish tongue, its phonetics and orthography, declension, syntax, nuance and style.

This "golden book" lay in the deepest obscurity until rescued by the philologist Gregorio Mayáns in 1737. In the late nineteenth century, at the time he produced the *Heterodoxos,* Menéndez Pelayo himself complained of its exclusion from the Biblioteca de Autores Españoles, "nor is there mention of Valdés in any of the histories of our literature." [35] Today the book circulates in an excellent paperbound edition whose blurb unfortunately glosses over the author's heterodoxy in one empty sentence: "A short time later there appeared his first book, the *Dialogue of Christian Doctrine,* which was the cause of his expatriation to Italy." [36]

In Naples, Valdés was soon surrounded by the leading lights of the Italian Reformation. Bernardino Ochino, Pietro Martire Vermiglio, Marcantonio Flaminio and Pietro Carnesecchi were part of the evangelical movement which he joined or, one might say, led. For his most celebrated patroness, the gentlewoman Giulia Gonzaga, he wrote the *Christian Alphabet,* and in succeeding

[34] Menéndez Pelayo, *op. cit.,* I, 899.
[35] *Ibid.,* p. 893.
[36] Juan de Valdés, *Diálogo de la lengua.* 4th ed., Madrid: Espasa-Calpe (Colección Austral, No. 216), 1964.

19

years produced, among other works, a catechism, a commentary on St. Paul's Epistle to the Romans, and the famous *One Hundred and One Considerations on the Christian Life.*

Of the *Alphabet* Menéndez Pelayo remarks, condescendingly, that its doctrine is "not so Lutheran as other works of Valdés, as if his mind was hesitating between truth and error." [37] What is light and darkness to the pious historian (and to his intellectual descendants today) was, of course, nothing of the kind to Valdés: far from wavering between truth and error, the heretic from Cuenca simply envisioned a reformation of the Church from within. In this he stood solidly behind the Erasmists, the Humanists and all the pioneering Christians of the sixteenth century; not until the coming of Pope John XXIII was Catholicism to produce this brand of men again.

Valdés' true position has been admirably fixed by Benjamin Wiffen in the introduction to his 1861 edition of the *Alphabet:*

Nor are some writers, on the other hand, strictly correct in describing him as a Lutheran, and claiming him for a Protestant. Valdés entered less than almost any thoughtful man of his time into the battle of hierarchies. He was less a destroyer of error and evil, than a builder up of truth and goodness. He left not, himself, the profession of the Church of Rome, nor incited others to do so. This was no part of his religion. He looked beyond her ceremonies and pompous ritual. Taking the New Testament for his standard, he fixed his view upon the things signified, not upon the symbols exhibited; being aware, to use his words, "how outward ceremonies breed inward vices," and that the mind inclined to superstition is naturally inclined to persecution. He was more Erasmian than Lutheran.[38]

No one has seen better into this irenic middle way than Bataillon, who has defined Erasmism as "a positive movement of spiritual renovation, an intellectual effort dominated by an idea of piety." [39] The prayers composed by Erasmus and Vives, he states,

[37] Menéndez Pelayo, *op. cit.,* I, 912.
[38] Juan de Valdés, *Alfabeto Christiano. A Faithful Reprint of the Italian of 1546: With Two Modern Translations in Spanish and English.* (London: 1861), pp. xlix–1.
[39] Bataillon, *op. cit.,* I, 396.

"charmed clergymen who were also humanists. Sober, fervent, *impregnated with reason,* ever turned towards renewal of the soul through grace and not through private favor, they were to contribute to the birth of a current of enlightened piety." [40]

How much Valdés contributed to this current can be seen from Bataillon's own exposition of the *Diálogo de la doctrina cristiana:*

Valdés does not feel very happy with the moral code and its catalogue of sins and virtues. If he holds to the venerable rule of the Ten Commandments, he makes it clear that the first comprises all the rest.

Those of the faithful who fast as the Church has ordained will not [fall into] superstitious abuse, and will be persuaded that the principal fast of Christians should be abstinence from sin and vice.

The essential set of the religious life, according to Valdés, is prayer, [but prayer] understood as an act which is essentially private and interior; prayers are not magic formulas calculated to produce a given effect.[41]

The keynote of the three passages is the idea of the First Commandment comprising all the rest: as early as the *Diálogo de la doctrina cristiana* Valdés was feeling his way around the doctrine of justification. In the peace of his Neapolitan exile he was to elaborate his evangelical thought and, with the *Christian Alphabet,* bring it to its purest statement:

And this I believe St. Paul wishes to be understood where he says, that the Law is a schoolmaster or governor who leads and conducts us to Christ, although by means of faith we are justified (Gal. 3:24). Here you perceive the office of the Law. The Gospel executes the same office in those persons who receive it only as law; but in them who receive it as an ambassador or messenger of grace its especial office is to heal the wounds made by the Law, to preach grace, peace, and remission of sins; to calm and pacify the conscience. . . . And thus Christ comes to them compassionate, humble, pacific and full of love and charity, and not terrible and alarming like the Law. In this manner the Law teaches us what we have to do, the Gospel gives us

[40] *Ibid.,* II, 189–90. Italics mine.
[41] *Ibid.,* I, 407, 416, 417.

spirit by which we are enabled to fulfil it. The Law makes the wound, the Gospel heals it, and finally, the Law slays, the Gospel gives life.[42]

In 1541 Valdés died peacefully in Naples, a city where his prayer and discussion meetings had stirred up antagonism, but not persecution. His disciples did not fare so well. When the Inquisition bore down on the small evangelical group some years later, Vermiglio and Ochino (who was an ex-Capuchin) fled to Switzerland. Carnesecchi was beheaded and his body burned.

Today, unknown in his native land save for the *Diálogo de la lengua,* read abroad only by the scholar, Valdés survives in one of the most singular manifestations of mystical Christianity: Quakerism. One hundred years before George Fox, the Spaniard Juan de Valdés thought, wrote and lived as a Quaker. His prefiguration of this religious movement, one of the most remarkable aspects of his spiritual insight, was first detected by Boehmer.[43] Menéndez Pelayo underlines it sourly, noting, on the subject of the *One Hundred and One Considerations,* that

private fanaticism [and] individual inspiration similar to the Quakers' [are] the soul of the entire book, and emanate from the very first page.[44]

If Quakerism is indeed the "middle way" between Catholicism and Protestantism, it began with this Spanish exile in Naples. A theologian willing to uncover one more meeting ground between the two faiths might well look into the peculiarly Quaker characteristics of Spanish mysticism, from the rise of the *alumbrados,* through the doctrine of that prince among saints, John of the Cross, to the survival of Friends-type worship among Spain's Fundamentalist *evangélicos* today. Given a modicum of good will and the proper tools, he might have no choice but to document the fact that Quakerism, far from being a movement for and by Anglo-Saxons, is one more chapter in the continuum of the Universal Church.

[42] Juan de Valdés, *op. cit.,* pp. 33–34.
[43] Boehmer, *op. cit.,* I, 45.
[44] Menéndez Pelayo, *op. cit.,* I, 921.

2

During the first three decades of the sixteenth century, Humanism and Erasmism shared their rebellious progress with a small but significant dose of openly Lutheran ideas. In 1519 the printer Johann Froben of Basel (from whose shop was to come Erasmus' reply to the charges leveled at Valladolid), sent Spanish readers a Latin translation of several works of Luther, followed by another of Luther's answers to Erasmus in the matter of free will.[1] In 1521 Pope Leo X asked the rulers of Castile to be on the lookout for Lutheran books; by 1530 Inquisitor Manrique himself had ordered an inspection of all libraries with a view to confiscating heretical works.[2]

The extent to which Lutheran tracts circulated in Spain is evident from a communication sent to the Infante Don Fernando, Charles V's brother, by his retainer at the Emperor's court. This letter, written in Burgos in 1524, informs the prince:

Your Highness will know that from Flanders came a ship laden with merchandise for Valencia, and that besides this merchandise, it carried two *toneles* of Lutheran books; the ship was captured by the French and, after it had been recovered by ours and brought to San

[1] Thomas McCrie, *Historia de la Reforma en España en el siglo XVI*, translated by Adam F. Sosa (2d. ed.; Buenos Aires: Editorial La Aurora; Mexico City: Casa Unida de Publicaciones, 1950), p. 79.
[2] Menéndez Pelayo, *op. cit.*, I, 1045.

Sebastian, while they were making an inventory of its cargo, the books were found: which [books] were taken to the plaza and burned: but some books could not be taken, and [much] effort is being exerted in their recovery.[3]

The seed of Protestantism planted by such works was not to bloom until the legacy of Humanism had run afoul of the ortho-dox *Weltanschauung* and the Erasmists had been silenced. When it did bear fruit, Spanish Lutheranism, nourished by the intellectual and spiritual advances of the age, became a force so defiant, so stubborn and close-knit that only a machinery as ruthless as the Inquisition could wipe it from the face of the land.

A brief study of religious persecution in the Spain of Philip II must necessarily telescope the historical process and content itself with names, places and dates. In the interest of clarity it must also follow, wherever possible, Menéndez Pelayo's admirable schema of the age. Save for the transposition of Seville and Castile, the three sections of this chapter do so. Their sources also include Bataillon, whose study overlaps the Spanish historian's in many facets of the post-Erasmist scene, and a third book, on which a word of introduction is not amiss.

The *History of the Progress and Suppression of the Reformation in Spain in the Sixteenth Century* was first published by W. Blackwood in Edinburgh in 1829. It was written by the Reverend Thomas McCrie, a Scotsman who looked on the Inquisition with all the horror of a pious Protestant. Echoing as it does that ghostly white paper that is the Black Legend, the book is unavailable in Spain today; but Menéndez Pelayo knew it, and quotes it on several occasions.

It is salutary to read McCrie against Bataillon: though there is an abyss in scholarship and vision between one author and the other, the same air breathes through the two works. What McCrie denounces with bitterness, Bataillon censures without raising an eyebrow; what the Scot describes in terms of Popish wickedness is exposed by the Frenchman as the essence of all-too-human

[3] *Ibid.*

24

tyranny. As Menéndez Pelayo's own research makes abundantly clear, the line between black history and Black Legend is razor-thin.

I

Sometime in the 1540's there lived in Seville a rich young nobleman named Rodrigo de Valer (also known as Valera) who was frivolous and fond of pleasure until the day when, in Menéndez Pelayo's condescending words, "as if moved by supernatural impulse, he abandoned his old pastimes." [4] At first it looked like another religious conversion along the lines of St. Francis': a youth of pleasure and dissipation, a sudden call, a change of heart. But when young Valer came out of the monastery to which he had retired and began to spout Scripture in the streets of Seville, it was evident that this had not been a retreat *to* the Church, but away from her.

McCrie and other Protestants [5] allege that Valer worked out his doctrine in the quiet of his monastic cell, alone with a copy of the Vulgate Bible; but it is not unreasonable to assume that the seed of evangelism was already in him when he converted. At any rate, he went forth as a lay preacher, set up shop on the busiest street corners of the city, and sought out members of the clergy with whom to engage in lively debates on the nature of the primitive church and the corruption of the religious orders.

The time for airing such things in public was past, and the Inquisition soon called Valer to account. He did not fare badly at the hands of the Holy Office: the Inquisitors declared Rodrigo mad, helped themselves to part of his estate and set him free. And thereupon this "fanatic," clearly a forerunner of the more discreet but equally persecuted pamphlet-passer of modern Spain, went back to the streets.

By 1545 the Inquisition could take no more. It made Valer

[4] *Ibid.,* II, 61.
[5] Notably Cipriano de Valera. Cf. Menéndez Pelayo, *op. cit.,* II, 61.

25

recant, condemned him to wearing the *sambenito*,[6] and gave him a life sentence with the obligation of hearing Mass every Sunday. On the Lord's Day, at the Church of the Saviour, the infighter lived again: "Even there [at Mass] he used to get up and contradict the preacher. . . ." [7] Later he was transferred to a monastery in Sanlúcar de Barrameda, where he remained until his death at approximately age fifty.

Valer's epitaph in Menéndez Pelayo's *Historia* bears transcribing:

The fact that he was an Old Christian, without admixture of Jewish or Moorish blood, had much to do with the leniency of the sentence. He made a few proselytes, among them Dr. Egidio.[8]

With Egidio, whose given name was Juan Gil, we are back in the Erasmist tradition of the intellectual heretic. Unlike Valer, Egidio was from his youth a man of learning, schooled in philosophy and theology and polished at Alcalá de Henares. So great was his reputation as a scholar that, after his graduation from Alcalá in 1537, he was appointed Head Canon of the Cathedral of Seville without recourse to the usual public examination against the other candidates—a move which, Menéndez Pelayo points out, "cost him no little enmity." [9] Thereafter, as even the Spanish historian admits, human rancor and envy, those two great cogs of the Holy Office, paved his way to prison as much as his own boldness.

From his pulpit at the Cathedral, Egidio began to "spread cautiously the seed of the new doctrine in his sermons and even more in secret *conventículos*." [10] In 1550 the Emperor, unaware

[6] The *sambenito* was a pinaforelike garment worn, along with a dunce cap, by all of the Inquisition's victims. Those to be strangled wore *sambenitos* with inverted flames painted on them (to signify their escape from the fire); those to be burned wore the flames right side up, surrounded by painted devils who carried bundles of wood or stoked the fire. (McCrie, *op. cit.*, p. 164.)

[7] Menéndez Pelayo, *op. cit.*, II, 61.

[8] *Ibid.*

[9] *Ibid.*, p. 62.

[10] The Spanish Academy Dictionary defines a *conventículo* as "an illicit and clandestine meeting."

of the trouble the preacher was making in Seville, proposed him for the bishopric of Tortosa. In so doing, Charles unwittingly delivered the doctor's *coup de grâce*. Egidio's antagonists knew that Tortosa was a gem among Spanish bishoprics; upon the Emperor's designation, they rose in a body and denounced the Canon to the Inquisition. The suspect was promptly clapped into the Holy Office prison and the Emperor's appointment went begging.

Once more Charles had put his trust in one of his brightest men; once more the shadow of heresy had fallen across his judgment.

The charges brought against Egidio included his teachings on "justification, the certainty of salvation, human merits, the plurality of mediators, purgatory, oral confession and the worship of images." [11] Not only had he defended Valer at his trial, but "he had been so bold as to urge the removal of a *lignum crucis* from the Cathedral, which [relic] he smashed to pieces, along with an image of the Virgin which St. Ferdinand carried in his campaigns." [12]

In prison Egidio followed the time-honored custom of writing a useless Apology, and asked that both Dr. Constantino and Bartolomé Carranza be allowed to speak on his behalf at the trial. Carranza, whose own spectacular process was to start a few years later, was in Flanders with the Emperor and could not accede to the request; it was agreed that Garci-Arias, a monk of the Order of St. Jerome, from the Monastery of San Isidro, would act in his place and stead. Though he seemed to play no great part in Egidio's trial, it is well to note that there are two schools of thought on Garci-Arias. Menéndez Pelayo finds him despicable; McCrie admits he was a man given to vacillation, overcaution and a tendency to play both sides against the middle, but points to the fact that it was he who introduced Reformed doctrine into San Isidro, where it spread like wildfire.

Egidio's trial did not go well. There is an apocryphal story, disclaimed by Menéndez Pelayo, of his betrayal by Fray Domingo

[11] McCrie, *op. cit.*, p. 98.
[12] Menéndez Pelayo, *op. cit.*, II, 63.

de Soto, a Dominican who had also agreed to undertake his defense. Whatever the truth of this anecdote, Egidio recanted and abjured ten of the "heretical" propositions put before him. Like Carranza, and like the many who were later to confess their guilt at the stake in order to gain the privilege of strangulation, Egidio's spirit crumbled before the might of the Holy Office.

But once again the sentence was lenient: the accused was given a year in jail with the suppression of his priestly duties during that period. He was also excluded from public acts for a decade and forbidden to leave Spain for the rest of his life. Four years after his conviction and shortly before his death, Egidio visited Valladolid's Protestant community and its leader, Dr. Agustín Cazalla. The trip brought him posthumous fame. When the Valladolid Protestants were discovered and it was found that Egidio had consorted with them, his remains were exhumed and burned, his property seized by the Holy Office and, in the *auto de fe* of 1560, his effigy fed to the flames.

Egidio's two partners in heresy had been Dr. Vargas and Constantino Ponce de la Fuente, old classmates from Alcalá de Henares. Constantino, as the latter is known, had early made his mark as a preacher and, having been chosen by Charles V as his personal chaplain, traveled with the imperial court through Germany and Flanders. On his return to Seville he continued to preach with great success and in 1556 he applied for the Head Canonry of the Cathedral, which had become vacant on Egidio's death.

He was elected to the post, though not without some difficulty. The Vicar-General of the Cathedral, one Francisco de Ovando, warned the Canons of a rumor that "Dr. Constantino was married," [13] and saw fit to remind them that "according to the statute of the Holy Church of Seville, no descendant from parents or grandparents of doubtful faith [i.e., of Jewish or Moorish lineage] could take a seat in the chapter." "The shot," says Menéndez Pelayo, "went straight towards Constantino, whose blood was Jewish." [14]

[13] *Ibid.*, p. 77.
[14] *Ibid.*, p. 76.

The other Canons hastily formed a commission for the heretic's defense, declared his sexual life to be in order, i.e., nonexistent, and pointed out that the statute on purity of blood did not apply to candidates to the Cathedral post: only those who had been "condemned, reconciled, etc." [15] by the Inquisition were barred from office.

Thus, as the heretic took his seat in the Cathedral chapter, the Church in Seville found herself giving sustenance—and a pulpit— to a man whose orthodoxy was at best doubtful.

But the infant Society of Jesus "was to put an end to the harm done by Constantino's preaching and reveal his covert wickedness." [16] Constantino must have very soon detected the Jesuits' enmity. For a while he answered in kind, casting all manner of aspersions on the Society; then, in a remarkable about-face, he solicited admission to it. Both tactics proved disastrous. The Jesuits' animosity was aroused by the former, their darkest suspicions by the latter. When the heretic insisted in his desire to join the Order, "the Fathers received him more sullenly each time and finally denied him his request, advising him that, in order to avoid gossip, he should visit [their] house as little as possible." [17]

Meanwhile, the Dominicans and other religious orders had awakened to the menace Constantino and his preaching represented, especially in view of its power to attract the common people.[18] As if all this were not enough, a final calamity overtook the Canon when the widow Isabel Martínez, in whose house he had secreted all his forbidden books and documents, was arrested by the ever-watchful Inquisition. Among other works, the cache at Widow Martínez's yielded the famous *Treatise on the Mass and the Pope,* possession of which was enough to seal any man's doom.

Constantino died two years after his arrest, still a prisoner at Triana Castle. His remains were exhumed and burned, along with an effigy, in the second of Seville's *autos de fe.*

[15] *Ibid.,* p. 77.
[16] *Ibid.,* p. 78.
[17] *Ibid.,* p. 81.
[18] *Ibid.,* p. 79. See also McCrie, *op. cit.,* p. 97.

His literary works included a *Summa of Christian Doctrine,* a translation of *The Sermon on the Mount,* a catechism, and a treatise entitled *The Sinner's Confession* which Menéndez Pelayo describes as "a beautiful piece of ascetic eloquence." [19] Of his *Summa,* in a statement echoing Wiffen's evaluation of Valdés, Thomas McCrie says: "The purpose of the author was not to defend Protestant doctrine, but to reveal the great truths of the Gospel, taking them directly from Scripture without linking them to the current controversies." [20]

II

Valer, Egidio and Constantino had not sown on barren ground: by the late 1550's Seville throbbed with Protestants of every social and intellectual station. Heresy spread through contacts and secret meetings. It took root in monasteries, private homes and above all in *conventículos,* those clandestine churches—hidden away, unmarked, anonymous—which were to be the prototypes of evangelical chapels in centuries to come.

Among the first arrested was Julián Hernández, called Julianillo on account of his short stature, a man of humble origins who took it upon himself to smuggle books and Bibles for the budding congregations. Julianillo was the patron saint, so to speak, of every Protestant colporteur who has ventured into the Peninsula with copies of Holy Writ in Spanish; perhaps the large lot (two *toneles*) of New Testaments which he brought in from Geneva in 1557 was the first consignment of such contraband ever to reach Spain.

One of the books he handled, a treatise against the Papacy entitled *The Image of the Anti-Christ,* seems to have come into the hands of a woman who had no relations with the heretics and who immediately turned it over to the Inquisition. Arrest followed arrest until "the prisons were full of people" [21] and the time had come for the Final Solution of the Protestant problem.

[19] Menéndez Pelayo, *op. cit.,* II, 73.
[20] McCrie, *op. cit.,* p. 131.
[21] Menéndez Pelayo, *op. cit.,* II, 89.

Seville's first *auto de fe* was held in the Plaza de San Francisco on September 24, 1559. Condemned to death by fire or strangulation—the latter if they "repented" and confessed to the attending priests—were the following:

Isabel de Baena, a rich woman whose house had served as a *conventículo;* burned.

Don Juan Ponce de León, son of the Count of Bailén; strangled.

Juan González, a priest of Moorish blood; burned.

Garci-Arias; burned.

Fray Cristobal de Arellano, Fray Juan Crisóstomo, Fray Juan de León and Fray Casiodoro, monks from the Monastery of San Isidro; all burned.

Cristobal de Losada, a physician, pastor of the most important of all *conventículos;* burned.

Fernando de San Juan, former rector of the Colegio de la Doctrina, a children's catechism school; burned.

Doña María de Virués, Doña María Coronel and Doña María de Bohorques—known thereafter to Spanish Protestants as "the three Marys"—members of the aristocracy, the last a bastard daughter of nobleman Don Pedro de García Jerez; all three strangled, "though they gave little sign of repentance." [22]

A priest by the name of Morcillo.

Francisco Zafra, another heretical priest, managed to escape from Triana Castle before the executions, and was destroyed in effigy.

In fifteen months' time, three days before Christmas, 1560, there came the turn of:

Julianillo (whose imprisonment had lasted three years).

Doña Francisca de Chaves, a nun from the Convent of Santa Isabel.

Ana de Ribera, widow of Fernando de San Juan.

Fray Juan Sastre, lay brother from San Isidro.

Francisca Ruiz, a constable's widow.

María Gómez, who, after having denounced Francisco Zafra, converted to the Reformed doctrine.

[22] *Ibid.,* pp. 91–92.

Her sister, Leonor Núñez, wife of a Seville physician.
Leonor's daughters, Elvira, Teresa and Lucía.[23]

All of the above were burned, as was Nicholas Burton, a hapless English merchant who, while visiting Cádiz and Seville, had the audacity to speak favorably of the Reformation. His nationality did not save him; his ship was confiscated by the Holy Office and his person fed to the flames.

One victim who never made it to the stake is worth a few lines of remembrance. Just before the 1559 *auto,* María de Bohorques had admitted under torture that she and her sister Juana had often discussed the new doctrine together. Juana, who was Baroness de Higueras, was six months pregnant when brought to the public prison. Eight days after she gave birth, the child having been taken from her, she was removed to a dungeon to await her turn at the rack. One session on *el potro* ("the colt") was enough: unconscious, hemorrhaging through mouth and nose, she was carted back to her cell, where she died a few days later, never to know that, at the great Christmastide *auto,* the Inquisitors were to find her "innocent." [24]

The twenty-eight leaders of the Protestant community put to death in the two *autos* were, of course, only part of the dramatis personae. Lesser sentences were imposed to *penitenciados,* who also walked in the ritual processions wearing *sambenitos.* In the *auto* of 1559, counting both Lutheran and non-Lutheran felons, the *penitenciados* came to eighty; in 1560 there were thirty-four.

"Here ends," says Menéndez Pelayo after detailing the *auto* of 1560, "the history of the Reformation in Seville. An energetic Catholic reaction wiped out the last vestige of the epidemic [*el contagio*]. The Monastery of San Isidro was purified; the Catholic monks who were left behind begged the Jesuits to come and indoctrinate them with good sermons. . . ." [25]

It remained for a seventeenth-century Jesuit, Father Martín de Roa, to render the most accurate account of Seville's purification.

[23] *Ibid.,* pp. 92–93. McCrie, *op. cit.,* 187–88.
[24] Menéndez Pelayo, *op. cit.,* II, 94. McCrie, *op. cit.,* pp. 187, 188.
[25] Menéndez Pelayo, *op. cit.,* II, 94.

THE CITY OF GOD

His description of Julianillo's end is perhaps the greatest, most eloquent manifesto of the Spanish mentality vis-à-vis Protestantism:

This damned beast had been turned over by the Inquisitors to Fr.
Francisco Gómez, who did everything in his power to bring him out
of his madness [and to] his senses. But seeing that [his madness] answered only to his shamelessness and obstinacy, . . . he determined to
break down his pride forcibly, so that, even if he could not make
him surrender to the faith, at least he could make him confess his ignorance and become convinced of the truth, if only because he found
himself beleaguered, without knowing what reply to give to the reasons adduced by Catholic teaching. And it was thus that, when he
began to argue with him by the stake, in the presence of many important and learned persons, and a great crowd of the common people,
the Father pressed his reasons and arguments upon him with such
power, that he convinced him of the evidence; and [Julianillo], his
hands and feet bound, not having or knowing anything to reply, grew
dumb.[26]

The epidemic which was spreading in Spanish territory was also
claiming victims among Spaniards abroad. One of the most
poignant cases was that of Juan Diaz, a Cuencan who spent more
than thirteen years at that focus of contagion which was the Sorbonne. Menéndez Pelayo states that it was "the reading of bad
books, especially those of Melanchthon, and contact with Jaime de
Enzinas around 1539 and 1540, which made him a Protestant"; [27]
he also accuses Diaz of being a paid spy in the service of the
French Reformers.[28] But Bataillon writes: "In Paris [Diaz] carried
on solid studies of Greek and Hebrew which were the basis for his
meditations on Scripture, particularly on St. Paul, and for his
conversion to justification by faith." [29]

When word of Juan's apostasy reached Spain, his brother Alfonso decided to take matters into his own hands. He hastened to
Ratisbon and beseeched Juan to return to the Catholic faith; but
the plea availed him nothing. "Nothing," says Menéndez Pelayo,

[26] Quoted in Menéndez Pelayo, *op. cit.*, II, 93.
[27] *Ibid.*, I, 938.
[28] *Ibid.*, p. 939.
[29] Bataillon, *op. cit.*, II, 99.

"could conquer that soul, blinded by error or sold out to sordid interest." [30] Thinking that the air of orthodox Italy would bring his brother to his senses, Alfonso then pretended to have been converted to Protestantism himself and proposed that Juan travel south with him in order to preach the new doctrine. Juan agreed, but later, sensing the ambush, changed his mind.

It was then that Alfonso decided murder would be the only solution. He hired an assassin and accompanied him to the village of Feldkirchen, where Juan was staying. The two men reached the house at dawn. The henchman lured Juan out of bed with word that he had brought a letter from his brother. Diaz came running and, as he stood by a window scanning the document "in the morning light," [31] he was cut down by the first blow of the assassin's ax, while Alfonso watched and waited at the bottom of the stairs.

The murderers were arrested near Innsbruck, but Alfonso appealed to the Cardinals of Strassburg and Trent and insisted that the case lay within the jurisdiction of the ecclesiastical, not the secular, authorities. Charles V interceded for him before the Palatine; the Bishop of Trent was entrusted with the matter and Alfonso went scot free. [32]

His brother left one book, the *Christianae religionis Summa,* whose substance is thoroughly Protestant.

Diaz's contemporary Francisco de San Román also converted to the Reformed faith around 1540. Burgos-born, he was a rich merchant who went to the Low Countries and Germany on business and who made the city of Antwerp his base of operations. It was from there that he traveled to Bremen in 1540, "to collect a certain debt from a banker on behalf of some merchants of Antwerp." [33] He chanced into a Lutheran church, heard a sermon by Jacobus Spreng, a Dutch ex-Capuchin, and, with typical Spanish impetuosity, became instantly enamored of the Reformed doctrine. One must consult both Menéndez Pelayo and McCrie to get

[30] Menéndez Pelayo, *op. cit.,* I, 942.
[31] *Ibid.,* p. 944.
[32] *Ibid.,* p. 946.
[33] *Ibid.,* p. 951.

the proper perspective on San Román's apostasy: the first finds it
outlandish that the man should have been so inspired by the
sermon, "as he understood very little of the German tongue";
the second declares without hesitation that the homily so impressed
San Román that he sought Spreng's counsel immediately.

Subsequent facts bear out McCrie. San Román must have understood enough German to get the substance of Spreng's message,
accept it, and cherish it for the rest of his life. On the other hand,
he may have actually spoken the language, as became a man who
did business abroad: here one must remember Menéndez Pelayo's
prejudice against "unlearned" men and the fact that he deems the
merchant from Burgos "utterly bereft of letters."

Though Spreng counseled prudence, San Román wrote back
to Antwerp with news of his conversion. On his return to the city
he was promptly apprehended by Spanish authorities and saved
from prison only by the intercession of friends. He went to Louvain and met fellow convert Francisco de Enzinas, who also
advised him to temper his ardor with caution. But having heard
that the Emperor was lenient with Protestants,[34] San Román,
who was becoming a species of Valer of the North, determined to
speak openly before him. He obtained an audience with Charles at
Ratisbon, and another, and another; though the Emperor himself
was patient enough, San Román so exasperated the court attend-
ants that he barely escaped being thrown into the Danube.[35]
Charles, with typical pusillanimity, finally washed his hands of the
heretic and ordered that he be judged "according to the laws of the
Empire."[36] The "laws" meant chains. After wandering through
half of Europe as the court's captive and having even been dragged
to Africa, San Román was burned in Valladolid at an *auto* whose
date remains unknown. Both McCrie and Menéndez Pelayo document the fact that the preacher at the *auto* was none other than
Bartolomé Carranza.[37]

Dominican Carranza, not yet a heretic, was only one of the

---

[34] McCrie, *op. cit.*, p. 106.
[35] Menéndez Pelayo, *op. cit.*, I, 953. McCrie, *op. cit.*, p. 107.
[36] Menéndez Pelayo, *op. cit.*, I, 953.
[37] *Ibid.*, II, 8. McCrie, *op. cit.*, p. 107.

many Spaniards who were crisscrossing the Empire on affairs of Church and State. Students, businessmen, exiles and migrants from the Peninsula swarmed all over the North. In a study on Vives, Marañón draws a lively picture of Bruges at the time of the Spanish hegemony:

The master [Vives] lived his longest years in Bruges, the divine Flemish city which was full of the Spanish spirit. The clear language of Castile could be heard on its streets at all times. It floated out of a window in song; it erupted from a quarrel in a tavern; it rose above the clash of coins in the depths of a small store. This was the clear language which the half-grown Emperor, Charles V, was already learning so he could address his universe in it.[38]

Charles' universe did not seem to understand Spanish; nor was the presence of Spain to be tolerated much longer in the Netherlands. But during the Emperor's lifetime, Bruges heard Spanish in her streets while Louvain welcomed eager young Spaniards who seemed more than ripe for the "bad books and bad doctrines from Germany" which, according to the *Heterodoxos,* circulated in the bosom of that most Catholic of universities.

One of these young people was Francisco de Enzinas, who translated his surname into various languages, as was the custom at the time (it will be remembered that Erasmus was born Gerhard Gerhards). "Dryander," the Greek version of the Castilian "Enzinas" (oak) seems to have been the Spaniard's favorite, although he also called himself "Duchesne" and "De Houx" in France, "Van Eyck" in the Netherlands and "Eichmann" in Germany. He was the son of wealthy parents who had sent him to Flanders, "where they had highly esteemed relatives." Pedro de Lerma, the Erasmist who spent his last years in Paris, was an uncle of Enzinas' and, as Menéndez Pelayo suggests, may have been responsible for predisposing young Francisco to Protestantism around 1537.[39] At any rate, the youth came to the Low Countries and registered at Louvain in 1539. After a sojourn in Paris

[38] Gregorio Marañón, *Españoles fuera de España* (5th ed.; Madrid: Espasa Calpe, S.A. [Colección Austral, No. 710], 1961), pp. 160–61.
[39] Menéndez Pelayo, *op. cit.,* I, 954–55.

(where he attended Lerma's funeral) and another in Wittenberg as a guest in Melanchthon's house, he resolved to translate the New Testament from Greek to Spanish.

Enzinas had the work printed in Antwerp in 1543 and, hoping to obtain the Emperor's blessing, presented him with the first copy. After a singular lunchtime interview between His Imperial Highness and the young heretic—singularly detailed by both Boehmer and Menéndez Pelayo—Charles handed the book over to his confessor, Fray Pedro de Soto.

Once again the result could have been foreseen: Soto, a Dominican, could find no virtue in the act of rendering Scripture into Spanish, or indeed into any language readily understood by the populace. He had Enzinas arrested and imprisoned in Brussels.

Fortunately, his friends came to the rescue. No one is quite sure just who was responsible for Enzinas' escape, but one day he pushed open his cell door and walked out of the prison. He made his way to Wittenberg, where he lodged with Melanchthon once more. Subsequently he traveled the length of Europe, met Calvin in Switzerland and even took a professorship of Greek at Cambridge at Cranmer's behest. He married one Margaret Elter in Strassburg in 1548 and died of the plague in that city in 1552.

Much less is known, paradoxically, of his elder brother Jaime, who was executed in 1547.[40] It appears that Jaime had first gone to Louvain and then, at his parents' request, transferred to the Sorbonne. There he was in close contact with both his kinsman Lerma and with the Flemish theologian Georg Cassander, whose works were to be put on the Index in 1617. There, too, he must have met Diaz, in whose conversion he was instrumental.

In Paris the elder Enzinas was especially affected by the spectacle of Protestants going to their death for the faith. It was precisely the sight of an execution in 1540 which, according to both Boehmer and Menéndez Pelayo,[41] made the Spaniard turn his back on France forever and return to Louvain. Nothing more was heard of him until he turned up in Rome. There, according to

[40] The date is Boehmer's. Menéndez Pelayo (*op. cit.*, I, 950) gives it as 1546.
[41] The victim was a young French heretic named Claude Lepeintre.

the *Heterodoxos,* having been processed and sentenced because "he had dogmatized and begun to spread his doctrine in private chapels," [42] Enzinas was burned at the stake.

Six years later, further north, the same fate was to befall Miguel Servet, one of Spain's Humanist glories. This time the flames rose in Geneva, and the éminence grise behind the murder was none other than John Calvin.

It was a wanton and a tragic killing. In his many and dazzling talents, the Spaniard Servet had typified the Renaissance genius: he was a theologian, a linguist, a cartographer, a writer, a physician, a student of the scientific method, a tireless researcher and above all an independent thinker. His life has been captured with skill and insight in a biography by Roland Bainton, who in the first chapter states:

John Calvin is the granite block from which we of Puritan tradition have been carved, and precisely because of our loyalty to the rock from which we are hewn, we would not disguise the flaws. To point them out is not so much to reproach a spiritual ancestor as to engage in searching of heart lest we perpetuate only the vices of our forebears. In this our day, religious liberty is in peril. This study may be revealing as to the reasons why men persecute and the reasons why, as Christians, they should not.[43]

Why was Servet persecuted? Why did he, as Bainton wryly remarks, have "the singular distinction of having been burned by the Catholics in effigy and by the Protestants in actuality"? [44] The answer is simple: because he dared to think for himself, and, having thought his way out of *both* faiths, found himself up against the very one which upheld his right to freedom. With the murder of Servet Protestantism trespassed, openly and without shame, onto the green fields of self-righteousness which the Catholic Church had staked out for herself.

Servet (also called Servetus and Serveto) had been born in

[42] Menéndez Pelayo, *op. cit.,* I, 950.
[43] Roland H. Bainton, *Hunted Heretic: The Life and Death of Michael Servetus—1511–1553* (Boston: Beacon Press, 1960), pp. 3–4.
[44] *Ibid.,* p. 3.

Navarre, probably of Aragonese parents. In 1528 his father sent him to study law in Toulouse, where his quest for spiritual and scientific truth began, in the classic style, with "the crumbling of his Catholic faith." [45] He read Melanchthon, he read the works of the German Reformers and, inevitably, he began to elaborate his own religious thought. Soon, as so many of his fellow heretics, he was serving his apprenticeship in the entourage of Charles V. As secretary to Charles' then confessor, Fray Juan de Quintana, he traveled with the court to Italy and Germany and attended the imperial coronation at Bologna in 1529, and the Diet of Augsburg in 1530. Years later he was to remember Charles' coronation at the hand of Pope Clement with something quite like despair:

With these very eyes we have seen him [the Pope] borne in pomp on the necks of princes, making with his hand the sign of the cross, and adored in the open streets by all the people on bended knee, so that those who were able to kiss his feet or slippers counted themselves more fortunate than the rest, and declared that they had obtained many indulgences, and that on this account the infernal pains would be remitted for many years. O vilest of beasts, most brazen of harlots! [46]

Barely two years after Bologna, Servet produced the first fruit of his theological meditations: *On the Errors of Trinity*. It was a Unitarian tract. Servet's "biographers and critics," says Menéndez Pelayo, "have admitted that [he] fixed his attention exclusively upon the *historical Christ*, which means that he intended to attack [Christ's] divinity; his work is thus the first, among modern theologians', to pursue this idea with insolence." [47]

The idea seemed insolent enough to Johannes Oecolampadius, the stern Reformer of Basel, who complained to Zwingli that Servet was "so haughty, so proud and contentious that nothing can be done about him." "Such pestilence is not to be suffered in the Church of God," answered Zwingli, "he who so blasphemes

[45] Menéndez Pelayo, *op. cit.*, I, 983.
[46] Miguel Servet, *Christianismi Restitutio*, p. 462, quoted in Bainton, *op. cit.*, pp. 18–20.
[47] Menéndez Pelayo, *op. cit.*, I, 985.

is unworthy of existence." To this exchange, transcribed here from Menéndez Pelayo, the Spanish historian adds his own pious aside: "What evangelical tolerance is shown by these mutineers against Rome!" [48]

Servet had the *Errors* printed in Hagenau, a village near Strassburg. The book's publication brought down upon his head the ire of the Reformed leaders and the far from wholesome interest of both the French and the Spanish Inquisition. Thereafter the Spaniard became the "hunted heretic" of Bainton's title—continually on the move, changing names, working at a variety of trades, always putting his myriad talents to use. Under the name Michel de Villeneuve he was corrector and editor for the firm of Trechsel in Lyons, for whom he edited Ptolemy's *Geography*. He studied medicine in Paris and became the first man to describe the nature and function of the circulatory system. And he continued to write. The appearance of his *Christianismi Restitutio* (*Christianity Restored*) in 1532 earned him a brief stint in a prison of the French Inquisition. After escaping he decided to move to Naples and practice medicine there. While passing through Geneva he was recognized and, at the behest of Calvin, with whom he had had numerous contacts, Servet was apprehended and charged with heresy.

All appeals to Calvin having failed, Servet went to his indescribably cruel death (the torment lasted half an hour) on October 27, 1553, leaving those inclined to marvel at the ways of Providence to ponder his rise and fall. Spain, his native land, was soon to begin her decline into that dark night of Catholicism in which the magical and the obscure, worshiped with primitive fervor, were to kill the life of reason, the roots of science, and, save for sporadic outbursts in the eighteenth and nineteenth centuries, the last vestiges of enlightened Humanism. Servet might have been Spain's magnificent, if unwilling, gift to Europe. But the man was destroyed in what is today Switzerland, a nation imbued with that political stability and terrestrial well-being that Spaniards are still striving for.

[48] *Ibid.,* p. 984.

3

The pyres were still burning in the Peninsula. Now they illumined the Castilian plain surrounding Valladolid, where an outbreak of Protestantism as alarming as Seville's was uncovered in the 1550's. Its central figure was Dr. Agustín de Cazalla, born in 1510 the son of Pedro de Cazalla and Leonor de Vibero, both of whom, though rich, had "been defamed as relapsed Jews by the Inquisition of Seville." [1] At seventeen Cazalla entered the Colegio de San Pablo in Valladolid and came under the tutelage of the ill-starred Bartolomé Carranza. In the late 1520's, the heyday of Erasmism, young Agustín registered at Alcalá de Henares, where he remained until age twenty-six, having received the degree of Master of Arts in 1530.

For a time Cazalla was a canon at Salamanca. In 1542 he joined that school of heretics which was the Emperor's court and, as Charles' preacher and chaplain, traveled through Germany and the Low Countries for nine long years. "It is commonly held . . ." states Menéndez Pelayo, "that when he came [back] to the Peninsula he had already contracted the Lutheran leprosy."

[1] Menéndez Pelayo, op. cit., I, 1047. McCrie (p. 136) states that the Inquisition had launched a process against Constanza Ortiz, Doña Leonor's mother, for "having died a relapsed Jewess." This is an interesting parallel to the case of Blanca March, Vives' mother, who, as we shall see, was also posthumously disgraced.

Cazalla's moves from 1552 on are certainly suspicious. Before long he was conferring with Carlos de Seso, a gentleman who had heard the doctrine of justification preached in Italy and who wanted, as Menéndez Pelayo acidly remarks, "to be in Spain what Luther had been among the Germans." [2] Seso had been *corregidor* in Toro, a city near Zamora which was to produce the key figures of the Reformation in Castile.

Soon there were converts by the dozen. Pedro de Cazalla, Agustín's priest brother, embraced the faith in Toro, as did his friend Antonio Herrezuelo. Leonor de Vibero and her three sisters converted in Valladolid. The Rojas, one of Castile's leading families, gave the new doctrine some of its most distinguished followers, among them Fray Domingo de Rojas and Don Pedro Sarmiento, the latter son and heir to the Marquis de Poza. Doña Ana de Enríquez, daughter of the Marquis de Alcañices, came by a copy of Bartolomé Carranza's *Catechism* which had been sent to her mother from Flanders; Ana soon convinced her cousin Doña María de Rojas, a nun of the Convent of Santa Catalina, that "there was no purgatory." [3] Another religious house, the Cistercian Convent of Belén, also "fell in the same heresy; both convents received and read books by Carranza and by the Valdés [brothers], and other suspicious doctrine." [4]

Doña Leonor de Vibero's house became the meeting place for the Protestant *conventículo*. How long the small church functioned is hard to say, but in the first months of 1558 it had already been infiltrated by the Inquisition's agents. In June of that year, Inquisitor Fernando de Valdés, Archbishop of Seville, had already written to the Emperor at Yuste giving him details of the *conventículo*'s discovery and the arrest of some of its leaders. Valdés' document, quoted at length in the *Heterodoxos*, [5] is a step-by-step lesson in the Inquisition's use of spies and, what is more remarkable, its readiness to act on anonymous denuncia-

---

[2] Menéndez Pelayo, *op. cit.*, I, 1048. Both McCrie (p. 141) and Menéndez Pelayo state that Seso was born in Verona.

[3] Menéndez Pelayo, *op. cit.*, I, 1053.

[4] *Ibid.*, p. 1053.

[5] *Ibid.*, p. 1058.

tions. This anonymity on the part of the accuser is, as we shall see in subsequent chapters, still a feature of the Spanish scene where the policing of Protestant activities is concerned.

The first raid, according to Archbishop Valdés' letter, netted "Dr. Cazalla and some brothers and sisters of his, and his mother, and Dr. Pedro Sarmiento, and his wife, and Doña Ana de Enriquez, his niece, daughter of the Marquis of Alcañices, and D. Luis de Rojas, grandson of the Marquis de Poza and heir to his house, and some other neighbors of Valladolid and of Toro. . . . And with great diligence they also sent [people] to the mountain passes to apprehend those who had fled, and it pleased God that in Navarra they arrested D. Carlos de Sesso, from Logroño, who had been *corregidor* at Toro, and Fr. Domingo de Rojas, who was dressed as a layman; which was a great boon, for they had license from the King of Navarre to cross into France, and carried letters of recommendation to the Princess of Bearne." [6]

The "neighbors of Valladolid and Toro" caught fleeing and those arrested at their homes must have come to a good number, for, as Menéndez Pelayo assures us, "the jails were seething with prisoners." [7] Valdés himself informed Charles that "Each day new witnesses come forth who are examined with great diligence and secretiveness. One gentleman from Toro named Juan de Ulloa Pereyra appeared and was imprisoned by the Inquisition, and there are others who have not been apprehended because there are no jails where they can be held and properly watched." [8]

Cazalla was interrogated on September 20, 1558, and tortured on March 4 of the following year. The Inquisition then "determined . . . to celebrate the most solemn *auto de fe* ever seen in Spain." [9] The rite was held on Trinity Sunday, May 21, 1559, in Valladolid's Plaza Mayor.

The reins of government had already passed from Charles'

[6] *Ibid.,* I, 1059.
[7] *Ibid.,* p. 1062.
[8] Louis Prosper Gachard, *Retraite et mort de Charles Quint au Monastère de Yuste* . . . (Bruxelles: C. Muquardt, 1855), II, 423, 424. Quoted in Menéndez Pelayo, *op. cit.,* I, 1062.
[9] Menéndez Pelayo, *op. cit.,* I, 1067.

hands to his son's. The old emperor, nearing the end of his days at the Monastery of Yuste in Extremadura, seemed far removed from the tumult at Valladolid, though, if Menéndez Pelayo is to be credited, "he followed avidly . . . all the actions of the Holy Office in the persecution of the accused, and urged that they be punished promptly and terribly." Further, "talking to the prior of Yuste, Fr. Martín de Angulo, he [Charles] lamented the fact that he didn't have Luther put to death when he had him in his power at Worms." [10]

Charles' son wouldn't have hesitated at Worms or anywhere else: with Philip the fight against Protestantism went into its bloodiest phase. But it was not simply the King's temperament (as the Black Legend would have it) that brought on the debacle. It was the course of history. Philip inherited the Protestant problem without any of its complications: the social, political, even personal considerations that surrounded heresy in Charles' time were totally unknown to him. Born and educated in Spain, pledged to the most ruthless orthodoxy from childhood, Philip picked up the pieces of his father's vacillation and with them built a lasting monument to the God of Rome. It was the proper, the fitting thing: he thought himself a Christian doing his Christian duty. Nothing more. In this sense Philip was a symptom of Spain's sickness, not its cause. He did not lead his nation to hate so much as he followed her there. As Bataillon makes clear:

Between 1556 . . . and 1563 . . . rapid and profound changes are wrought in the spiritual climate of Spain. [But] It would be a great error to attribute these changes to the accession of Philip II to the throne: the aging Emperor had retired to Yuste *and his entire generation had aged with him.*[11]

Furthermore, the new Inquisitor, Fernando de Valdés, was a man whose ruthlessness was matched only by that of his theological advisor, Melchor Cano. It was Cano who, as we shall see, framed Carranza. And it was Valdés who, personally or by dele-

[10] *Ibid.,* pp. 1063, 1066.
[11] Bataillon, *op. cit.,* II, 311. Italics mine.

THE CITY OF GOD

gation of his powers, chastised every heretic who disturbed the peace of His Catholic Majesty's kingdom in the latter half of the sixteenth century.

The *auto* held on Trinity Sunday, May 21, 1559, was duly solemn. "In those days," says Menéndez Pelayo, "people rose very early. At one o'clock Masses began to be said in churches and monasteries, and it wasn't five in the morning when there appeared at the Consistory Doña Juana, the Regent Princess, dressed in *raja* [a thick cloth] with a cloak and headdress of black Oriental crepe in the Castilian style, a satin waist, white gloves, carrying a gold and black fan in her hand; and the weak and sickly Prince Don Carlos in a cloak and doublet of black *raja,* knit stockings, velvet thigh-pieces, woolen cap, sword and gloves." [12]

Condemned to death before the distinguished assemblage and an enormous crowd ("It looked like a general congregation of the world," says another account quoted by Menéndez Pelayo, ". . . a proper picture of the Last Judgment" [13]) were the following:

Dr. Agustín de Cazalla.

Doña Beatriz de Vibero, his sister.

Alonso Pérez, a clergyman from Palencia.

Juan García, a silversmith from Valladolid.

Cristóbal del Campo, of Zamora.

Cristóbal de Padilla, of the same city.

Antonio Herrezuelo of Toro.[13a]

Catalina Román, Isabel de Estrada, Juana Velázques, all from the town of Pedrosa.

Catalina Ortega, of Valladolid.

A man named Herrera, of Peñaranda de Duero.

Gonzalo Váez, a relapsed Jew from Portugal.

Doña Leonor de Vibero, Cazalla's mother, had died several years before. Her body was exhumed and burned, her house razed to the ground and a marble wall with a defamatory inscription built on the site.

[12] Menéndez Pelayo, *op. cit.,* I, 1070.
[13] *Ibid.,* p. 1070.
[13a] Herrezuelo's widow, Leonor Cisneros, was burned alive in 1568. McCrie, *op. cit.,* p. 172; Menéndez Pelayo, *op. cit.,* I, 1083.

Condemned to life imprisonment and perpetual wearing of the *sambenito,* were:

Doña Francisca de Zúñiga, of Valladolid.

Don Pedro Sarmiento, *comendador* of Alcántara.

Doña Mencía de Figueroa, Sarmiento's wife.

Don Juan de Ulloa Pereyra, of Toro.

Leonor de Toro, from Zamora.

Gabriel de la Cuadra of the same city.

Of the remaining prisoners, Don Luis de Rojas, Marquis de Poza, was "banished from the kingdom forever." Doña Ana de Enriquez was ordered to return to jail wearing the *sambenito* and there remain three days; "she gave indications of repentance and seemed very beautiful to all," adds Menéndez Pelayo of the twenty-three-year-old aristocrat. Doña María de Rojas, the nun, daughter of the Marquis de Poza, was ordered back to her convent, where she "would take no vows, actively or passively, and would occupy the last place [of the community]." Antón Dominguez, of Pedrosa, was given three years in jail, with confiscation of his goods. Anton Ansel, French page to the Marquis de Poza, was condemned to wearing the *sambenito* for life.

A second *auto* took place on October 8, 1559. "Released to the secular arm" for burning were:

Don Carlos de Seso.

Fray Domingo de Rojas.

Pedro de Cazalla, Agustín's priest brother.

Juan Sánchez, gagged so that he wouldn't blaspheme.

Domingo Sánchez, a priest from Villamediana del Campo and a disciple of Seso's.

Doña Eufrosina Ríos, a nun from Santa Clara Convent in Valladolid.

Doña Catalina de Reinoso, age twenty-one, a nun from the Convent of Belén in Valladolid. Doña Catalina's background is a typical sixteenth-century tangle of bloodlines and religions. Her father was the Lord of Astudillo de Campos, her brother Don Francisco was bishop of Córdoba, her mother, Doña Juana de Baeza, had Jewish blood.

Doña Margarita de Santisteban, another nun from the same convent.

Doña Marina de Guevara, *idem.*

Doña María de Miranda, *idem.*

Pedro Sotelo, of Aldea del Palo, Zamora.

Francisco de Almarza, from the town of the same name in Soria.

Juana Sánchez, also condemned to death, committed suicide in prison; her remains and effigy were burned instead.

Life sentences and *sambenitos* were meted out to:

Doña Isabel de Castilla, Seso's wife.

Doña Catalina de Castilla, her niece.

Doña Francisca de Zúñiga y Reinoso, sister to Doña Catalina, and like her a nun at Belén.

Doña Felipa de Heredia and Doña Catalina de Alcaraz, two other nuns from the same religious house.

This *auto,* presided over by Philip himself, was the setting for a memorable exchange between the monarch and Don Carlos de Seso. When Seso asked the King "how he could allow them to burn him," His Majesty answered with the now-famous dictum: "I'd bring on the firewood to burn my own son if he were as wicked as you." Having asked permission to address the King, Fray Domingo de Rojas also spoke: "Though I come here a heretic in the eyes of the populace," he said, "I believe in Almighty God, Father, Son and Holy Ghost, and I believe in the passion of Christ, which is enough to save us all, with no other justification of the soul before God, and I hope to achieve salvation in this faith." Fray Domingo did not get an answer to his brief harangue. "They ordered him gagged," says Menéndez Pelayo, "and went on with their business." [14]

The wrath of the Spanish God knew no bounds. In August of that year the Inquisition had closed in on Bartolomé Carranza— Archbishop of Toledo, Dominican friar, Censor of the Holy Office, theologian at Trent, scourge of heretics, friend of the Emperor,

[14] Menéndez Pelayo, *op. cit.,* pp. 1071–73, 1081–83.

scholar, teacher, writer, "noble and of clean blood." [15] When placed under house arrest at Torrelaguna, Carranza's case was already hopeless. Valdés quite simply hated him, while fellow priests, like vultures flying in for a feast, had declared against him in the most injurious terms. Melchor Cano in particular relished the opportunity of finishing off his longtime rival. The two men's enmity went back to their seminary days, when they had vied for top honors in scholastic jousts, and had ripened at the time both aspired to the post of Provincial of the Dominicans' Valladolid chapter (Carranza captured it). When Inquisitor Valdés asked him to censor the Archbishop's *Catechism*, Cano fired off six charges which, as Menéndez Pelayo points out, were the "keystone of [Carranza's] process." [16]

An appeal by the Archbishop to the dead Emperor's son was a waste of time: Philip, remote and forbidding, refused to lift a hand in his defense. In the ensuing decade all the efforts of Carranza's only defender, the brilliant Martín de Azpilcueta, proved equally fruitless. Seventeen years after his arrest Fray Bartolomé died in an Italian prison, still a pawn of the Holy Office.

Born in Navarre in 1503, Carranza had joined the Dominican order at seventeen. In 1523 he entered the Colegio de San Gregorio in Valladolid, "preceded by the required information on *moribus et genere* [customs and blood]." [17] He read theology there and shortly afterwards taught at the Colegio de San Pablo in Valladolid, where young Agustín Cazalla confessed with him. Carranza's star was soon rising: in 1539 he was sent to his Order's General Congregation in Rome. Not long thereafter he began to serve the Inquisition as Censor. And in 1545 the Emperor dispatched him to Trent, where his fine-honed Thomism and superb oratory aroused the admiration of all.

At his second appearance before the Council in 1551, Carranza

[15] *Ibid.*, II, 6.
[16] *Ibid.*, p. 26.
[17] *Ibid.*, p. 7. The words are in quotes though the writer gives no source. If they are taken from school records, they are a significant confirmation of Menéndez Pelayo's earlier statement as to the "cleanness" of the Archbishop's blood.

once again took a Catholic stand on justification, censored books with relish and burned a number of Lutheran tracts. In 1555, two years after his return to Spain, Crown Prince Philip summoned him to England "to convert, with the prestige of his doctrine and the power of his eloquence, the subjects of Queen Mary. . . ."[18]

Fray Bartolomé took England by storm. "He visited the University of Oxford and all thirteen of its Colleges," says Menéndez Pelayo, "and found it Catholic." Further,

He had the remains of Peter Martyr Vermigli's wife, which were buried in the main chapel of Oxford Cathedral, exhumed and burned; he pressed for the execution of Archbishop Thomas Cranmer; with the Bishop of London and Drs. Storius and Rochester, who functioned as Inquisitors, he worked for the chastisement of heretics, and he brought upon himself the hate of the sectarians [i.e., Protestants] to such an extent, that they tried to kill him several times, and called him the *Black Friar*.[19]

From England he went to Flanders, where "he sought out heretics and burned books." When Philip came to Brussels on All Saints' Day, 1557, this pious whirlwind

informed him of some Spanish students at Louvain whose faith he thought suspicious, and of some Protestant fugitives from Seville who came to Germany and Flanders bringing many harmful books, which they sold publicly before the palace door and even inside the premises.[20]

It is difficult to say just when Carranza's conduct began to veer from the Orthodox pattern, for once he stood accused, it all seemed a matter of *arrière-pensée:* hadn't he been unusually independent, unusually bold, unusually close to the fountains of damnation? Hadn't there been rumors—in the best tradition— that "the Archbishop was returning [to Spain] tainted with heterodox opinions born of his dealings with German and English Protestants, and the reading of their books"?[21]

[18] *Ibid.,* p. 10.
[19] *Ibid.,* p. 11.
[20] *Ibid.*
[21] *Ibid.,* I, 15. One accusation, made by Don Diego Hurtado de Mendoza, stated that the Archbishop was "the friend of heretics and read books by Juan de Valdés." *Ibid.,* p. 37.

There was, in fact, much more than that: there were solid theological charges to be made before the Archbishop in the name of the Church of Rome. His *Commentaries to the Christian Catechism,* published in Antwerp in 1558, was a case in point. Menéndez Pelayo reminds the reader that Fray Bartolomé's book "was ostensibly written to warn people against Lutheran error," but then adds:

The intention of the author might have been praiseworthy, but the fact is that the book gave rise to significant objections. In it Carranza announced his intention to revive as far as possible the ancient Church, for "it was the best and the cleanest"; and he constantly spoke of faith and justification in almost Lutheran terms, as, for example: "Faith without works is dead, not because *works give life to faith, but because they are the certain sign that faith is alive.*" [22]

It was the proofs of this catechism which Carranza had sent to the Marquesa de Alcañices, Doña Elvira de Rojas, in Valladolid. And it was in her mother's house that Ana de Enriquez found them, read them, and went the way of all Castilian heretics. On April 29, 1559, Doña Ana declared before the Inquisition's tribunal:

I said to Francisco Vibero that I had read a book of the Archbishop's on the Christian doctrine, where it said in one passage that Christ satisfied all blame and all punishment, and in another passage that we should remove the vestiges of sin by works of penance. And I said to myself: "In one passage he says one thing, and in the other he contradicts it, and I certainly think he is speaking foolishness." [23]

The lovely Doña Ana was not the only one who was weakening under pressure. Fray Domingo de Rojas related a conversation between himself and Fray Bartolomé on the subject of purgatory.

ROJAS: Well then, Father, what of Purgatory?
CARRANZA: Alas!
ROJAS: Father, I am very much afraid of it.
CARRANZA: You are not competent enough for such matters now.[24]

[22] *Ibid.,* II, 15–16.
[23] *Ibid.,* p. 17.
[24] *Ibid.,* p. 18.

As if this ambiguous but incriminating statement on the doctrine of purgatory were not enough, Fray Domingo declared that he had seen a letter Juan de Valdés had sent to Fray Bartolomé in Rome, in answer to another which the Archbishop had written to the heretic. "Contagion," to use Menéndez Pelayo's word, was in the air.

Even worse was the testimony on the Archbishop's "Lutheran" conduct at the death of Charles V when, according to witness Juan de Regla (a friar as well), the Archbishop, "having entered several times in [Charles'] chamber, without having heard anything in confession, absolved him several times of his sins, which seemed to this witness to be a mockery of the Sacrament, or an abuse of the same, for certainly he could not have done it out of ignorance." [25] Another witness, Fray Marcos de Cardona, accused Carranza of having said to the Emperor: "Let your Majesty have great confidence, for if sin exists, and if sin existed, the passion of Christ alone suffices." [26]

Carranza was doomed. He insisted on his Catholicity, he appealed to his friends, he begged the King for justice—all to no avail. During this time, and more so as the years wore on, his inner torment must have been the greatest of any Spanish heretic. He had thought the Faith to be a rock: he found it to be quicksand.

On September 1, 1563, Licenciado Ramírez, prosecuting attorney for the Holy Office, drew up the first accusation against Carranza. The Archbishop was charged with:

1. Having believed and taught the article on justification in accordance with Lutheran doctrine.

2. Having denied, in the course of private conversations, the existence of purgatory.

3. Having preached [that] satisfaction was obtained only by the merits of Christ, saying and holding that there was no sin for those who did not believe in it, nor death, nor devils.

4. Having said and held that on his deathbed, and in public, he wished to renounce all his good works and limit himself to the benefit of Christ.

[25] *Ibid.*, p. 21.
[26] *Ibid.*, pp. 21–22.

5. Not having denounced a certain heretic [Carlos de Seso].

6. Having given his pupils a *Notice* [Juan de Valdés' *Notice on the Interpreters of Sacred Scripture*] which was full of Lutheran heresies.

7. Having believed and stated that the Hail Mary and the Our Father should not be said to the saints.

8. Having defended the certainty of salvation.

9. Having pronounced the words *Ego haereo certe* [I am certainly a heretic] when Lutheran controversies were being discussed.

10. Having possessed and read heretical works and books forbidden by the Holy Office, and having given and explained them to his disciples.

11. Having spoken with little reverence of the Most Holy Sacrament of the Altar.

12. Having been close to and familiar with excommunicated heretics.

13. Having underrated the discipline and ceremonies of the Church and the power of the Pope.

14. Having defended Erasmist doctrines on confession and on the authorship of the Apocalypse.

15. Having refuted Lutheran errors with very brief arguments after having exposed them at great length.

16. Having said that litanies should have this phrase added to them: *A Concilio huius temporis libera nos, Domine* ["From a Council at this time, deliver us, O Lord"].

17. Having steadfastly defended the heretical propositions of [his] Catechism, casting about for arguments and testimonies.[27]

Witnesses came forth literally by the scores; when transcribed, the trial took up twenty-one bound volumes. Carranza's lawyers were Dr. Alonso Delgado, a Canon of Toledo; Dr. Santander, Archdeacon of Valladolid; and Dr. Morales of the same Chancery. But his most ardent defender was the Basque theologian Martín de Azpilcueta, who took the case in 1561.[28] It was Azpilcueta

[27] *Ibid.*, p. 45.
[28] Azpilcueta, known as "the Navarrese doctor," was one of the most brilliant theologians of his time. Bataillon points out that one of his books—the *Commentary*—aspired to be a reply to Erasmus but is in fact "solidly based on Erasmus' spirit." Bataillon, *op. cit.*, II, 177.

who transmitted the Archbishop's futile plea to Philip, and it was he who insisted all along that the matter of the prelate's apostasy lay within Rome's and not Spain's jurisdiction.

Rome was of the same opinion; indeed, the Holy See had long been clamoring for its right to try Carranza. But the Spanish Church had refused the Roman overtures point-blank: "the Inquisition had taken it as a matter of honor that the case be resolved in Spain, and did not want to yield a single point on its jurisdiction." [29]

Seven long years after it was opened, the Carranza case was at last turned over to the Pope. The Archbishop sailed for Rome on April 27, 1567, on board a ship which, by coincidence, also carried the Duke of Alba, Governor of Flanders—he of unhappy memory in the countries of the North.

In Rome, Pope Pius V was favorably disposed not only towards the Archbishop, but towards his "heretical" *Catechism*. Unfortunately the case languished in the hands of seventeen eminent consultants and Pius died in 1572 without having absolved the prelate. His successor, Gregory XIII, took four years to make up his mind on Carranza. When he did so, Gregory declared that the Archbishop "had drunk the depraved doctrine of many condemned heretics such as Martin Luther, Oecolampadius and Melanchthon . . . and taken from them many errors, phrases and manners of speaking which they had used to confirm their teachings." [30]

The Pope's declaration was made on April 14, 1576. Carranza died just over two weeks later, having abjured sixteen heretical propositions put to him by Gregory in the name of the Church Triumphant.

In a few more years Spain had been wiped clean of Protestants. Those heretics who could escape did so, among them Casiodoro de la Reina and Cipriano de Valera, whose work we shall deal with in a subsequent chapter. Purified of all heresy, the country took

[29] Menéndez Pelayo, *op. cit.*, II, 47.
[30] *Ibid.*, p. 52.

on a new look, a new style, a new faith. Henceforth, and even more intensely than in the days of the Moorish wars, Catholicism would be the quiddity of Spain. More than a set of ethical rules, more than a statement of man's relation to God, the Faith would confer *nationhood*—like the Children of Israel's.

4

Every scholar who has looked into the history of the Inquisition
has been struck by one peculiar fact: the high incidence of Moorish and also Jewish blood among the accused. As far back as the
1880's Menéndez Pelayo stopped to consider the matter:

It is remarkable how many proselytes the Reformation made among
the New Christians [i.e., converts from Islam or Judaism], but the antievangelical discrimination engendered by the Statutes on Purity of
Blood, which fed the blind hate of the populace against the converts'
kin, couldn't help but produce such un-Catholic results. Mark this well:
the Cazallas were *judaizantes* [relapsed Jews]; so was Constantino;
Juan González and Casiodoro de la Reina were of Moorish blood.
The racial question explains many phenomena and resolves many
enigmas in our history.[1]

But the racial enigma of the Inquisition and the meaning of the
Jewish factor were far from resolved by Menéndez Pelayo.
Américo Castro, the distinguished historian who became a self-
exile after the Civil War, has shed more light on the role of the
Jews in the Great Purge. Castro's *The Structure of Spanish History*
is an exhaustive, almost anthropological examination of the Moorish and Jewish antecedents in Spanish society. His insights into the
linguistic, social and temperamental legacy of Islam are matched
by a brilliant study—one chapter long, but just as well documented

[1] Menéndez Pelayo, *op. cit.*, II, 88.

—on the Jewish influence *within* the Holy Office itself. Even out of context, this segment of Castro's work—Chapter II of the book's Mexican edition [2]—is required reading for the student of the modern Spanish Church and its indomitable ways.

Castro begins by attacking the notion that the Spanish conscience came into being as a result of a Holy War, i.e., a war waged for the sole purpose of converting the enemy:

the war against the Moor was not waged with a religious purpose, to exterminate a belief adjudged false (as did the Crusades of the French against the Albigenses or the wars between Catholics and Protestants in the 16th and 17th centuries). The "Christians," in our case, were fighting men informed and sustained by a religious belief which was no less effective in a *military* and *political* sense than the enemy's. Faith in Christ "nationalized" as much as faith in Mohammed, under whose auspices almost all the Peninsula had fallen into Saracen hands. Making the national (or political) dimension coincide with the religious was thus the consequence of a primary and basic *correlation* between Al-Andalus and the infant Christian kingdoms. . . .[3]

It was this correlation that nourished the caste system in whose rise and fall Castro finds the roots of the Inquisition. (He makes it clear that he is using the word "caste" in its original Spanish connotation, and not in the modern, Indian sense: the Portuguese took the term to India and there applied it to a system which bore no resemblance to Spanish society.) Castro's hypothesis, in brief, is as follows: After the Moslem invasion, three castes of believers shared the Peninsula—Moors, Christians and Jews. The Moorish kingdom of Al-Andalus, where Jews and Christians lived and worked peacefully alongside the Moslem majority, was itself the pattern for this tripartite way of life. "The idea of 'caste' founded on religious faith," writes Castro, "began to project itself over the future of Spanish life during the centuries of [the Christians'] struggle to reconquer lost territory, and in the light of the example offered by Al-Andalus." [3a]

[2] Américo Castro, *La realidad histórica de España*. Mexico City: Editorial Porrúa, 1962.
[3] *Ibid.*, p. 30. Italics mine.
[3a] *Ibid.*, p. 33.

Until the fifteenth century, the three castes lived side by side, interlocking and mutually dependent, unhindered in their individual growth by any measures from within or without.

Laws dictated to forbid Christians from using the services of Moors and Jews were useless. The tolerant measures of the *Partidas* (an otherwise theoretical code of the thirteenth century) accepted the existence of the Jews, though they did not suggest that Christians should bow to their occasional superiority. Jews were tolerated so that "they should live in captivity as always, and serve to remind all men that they came *from the lineage* of those who crucified Our Lord Jesus Christ." (*Partida* VII, 24, 2.)[4]

The deicide charge is, this once, beside the point. Whatever the individual Christian thought about it, he not only coexisted with the Jew, but availed himself of his services. "Living as an intermediary between Moor and Christian, the Jew had a 'Western' temper which the Moslem lacked. Proficient in foreign tongues, hard-working, fond of moving about and always on the alert, he got on with the Christian [community] much better than with the Moslem." [5]

Intermarriage was not uncommon in the highest strata of Christian society:

Illustrious Christian families had married into the Jews in the Middle Ages for economic reasons or because of the frequent beauty of [Jewish] women; but before the fifteenth century no one was shocked by this, or, if there was any shock, it found no echo in literature aside from the legendary romance of Alfonso VII and the Jewess of Toledo.[6]

Even royalty was tinged with Judaism. The daughter of Jaime II of Aragon sought and followed the counsel of Jews in bringing up her children; and Ferdinand the Catholic, who with his wife Isabella was to exile the Jews from Spain forever, had, on his mother's side, the Jewish blood of the Henríquezes.[7]

But the Jewish caste, while marrying into royalty and min-

[4] *Ibid.,* p. 44.
[5] *Ibid.,* p. 43.
[6] *Ibid.,* p. 48.
[7] *Ibid.,* pp. 43, 49.

gling with plebeian blood, *had always boasted of the purity of its lineage*. In fact, prior to its assimilation by the Catholic Inquisition, the concept of "clean descent" was exclusively Semitic. For what, in the relatively peaceful Middle Ages, had been "purity of lineage" if not proof of unmixed Jewish blood? Castro quotes a document published by A. A. Neuman as the first record of this phenomenon in the history of Spain. It is dated sometime between the thirteenth and fourteenth century, and it reads:

Let all those who see this letter authorized by my signature know that certain witnesses have appeared before me, master Rabbi Isaac, president of the assembly, and made known to him the faithful and legal testimony of elderly and venerable persons. According to these [persons] the family of the brothers David and Azriel is of clean descent, without familial stain; David and Azriel are worthy of marrying into the most honorable families of Israel, since there is not in their ascendence any admixture of *impure blood* from the paternal, maternal or collateral sides. Jacob Isaachar.[8]

In 1492 Ferdinand and Isabella decreed the expulsion of the caste which, through intermarriage and the capture of the highest positions in commerce and the arts, had become *de facto* superior and, as such, a threat to Catholic power. The Jews left or were reduced to Catholicism; but the idea of "clean descent" remained behind. This, in sum, is the heart of Castro's thesis: that the Statutes of Purity of Blood invoked by the Iberian Inquisition were the direct result of Jewish influence on Spanish life. "The Hispano-Christian," he states, "copied a system of individual and collective values which was peculiar to the Hispano-Hebrew." Or, in other words, "The more he persecuted the Hispano-Hebrew, the more did the notion of purity of blood become incarnate in the mind of the Hispano-Christian." [9]

The premise is worthy of consideration. Sixty-seven years elapsed between the expulsion of the Jews in 1492 and the first *auto de fe* of 1559, time enough for two generations to ripen in a society virtually bereft of practicing Jews (the penalty for re-

[8] A. A. Neuman, *The Jews in Spain*, II, 5, quoted in Castro, *op. cit.*, p. 51.
[9] Castro, *op. cit.*, pp. 44–45.

lapsing was death) but alive with ex-Jews who had chosen conversion over exile. By the time the Protestant rebellion erupted, it is little wonder that there were men of Jewish blood not only at the stake—guilty of having chosen a more rational, more intellectual content for the religion their forebears had arbitrarily embraced—but, what is more important, that Jewish blood ran through the veins of Inquisitors great and small (Torquemada is a case in point)[10] who meted out sentences with a fury proportionate to their sense of guilt and self-hate.

In Américo Castro's own words:

The [notion of the] Church-State sprang from the minds of those who found themselves in a position to give way to [feelings] they had harbored within themselves for a long time; it was an almost revolutionary conquest carried out by resentful masses, by converts and descendants from converts who were anxious to forget what they had been. The structures of the former Jewish society were now saturated with anti-Jewish meanings and plans, [transformed] with an anger which was proportionate to the desire of eradicating all [Jewish] origins. . . . My idea that Spanish Christianity became fanatical in the measure that the Jews disappeared and were Christianized is, therefore, not a paradox but an elemental reality. Spanish Catholicism of the sixteenth century, totalitarian and federated, bore no resemblance to the Catholicism of the Middle Ages, nor to Europe's, nor even to that of Pontifical Rome who had no qualms in giving asylum to many Jews expelled from Spain.[11]

As we shall see, the contemporary historian Julio Caro Baroja has taken exception to Castro's thesis. And the bibliography on Spain from the American Historical Association's *Guide to Historical Literature* warns that Castro's book "should be used with caution." [12] But granting all reservations, the premise put forth in *La realidad histórica de España* warrants study. If modern

[10] *Ibid.*, p. 54. Castro quotes a document of Hernán Perez del Pulgar (himself a Spanish Semite) to the effect that the Torquemadas were descended from converted Jews.
[11] *Ibid.*, p. 53.
[12] The work was translated by Edmund L. King and published by Princeton University Press in 1954 as *The Structure of Spanish History*.

Spanish Catholicism bears little resemblance to that of any other country of Western Europe—with the possible exception of Italy —it may be that the Messianic nature of the Iberian Church cannot be understood without reference to its Semitic root. Only a Spaniard could, in the middle of the twentieth century, identify "the rights of God" with the rights of his own faith—as Spanish Council Fathers did consistently at the Vatican in the autumn of 1965. Only a Spanish mind could openly, indeed sincerely, conceive of its Church as "God's Church" much as an Old Testament Jew thought of his people as "God's People." Why?

Today the effects of the Inquisition on the Spanish mind can best be seen in the climate of opinion surrounding the sixteenth century. A brief comparison with France, however obvious, is not amiss. France was fully as guilty of religious persecution in her own 1500's, if indeed not more: there was no St. Bartholomew's Day in Spain. But through the social and intellectual turmoil of the seventeenth and eighteenth centuries—particularly the Enlightenment—she expunged the idea of sacral Christendom from her conscience forever. Not so Spain. Ever returning to the principle of religious "unity" as the cornerstone of her political existence, Spain is still, in the twentieth century, officially engaged in a "historical defense" of the Inquisition.

Turning from the world of Américo Castro, with its racial and cultural co-ordinates, it is well to examine a slim volume which appeared in Madrid in 1964. Its title is *The Inquisitorial Processes Against the Jewish Family of Juan Luis Vives*.[13] It was published by the Council of Scientific Investigations, a government institution responsible for a good many treasures of Spanish scholarship. It bears an introduction by Father Miguel de la Pinta Llorente, O.S.A., who unearthed its extraordinary documents, and a report

[13] *Procesos inquisitoriales contra la familia judía de Juan Luis Vives. I. Proceso contra Blanquina March, madre del humanista*. Introducción y transcripción paleográfica de Miguel de la Pinta Llorente, O.S.A. y José María de Palacio y de Palacio, Marqués de Villareal de Alava. Madrid: Instituto Arias Montano, Consejo Superior de Investigaciones Científicas, 1964.

by Señor José María de Palacio, Marqués de Villareal de Alava, the paleographer who transcribed them.

The book confirms Américo Castro's belief that Luis Vives was a full-blooded Jew. In a prefatory note, Father de la Pinta quotes Castro's fullest declaration on the subject, contained in the 1954 edition of *The Structure of Spanish History:*

The idea [I] expressed as a reasonable conjecture in *España y su historia* (1948, pp. 682–85) has now received full documentary confirmation: the paternal and maternal ancestors of Luis Vives and his wife were Jewish. The documents will be published by Sr. Abdón M. Salazar, whom I duly thank for having shared with me the essentials of his sensational findings. Until he was ten years old, Luis Vives attended, with his family, the clandestine synagogue of his great-aunt Leonor Castell; i.e., until [the synagogue] was discovered in 1502. . . . Luis Vives' father was burned [alive] in 1526; his mother's remains were exhumed and burned.[14]

Having quoted Castro, Father de la Pinta, one of the best scholars on sixteenth-century Spain, goes on to state that, as no documents were forthcoming from Señor Salazar, he took it upon himself to do the pertinent research in the matter of Vives' lineage. The first part of his findings is the trial against the "memory and fame of Blanquina March," Vives' mother, whose remains were exhumed and burned in Valencia in 1530, ten years before the Humanist's death in Bruges. Father de la Pinta adds a foreword to this trial, and this foreword is, for our purposes, the most important part of his work.

But the meaning of the trial itself is not to be overlooked in any study of Spanish religious dissent. Until Castro voiced his suspicion in 1948 few scholars guessed what lay behind Vives' brilliant but melancholy life abroad. The suggestion that he had an admixture of Jewish blood would have surprised no one, given the facts of intermarriage in the fifteenth century; but the revelation that both his parents were Jewish, that his father had died on an Inquisition pyre and his mother's remains were exhumed and

[14] *Ibid.,* p. 9.

burned, would have shed a different light on the works of this extraordinary man.

Born in 1493, Vives left Spain at the age of fifteen, never to return. He studied at the Sorbonne, taught at Louvain, lived in England and, in 1527, settled in the Netherlands. As a philosopher and psychologist he had few peers: his contribution to the latter science, *The Treatise on the Soul,* is a milestone in the study of rationalization, judgment, memory, habit and feeling as they relate to the psychic whole that is man. He dedicated his commentaries on St. Augustine's *The City of God* to Henry VIII. *An Introduction to Wisdom* and *On the Decay of Learning* are among his many works on education. His *Instruction of the Christian Woman,* dedicated to Catherine of Aragón, is a paean to the sexual repression which still passed for virtue in the Humanist's time. An enterprising scholar with the proper Hebraeo-Christian tools might well look for the Jewish influences in this moral study written by a Catholic who as a child was led to the synagogue by his mother's hand. *Scenes of School and College Life,* designed to entertain children and simultaneously exercise them in Latin, are lively vignettes of sixteenth-century life cast in the mold of the classic Renaissance Dialogue. One of them, *On Orthography,* contains a reference to Vives' own Spanish school days "at the school of Antonio Nebrija."

Spanish writers have ever gloried in Vives. Menéndez Pelayo, for one, cannot contain his admiration for this Spaniard in exile. He calls him a better philosopher than Erasmus and "the most pious of all the Humanists." [15] More recently Marañón produced a delightful essay on the hygienic and nutritional realities of Vives' world which might have well been called "Variations on the Theme of Gout." [16] But the distinguished Don Gregorio— in his wit, his compassion and his profound medical and psychiatric learning one of the great Humanists of modern times— missed, through no fault of his own, the essence of his compatriot's melancholy.

[15] Menéndez Pelayo, *op. cit.,* I, 766, 774.
[16] Marañón, *op. cit.*

In 1940, however, Ortega y Gasset was writing:

Whether or not Vives was a Christian is not the point to be debated; but rather what kind of a Christian he was. The deepest recesses of his life were informed by a full, unwavering faith in the God of the Bible. To narrow it down even further: in the three preceding generations the gravitational center of the faith had shifted from the Old Testament to the New. It is not the God of Sinai, the transcendent God, the God of Oriental and Augustinian Christianity, and above all [not] the mysterious ultra-being of the Trinity that the fifteenth century is interested in and adores; it is the God who comes down to the world; . . . if I have made myself clear, more than God, it is Jesus, [it is] Christ.[17]

The God who comes down to the world: in this beautiful phrase Ortega captures the essence of Christian Humanism with its faith in man and man's redemption in the here and now. And with it he defines the greatness of Vives who, having shed the myths of Judaism, gravitated to the bosom of a progressively de-mythologized Christianity. Vives is the New Christian (let us remember it was a term of derision) whose Christianity flowers with a truly new, first-generation splendor: objective, natural, terrestrial, anchored in the dignity that Bethlehem conferred on man forever. He lived at the dawn of the Modern Age and, as Ortega states, he looked ahead:

He was the first man in whom there awoke the *slightest* suspicion that beyond the culture of the Middle Ages and the pseudoculture of his time, with its revival of antiquity, there lay something else. He foresaw, he groped his way to the fact that this something else, this possible future culture . . . would be centered on man and on the world, both as pure nature; that it would be a culture inspired on utilitarian knowledge and not on useless contemplation; in sum, that its method would rest on experience.[18]

But Vives' intellectual triumphs pale beside the victory he won in the depths of his own soul. To the end of his days in Bruges,

[17] José Ortega y Gasset, *Obras inéditas: Vives-Goethe* (Madrid: Revista de Occidente, 1961), p. 47.
[18] *Ibid.*, p. 61.

where he lived modestly with his Jewish wife, he remained a man at peace. How much that peace cost him can be known only today, in full view of the documents published by Father de la Pinta and Señor de Palacio. His anguish knew no end; but neither his continued separation from his kin nor the news of his mother's posthumous disgrace, nor reports of subsequent misfortunes (the family property was confiscated and a brother-in-law processed as a *judaizante*), nor even the memory of his father's death could alter his irenic turn of mind. Earnestness, says Ortega, was his first great virtue.

Serenity was the second. That is why he chose as his motto the phrase *Sine querela* ["without grievance"]. It does not matter much that Vives was by temperament calm and quiet. His motto, and all his works, reveal to us that this calm and serenity, [this] not looking about for grievances, not complaining, not feeling self-righteous, not being mistrustful—how many times he repeats this advice: don't be mistrustful: i.e., don't always walk about thinking others are persecuting you—all this was in him the result of a perfectly thought out . . . technique or method and not the spontaneous [fruit] of his temperament.[19]

Such was Luis Vives, the ex-Jew who found his peace in Bruges. In Madrid, four centuries later, very little peace is to be found in Father de la Pinta's introduction to the trials of Blanca March.[20] The Augustinian scholar begins by referring to the vast, relatively untapped wealth of materials on the Jewish question, and to the need for "a systematic investigation conducted on behalf of our culture and of the structures of ancient Spanish society." Then he continues:

For the international masses, and for so many ignoramuses and cretins bent on a delirious and absurd anticlericalism, the Inquisition is the exclusive invention of the Iberian, a "choleric and rambunctious" man, a prowling monster of cruelty, fanatism and barbarousness. And yet this Institution was not altogether new when it was established

[19] *Ibid.*, p. 67.
[20] Spanish women do not lose their maiden name upon marriage; hence the Humanist's mother remained a March after she married Luis Vives Valeriola.

by the Catholic Sovereigns in the fifteenth century, since in the twelfth it already existed as a diocesan tribunal. . . . The use of force to implement [policies of] intolerance originates in antiquity; it is the fruit of the Roman tradition, which regarded heterodoxy as a religious and civil crime.[21]

He goes on to cite the establishment of the Holy Office under St. Louis in France and the chastisements visited on German, English and French Jews in the Middle Ages. In Spain, he states, the Jewish and Moorish problem "affected the marrow, the deepest recesses of the Spanish soul."

The Spanish Inquisition was a tribunal of justice . . . devoted to the investigation, definition and persecution of crimes against religion, heresy being considered a political offense, a crime of high treason. The nonnational character which was attributed to the Jewish race, its propensity to liberty of thought, have survived across the generations and [made it] weaken the lineages with which it coexists.[22] In Spain, however, it was not the Jew as such who was persecuted, but the *judaizante,* the astute convert who, behind the mask of a pretended conversion to the Church, lived, traded and climbed to the highest positions while in secret he held on to Mosaic practices and beliefs, and simultaneously engaged in proselytism, with the attendant and most serious danger to dogmatic principles and social stability. . . . A long time ago Don Américo Castro wrote: "the extermination of the Hebrews, and its sequel, the Inquisition, are not the fruit of the sovereign's intolerance, but only a great chapter in the tenacious defense of the popular Spanish spirit." [23]

For all his scholarship, Father de la Pinta is, like Menéndez Pelayo, one of the great representatives of that spirit. In this sad introduction to the trials of Blanca March he comes to a con-

---

[21] *Procesos inquisitoriales,* pp. 13–14.

[22] I had to take counsel with a philologist in translating this important phrase of Father de la Pinta's: *desvirtuando los linajes con quienes conviven.* The verb *desvirtuar* means "to deprive of efficacy, substance or vigor" and is usually employed with intangibles such as laws and principles. Hence "to weaken" (in the sense, perhaps, of diluting) would seem the correct English equivalent.

[23] *Procesos inquisitoriales,* pp. 15–16.

clusion which is worth quoting in full, so much light does it shed on the problem of tolerance in modern Spain:

For us, however, the Inquisition is indefensible. As a member of the clergy and a modern man, enemy of all interior coercion and all stifling of the intellect, we could never canonize Institutions such as the one we are writing about; but it is one thing to say this and another to carry out a "historical" defense of the Inquisition, which is very different and perfectly viable. We defended our popular conscience against [a] dismemberment which would have fragmented the Spanish masses [and produced] a continuous and progressive deviation [among them], sweeping away our cardinal doctrines and our operative philosophy with its own tone and character, [which is] one of the vital elements of any nation.

On the other hand, the problem of tolerance from the Catholic point of view offers no complications. Dogmatic tolerance is one thing, civil tolerance is another. The first gives rise to the following questions from the orthodox side: has man the moral obligation of finding the true religion, and having found it, of joining it? Certainly yes. Does the Church have the right to condemn all heterodoxy which opposes the Divine revelation with which she has been entrusted? Indubitably yes. Let us broach, now, the problem of "civil tolerance": Should society respect the individual conscience and abstain from imposing a religious creed by force? Again yes. That is all.[24]

It is, indeed, all. All the Spanish philosophy on tolerance is summed up in this brief statement appended to the trials which the Inquisition visited on an unhappy Jewess. The same rationale exactly rang out over the Vatican on September 17, 1965, when Archbishop Cantero of Zaragoza spoke of the Schema on Religious Liberty:

The matter under discussion is religious liberty, not liberty in matters of religion: it is not religious liberty before God, but before Caesar and society; it is religious liberty as a civil right to immunity from the coercion of the State or society. . . .[25]

It would not be fair to omit Father de la Pinta's heartfelt tribute to Vives. He speaks with admiration of the Humanist's serenity in

[24] *Ibid.*, p. 18.
[25] Communiqués from the Second Vatican Council's Press Office as reported in *Ecclesia,* September 25, 1965, p. 30.

the middle of his "moral Calvary." "Vives," he states, "was a sincere Jewish convert, a Hispano-Hebrew of surprising depth and breadth." He finds his Humanism "integral," "harmonic," and not at all suggestive of "man's vanity."

I would say that he was an extraordinary man who, as Goethe would, reached the infinite because he knew how to concentrate humbly and lovingly on his own finiteness. This is the lesson [contained] in some of his Treatises, written in the midst of confusion and bloody wars, [but written] in search of concord and civility, of tolerance and Christian piety. From all accounts it appears that Vives did not revile his homeland. Considered thus, he is for us a man *who lived his life fully.*[26]

There is no doubt that the Jewish question holds the key to Spain's ruthless stand against heresy since the sixteenth century. Whether Spanish bigotry answers to an ill-digested Semitism, as Américo Castro postulates, or whether it is the product of other cultural and temperamental factors, the expulsion of the Jews in 1492 was Spain's first and decisive stand on the subject of religious dissidence. All the tragedies that followed sprang from the very same thirst for "unity" which made the Jew unwelcome in a Christian society.

Castro's study on the subject (a second volume is yet to come) is now complemented by a more extensive work, *The Jews in Modern and Contemporary Spain,* by Julio Caro Baroja, professor at the University of Madrid (and a nephew of the late Pío Baroja). More than an exploration of a Spanish theme, Professor Caro's three-volume work is a major contribution to the historical literature of the West. The universality of its theme rings out from the very first sentence of the very first volume:

Why have the Visigoth, the Medieval Moor, the Spaniard of the late Middle Ages, the German, the Russian, the Berber and many other nations hated the Jew so continuously and systematically across the centuries and down the generations? [27]

Professor Caro tracks down that "why" in the social, religious, economic and, as he says, "even the physical and temperamental"

[26] *Procesos inquisitoriales,* pp. 31, 32.
[27] Julio Caro Baroja, *Los judíos en la España moderna y contemporánea* (Madrid: Ediciones Arion, 1961), I, 21.

phenomena of Jewish life in Europe, and particularly Spain. As regards the Spanish picture, he makes clear that he intends to steer a path between the extreme positions taken by his two predecessors:

Don Américo Castro holds . . . that the history of Spain as regards the Jews is, by reason of their importance thereto, essentially *different* from that of any other nation where they existed. I would not go so far as to say this. But neither would I indulge in another species of historico-cultural simplification conditioned by a line of thought quite different from his.

When Don Marcelino Menéndez Pelayo wrote the *Historia de los heterodoxos españoles*—a book which is, for me, as admirable as it is irritating—he said in a certain passage; "A *judaizante* was never missing from any of the *autos de fe* celebrated during the 16th and 17th centuries; but it would be altogether useless and vexatious to identify [these individuals], who were for the most part obscure people, without any resonance in [the] literature [of the times]."

I don't believe I have ever come across such professional haughtiness, nor such a specious way of eluding an important subject in a book which does not purport to be literary criticism, but religious history. . . . No, between Castro's categorical and heated assertions and Menéndez Pelayo's disdainful grimace there lies an entire world whose presentation [by these two authors] cannot find favor in the eyes of a cultural historian. . . .[28]

No mention of Caro Baroja's work—or of any similar study—should end without an important clarification. In Spain the Jew, like the Protestant and the *morisco,* was persecuted for his religion, never for his race. From the very first days of the Inquisition "purity of lineage" meant freedom from doctrinal, not genetic contagion: in a country where Jewish blood ran through the veins of courtiers and kings, merchants and warriors, preachers and scholars, a racial standard was absolutely meaningless. Américo Castro himself makes this abundantly clear:

Given the prejudices, the confusion and the subterfuges that reign in this field, it is well to insist on the special character of Spanish "purity of blood." Some Germanic peoples have created for them-

[28] *Ibid.,* I, 14.

selves a physical prototype of the perfect individual of their race. The physical and biological notions embodied in Western mythologies functioned within the German ambiance in a way unknown to the Spaniard. There is no physical, racial type of "Spanish man." From the 15th century on, "purity of blood" functioned as consciousness of caste, of descent from a people that 16th-century Spaniards deemed Chosen by God—itself a Hebraic standard.[29]

Hence the anti-Semitism of the West, with its ethnic overtones, was, and is, completely unknown in Spain. The Spaniard may be a monumental bigot but he has never been a racist: his lingering hatred of Jewry (it does linger), like his incurable hatred of Protestantism, is born of an *ideological* repugnance to a creed he deems false and therefore despicable.

In place of Aryan features and blue eyes the Spaniard worships an abstraction. Its name is "unity." "Unity" means uniformity of thought, unanimity of opinion, coincidence of ideas, blind obedience to a divinely ordained authority. For "unity" the Crusade [30] was fought; in "unity" the Church-State rose.

[29] Américo Castro, *op. cit.*, p. 45.
[30] The Civil War of 1936–1939 is officially known in Spain as the "Crusade of Liberation." Hereinafter we shall refer to it by that name.

5

In a study entitled *Religion and State in the Spain of the Sixteenth Century,* Fernando de los Ríos transcribes segments of an interview between Anne O'Hare McCormick and the Fascist philosopher Giuseppe Gentile published in the New York *Times Magazine* in September, 1926. De los Ríos—another post-Civil-War exile—expounds the thesis that the Ecclesiastical State is a "lasting" phenomenon in the history of Spain and, indeed, of Europe. To support his thesis he quotes the Italian's declarations to Miss McCormick:

The Fascist State is a super-State. . . . The Fascist idea of "hierarchy" is partly military but mostly ecclesiastical. Fascism has under its eye the oldest governing organization now existing: a Pontificate that dealt with and inherited from the Roman Caesars; and it is not averse to adapting for its own ends a structure that has proved so elastic and so invincible.[1]

Gentile's declaration is invaluable to an understanding of the present Spanish government. Where the Fascist states of Europe have long withered away, Spain's regime remains virtually unchanged: still monolithic, still patterned on the invincible authoritarianism which has always been the hallmark of the Catholic

[1] Fernando de los Ríos, *Religión y estado de la España del siglo XVI* (Mexico City: Fondo de Cultura Económica, 1957), p. 47.

Church. As the Church is "One, Holy and Catholic," so does Spain proclaim herself, in her own motto, "One, Great and Free." Both structures are informed by the idea of "unity," or, as we have said, uniformity, as the basis of their very existence.

Generalísimo Franco's statement of the nation's "Fundamental Principles," contained in the Law of May 17, 1958, bespeaks the ecclesiastical flavor of the Spanish power structure. The preamble and the first two points of the law read as follows:

I, Francisco Franco Bahamonde, Caudillo of Spain,

Conscious of my responsibility before God and before History, in the presence of the Cortes of the Realm, DO PROMULGATE, as principles of the National Movement, construing [as such] the union of all Spaniards in the ideals which gave life to the Crusade, the following [points]:

1. Spain is a unity of destiny in the universal [sphere]. To serve the unity, greatness and liberty of the Motherland is the sacred duty and the collective task of all Spaniards.

2. The Spanish nation considers as a badge of honor the submission [acatamiento] to the law of God according to the doctrine of the Holy, Catholic, Apostolic, Roman Church, the only true faith, inseparable from the national conscience, which shall inspire its legislation.

Not until the Second Vatican Council did the Church envision a change in her rigid, quasi-military government; and coincidentally, not until the 1960's, when European capital and ideas began to infiltrate an impatient country, did the thought of a change in the "Fundamental Laws" occur to the Spanish regime. Today, happily, the Church is in ferment while Spain is obviously in transition.

But where, in the absence of any effective form of self-determination, is Spain's transition leading? How and when will she abandon her Catholic Fascism and lead her people to a saner, more secular and human fulfillment? The answer to the question lies within the realm of practiced—and imaginative—historians and political scientists. All that the student of the Protestant problem can do is review the historical and temperamental antecedents of the Spaniard's thirst for "unity," and measure them against the new, unmistakable signs that Spain is at last awakening to the "sinful," "materialistic" world of the twentieth century.

I

Salvador de Madariaga has shed more light than any other writer on the phenomenon of Spanish individualism and its corollary, the worship of authority.

Whether consciously or not, the Spaniard lives against a background of eternity, and his outlook is more religious than philosophic. Hence it is that the two poles of his psychology are the individual and the universe; the subject and the Whole; and that life for him should consist in the absorbing of the universe by the individual, the *assimilation* of the Whole by the subject.

The individual thus becomes the standard of all life—an individual voluntarily stripped of all but essential tendencies. Instinctively at home in essential things, the Spaniard is therefore apt to evade the grasp of things which are less high up in the scale—things merely necessary or useful or advisable.

Moreover, the instinct for preserving his own liberty makes him eschew all forms of social cooperation, since all collective work tends to enslave the individual and to reduce him to the status of a piece of machinery. His anti-cooperative instinct comes to reinforce his tendency to dwell on the two poles of his psychology—man and the universe—leaving uncultivated the middle stretches in which social and political communities lie.[2]

It is precisely because these "middle stretches" lie uncultivated that Spaniards have always yearned for, and supported, a strong, centralized authority which will shape Spanish society and hold it together. Franco's cry that he is "responsible before God and before History" is perhaps the most supremely Spanish utterance of modern times. It is defiant, it is redolent of that abnormal spirituality that looks *past* the world to eternity and, what is per-

[2] Salvador de Madariaga, *Spain, A Modern History* (London: Jonathan Cape, 1942, 1946), pp. 21, 22.

72

haps most important in a Spanish context, it has undoubted style. This single statement may well explain Franco's continuing sway over a permanently disenfranchised country, and his ability to muster a crack police force whose loyalty and devotion can only be matched with Mussolini's or Hitler's in the late thirties.[3]

By assuming the very title of *"Caudillo"*—and assuming it for life—Franco paid homage to that tradition of absolute power that lies at the heart of Spanish politics. The word *"caudillo,"* which means "chieftain" or "leader," is defined by the Spanish Royal Academy Dictionary as "he who, as head or guide, sends people to war"; and, "he who directs a guild, a community or body." Speaking of the *caudillismo* which emerged in the Peninsula after the French invasion of 1808, Américo Castro writes:

The *caudillo* is he who, with no more law than that of his strength or personal appeal, organizes guerrillas in Spain or mounted raids in Spanish America; he who commands and is obeyed . . . ; for centuries he has been dazzling and bewitching those who are responsive to a

[3] Two things are still sacrosanct, and unassailable, under Spanish law: the Chief of State and the Police. The supremacy of the Police continues unabated, although the democratic ferment now at work in the country is indirectly tempering the rigors with which the Penal Code chastises "illegal propaganda." On November 13, 1965, the newspaper *Ya* published the news of a one-year jail sentence imposed upon a Madrid lawyer who wrote letters to the Bishop of Madrid, the Apostolic Nuncio and the Secretary of State at the Vatican, complaining of the mistreatment of clients of his at the hands of the Police. Señor Eduardo Cierco Sánchez, the accused, also made the text of his letter available to the French newspaper *Le Nouvel Observateur*. The French paper printed the text in full; thereafter it appeared in the *Bulletin* of the Unión General de Trabajadores (General Workers' Union) and *España Libre,* organs of anarchical, anti-Spanish elements abroad. Although it was not proved that Señor Cierco made the letter available to the newspapers, the prosecution requested a sentence of nine years in prison for violation of Article 252, Paragraph 2, of the Penal Code. When the sentence was handed down the penalty was fixed at one year because, "considering the frequency of news of this type in the foreign press, and the fact that readers have become inured to them, their psychological impact on the public has diminished, downgrading the importance of the crime."

power . . . granted from above, and not to horizontal "considerations" which are visible and ever open to revision.[4]

The power from above he speaks of is, of course, equivalent to the divine right of kings; visitors to Spain can note its modern application by examining Spanish coins, all of which bear the effigy of Franco and the legend, *"Francisco Franco, Caudillo de España por la G. de Dios"* ("Francisco Franco, Caudillo of Spain by the Grace of God"). The horizontal considerations, on the other hand, are the social and economic factors—ever open to revision—which move the voting masses in the "liberal" democracies and which underlie the strictly pragmatic party system of the West.

Spain, be it said, thinks of itself as a democracy; but an "organic" or "representative" one. In an organic State, citizens cluster in miniature nations, each headed by a *caudillo* whose authority is granted by the *caudillo* above him, whose authority is in turn granted by the one above him, and so on in a chain of command that leads inexorably to the absolute *Caudillo* at the top. It is a truly vertical system under which power is entrusted to reliable, hand-picked chieftains whose loyalty to the moral and ideological "unity" of the nation has been proved beyond shadow of doubt. Franco and Madariaga explain it thus:

Franco:

For us, democracy is not the exploitation of man, it is not the hunger, misery and despair [fostered] in homes by the formula of presenting a few names every four or five years and asking [them] which they wanted, so that the masses, deceived, would answer as at that sad first election, saying: Barabbas! No; we do not submit the fate of the Motherland to such wretchedness; by democracy we understand the real participation of man in the tasks of the State. But man can only be effective and intervene in the affairs of State through his natural organizations; through the family: he who creates a family, he who supports it and presides over it, is he who should speak, and not those who depend on him. Through the Municipality, as the first association with which he has contact; through the [State-controlled] labor union to which he belongs. . . . It is through the Municipalities and the

[4] Américo Castro, *op. cit.*, p. 277.

labor unions that men take part in the life of Spain today, and not through that false, exploiting democracy which asked for their vote today to deceive them tomorrow. That democracy we repudiate.[5]

Madariaga:

The individual, moved by stronger vertical than horizontal impulses, i.e., by natural forces expressed in him rather than by forces transmitted by tradition or absorbed from the environment, tends to assert his personality and (like a bottle already full of its contents) to refuse other influences. This leads to dictatorship, observable not merely in the public man, statesman, general, cardinal or king at the head of the state, but in every one of the men at the head (or on the way thereto) of every village, city, region, business firm, or even family in the country.[6]

As the new Catholic State rose from the ashes of the Civil War in 1939, its philosophy of government slowly found shape and direction. Internally, all measures were taken to ensure the moral, religious and ideological "unity" of Spaniards; meanwhile the battle to defend Spain from her "enemies" in the outside world began in earnest. And of all the anti-Spanish demons prowling abroad, the most formidable was "inorganic democracy"—a materialistic, immoral way of life which, in the Spanish rationale, would eventually spell the ruin of Europe and all Western civilization.

The Spanish position before "liberal" democracy (another term for the Western system) followed two lines. The first, evident in Franco's speech quoted above, impugned the party system as a moral abomination. The second, which emerged almost simultaneously and snowballed into a face-saving tenet, held that political parties abroad were insignificant accessories of essentially "organic" regimes—in other words, that "liberal" democracies were "organic" at heart.

The party system came in for its worst beatings in the forties

[5] Speech in Huelva on April 25, 1956. Quoted in *El pensamiento político de Franco*, with texts selected and arranged by Agustín del Rio Cisneros (Madrid: Servicio Informativo Español, 1964), p. 251.
[6] Madariaga, *op. cit.*, pp. 22–23.

and fifties. In his 1955 end-of-year address, Franco recapitulated thus:

The fact that we have put aside the party system whose history has been so sad and whose results have been so catastrophic, and channeled [the people's] participation in public affairs through those natural organizations in which the life of men unfolds—as His Holiness reminded us in his last message—it was this which permitted us to redeem ourselves from the wretched and artificial fruits of the party system, so closely linked to the tragedies [which have befallen] our nation.[7]

His allusion to the Pope was not gratuitous. Pope Pius XII, whose *affaire de cœur* with prewar Nazism ended so dismally, found salve for his ascetic, aristocratic soul in the continuing success of the Spanish regime. In a message to the Spanish Minister of Foreign Affairs a year after the above speech of Franco's, Pius again spoke of that "structuralization" of Spanish society so dear to his heart:

Catholic Spain has lived through certain horrors, and this very experience might be a special grace from above which has kept her from not inconsiderable perils. Our fervent wish is that she know how to make use of this singular blessing, progressing continuously in the reorganization of her means of production, in the structuralization of her fundamental institutions, in the practical regulation of the principles she has always acknowledged and accepted. . . .[8]

Slowly, in the wake of postwar Europe's recovery and the emergence of strong, prosperous states all over the western part of the Continent, the Spanish line began to change. As far back as 1943, Franco had spoken of a "third system" which, repudiating both Communism and capitalism, made clear the path of "Christian morals": "There is a third system born of Christian morals, of the history and tradition of peoples, [and] that is the system we have established." [9] In 1943 Spain was only beginning that long

[7] *El pensamiento político de Franco,* p. 251.
[8] *La iglesia habla de España* [*The Church Speaks of Spain*] (Madrid: Servicio Informativo Nacional, 1964), p. 79.
[9] *El pensamiento político de Franco,* p. 263.

period of isolation and suffering when, materially and intellectually destroyed, she would feed on her "Catholic" pride and her resentment of the hostile world outside. The "third system" was, for her, a *punto de honor*. But as the years went by and Western Europe not only stood firm, but prospered under its "liberal" system, the Spanish premise began to change. It had first been held that Spain was uniquely Christian and uniquely endowed to lead Europe to salvation; now the official line contended that Europe had adopted the Spanish system all along. Parties and other impedimenta were not important: all Western nations were governed by a single political "movement" which remained constant even if the rulers changed.

I first heard the theory from a Spanish student in the United States in the early fifties. Democrats and Republicans were all the same, he told me quite solemnly. There was no real, essential difference between them: weren't they all American? The reasoning, which he had acquired through the Fascist indoctrination that goes hand-in-glove with Spanish education, has proved unusually hardy, and survives to this day in the Spanish press. When, having defeated Senator Goldwater at the polls, Lyndon B. Johnson adopted a "get-tough" policy in Vietnam compatible with what the Senator had recommended in his campaign, the "organic" nature of the American system was derisively underscored in Spanish newspapers. One year later, reporting on the fiercely contested German elections, *ABC* [10] ran pictures of Candidates Erhard, Brandt and Mende with a text that began: "On the eve of the [elections], the electoral climate in Germany is bereft of passion. There are hardly any differences in the parties' policies regarding international affairs, and their positions on domestic matters are very similar."

Twenty-five years of such pat reasoning, complemented by the most rigid censorship in postwar Europe, brought about the truly organic, pyramidal society that is Spain today. In the religious sphere, the search for "unity" resolved itself along similar lines, and for similar reasons. Menéndez Pelayo is speaking of the temperamental no less than Madariaga when he states:

[10] September 18, 1965.

77

The rapid propagation of Protestantism must be attributed, among other causes, to the inveterate hate of the Northern countries towards Italy. . . . The blood of the Germans is that of Arminius, who destroyed Varro's legions. There is in them a tendency towards division which has always stumbled against Roman and Catholic Unity. That is why the nations of the South have rejected and energetically continue to reject the Reformation.[11]

This "tendency towards division" and its social and political consequences are, of course, not only at the heart of Protestantism, but of all Western civilization. Yet in Spain, in the middle of the twentieth century, the intelligentsia continues to denounce "inorganic" democracy as corrupt. An articulate defense of a system based on a "differentiated," "separate," "privileged-by-act-of-God" oligarchy was to be found in *ABC* on November 10, 1965. The author was Father de la Pinta Llorente, whose judgment on the Jewish question we have already studied. In his article, entitled "Masses and Minorities," he assails the "horizontal" system of modern nations in the name of Nature:

Every civilized act is an act of differentiation, of segregation. To attend a University, to read authentic literature, to hear good music, each and all of these acts of separation, of separation from the "mass," as Ludwig Lewisonh [sic] has written. And he added: "All these acts are becoming more and more necessary for the survival of civilization."

Natural Law and the Christian conscience certainly demand that all members of a community be guaranteed the material and mental means to solve those basic needs which enrich the human personality and, consequently, society. But to work from the premise or norm that "we are all equal" is completely unacceptable, and leads eventually to the disintegration and crumbling of the foundations of society. Differentiated existence is a decree of Nature. We are all equal as regards our "human nature" [sic], which was created by the Maker. But nothing more. Each human being is unique in its psychological richness, its mental qualities, its moral excellence—not forgetting, as Alexis Carrel wrote—"that the most humble task is no less noble than the most lofty."

As we have written before, there is no greater stupidity than that

11 Menéndez Pelayo, *op. cit.,* I, 743.

shown by rulers of modern countries who permit the participation of certain structures in the lives of [their] nations. This is the punishment which Europe had to pay, and which she will pay with high interest; a continuous disintegration in the name of a "mass" which anathematizes and attacks wealth [*riqueza*], rank, or culture as antidemocratic and antiliberal values. Historical Marxism, economic socialism, the Humanist and Protestant revolt—in other words, the headiest wines —are at work in modern countries, co-operating with all extremism and all violence in the pretension that "quality" and "numbers" shall do away with all cultivated minorities. . . . This tragic disintegration of the classic European synthesis has gradually given rise to a lack of cultivation among humans, individually and collectively: to the absence of egregious and august personalities, to the definition of human conduct as a jostling of others, as coarseness, as resentment of all those who treasure a difference: culture, money [*fortuna*], manners or rank.

In positing a society where a "coarse," "jostling" mass encroaches upon the privileges of a "cultured minority," Father de la Pinta is giving us the antithesis of post-Civil-War Spain. His text, incomprehensible to anyone who has been exposed to the masses of Germany, France, Scandinavia, etc., not to mention the constant mobility of the lower and lower-middle classes of the United States, must be read against the realities of the Spanish world. In Spain "culture" is, in actual fact, the prerogative of a few: it is not *acquired,* it is *born* to. Cultured Spaniards may be found in the aristocracy, the upper bourgeoisie and the relatively small middle class, where they occur genetically, much as brown, blond or red hair can result as it will given the Mendelian requirements. Beneath the middle class, the human condition falls off abruptly. The peasant, the worker, the great legion of functional illiterates, dignified as they undoubtedly may be, stand bereft of any intellectual, social or civic awareness. With the possible exception of highly industrialized Cataluña, in all Spanish regions books and records ("authentic literature" and "good music," those commonplaces of life in Europe and America) are still beyond the intellectual and economic reach of the masses. Hence the intervention of these "structures" in the life of certain countries horrifies Father de la Pinta in the name of Nature.

His defense of the power system also echoes the firm alliance between the Church and the aristocracy which began in 1939, and which has been a factor in the continuing "invisibility" of the Protestant minority.

The swing to the Right after the Civil War brought with it the rehabilitation of all traditional values, beginning with the most traditional of all: the hegemony of an aristocracy of the blood, titled and otherwise, which, after having recovered the immense landholdings expropriated by the Republic, divided among itself Father de la Pinta's differentiating emblems of "wealth," "culture," "manners" and "rank." Thus, if politically and theologically Spain emerged from the Civil War an extraordinarily centralized country, socially she was tidier still: she was a nonconstitutional kingdom without a king. (In the 1960's Franco is still advised by a body called the "Council of the Realm.")

From the very beginning Catholicism—itself an orderly vertical structure—blessed and shared in the joys of nurturing an intellectual and social elite. And having aligned herself with the aristocracy, the Church found one more "natural" reason for looking down on native Protestantism, which, as it was not beyond stating time and again, drew the bulk of its members from the lowest classes of Spanish society. Even in the post-Johannine days of cautious good will, the idea of Protestantism as a movement strictly for and by the "uncultured" was hard to get rid of. Writing in a religious magazine [12] in March, 1965, Father Ricardo Sanchis, S.J., a Jesuit of the liberal persuasion, unconsciously falls into this cavalier attitude. His story, "A Protestant Cop" (see Appendix, pp. 368–70), is aimed at children; it praises the kindness and efficiency of a much-taunted (and presumably real) policeman who happens to be an *evangélico*. "Catholics," he writes, "have learned not to be cruel to our separated brethren, even if the heritage of the Inquisition has not disappeared completely." Then he adds: "Does it make sense to speak of ecumenism in Spain? The dissident minority is so small and is rooted in such

[12] *El reinado social del Sagrado Corazón*, p. 14.

low cultural strata, that we always think of ecumenism as something to be fostered abroad. . . ."

II

At the end of the Crusade the situation of the "dissident minority" was critical. Such tolerance as was extended to the *evangélicos* by the Church-State allowed them to practice their rites only in the strict seclusion of unmarked churches and private homes. For by professing Protestantism a Spaniard was automatically a subversive element in the eyes of the authorities, of the all-powerful Church and above all of the rank and file of victorious Crusaders. During the forties, fifties and part of the sixties, Spanish Protestants were—to use a magnificent term of Madariaga's—"religious aliens" in their own homeland.[13]

Morally, in the official view, the *evangélicos'* condition was altogether hopeless. Between the end of the Crusade and the advent of Pope John, the Spanish Church did everything in its power to defame the handful of natives who held on to their "erroneous" beliefs. Looking back over those years, one is struck by the fact that the moral climate surrounding Protestantism—created and carefully nurtured by the hierarchy—was the exact complement to every Government measure taken against Protestants. Here is the Church speaking to her faithful in 1947:

Some time ago, in the garden of our Spain, a snake appeared and is still hiding in the grass. This snake is Protestantism. Enemy nations who have done nothing to help us, but a great deal to harm us, have offered us this rotten bit of goods. . . . It is corruption under a gilt cover, presented with phrases from a desecrated Bible. Their Bibles and Gospels are not the word of God, for they do not come to us by the way shown by Christ himself. To read or distribute them is a

[13] Madariaga uses the words to describe the *moriscos* expelled in the seventeenth century. They apply to every Spaniard—Protestant, Moor or Jew—who does not profess the racial faith.

mortal sin. . . . The Immaculate Virgin, our Patroness, once more will crush the head of this serpent.[14]

The above notice appeared in *My Parish,* a publication of the diocese of Zaragoza, on December 2, 1947. It is only one of the many such warnings circulated by the Church, officially and un-officially, in the forties and fifties (see Appendix, pp. 350–54). The Zaragoza tract, rescued for posterity by Huguenot Jacques Del-pech, sounds the leitmotiv of the entire campaign: Protestants are agents of a foreign, inherently evil power, which has intruded upon the sanctity of the Spanish nation.

Three years later, a Barcelona Jesuit wrote a 68-page "cate-chism" on Protestantism for the use of Spanish children. The late M. Delpech included excerpts from this primer on hate in his small but well-documented book on the Spanish situation. The text he reproduces is as follows:

Q. Is becoming a Protestant equivalent to losing the faith?

A. Yes, certainly; to become a Protestant is nothing else but open apostasy against the Christian religion; it is to reject the faith of the true doctrine of Jesus Christ, the Apostles and the Church.

Q. Are these doctrines not worse, in a certain sense, than those of the pagans?

A. You are right; many pagan doctrines are far less impious.

Q. Who are those who favor Protestantism?

A. Disregarding demagogues, revolutionists of all breeds and mem-bers of secret societies, which are in league with Protestantism, the most enthusiastic abettors of the Reformation are generally bad Catholics, and those who neither profess nor practice any religion.

Q. Have they not special motives for leading young people astray?

A. Quite so; young people constitute the special objects of their apostolate, because they know very well that youth lacks experi-ence. . . .

Q. What is the conduct of these unfortunate young people?

A. They manifest to the world what they are like inwardly, and

[14] Quoted in Jacques Delpech, *The Oppression of Protestants in Spain,* translated from the French by Tom and Dolores Johnson (London: Lut-terworth Press, 1956), pp. 38–39.

leave everywhere the fruit of the pestiferous seeds sown in their spirits and in their hearts.

Q. Are the propagators of Protestantism trying to spread socialism and communism?

A. That is the sole reason for all their painstaking efforts. Protestantism is nothing but a vague voice, a negation of the true religion; that is why it suits them best for the purpose of covering up their designs whose aim is nothing else but the destruction of society.

Q. By what signs can one recognize the propaganda of Protestantism?

A. By various signs, as some are foreigners and some are Spanish. The former are generally English. The latter are usually sectarians, apostate monks or clerics, or dissolute young people led astray by the others.

Q. How can foreign propagators of Protestantism be recognized?

A. As for the English, who are like birds of prey who swoop down everywhere to seize their victims, they appear at first sight to be devout and religious . . . and always carry their Bibles or prayer-books under their arms.[15]

Such was the moral climate surrounding "heresy" in the days before the signing of the Concordat with the Holy See. The legal situation of the *evangélicos* was no less discouraging. Only by virtue of Article 6 of the *Fuero de los Españoles* (Spaniards' Bill of Rights) were they allowed to open "private" chapels for what was, in effect, the hidden practice of their religion. The *Fuero,* drawn up in consultation with the Holy See, delves into the sacral in its preamble:

The Spanish State proclaims, as the guiding principle of its acts, respect for the dignity, integrity and liberty of the human person, and acknowledges man, *qua* bearer of eternal values and member of national community, as the holder of rights and duties whose exercise the State guarantees in accordance with the common good.

The key words, as regards freedom of worship, are "eternal values" and "common good"; their import is hammered home in Article 6, which states:

[15] Juan Perrone, S.J., *Catechism on Protestantism* (Barcelona: 1950), pp. 14–15, 24, 25, 28, 30, 32. Quoted in Delpech, *op. cit.,* pp. 40–41.

The profession and practice of Catholic religion, which is that of the Spanish State, shall enjoy official protection. No one shall be disturbed because of his religious beliefs or the private practice of its ceremonies. No outward ceremonies or demonstrations other than those of the Catholic religion shall be permitted.

Hanging on the slender hope offered by the *Fuero,* which was implemented by Circular Order on November 12, 1945, approximately twenty-five Protestant chapels opened between 1945 and 1948. Housed in unmarked buildings, often clandestine (i.e., without the official government permission required by the above-mentioned order), poor and ill-equipped as these meeting places were, their existence soon alarmed the Church. On February 23, 1948, the Ministry of Government drafted a Circular Order to all Civil Governors of Spanish provinces which stated:

So great have been the abuses committed under the protection of the tolerance established in Article 6 of the Spaniards' Bill of Rights; and so many have been the protests of Ecclesiastical and Secular Authorities on the subject; and in view of the fact that before our Crusade Protestant chapels were hidden centers of Masonry which conspired against public order; the differences between (a) the private exercise of worship and respect for the [dissidents'] conscience, and (b) abuses and infringements committed under the cloak of toleration must be determined. It must be made clear that the text of the law, both in letter and spirit, admits only the following interpretation and application:

First: The exercise of private worship of non-Catholic religions is recognized.

Second: By "private worship" is meant strictly personal worship, or worship carried on inside buildings of the denomination in question.

Third: This worship may in no case be manifested outwardly or publicly, in the first place because it would [thereby] cease to be private, which is the only modality allowed; and in the second place, because no outward ceremonies or manifestations are allowed other than those of the Catholic religion.

Fourth: Consequently, all propaganda or proselytizing for non-Catholic religions is illicit, whatever method may be used, such as, for instance, the founding of schools for teaching; the distribution of gifts, supposedly for charity; the operation of recreational centers, etc.; for these would obviously be outward manifestations, which are not allowed. For these reasons Your Excellency will proceed most zealously to keep under strict vigilance the activities of the religious denominations mentioned above, curtailing with the greatest alacrity any infringements of the law, and informing me immediately of the transgressions found and the sanctions imposed. . . .

In the years leading up to the Concordat of 1953 the Civil Governors' vigilance did not lag. Neither did the special section of the Dirección General de Seguridad (Spanish F.B.I.) charged with policing "Freemasons, Communists and Protestants" fail in its investigative and punitive mission. To these two agents must be added a third: Fe Católica, a three-Jesuit team described by one of its collaborators, Father Francisco Peiró, S.J., as a "center of religious information and orientation." The organization (which still exists, with headquarters in Madrid, at No. 1 Maldonado Street) for many years kept the official police files of all Protestant churches in Spain, their pastors, membership and activities. Today its fight against Protestantism is carried on in *ABC,* the nation's leading paper.

Those inclined to puzzle at the fact that fourteen years elapsed between the end of the Crusade and the signing of the Concordat must note that Rome had negotiated a provisional convention with Spain on June 7, 1941, and that the last two articles of this document left no room for doubt as to the relations between Madrid and the Vatican, and their outcome in future years:

Article 9. Until the conclusion of a new Concordat, the Spanish government agrees to abide by the provisions contained in the first four articles of the Concordat of 1851.[16]

[16] As transcribed in Menéndez Pelayo (*op. cit.,* II, 996), the first article of the 1851 Concordat reads: "The Roman, Catholic, Apostolic Religion, [which,] to the exclusion of any other, continues to be the only one of the Spanish nation, shall always be preserved in the domains of Her Catholic Majesty with all the rights and prerogatives which it would enjoy according to the Law of God and the dispositions of the holy canons [i.e., Canon Law]." By virtue of the Concordat, Bishops were given the right to control education and ban all harmful books. There was also provision for the payment of the clergy (today the Franco government still pays the salaries of secular priests).

Article 10. During that time, the Spanish government agrees not to legislate on matters that could affect the Church, without first obtaining the approval of the Holy See.

The outbreak of World War II and Europe's agonizing period of recovery, with its attendant strain on the allegiances of Pope Pius XII, delayed negotiations for a Concordat. In the meantime Spain—materially undone, intellectually sterile and spiritually putty in the hands of her hierarchy—was turning more and more fiercely Catholic. All news was censored and all newscasts were begun with an evocation of the Crusade's martyrs. As Protestantism became synonymous with perfidy, so was religious liberty equated with perdition. The Metropolitan Conference of Bishops, in its Instruction of May, 1948, stated plainly that

Freedom of worship for individuals is false, if it is considered as the right of each person to practice the religion that he chooses or deems proper. For the faithful there should be no freedom of choice between one church and another, since they have the sacred duty to become members of the only Church founded by Christ, which is easily recognized by its signs and marks of unity, sanctity, Catholicity and Apostolicity. . . .[17]

Three years later, the marriage between the Regime and the Church was solemnly ratified. Pope Pius XII signed the Concordat in Rome on August 27, 1953; on October 25 of that year Franco presented it to the *Cortes* in Madrid. In his speech to the Spanish Parliament, the Generalísimo drew a dazzling portrait of the fourteen-year-old union and its exotic outcome: a sacral State of medieval proportions in which civil legislation points the way to Heaven:

For Catholic nations, matters of Faith assume a foremost place among the affairs of State. The salvation or the loss of souls, the expansion or inhibition of the true faith are capital problems before which [the State] cannot be indifferent. That is why we cannot judge the Concordat by thinking of our Catholic faith in the abstract, with the erroneous mentality of lay states, or [with] those liberal concepts

[17] Quoted in Delpech, *op. cit.,* p. 31. Cf. also *Ecclesia,* June 19, 1948, p. 5.

[epitomized by] a haggling between strange powers, [and] suggestive of a compromise or a settlement between enemies. If, by virtue of the Concordat we have signed, we serve the transcendental ends of the Church of Christ, we are serving ourselves and the spiritual welfare of our souls. . . . The Spaniard cannot conceive of a stable, much less a prosperous, national situation, if it is not based on a perfect co-ordination between the respective mission and ends of the Church and the State.[18]

In Chapter 13 we shall see how laws designated to effect "the salvation of souls" impinge on the lives of Spanish Catholics. What must be noted at this point is that, once proclaimed, the Concordat became the basis for an unrelenting, systematized harassment of all "heretical sects." Article 6 of the *Fuero* was, in Franco's words, "accorded the high honor of being incorporated into the Concordat's Final Protocol." To implement the old call to battle, Articles 1 and 2 of the Rome-Madrid agreement left no doubts as to the absolute dominion of the Church in the national territory:

1. The Roman Catholic and Apostolic Faith will continue to be the only religion of the Spanish nation, and will enjoy all the rights and prerogatives that are due it, in accordance with divine law and canon law.
2. The Spanish State recognizes in the Catholic Church the perfect type of society and guarantees its right to free, complete exercise of its spiritual power and of its jurisdiction, as well as the right to free public worship.

In November, 1949, Cardinal Tedeschini had addressed a few words of encouragement to a group of Spanish seminarians in Rome:

[18] The speech of Don Esteban Bilbao, President of the *Cortes* until 1965, is no less characteristic. One passage states: "All those who revile us abroad can go on doing so. No matter. Our triumph is measured by its own importance. While they [the enemies] clamor, Spain, exiled from international circles, yesterday the widow of nations like Biblical Jerusalem, dons her imperial cloak and, remembering the paths of her greatness, crosses herself to enter triumphantly in a new age of history."

Praise be to Spain, a Catholic nation, whose material and moral realities I am, and have been, aware of. With only a few [more] nations like her, the world would be saved. She teaches us how to govern in the Catholic way. If Rome is a promise, Spain and her Catholic government are a reality. Praise be to Spain! [19]

[19] *La iglesia habla de España,* p. 40.

II

A Snake in Eden

6

As we have seen, it is impossible to understand the Church-State without a basic knowledge of the Spaniard's ethnic background, his culture, history and temper. By the same token it is impossible to fathom the Spain created by the victorious Crusaders without reference to the regime against which they took up arms. All of Spanish history has been a continuous and violent zigzag between authoritarianism and anarchy. On the religious level—where it is no less evident than in politics—Madariaga describes this phenomenon as the "familiar rhythm of the Spanish spirit, oscillating from extreme to extreme without a position of equilibrium in the middle term." [1]

The "Republic of Workers" which came into being in 1931 sought to break the centuries-old power of the Church and channel Spaniards' psychic and intellectual energies towards those secular, human, nonreligious achievements which are the backbone of the modern world (and which, thirty-four years later, were to be ticked off so thoroughly in the Second Vatican Council's Schema XIII). The Republic wielded the ax against *all* religion with evident relish; but it took special pains, and pleasure, in disestablishing the Catholic Church. Article 3 of the Law of Religious Conferences of May 17, 1933, held:

[1] Madariaga, *op. cit.*, p. 159.

The State has no official religion. All "confessions" can perform their services freely within their churches. To perform them outside the same, they will require previous authorization in each case. . . .[2]

Article 11 nationalized all Catholic property. Article 12 forbade the Church from disposing of any of its assets. Article 10 decreed that the Catholic Church and other religious confessions could "acquire by any title buildings and real estate; but they can only hold them to such an extent as may be necessary for their religious duties. . . ."

The disabilities imposed upon the Church by the Law were many and onerous. *Evangélicos* came in for trouble, too, in constitutional measures forbidding religious education; furthermore, Article 7, by requiring that all religious "ministers, administrators and holders of office be Spaniards," dealt a blow to the work of foreign missionaries. But the Protestant bodies, emancipated and freed by the Lay State, took an attitude of watch-and-wait before the new difficulties. Not so the Catholic Church, which had suffered a staggering blow to its pride and self-sufficiency.

Quite naturally the fires of reaction were soon burning. When the Republic, "oscillating" in the best Spanish form, degenerated into lawlessness and terror, the conflagration was inevitable. In 1939 the three-year Crusade was at last over, one million people lay dead, the Government was Fascist, and the Church supreme once more.

It was then that "Rome's promise" became a reality. Our study of that sad fulfillment begins in the dismal forties when "unity" reigned over a devastated, poverty-stricken land, and when Protestants—called by one Roman pontiff the "enemies of the Cross of Christ"—found themselves unable to open a place of worship without the authorization of the Church-State.

I

From the early days of the new Regime, the opening of a clandestine chapel was considered a violation of Article 16 of the *Fuero:*

[2] Quoted in C. Araujo García and Kenneth Grubb, *Religion in the Republic of Spain* (London, World Dominion Press, 1933), p. 49.

Spaniards shall meet and assemble freely for licit purposes and in accordance with the provisions of law.

Any chapel opened without express Government authorization was both "illicit" and against "the provisions of law." Authorization, on the other hand, was granted only when four points had been proved:

(1) That there were enough Protestants to justify the petition;
(2) That the church had existed before the Crusade;
(3) That the group had not been previously penalized for abuses of "proselytism";
(4) That the church had no politico-criminal record.[3]

An analysis of these four points sheds much light on the long-range objectives of Church and State in suppressing all forms of Protestantism. In June, 1952, writing in the magazine *Razón y Fe,* a Jesuit had admirably depicted the Spanish situation: "In our country Protestantism hardly exists at all. It is not an established fact. It is a threat."

He was right on all accounts. After the Crusade, Spanish Protestants numbered five thousand, or roughly .004 per cent of the total population. They were scattered to the four winds, disorganized and churchless. Their schools had been closed, their publications banned. Many of their ministers had come through the Crusade with politico-criminal records (a good many served jail sentences); as such they were barred from the exercise of their ministry and, in fact, from participation in any phase of the new, all-Fascist Spain. Under these circumstances Protestantism was certainly *not* an established fact. But it was still a "threat."

The successful fight against this threat thus required: (1) the containing of all Protestant growth; and (2) once the growth was stemmed and the spiritual and intellectual currents blocked, the gradual dwindling of Protestant congregations and their eventual absorption into the Catholic "unity" of Spain.

[3] The Spanish phrase (*antecedentes políticos*) is difficult to translate. It means any record of allegiance to a government, such as the Republic's, or a political ideal, such as socialism or Communism, opposed to the National Movement (Falange), under which Spanish society was constituted after the Crusade.

Curbing the *evangélicos'* expansion was hence the first order of the day; the restrictive measures imposed after the Crusade had this sole finality. Indeed, the four points submitted to would-be worshipers had no other aim but to make "authorization" of a chapel well-nigh impossible:

1. *That there were enough Protestants to warrant the petition.* The number of worshipers who constituted a congregation was not defined until 1961; before that, authorities could arbitrarily turn down a request on the grounds that it violated this rule. On the other hand, drawing on a national membership of five thousand, few evangelical groups could muster a sizable showing in the days following the end of the Crusade.

2. *That the Church had existed before the Crusade.* Under this ruling, even if a minister assembled a good number of Protestants and presented the required guarantee of political "loyalty," he could not house a congregation in a new building. In other words, only churches which had physical existence before 1936 were allowed to reopen: new ones were illegal.

3. *That the group had not been previously penalized for abuses of "proselytism."* Since such abuses include the passing of leaflets, New Testaments, or any other written propaganda; the displaying of any "external" signs in a place of worship; the singing of hymns so loudly that they could be heard in the street; the bringing of a body to church or the formation of a funeral procession and many other acts considered offenses against Catholic "unity," dozens of Protestants who had been found guilty of them had effectively disqualified themselves for any "authorization."

4. *That the Church had no politico-criminal record.* The allegiance of a church's pastor, or any of its members, to a non-Fascist cause or government was enough to bar the church from "authorization." And the number of Protestants who had openly supported the anticlerical Republic—and its policy of religious liberty—was extremely high.

"Authorization" was likewise required—and still is—if an "authorized" church wishes to move to another building. Furthermore, when permission is requested for building a new church on the site of an old, "authorized" one, the legal obstacles are, once more, nearly insurmountable. Since there is no law covering non-Catholic churches, the work must be carried out in accordance with regulations governing commercial structures. These regulations require proof of the specific commercial activity envisioned before a building license is issued. An evangelical group, unable to prove any such commercial motive as a subterfuge, was nearly always unable to obtain the license.

A church may also be "authorized" to move to a new site, but on the express condition that its old building be closed down and abandoned. One of the latest cases of this kind involved a Barcelona Baptist chapel which requested permission to move from No. 20 Montsant Street to No. 15–17 Montmayor Street in that city. In a document dated November 29, 1965, and signed by the Civil Governor, permission is granted in the following words:

This Ministry, in accordance with the report issued by the Civil Government and the provisions of Article 6 of the *Fuero de los Españoles* on the private practice of dissident religions, has seen fit to grant the requested authorization, whose validity shall be conditioned by the fact that the director and members of the group served by the center in reference shall abstain from undertaking any activities of proselytism, or from carrying out external manifestations or celebrating religious ceremonies at the aforementioned site, No. 20 Montsant Street, or in any other unauthorized location.

The *evangélicos'* last resort, that of meeting in their own houses, has come up against the law of the land on repeated occasions, most notably in Ubeda, Jaén, in 1961. The file on this case opens with a communication from the Civil Governor of the Province dated May 5, 1961:

In view of the accusation brought against you by the Civil Guard of Jordá, and
WHEREAS on the seventh day of the month of March past, in the tailor shop belonging to the resident of that vicinity Andrés Pérez León, and in the presence of employees of the same, you showed a film on the Gospels, simultaneously explaining the same, [and thus] propagandizing for the Protestant religion . . . [*there follows a list of the laws violated, with the articles and provisions thereof*] I have decided to impose upon you the fine of FIVE THOUSAND PESETAS.
God keep you many years.
[*signed*] The Civil Governor

The recipient of the communication was Pastor Narciso Núñez Moreno, who appealed promptly through Madrid's Evangelical Defense Commission. His defense, drafted by Señor José Cardona Gregori, the Commission's Executive Secretary, makes clear: (1) that the tailor shop was the home of one of his parishioners; (2) that the alleged "film" was a series of slides produced and sold for the use of Roman Catholic children in Roman Catholic schools ("since the faith in and contemplation of the miracle of Our Lord Jesus Christ . . . is common to all Christians without distinction"); (3) that, besides himself, seven people were present, all parishioners of his church, whose names and addresses he appends; and, (4) that in any case he considered the fine excessive for a man who lived on the modest income of a *bracero* and doubled as pastor of the local Protestant church.

This document earned Señor Núñez a reduction in the fine; on July 24, 1961, he was notified by Madrid's Dirección General de Seguridad that he would have to pay only 500 pesetas.

The case did not rest there. Eager to wipe out the entire indictment, Señor Cardona and Pastor Núñez appealed once more— fruitlessly but, as it turned out, providentially. While poring over the laws of Spain, Señor Cardona had come across a Law of Meetings of June 15, 1880, which had somehow never been repealed. For a man who was not a professional lawyer it was a remarkable feat of legal sleuthing. The law had slipped through the fingers of the Fascist authorities and still stood in all its glory, providing a gigantic loophole for Article 16 of the *Fuero*. The pertinent provision of this legal godsend stated:

Article 2. A public meeting, for the effects of this law, shall be any attended by twenty persons, and celebrated in a building which is not the habitual residence of those who convene in it.[4]

If a public meeting was thus one attended by twenty people, any meeting with an attendance under twenty was private and therefore not subject to the rigorous provisions governing public assemblies.

[4] León Medina and Manuel Marañón, eds., *Leyes penales de España* (Madrid: Instituto Industrial Reus, 1947), p. 51.

Núñez's second appeal duly cited the dusty Law of Meetings. But on September 1, 1961, the Directorate General of Interior Politics of the Ministry of the Government replied stating that investigations had shown the pastor's income to be 4,000 pesetas ($66) a month, and hence "much superior" to that earned by a *bracero*, and that in any case no review of the case was possible since Señor Núñez had in effect committed an act of proselytism. Madrid's reluctance to strike the indictment from the books was nothing but the wish to save face. Time and again, as we shall see, authorities have turned deaf ear to all appeals, refused to grant audiences to those accused or in any way make possible an exchange of views on the alleged Protestant crime.

The last chapter of Man and God at Ubeda thus closes with the payment of a 500-peseta fine for having shown slides of: (1) the healing of the leper; (2) the healing of the man afflicted with palsy; (3) the resurrection of Jairus' daughter; (4) the resurrection of Lazarus; (5) the healing of the blind man Bartimeus.

This Biblical cast of characters had nevertheless done its bit for the freedom of Spain's Protestants. Having once turned a deaf ear to the Law of 1880, Madrid's authorities found themselves unable to do so when, in 1962, another case of "illicit assembly" came before them.

Early that year, in Madrid, Pastor Luis Poveda had been fined for holding a meeting at the house of a parishioner. The number of Protestants gathered together was again eight. No films or slides were shown: the accusation simply stated that a "clandestine meeting" had taken place. When Señor Cardona again cited the eighty-year-old law, the authorities found themselves without a leg to stand on. On the 21st of March, 1962, the Dirección General de Seguridad reversed itself for the first time in the history of post-Crusade Spain:

Since it has been proved that the persons assembled were only eight, and that they held the meeting in the home of one of them, under which circumstances, according to the provisions of law now in vigor, such meeting cannot be deemed "public" . . . [and] in view of the Orders of July 20, 1939, April 18, 1940, the *Fuero de los*

Españoles and the Law of July 15, 1880 . . . the fine is ordered refunded. . . .

It was a record-making precedent: for the first time in the history of the Franco regime, the number of persons who constituted a "public" assembly had been defined. Henceforth all Protestant meetings in private homes would not be disturbed provided their attendance was under twenty.

Another and even more bizarre attempt to protect the "spiritual unity" of Spain occurred in Valencia in 1953, when a total of 9,000 pesetas in fines rained down on the head of a pastor for refusing to *move* from a house he had rented in the town of Navarrés. Be it said in passing that 9,000 pesetas ($150 at the present exchange rate, $209 in 1953) is a sizable sum in the Spanish economy.

The pastor, Aurelio del Campo Santamaría, had been traveling to Navarrés from a nearby town to minister to the local Protestants in their own homes. All was well while he limited himself to periodic visits and held services in private houses. But when he decided to move to Navarrés and make his home there, his presence in the town became the classic "threat."

The accusation against del Campo was made by the parish priest to the Mayor, and by the Mayor to the Civil Governor. There is no record of it. In the extensive documentation which Señor Cardona has collected for the Evangelical Defense Commission over the years, there is nothing to substantiate a single accusation: anonymity has cloaked every man, woman, child, priest or nun who has denounced any Protestant activity to the civil authorities. Restored after 1939, the tradition of the sixteenth century remains intact.

The Civil Governor summoned Señor del Campo and informed him—in the presence of Señor Cardona, who had opened a file on the case—that no harm would come to him if he left the town of Navarrés. If he chose to stay, however, he would be subject to fines, sanctions, harassment and the eventual closing of his private chapel.

Del Campo's case is one of the most striking manifestations of the plight of "unpersons" in the political and religious unity of Spain. Article 14 of the *Fuero* states:

All Spaniards shall have the right to fix their residence freely within the national territory.

But in the Fascist context the word "all" encompasses only those in communion with the Church and the Regime. Outside this "unity," no rights obtain. Not only did the Civil Governor of Valencia flout Article 14 in his desire to rid Navarrés of the Protestant minister, but he in fact penalized the man for his refusal to go.[5]

When it was evident that Señor del Campo was intent on staying in Navarrés, the Governor sent a teacher to the dwelling the minister had rented, with orders for the landlady to evict the minister and house the newcomer. The landlady—a Catholic—refused.

Three of the fines are on file in Señor Cardona's office:

To Aurelio del Campo Santamaría, Proceedings No. 2535, dated December 17, 1953, because "You have been distributing non-authorized publications" .... 1000 pesetas
To Aurelio del Campo Santamaría, Proceedings No. 2534, dated December 17, 1953, because "You have been responsible for scandals that have been committed" .... 1000 pesetas
To Doña Milagros Calatayud [the landlady], Proceedings No. 2532, dated December 17, 1953, because "You refused to rent [your] house to the teacher" .... 1000 pesetas

II

The Núñez and del Campo cases are only two variations on the most widespread practice of all: the forcible closing of dis-

[5] Another provision of the *Fuero* which falls by the wayside when Protestant homes are raided is Article 15: "No one shall enter a domicile without permission from the owner, unless he possesses a warrant issued by the proper authorities, within the limits and according to the form established by law."

sident churches. By far the worst blow dealt Protestantism by the Spanish Church-State since 1939 has been the disbanding of dozens of chapels and units of worship throughout the length and breadth of the country. Some of the closings made news. Tucked here and there in the pages of American newspapers in the forties and fifties were small items about chapels ransacked and closed, Bibles confiscated, ministers manhandled. Dr. Santos Molina, the late Bishop and President of the Spanish Reformed (Episcopalian) Church, was beaten and knocked to the ground by a band of Catholic boys in a particularly bitter raid in Seville in March, 1952. The New York *Times* picked up the story.

Generally speaking, the news from Spain created little stir in the United States. Southern Baptists and other militant groups, aided and abetted by Paul Blanshard's rabid Protestants and Other Americans United for the Separation of Church and State, did nothing to enlist the sympathy of American Catholics; and American Catholics, snug and prosperous in an open society, couldn't care less about Spanish Protestants. (During my parochial high school days, I can remember few people who incurred the good Sisters' displeasure so much as Mr. Blanshard and his associates.) But America was not alone in her apathy. Throughout the world the Church was sleeping its pre-Johannine sleep and in no mood to inveigh against Holy Spain. When the "incidents" erupted and Spain deigned to make a statement, people were inclined to take her at her word: the problem of Iberian Protestants was an "artificial" problem stirred up by mountebanks and troublemakers on both sides of the frontier.

If it had to face an actual complaint, the Spanish Government could hardly contain its impatience. One Southern Baptist, the Reverend Paul E. Freed, visited Spain in 1952, shortly after the Seville incident involving Dr. Molina. He submitted to Don Blas Piñar, then Minister of the Interior, a questionnaire on the status of Protestants and the issue of religious liberty in Spain. Mr. Freed received no reply. His document evoked that ominous stillness—called by Spaniards "administrative silence"—which has been the all-too-usual reply to the appeal of an unperson. When

Mr. Freed pressed his inquiry, he was told the matter came under the jurisdiction of the Minister of Foreign Affairs, Don Alberto Martín Artajo—to whom the Baptist preacher, undaunted, addressed a memorandum.

Martín Artajo's answer to Freed is a classic document couched in classic terms. Of the five points he makes, numbers three, four and five and the final paragraph are especially aglow with that mixture of xenophobia and arrogance which characterized all defenses of "religious unity" at the time:

(3) It must be borne in mind that neither the Bill of Rights, the basic constitutional charter of the Spanish people, nor our Concordat with the Holy See, gives the Government power to authorize Protestant proselytism, meaning by this the capturing of new proselytes. The Government can go no further than what is authorized by the legal text.

(4) It is an indisputable fact that national public opinion looks with the greatest distaste upon foreign intervention in these matters, because this intervention only confirms what most Spaniards believe: that Protestant propaganda in Spain is an attempt by foreign nations to penetrate into the national life, *directed with political aims* at the destruction of the religious unity that substantially exists in Spain and that is recognized by all Spaniards.

(5) There is no doubt that the few Spanish Protestants and the foreign Protestants who reside in Spain can use legal channels to resort, as Spanish citizens or as authorized residents, to the Spanish authorities in case they believe that the rights conceded to them by law have not been recognized.

Thus it is clear that they have no need for the backing and the support of foreign religious and political organizations, whose intervention in Spanish affairs might prove not only useless, but actually prejudicial to the protection sought by these organizations.[6]

The threat in the last sentence was real; in the wake of protests like Mr. Freed's dozens of churches were summarily closed. Perhaps three-quarters of today's Thirty Thousand have seen their place of worship fold overnight, or have friends who were left

[6] Delpech, *op. cit.*, pp. 48–49. Italics mine.

churchless time and again. The very first congregation I called on had been turned out on the street three times, although I did not know it at the time of my first visit. On the cold, drizzling night of November 1, 1964—All Saints' Day, which also happened to be Sunday—when I made my way to the chapel at No. 10 Ros de Olano, Madrid, seeing a group of Baptists at prayer was all I had bargained for.

Ros de Olano is a side street in a working-class neighborhood known as "Prosperidad"—an ugly, unplanned, utterly treeless and shrubless quarter where buildings of graying cement are jumbled against one another, spaced here and there by garish shoe or clothing stores. The street where the chapel is located branches off from the main artery, López de Hoyos; turning right on the latter, and walking some three hundred yards, one will come to No. 10.

There is nothing to indicate the presence of a church: No. 10 is a drab, good-sized, two-story house surrounded by a high fence. (Later a Protestant was to tell me, half-jokingly, that I must learn to look for the doorbell, find it, and check the type-written-sized characters underneath which spell out "CHAPEL." This is the only "external sign" allowed by the law.) In the darkness, I hesitated for a few minutes. A gate on the far end of the wall seemed closed. While I was looking for another door two men and a woman came up from the opposite end of Ros de Olano, pushed the gate and went in. I scrambled behind them, followed along a short driveway and came upon double doors which opened into a rectangular cement shed literally packed with people. It was the church.

There were two rows of battered pews. The walls were painted blue. At the altar end stood a lectern covered with a cloth on which was embroidered the legend, *"Dios es amor."* The wall behind it was hung with yellow drapes joined by a valance with the words: *"La paga del pecado es la muerte; pero la dádiva del Señor es la vida eterna en Cristo Jesús"* ("The wages of sin is death, but the gift of God is eternal life in Christ Jesus." Rom. 6:23).

The preacher stood silhouetted against the drapes, a Bible open on the lectern before him. Below him was a table on which several objects had been placed and carefully covered with a white cloth.

Despite the furnishings, the place looked so much like a garage—it could have housed four or five large American cars—that one almost expected to smell grease and gasoline.

A row of worshipers squeezed together and made room for me in a back pew. As I sat down, my first and only thought was to count the house.

I looked over a sea of drabness. Nothing seemed to break the monotony of the dark blues, dark grays, faded blacks and chocolate browns of the congregation's coats and suits. In one pew sat an American woman with a little blond boy beside her; though she was plainly, indeed soberly, dressed, her clothes stood out. (I never learned her name, but I was to see her at the church on various occasions and, after the services, watch her greet friends with evident affection and in fluent Spanish.) In another pew sat a young sailor in the uniform of the Spanish Navy. Several men and women had brought their children along, some of them toddlers.

Counting the children, my tally came to just over one hundred. After a second count had given me one hundred two, it occurred to me that the air was very close. There was no heat and, with the center and back door made fast, the congregation's breath seemed to have solidified all around us.

I had missed the preacher's text, but he had been illustrating it with the story of a divided family whose sons left home to seek adventure in a big city and later returned to their parents, contrite and disillusioned. When the sermon was over he announced that the "young people's choir" would sing an appropriate hymn. A girl who had been playing a harmonium left her place to a bespectacled lady and faced sixteen youngsters who had come forward from the front pews. The girl, I learned later, was the pastor's fourteen-year-old daughter. She raised both arms and, tracing long horizontal curves with her hands, led the choir in "Home, Sweet Home" (*Hogar, Dulce Hogar*).

Communion concluded the service. Four elders joined the min-

ister before the table, the white cloth was removed and two trays
—one bearing bread cubes, the other small glasses of wine—were
passed among the congregation. Fifteen or twenty minutes later
the *evangélicos* were on the way home after pausing at the chapel
door for the traditional handshake with their pastor, José Núñez
Moreno (who, as it turned out, was a brother of the Ubeda
Núñez).

A few days later, when I told Pastor Núñez that his was the
first evangelical chapel I had ever visited, he smiled and said, "You
have started with the humblest." When I asked if he had had any
difficulties with the law, he smiled again. In 1958, he told me,
he had been processed for reopening a chapel at Usera, another
working-class suburb of Madrid.

The Usera case is one of the many that had leaked out. Paul
Blanshard himself witnessed Pastor Núñez's trial; P.O.A.U. asked
Secretary of State Herter to lodge a formal protest with the Spanish government, while newspapers in Europe and America carried
details of the courtroom scenes. It may have been another such
"mock trial," as an American periodical [7] called it; but looking
back on it, one is struck by its timing. With the election of Pope
John XXIII on October 28, 1958, Roman Catholicism had entered a new era: Pastor Núñez, tried for a transgression of "divine
law," would live to see his cause placed before the world by the
very Church that prosecuted him.

On October 7, 1959, when he was sentenced, Núñez, of course,
couldn't see anything of the kind. He had been haled to court
for having broken the seals on the Usera chapel and having held
two services there.

To understand the nature of his offense, one must be familiar
with the terms *iglesia* and *templo* as used in the legal language
of Spain. *Iglesia,* the Castilian word for "church," is applied by
law to a group of believers who meet in private; *templo,* the Jewish terms Spaniards frequently use in designating their places of
worship, is construed legally to mean "structure" or "building."
The Usera chapel, having been closed, had passed from *templo* to

[7] Dallas *Baptist Standard,* November 11, 1959.

iglesia: its faithful could continue to meet as long as they did so in the strict privacy of their homes.

Opened in 1949, the small Baptist meeting place at No. 41 Mother of God Street [8] had been raided by the police on July 17, 1954. The request for its closing came from a group of nuns who held a *catequesis,* or catechism school, very close nearby. The charge was "proselytism." According to Pastor Núñez, the nuns charged that three girls from their classes had been physically coerced to attend the Protestant Sunday school; the information that he [Núñez] had been given was that the children did in fact talk to a member of the church outside the building and entered the same.

The only written evidence of the charge available today is a document dated October 26, 1954, which contains the declarations made by the chapel's pastor, José Beltrán Ferrándiz, at the Dirección General de Seguridad. In this informal deposition Ferrándiz states that he had been charged with "irregularities and proselytism, consisting in giving toys and candy" to the children. He does not bother to deny the charge; it is a standard accusation, one of the oldest brought against Protestants by the guardians of the spiritual unity of Spain. Bribery is, indeed, the classic construction of the term "proselytism" in the eyes of the Spanish Church-State. In his Concordat message of 1953 to the *Cortes,* Franco himself had referred to those who make use of "gratifications [*dádivas*] to divert Catholics from their religious duties."

(His point was well taken: the document he brought before Parliament for ratification provided for rigid Catholic control of Spanish hospitals, orphanages, sanatoria and beneficent institutions of all kinds. If one must leave behind most Western criteria in judging the Spanish religious spirit, nowhere more so than in this area of licit and illicit charity. To a Spaniard, a Protestant

---

[8] The street was originally known as Calle de Egoscozábal. When the Protestant chapel was first opened, the municipal government changed its name to Madre de Dios. Neighbors, whose rent receipts, tax statements, etc., had been made out under the old name, complained to the authorities of the confusion the change was occasioning. The street was renamed Egoscozábal, only to revert, sometime later, finally and definitely, to "Mother of God."

hospital is in and by itself an offense against the country: Protestant medicine is a *dádiva* and, as such, evil. The same thinking applies to orphanages, recreational clubs, summer camps, etc. In Madrid one young minister *has* been bold enough to open an evangelical old people's home; it operates clandestinely in the outskirts of the city.)

The Usera chapel remained closed until Pastor Núñez decided to request its rehabilitation. He wrote to the Chief of Police, to the Dirección General de Seguridad and to the Civil Governor. "I wrote to everyone within my reach," he says. "And all I got was administrative silence. I asked for interviews, but never got a single one. I never had a chance to express my views or listen to theirs."

Early in October, 1957, Núñez rallied the congregation, reminded them of the Spanish saying, *el que calla otorga* ("he who is silent accedes"), and marched into the chapel with them. He knew perfectly well that in the case of *evangélicos* silence granted nothing at all, and that he was risking arrest.

"We scrubbed the place and cleaned it up," he says. "I think we held two services—one a prayer meeting and the other one the regular Sunday service. Next morning, Monday, the police arrived."

When Núñez refused to sign a document drawn up by the police on the spot unless they gave him a copy, he was taken to the Dirección General de Seguridad's headquarters at the Puerta del Sol. There he faced the Chief Commissioner of the Social Brigade, who also asked him to sign. Again he refused.

"He warned me that if I didn't sign I would be declared 'rebellious' [the Spanish equivalent of resisting arrest]. After calling me many names which I will not repeat before you he asked that I be taken downstairs and 'dealt with.' "

The "dealing with" turned out to be lunch in the pleasant employees' lunchroom: as in many such cases, holy zeal was only bravado in disguise. "After lunch I was taken to a comfortable room and given magazines to read. *Protestant* magazines.[9] They

---

[9] The Dirección General de Seguridad keeps a complete file of all Protestant and other non-Catholic publications which circulate in Spain. In the forties and fifties it also intercepted mail addressed to evangelical pastors.

gave me one put out by the Jehovah's Witnesses and another one of the Seventh-day Adventists. I told them I had nothing to do with either group. Then they brought our own Baptist magazine. It was the latest issue, which hadn't reached me yet. I thanked them and read it."

When he failed to come home, Núñez's wife alerted several of his fellow pastors who, in turn, contacted their lawyer. Núñez finally agreed to sign the police document and was taken to the Ministry of Justice—known informally in Madrid as *"las salesas"* —for arraignment. His lawyer was already there. The *juez de primera instancia* took a declaration from Núñez and told him to go home. "I asked him, 'You mean I'm not supposed to stay here?' 'No, of course not,' he answered. 'Just come back every two weeks.' I was free on probation until the day of the trial." According to Núñez another official offered to waive the fine. " 'You probably make as little money as we do,' he told me. 'You don't have to pay anything.' " Núñez did not pay.

There were two trials. The first was suspended for lack of documentation on the original closing of the chapel. When some of the pertinent papers had been located, the second trial got underway. A typed translation of a Reuters dispatch in Pastor Núñez's file (he could not tell me where or when it had been published) states that four hundred Spanish Protestants attended the trial, as well as Mrs. Nella Dean Mitchell, representative of the Southern Baptist Convention, and an official of the U.S. Embassy. The dispatch, dated October 3, 1959, also declared:

When Mr. Núñez's lawyer cited Article 6 of the *Fuero de los españoles,* to the effect that "No one shall be bothered on account of his religious beliefs or the private practice of its ceremonies," the Judge asked him to limit his remarks to the case at hand.

The judge, in fact, repeatedly silenced both lawyer and client when they brought up the issue of religious liberty. If the attorney did so, the bench called him down. If Núñez mentioned his duties to his flock, the same thing happened. "Every time they asked me why I had broken the seals, I answered that I had not *broken* them, as the wind and the rain had already torn them apart; that

I had merely opened the door and gone in to give spiritual assistance to my congregation. And every time I said this the presiding
judge would ring the bell and say: 'Limit yourself to answering
the question put to you by the prosecutor.' And again the prosecutor would ask: 'Why did you break the seals?' And again I said
that I had opened the church to give spiritual assistance to my
people, and again the judge rang the bell. And so it went." More
than a text for a news agency, it was a scene for a Daumier or a
Rouault.

The sentence, dated October 7, 1959, finds Núñez guilty of that
most Spanish of sins: "Disobedience." Though no one could have
thought it significant at the time, the pastor was saved from two
months in jail by a general amnesty granted in celebration of
Pope John XXIII's coronation. It was thus that the man whom
evangélicos call "of blessed memory" unwittingly rescued his first
Spanish heretic.

Once the Usera chapel was closed for the second time, its
congregation transferred to a storefront church at Perez Ayuso
Street, in the Prosperidad section. The storefront, too, was closed
by the police and remained sealed for a year. Finally the Baptists
obtained permission to transfer to the premises at No. 10 Ros de
Olano, where, one year after my first visit, on Sunday, November
21, 1965, Pastor Núñez was preaching with more vigor than ever.
After the sermon he announced a fund-raising campaign for a new
building and showed the faithful an architect's model, which, he
said, they could inspect at their leisure after the service. "It is
not a model of our church, of course; it is a model of a church
planned for Elche [Alicante], which for some reason or other was
never built. But ours will look something like this."

7

During my first visit to Pastor Núñez's church, I noticed a boy in the uniform of the Spanish Navy in one of the jam-packed pews. The prayerful and attentive sailor, wearing his country's uniform to a subversive rite, brought home very vividly the peculiar conflicts young *evangélicos* are heirs to. One of these is the peril of service in the Spanish Armed Forces; the other is the possible (and frequent) humiliation of being denied the right to marry.

The Armed Services question has been fraught with difficulties and liberally peppered with jail sentences since the end of the Crusade. Jacques Delpech speaks of it briefly, citing one case of military "insubordination" whose punishment, very exceptionally, degenerated onto a physical plane. As we shall see, the case of sailor José Morado is a fitting preamble to a chapter on military ecumenism.

Delpech's text is as follows:

A writer named P. Cantero, in a long article in the Madrid daily *Ya* on the subject of "Religious Freedom in Spain" (February 12, 1950), tried to show that Protestants enjoy all necessary freedoms. In regards to military service, he said:

The Spanish Army, being part of the Spanish State, protects the Catholic form of worship. The attendance of commanders, officers, and soldiers is required at all religious ceremonies which are a part of their military duties. . . . What an outcry was made by the foreign press over a slight punishment inflicted in the 8th military district (Galicia) on a soldier who, while on duty, disobeyed the order of his superiors to honor the Blessed Sacrament during a Catholic procession!

The event to which the writer so lightly alluded was, in fact, much more serious. On May 12, 1945, a young sailor, José Morado, refused to kneel before the Blessed Sacrament during a ceremony, saying he was a Protestant and that such an act was contrary to his conscience. He was then beaten by order of the colonel [*sic: there is no explanation of the officer's Army rank*] and had to be removed to a hospital in serious condition. Later he was tried before a military tribunal and sentenced to a year in prison. Evidently Morado's health was fatally weakened by his severe treatment and by his imprisonment. [*In a note, Delpech states that Morado died on October 16, 1948.*] [1]

I

The Armed Forces of Spain, as the State they serve, are Catholic: one might say "militantly" Catholic without indulging in a facile pun or in idle sarcasm. The fighting nature of the soldiers' Catholicism is evident in an instruction on the "Norms to be applied to non-Catholic individuals of the ranks," contained in the Official Bulletin of Military Ecclesiastic Jurisdiction (roughly equivalent to the Chaplain Corps) for July–August, 1962. "The norms [previously] dictated in some concrete cases," states the *Bulletin,* "have given rise to some doubts as to the manner of their application. Hence it seems advisable to determine how they should be interpreted in the future, bearing in mind that the exemption from assistance at certain religious acts granted to non-Catholics shall never be a pretext for their eluding the hardships or exertions of an obligatory duty, nor an occasion for them to forget the respect they owe to the religion professed by Spaniards." [2]

It will be noted that the chaplains mince no words. The religion professed by "Spaniards" is not the religion professed by non-Catholic servicemen.

[1] Delpech, *op. cit.,* pp. 82–83.
[2] *Boletín oficial de la Jurisdicción eclesiástica castrense,* Año XXVI, No. 301, Julio-Agosto, 1962, p. 215.

But the Instruction should be examined from the very beginning:

> The assistance at some acts of doctrinal education and worship of the Roman Catholic, Apostolic Religion is obligatory in the Army, since it is the official religion of the State, the only true one, and a faith inseparable from the national conscience, professed and practiced by almost the totality of Spaniards. Such acts consist of religious lectures, pious obligatory worship [i.e., Mass on Sundays and holy days of obligation] and the religious ceremonies which are part of essentially military functions.
>
> Nevertheless, very exceptionally and sporadically, some individuals in the ranks do not profess the Catholic religion. . . .[3]

The Instruction goes on to issue certain rules which exempt non-Catholics from religious services "in order not to do violence to their erroneous beliefs, as well as to avoid insubordinate attitudes which merit punishment as offenses against military discipline, but which punishment may be ascribed—as has been done in bad faith—to intolerance and religious sectarianism."

As in the case of church closings, the thought of undue attention on the part of Spain's "enemies" abroad colored the Church-State decision on the handling of recruits who profess "erroneous" beliefs. Still another parallel to the church regulations may be found in the norms set down within the same Instruction regarding non-Catholic recruits' formal oath of allegiance. The ceremony, known in Spain as the *jura de bandera,* or oath to the flag, consists in an exchange of formulas between the soldier and the inducting officer, after which the former kisses the national standard. As dissident worship must be carried out in strict seclusion, away from the eyes of the faithful, so must the swearing in of the non-Catholic recruit be performed without giving scandal to the troops who profess the "true" religion. When the inductee is not a Catholic, the act of allegiance

> shall be carried out on a different day from that set aside for the [oath] of the Unit's soldiers. The ceremony of the oath shall take place without publicity in closed quarters, if possible in the same

[3] *Ibid.,* p. 214.

111

ones where the Flag or Standard is deposited for safekeeping, or in any others which may be set up for the act, provided they meet the conditions for its celebration, which shall always be of a private nature.

The Instruction had been inspired by a spate of "indisciplinary acts" since the end of the Crusade, some of which, like sailor Morado's, had attracted unwelcome publicity. In 1958, when the Evangelical Defense League was founded, it began to keep its own files on all the trials and courts-martial of Protestants in the Armed Forces. And in every serious military case the difficulty revolved around the same circumstance: the *evangélicos'* forced attendance at Mass and their un-Catholic behavior at the climactic moment of the rite.

Until the Instruction was issued, the Protestant draftee had to attend the Holy Sacrifice with the rest of the troops. The *evangélico* so compelled marched into the church, sat, knelt and stood in unison with his companions for three-quarters of the rite. But when the Elevation came, so did the Protestant's downfall. At this highlight of the Mass, when according to Catholic dogma the Host is transubstantiated into the Physiological Christ, the commanding officer of the Spanish troops calls out *"Rindan"* and the servicemen lower their rifles in homage to the Real Presence.

In every case brought before a court-martial the *evangélico* was accused of having remained at attention (called in Spanish *firme*). The 1961 report of the Evangelical Defense Commission lists three typical arrests, carried out after the three soldiers in question had unsuccessfully requested that they be excused from attending Mass:

Juan Tonés Costa, Case No. 1115/57 brought before the Supreme Court of Military Justice.

Joaquín González Fernández, case brought before the Generalship of Palma de Mallorca on June 6, 1960.

Samuel Pérez Hernández, case brought before the Generalship of Santa Cruz de Tenerife (Canary Islands) on June 5, 1960.

Young Samuel's father addressed a letter to the colonel who

commanded his son's unit explaining that the boy had been brought up a Protestant. The officer wrote back to Pérez senior:

I must inform you that your son Samuel was not arrested because he did not kneel before the Most Blessed Sacrament, but because he disobeyed a bugle call, which is a Superior Order, thereby committing an act of indiscipline; one must bear in mind that he assumes that position [i.e., *Rindan*] every day during the course of his instruction, and, therefore, to have done so should have presented no problem to his conscience, either as a good Protestant or a better soldier.

On the other hand, I must tell you that your son's case is no longer under my jurisdiction as, by virtue of a Superior Order, it has been turned over to a Judge. I regret that I cannot do anything more for you on this occasion.

A year later, the son of the evangelical pastor in Castellón (Province of Valencia) asked to be excused from attending Mass. Permission was refused and shortly thereafter the boy entered prison for the classic misdemeanor. He served a fortnight before the case was opened and it was discovered that he had not been baptized as a Catholic (i.e., that he was not an apostate), which information secured his immediate release.

On the very same day, in Melilla, Spanish Morocco, another *evangélico* had stated he did not want to attend a "soldier's farewell Mass" (an obligatory rite which marks the men's last day in service). Genaro Redero Prieto was marched into the church and—after the Elevation, of course—marched right out into the brig. His court-martial (No. 1187/61) ended on November 3, 1961, with a three-year sentence for the crime of "disobedience."

Redero's father appealed to Generalísimo Franco on January 4, 1962. But the man, who died three months later, never saw his son again. The boy served almost two and a half years in military prison before being granted an amnesty.

The 1962 Instruction put an end to the Blessed Sacrament courts-martial. But by virtue of an official Order of March 30, 1960, Protestants are to this day barred from serving in the Air Force.

The reason for this Order was the same which prompted the Instruction: a multiplication of incidents involving Protestant recruits at Mass. When, on May 17, 1959, Joaquín González Fernández informed his Air Force captain "that his religious beliefs forbade him from carrying out the *Rindan* during the Elevation at Mass, since he professed the Baptist Evangelical religion, the captain told the recruit that, nonetheless, he should enter the formation and follow the movements of the rest of the force." Came the Elevation and, shortly thereafter, the court-martial. The official Air Force document, bearing number 210, from which the above quotation is taken, goes on to state that the recruit was sentenced to one year and six months in jail, which penalty was reduced to six months and one day by the Supreme Court of Military Justice. "In order to avoid cases of this type, instructions are given on this date to the Chief of the Second Section, Duplicate, of this General Staff, that, in future, all his reports on applicants to this Force should state the religion they profess, so that Your Excellency may eliminate those aspirants who are non-Catholics."

Two *evangélicos* were denied admission to the Air Force in 1961. In the spring of 1965, a young Madrid Baptist slipped in; but a few days after his induction, when it was found that his application form said "Protestant," he was dismissed.

II

"I had a beautiful military service," Pastor José Palma López of the Pentecostal Church told me. "Not one incident, not one difficulty. It was incredible. Everyone was considerate and kind." When I asked him the date of his induction into the Armed Forces, he told me he had been drafted in 1959.

Our chat about his Army days—to which I shall return—was marginal to my visit. I had called on Pastor Palma to talk about a marriage case, a type of "incident" that comes up more frequently than courts-martial and causes far more grief. Where military justice is a businesslike and clear-cut process, Spanish legislation on civil marriage is a morass of laws, orders, regulations, circulars and prejudices in which the *evangélico* can sink up to his very soul.

If a Protestant seeking to marry submits his application to a liberal judge—and there are a number of liberal, or, at most, indifferent, men on the bench—he will marry without difficulty. But if the *evangélico* should run into a pillar of the Faith in magisterial robes, in nine cases out of ten the tight Church-State net will close around him and delay the wedding for weeks, months or, if need be, years.

The basis for Spanish marriage legislation is Article 42 of the Spanish Civil Code as it existed under the Monarchy:

The law recognizes two forms of marriage: the canonical form, which must bind all those who profess the Catholic religion, and the civil form, which shall conform to the provisions of the Code.

On March 22, 1938, the Government issued an order interpreting this measure for the new Catholic State which was rising from the ashes of the Crusade:

Inasmuch as Article 42 of the Civil Code clearly makes canonical marriage obligatory for Spaniards who profess the Catholic religion, in order to obtain a civil marriage license, it is necessary to demand an express declaration of nonprofession of the Catholic religion on the part of both parties to the marriage, or at least of one of them.

The order was, as we shall see, remarkably liberal: it requested only the "nonprofession" of the Catholic religion for parties wishing to contract a civil marriage. Protected by this provision, *evangélicos* began to marry without difficulty—and, in so doing, to alarm the Church, whose ascendancy over the Regime was more patent every day. On March 10, 1941, another interpretation of Article 42 was issued by the Government:

Municipal judges shall authorize no civil marriages but those for which the parties have proved by documentary evidence that they do not belong to the Catholic religion. If it is not possible for them to produce such documents, they must declare under oath that they have not been baptized as Catholics. The validity of the marriage shall depend upon the veracity of these declarations.

The 1941 measure marked the beginning of the ecclesiastical take-over. Thereafter a new, canonical test of non-Catholicity was applied, a test which, with the Concordat of 1953, became the law of the land. In its Article 23, the agreement between Rome and Madrid simply echoed Article 42 of the Civil Code:

The Spanish State recognizes the full civil effects of a marriage celebrated according to the norms of Canon Law.

But in the Concordat's Protocol, the Vatican makes a significant distinction as to the rights of non-Catholics to contract civil marriage:

In the juridical regulation of marriage for unbaptized parties, no impediments will be offered to natural law.

The civil measures after the Crusade had spoken of "nonprofession" of the Catholic religion; the Concordat referred to civil marriage between "unbaptized" parties. And an apostate was not considered "unbaptized." Thus, *evangélicos* who had left the Catholic Church found every obstacle in their way when they wanted to marry in their new faith. In January of 1966 I interviewed a young couple who, encouraged by rumors of a Statute of Religious Freedom, had abandoned the strict evangelical code of waiting—months and in some cases years—for Government authorization to marry. They had solicited such permission in May, 1965, and been denied it; they were wed at the Baptist Church on Madrid's General Lacy Street in August of that year. When I talked to them, the young wife was expecting the birth of her first—and illegitimate—child. The Church-State had determined that her conversion was invalid, and hence that she was still a Catholic, subject to Canon Law and unable to contract marriage under the provisions of Article 42 of the Civil Code.

As the strict conditions for opening a "private" place of worship looked towards the containing, and eventual destruction, of all "erroneous" beliefs, so the marriage policy of the Church-State was ever aimed at preventing the growth of Protestants.[4] Under the provision of official directives which we shall quote below,

[4] They have grown 600% in twenty-five years.

when all *evangélicos* come up before the authorities and request permission to marry outside the Catholic Church (i.e., in a civil ceremony), the magistrate must demand "proof of non-Catholicity" and, after having received it, must pass on its validity. Until the late fifties, the Church-State, through its judges, held up the "indelible" nature of Catholic baptism as proof that a Catholic could not legally or morally abandon the Church. Writing on this subject in the magazine *Ecclesia* in October, 1953, Judge José Peré Raluy stated:

Every baptized person is a Catholic, as well as every person converted to the true faith, adjuring schisms and heresies, even if he has not been baptized in the Catholic Church. The heresy, apostasy, or schism of any subject of the Catholic Church, while depriving him of his personal rights, does not relieve him of his obligations to the Church. The tie that binds the Catholic to the Church is indestructible, as it is based on the indelible nature of baptism. Thus every member of the Catholic Church, whether he be a baptized Catholic or a convert to the true faith, remains subject to the Church, even though he separates himself from the Church, and even if he is excommunicated.[5]

The judge's stand, based on Canon 87 of the Code of Canon Law, has been echoed in Protestant marriage cases throughout the years. Delpech transcribes a letter received by a Protestant girl who appealed to the Minister of Justice in her attempt to marry an ex-Catholic who had converted to Protestantism. The Ministry's Director General of Registries and Notaries answered her as follows:

With regard to the request addressed to His Excellency the Minister of Justice concerning an authorization to contract a civil marriage before the Justice of Peace:
The Director General informs you that in order to be married under civil law in Spain, in conformity with the decree of the Minister of Justice of March 10, 1941, it is necessary that neither of the parties have been baptized in the Catholic Church. The fact that one

[5] Quoted in Delpech, *op. cit.*, pp. 25–26.

117

may have gone over to another religion or may be practicing no religion at all is not sufficient to exempt those who have received Catholic baptism, because the Sacrament of baptism is indelible.

May God bless you and keep you.

The Director General

Madrid, September 17, 1946 [6]

Some marriage cases, like some church closings and military incidents, were picked up by the press of the "erroneous lay States." One of these was the fourteen-month ordeal of Pastor Francisco Manzanas and his fiancée, Carmen Pelegrina Jalvo, both baptized as infants in the Catholic Church, both converts to the Iglesia Evangélica Española (a merger of Lutherans, Presbyterians and Methodists and one of the country's most important Protestant groups). The first municipal judge the couple visited—in October of 1953, three months after the signing of the Concordat —was the magistrate for Señorita Pelegrina's district in Madrid. The dignitary denied them authorization on the grounds that they lacked proof of "nonbaptism" in the Catholic Church. The couple then applied to the judge for Señor Manzanas' district, who echoed his colleague's dictum. Señor Manzanas next took his plea to another Madrid district where his sister, also a Protestant, had been married without difficulty four years before. The judge, who was sympathetic, explained to Manzanas that after granting two or three authorizations following his sister's, he had been reprimanded by the authorities and told not to do so in the future: under the circumstances there was nothing he could do.

Manzanas went back to Alicante, where he had served as a minister for fourteen months (and where he is today pastor of the church at No. 32 Maestro Caballero Street) and there, for the fourth time since the beginning of his marathon, requested permission to marry. The answer, again, was no. Returning to Madrid, he called once more on the first judge he and his fiancée had visited and requested a denial in writing. With this document he applied to the next highest court, the *Tribunal de primera instancia.* It was already mid-1954.

The *juez de primera instancia,* after studying the case, declared

6 *Ibid.,* pp. 72–73.

that the documents submitted by Señor Manzanas and Señorita Pelegrina were proof enough of their "non-Catholicity" and that they were therefore entitled, under law, to be married in a civil ceremony. But the man dared not act without first consulting with the Ministry of Justice. The decision, though clearly within the provisions of civil law, was, in view of the newly approved Concordat, politically compromising before the Church authorities.

As it turned out, the magistrate's caution was an omen of the Ministry's disapproval. Weeks and months went by; a series of letters addressed by both Señor Manzanas and his fiancée to the Minister evoked only administrative silence. When a year had gone by, Manzanas, who was reaching the end of his rope, decided to lay the matter before the Chief of State. He wrote directly to Generalísimo Franco; after a visit from the secret police, the *Caudillo* himself, through the Presidency of the Government, granted the two Protestants permission to marry. The New York *Times* for February 5, 1955, carried a story by Camille Cianfarra detailing the case and its solution after Franco's personal intervention.

Pastor Manzanas' ordeal is a case history in the moral and legal sway of the Church over functionaries of the Ministry of Justice: although the *juez de primera instancia,* upon studying the documents, had decided that sufficient proof of "non-Catholicity" had been adduced by Señor Manzanas and Señorita Pelegrina, neither he nor any other judge who valued his career dared to make a move in the case. In sexual matters, more than in any other field, the chain of command leads directly back to Divine Authority. The judge answers to the Minister, the Minister to the Papal Nuncio, and the Nuncio to Rome.

The extent to which the Spanish power structure came under the Vatican's orders was made clearer three years later when the Nuncio, outraged at the continuing marriages of "apostates," issued a Circular to all Spanish Bishops giving them concrete instructions as to their duties when such cases came before them. The document, dated March 25, 1957, and bearing Protocol No. 559/57, is one of the most remarkable in the history of the Church-State. It reads:

THE THIRTY THOUSAND

The Spanish Government has disposed that those who, having been baptized, later unfortunately apostatize, and refuse to be subject to the canonical norms of marriage, shall, under certain conditions, be admitted to the covenant of the so-called civil act. . . . To avoid confusion or doubts in the practical sphere, I have deemed it convenient to call Your Grace's attention to the following norms, set down herewith so that the Ecclesiastic Authorities will proceed accordingly:

A) As soon as he has received the notification of the civil authorities, the Ordinary or Ordinaries in question will take great pains to determine if the abandonment of the Catholic faith by the wretches [*los desdichados*] in reference is genuine, and to prevent any [of them] from making rash statements as to their non-Catholicity, with the sole intention of evading canonical legislation on marriage, as this would be equivalent to opening a breach and [inviting] a multiplication of civil unions, with the doleful consequences that may be easily surmised. . . . The Most Reverend Ordinaries should ask the civil authorities for the documents presented by the interested parties to verify their abandonment of the Catholic faith in cases where [such documents] are not attached to the notifications.

B) When such [abandonment] is not factual, and it is determined that it answers to indifference or even hostility to the practice of the Faith, Civil Authority shall be informed accordingly. In cases of special importance, the Ordinaries may address the Minister of Justice directly, informing him of the results of their own investigations. . . .

C) At the same time, the Most Excellent Bishops, by means of the priests or other people they may deem adequate [to the task] shall try, with all clarity and prudence, to dissuade the interested parties from their deplorable intent, making them realize the moral and spiritual consequences of the act and threatening with the punishment cited by Canon Law.

D) When such actions do not give the desired result, no information will be given to the Civil Authority. But the latter shall not authorize the covenant [i.e., the civil ceremony] before an entire month has elapsed after its notification by the Ecclesiastic Authority.

(The Circular also speaks of "the scandal" produced by Catholic witnesses at non-Catholic weddings "in a Catholic nation like Spain," and urges Ordinaries to proceed against such witnesses by excommunicating them. Obedience has been prompt and thorough.

On June 4, 1961, in Cartagena, the Diocesan Authority even ordered that the excommunication of witnesses at a Protestant
wedding be broadcast over the radio and announced from all the
pulpits of the city's parishes on the following Sunday. It was so
done. The excommunication resulted in the firing of several of the
Catholics involved from the firm in which they worked, with the
attendant loss in salary; they were later reinstated in their jobs.)

No sooner was the Circular out than the Government sprang
into action. Three measures followed in quick succession, all aimed
at bolstering the Nuncio's instruction to the Spanish Bishops.
They were the Circular of the General Directorate of Registries
(a section of the Ministry of Justice) of April 2, 1957; the law
of June 8, 1957, on the Civil Registry; and the Rules for the application of the latter law, set forth in the Decree of November 14,
1958. The legal adviser of the Evangelical Defense Commission
has made an extract of the dispositions contained in all three
documents:

(a) The profession of the Roman Catholic Religion is presumed to
be valid in every person incorporated to it by [infant] baptism or
conversion.

(b) It is possible to apostatize at a given moment, but the imperative nature of Article 42 of the Civil Code demands that apos-
tasies which take place at the time of the desired marriage be
regarded as suspect, since they could well be motivated by the
desire of eluding the canonical discipline on marriage rather than
by the desire to change faiths.

(c) The interested parties shall be credited with nonprofession of
the Catholic faith "when it can be proved, through the means provided for by Law, that (1) they were not baptized in the Roman
Catholic Church, or (2) that they have apostatized materially
and formally."

(d) To demonstrate the negative fact of "not having been baptized,"
the declaration of the interested parties, ratified by two witnesses, will normally suffice; or any other way of proving that,
since he or she had not been born in a Catholic ambiance, baptism
in the Roman Catholic Church would have been anomalous.

(e) On the other hand, when it is evident that the party was baptized
in the Roman Catholic Church, he must present "sufficient and

121

adequate proof of his ostensibly separatist and apostatic attitude before the fundamental dogmatics of Catholicism." This proof should be made through the means allowed by law, and should be sufficiently convincing to fill the Judge's spirit with the certainty of an authentic apostasy; the Judge, on his part, will display the greatest zeal possible to expose any subterfuge through which the party may tend to evade the canonical bond of marriage.

I talked to María Luisa Ruiz, twenty, and her husband, José Moreno Fortes, twenty-three, after an evening service at the Baptist Church on Madrid's General Lacy Street. María Luisa's child, due in June, 1966, would be born illegitimate by virtue of paragraph (b) above. When, as a Protestant who sought to marry, she made the required visit to the judge's chambers, the girl was asked the date of her conversion to the Evangelical Church. She answered that she had formally joined the Baptist Faith on March 24, 1964. But the zealous judge pressed her further. How long had she been courted by Moreno Fortes before she had converted? One month, she replied. Then the conversion, concluded His Honor, was invalid, as it was influenced by her desire to marry a Protestant, and permission to carry out a civil ceremony was denied. By Judicial Decree of August 2, 1965, the denial is made formal:

CONSIDERING that, in accordance with the provisions of Article 42 of the Civil Code, Articles 243 and 244, and concordances, of the Civil Registry, and with the reiterated jurisprudence of the Supreme Court and the Resolutions of the Directorate General of Registries and Notaries, in order to celebrate a civil marriage between baptized parties it is necessary to furnish full proof of apostasy; and since, in the opinion of this Court, such [proof] has not been forthcoming in the present case, as the exclusion of the appellant from the Catholic Church has not been fully justified, and as the certificate of the Pastor has no validity, since he is not a public functionary, while, on the other hand, a short time has elapsed since the separation of the interested parties from the Official Church of the State, all of which makes the Court believe that their total separation from the Catholic Church does not exist, but that, on the contrary, there exists a

possibility that they simply wish to evade the existing marriage legislation. . . .
The authorization to contract a civil marriage requested by D. José Moreno Fortes and Da. María Luisa Ruiz Luna is denied. . . .

María Luisa told me she had started attending the General Lacy Street Church in the company of an aunt almost a year before she had become a Baptist. Of her marriage she spoke calmly; she seemed disturbed only by the fact that neither José's nor her own relatives had been told of the legal difficulties. The respective families had come to the church wedding and believed them fully married, and she was not anxious that they should find out the truth. She seemed very calm but very young—a frail girl with titian hair and dark blue eyes, a type fully as "Spanish," in this melting pot of European strains, as her Andalusian husband.

José is short, wiry and dark. Two years before, he had been through a military skirmish of a novel character. "I was in the mess hall," he told me, "when the lieutenant sent for me, and said that a Protestant book had been found in the infirmary. I told him I didn't know anything about it. He said, 'I'll give you until tomorrow to explain how the book got there.' Next morning he called me again, and again I said I knew nothing about the matter. He gave me fifteen days in the brig. From the brig I wrote to Señor Cardona and to my pastor, Don José Luis Rodrigo, who rushed over to the camp. They talked to the colonel, who knew nothing about what had happened. He let me out immediately, gave me back the leave I had lost and told me to let him know if I had any more trouble."

"What about the book?" I asked. "What sort of book was it?"
"They never told me. I never saw it."
"How long were you imprisoned?"
"Eight days."

He seemed more worried than his wife about their legal situation. When the child was born, he told me, he would legitimize it (i.e., acknowledge fatherhood) at the Civil Registry. But until such time as the authorities permitted him and his wife a civil ceremony, he was cut off from all social assistance. In order to qualify for social security, medical insurance and the family allowance granted by the Government to all married Spaniards (or, if unmarried, to bona fide dependents), the employer must present a *libro de familia* with the pertinent documentation. Since he is legally unmarried, Moreno, his wife and children were completely cut off from the Government's social bounty.

In April, 1966, the Church-State relented; María Luisa and José were married two months before the birth of their child.

A month later, the case which led me to Pastor José Palma López came up in Madrid. I learned of its antecedents on my way to visit the judge with Teresa Lerma, a twenty-four-year-old Pentecostal who sought to marry Jaime Guerrero, twenty-five, a member of the same church.

Teresa and Jaime were childhood friends in their home town of Villargordo, Jaén, where their respective families were very close. His relatives, like many country people, moved with him and their children to Madrid two years ago. Then, late in 1965, Jaime and Teresa, who had been courting for some time, decided to get married. Teresa came to stay with the Guerreros in Madrid while the wedding was arranged.

When I rode with Teresa to the *juzgado* with her on February 15, 1966, she had already been through a harrowing interview with a magistrate who refused to grant permission for the civil rite on the grounds that neither she nor her fiancé were residents of Madrid. That first examination had taken place in mid-January when the two young people, accompanied by Pastor Palma, had gone to the *juzgado* to present the pertinent documents.

Teresa, who was called in first, emerged in tears. After telling her she was "ignorant" and "had no studies" and therefore did not know what she was doing, the judge accused her of cohabiting with Guerrero. On a village girl with "virginity" written on every square inch of her body, the impact of the words was disastrous. When she came out into the hall, where Guerrero and the pastor were awaiting their turns, she was, as Palma told me, "tearful, choking and confused." Next Guerrero was equally abused as "ignorant"; then came the pastor's turn. The discussion, begun on a legal plane, with the judge insisting all the documents were false, soon degenerated. After telling the three visitors that the entire case was a farce, His Honor descended so low as to sing the nuptial march for their exit.

When I accompanied Teresa to the *juzgado* she brought an appeal drafted by the Evangelical Defense Commission. Señor Palma's wife, who accompanied us, remained unobtrusively in the hall while we were ushered before the judge.

The man, past middle age, bespectacled, dark, of military bearing, was dressed in a grayish suit and vest, and wearing a black tie. His face, from our entrance to our exit, was a superbly controlled mask half rent by an ironic grin. "Well, what is it?" he said.

"I've come to see about the papers," said Teresa.

"Do you think this is a slot machine, where you put in a coin and out comes the candy?" he told her. "A machine like they have in the subway stations?"

Teresa shot me a look.

The judge asked again: "Do you think this is a *tragaperras?*" ("bitch swallower," a "bitch" being slang for a ten-*céntimo* coin).

Teresa was silent.

"She has come to ask how the case is going," I said, hoping to prod her.

"I don't know how it's going. I have to study this [the appeal the clerk had handed him]. And who are you?" He had not taken his eyes off me since our arrival.

"A friend of the family's," I said.

"She came with me so I would not be alone," Teresa put in quickly.

"Ah, a friend?" the judge said, looking me up and down as though I were merchandise. "Well, you're not going to make us believe they live in Madrid. You're not going to make us take Communion with millstones."

The last expression—a distorted Eucharistic image—is a popular Spanish saying used to parry outrageous lies: it describes, quite simply, the impossibility of getting a millstone in the mouth as one would a Host. As it rang out from the judge not once or twice but three times during the course of the interview, I found it increasingly macabre that a Catholic should have been using such terms to belittle a Protestant's claim.

"It's all full of falsehoods, it's all false," said the judge, flipping the pages of the file.

Teresa had turned visibly pale; her brown eyes were wide open. The judge, fortunately, seemed to be addressing me exclusively.

"Could you tell me what is false?" I asked.

"Look at this," he said, pointing to Guerrero's *Fe de vida,* a document stating the place where he was officially inscribed. "This says he lives in Villargordo."

I meant to play dumb, but my ignorance was real, for I had not seen the file before. "Yes, I see. But since he lives in Madrid now, perhaps you could just overlook that certificate. Would its being there harm the case in any way?"

"I do not know. It might and it might not. . . . And then look at this," he said, turning to another declaration. "This says he lives in Coslada."

"No, he does not live there, he *works* there," I told him, for I did know of Guerrero's place of employment. "You will notice it says so. That firm," I pointed to the letterhead of a thermic-machine manufacturer, "is his employer."

"But why do they bring me these papers?" he asked in irritation, never losing the ironic grin. "What I can't understand is their ingenuousness in bringing me papers like this."

Again I suggested that, if the certificate of employment was not needed, he overlook it. "It wouldn't do any harm in any case, would it?"

"I do not know. It might and it might not." His Honor stood flipping more pages. All three of us were standing; in the fifteen minutes we spent together he did not once ask us to sit down. "Take this signature," he said, pointing to one that appeared on one of the last pages, "and this," singling out another one in the middle, "and this," flipping to another at the beginning. I looked at them carefully; by then it was evident he was addressing me, and not Teresa. Later I found that the clerk who had ushered us in, on coming out into the hall had said to his colleagues, meaning not Señora de Palma, but *myself* and Teresa: "It's the Protestant and the pastor's wife!" Whether or not we were so announced to His Honor, it was evident that he was deigning to speak to me rather than to the girl. "In my opinion, they look the same," I said, referring to the signatures.

"Are you an expert calligrapher?"

"No."

"I deal in calligraphic reports and I know what I am talking about. Look at this line, then look at this one."

He pointed to Guerrero's *rúbrica,* the flourish appended to Spanish signatures. In the last document the line under the name went in one direction, while in the first one it went in the other. From the *rúbrica* we passed to the shape of the "J" on "Jaime." Thick in one case, thin in the other.

"He signed that paper before me," said Teresa.

"I am not doubting that he signed it before you, señorita . . . or señora?" The smile and the implication were unmistakable.

Teresa changed colors. *"Señorita."*

"I am not doubting that he signed it before you. I am only saying that the signatures are different."

"Would that make any difference to the case?" I asked.

"I do not know. It might and it might not."

After another ten minutes inspecting the small letters, their comparative size and slant, we left His Honor. Teresa now clutched a copy of the appeal which the court had stamped for her. I wondered how much longer she would have to wait before she would be married. (It took her only four months.)

Pastor Palma wondered too. "What manners! What manners!" he said of the judge two days later. I was sitting with him—a bespectacled young man in a business suit—in the tiny living room of his apartment. He said he had helped Jaime get the necessary documents, had given him a certificate of membership in his church and had tried to help him and Teresa by coming with them to the *juzgado.* "Though, on the other hand, that is dangerous because it may look like coercion." He told me of the preliminary discussion with the judge on the "falsehood" of the documents and then related the end of the interview. "He told me I was fishing for

127

ignorant people, that they [the young people] were like fish which had fallen in my net. At the end he said, 'All this is a farce. A carnival. I am here talking to you because I am paid to do it, but it is all a lie. They [Teresa and Jaime] will go out of here as single as they came in, only a priest can marry them.' As we were leaving he began to sing to the tune of the nuptial march [from *Lohengrin*], 'They're already married! They're already married!' "

Palma himself is a quiet Andalusian who was born in Granada, converted to the Pentecostal Church in Ronda, and has lived in Madrid a number of years. He works in an opticians' supply house during the day, and tends his church in his spare time. During the negotiations for the church opening he was questioned by the police both at Central Headquarters and at his house ("The police inspector sat right in that chair where you're sitting"). The investigative sessions were long and thorough, but the inspectors, he says, were courteous at all times. In his experience, he continued, he had never come across such hostility as the judge's. Least of all in his own marriage case. "The judge who married us was kind," he said. "He took eight months, but he was *kind.*"

I was curious about the Pentecostals, known to most Americans as the redoubtable Holy Rollers. In Spain, Palma said, the Assemblies of God's worship and organization were identical to the Baptists': "A Baptist service and our service are exactly alike." In the matter of doctrine, Pentecostals differ from the Baptists by their interpretation of Acts 2:4 ("and they were all filled with the Holy Spirit"), which they believe signifies the Holy Ghost's continued and tangible presence in the modern church.

As for rolling—in Spain, he said quietly, it is simply not done. "I'll tell you, there was a police official here, one of the people in charge of Protestant churches, who went on a visit to the United States. And to our misfortune," Señor Palma brought his hands to his head, "he walked into a Puerto Rican Pentecostal Church in New York. . . . After he got back we told him, we showed him our church was different." Lately Pastor Palma's congregation has been increased by some Cubans who profess the faith. "One sister did begin with the hand clapping but we told her that it was not done here."

We then spoke of his military service. "I was lucky, I guess. I was assigned to the Engineer Corps and sent to the Engineering School. The officers were Academy people, professionals, men of culture. It makes a lot of difference when you get men like these, and not people who have been corporals or sergeants for twenty years.

"On my first day there I went up to the lieutenant and told him I was an *evangélico*. He put an arm on my shoulder. 'Look, boy,' he told me, 'when the unit is drawn up to go to Mass, or the religious lectures, or anything like that, you just stay behind.' " (I couldn't help thinking of one officer framing and jailing Moreno, and another protecting a Protestant: Spain and anti-Spain in the Army.) "He was so considerate," Palma continued, "that I used to go to the lectures from time to time, so as not to make my absence too obvious. And every time the priest saw me there," he said, smiling, "he'd start talking about Luther.

"Even the priest was nice. One day I was told the chaplain wanted to see me. Word spread all over the place. 'Palma and the chaplain!' 'The Protestant and the priest!' The priest put one arm around me—I remember it was a big esplanade—and we began to walk up and down. He told me, 'I don't want you to bring any books or propaganda here.' I told him I wouldn't, but that the other men were constantly bombarding me with questions, and that it would be impolite not to answer. 'Oh, that's all right, that's all right,' he said. 'Just don't bring any books.' And that was all.

"The thing I feared most was the *jura de bandera*. When the day came I told the lieutenant I wouldn't go to Mass. That I'd speak to the colonel if it was necessary but that I wouldn't go. He thought it over and said, 'Why don't you stay behind and then, at the end of the Mass, sneak into the last ranks?' [The Mass is a field Mass held on the camp grounds.] I knew he was putting himself out for me, that he was sticking his neck out before the other officers and the colonel. And if I stood in the last ranks,

129

since we were arranged by order of height, with the taller ones up front, I knew I'd stick out. So I said to him, *'Mi teniente,* what if I arrange it with some of my buddies up front, and when the Mass is almost over, have them make room for me at the end of their files?' He looked at me. He didn't say anything, but I think he could have given me a hug.

"No, I had no problems. Some people," said Palma, shaking his head, "think that Spain is a Black Hole."

8

Once they have obtained authorization from the Catholic Church and married in their own, Spanish Protestants face the problem of educating their children. The only institution available to them is the Sunday school of an "authorized" church; and the importation of Bibles for use in such schools—and indeed in all Protestant worship—is subject to regulations as stringent as those governing the existence of the church itself.

The social and intellectual barricade which the Catholic Church has thrown around Spanish Protestantism for the past twenty-five years is thus complete. An adult Protestant, the offspring of an "authorized" marriage, reading an "authorized" Bible in his private, unmarked, "authorized" chapel presents no grave problem to the Catholic unity of Spain. But a Protestant child or catechumen with access to a rich and steady supply of Bibles or other religious texts from abroad, whose perusal will help him grow in the evangelical faith and strengthen his witness of that faith in the Spanish community, is of course an outright "threat." Even worse, in Catholic eyes, is the notion of a Protestant school where the child will acquire a solidly "erroneous" education.

We shall address ourselves to the Biblical situation after a look at the problems presented by the Church-State's educational policy, and the efforts of one evangelical group to break down this solid, Rome-inspired barrier.

I

All Protestant schools are forbidden in Spain. The interdiction, like that on any "external manifestation" of Protestantism, is contained both in Spanish civil legislation and in the Concordat with the Holy See signed in 1953. Here, again, the civil measures ripened into the Concordat, while the Concordat ratified the civil measures.

The Law of Primary Education of July 17, 1945 (promulgated the same day as the *Fuero*), states:

Article 3. The Church has the right to watch over and inspect all teaching in both public and private institutions. . . .

Article 5. Primary education, drawing its inspiration from Catholic thought, in accordance with Spanish scholastic tradition, shall conform to the principles of Catholic dogma and ethics, and to the provisions of Canon Law in force.

The Law of Secondary Education of April 12, 1962, provides:

Article 2. Secondary education shall conform to the standards of Catholic dogma and ethics. . . .

Article 4. The State shall protect the spiritual and moral activity of the Church in all official or private institutions of secondary education. . . .

Article 34. [In classes of] up to 50 students, a teacher with a diploma in letters, a teacher with a diploma in science, and a teacher with a diploma in religion [shall be required]. . . . In agreement with the ecclesiastical hierarchy, the number of teachers of religion shall be established in proportion to the number of students. . . . Every center of secondary education shall have a chapel and a chaplain or spiritual director, named to the post on the recommendation of the proper ecclesiastical authority. . . .

Article 60. In all schools, inspections shall be carried out (a) by the State . . . ; (b) by the Church, in matters concerning the teaching of religion, the orthodoxy of doctrines, and the morality of customs. . . .

Article 84. The compulsory subjects shall be: Religion, Spanish language and literature. . . .

Article 96. Final examinations must cover all compulsory subjects. . . .
Article 105. There shall be in all examination juries an official teacher of religion who has been authorized by the bishop so to serve, and who shall examine in this subject exclusively.

The orthodoxy of higher education had been guaranteed by a law of 1943 which, coming in the middle of World War II, served as another reminder that Fascism was the Church's Fairy Godmother in the "third" world of Christian morals. Madariaga provides the best summary of this piece of legislation, which is in force even today:

The universities are ruled by the law of July 29, 1943, which declares its aim to be "to make the University the most solid bastion of Falangism." It declares explicitly that all education shall be subordinated to the teaching of Catholic dogma and to the program of the Falange. There is only one Association of Students, the Sindicato Español Universitario, of course, a Falange-led organization. Acceptance of the fundamental principles of the state (i.e., Falangism), duly certified by the General Secretary of the Movement, is required of anyone, no matter how competent, who wishes to become a professor. Chairs of religion have been set up even in highly technical schools, and the professor of religion can, by blackballing a candidate, prevent the most brilliant man from obtaining a diploma.[1]

By 1952 all primary, secondary and higher schools were thus securely in the Church's hands. One year later, the Concordat summarized the previous legislative measures and solemnly proclaimed the Church's *de facto* and *de jure* control of all education in Spanish territory:

Article 26. In all teaching centers of any kind and level, be they State-sponsored or not, the teaching shall conform to the principles of dogma and morals of the Catholic Church.
Ordinaries shall exercise freely their mission of watching over the

[1] Madariaga, *op. cit.,* p. 606. The student riots of the spring and fall of 1965 were provoked by the young people's desire to elect the officers of their own Association, in defiance of the Government ban on free elections. The riots, which started as peaceful demonstrations, were ruthlessly crushed. Five professors were expelled, scores of students arrested, and the dangerous precedent of "inorganic" democracy nipped in the bud.

purity of the faith, good customs and religious education in such centers.

Ordinaries may demand that books, publications and teaching materials contrary to Catholic dogma and morals be banned or withdrawn.

Article 27. (1) The Spanish State guarantees the teaching of the Catholic Religion as a regular and compulsory subject in all educational institutions, be they State-sponsored or not, of any kind or level. The children of non-Catholics shall be dispensed from such teaching if their parents or guardians so request.

(2) In primary State schools, the teaching of religion shall be entrusted to the regular teachers, except in cases where the Ordinary has any objections against any of them, for the reasons cited in Canon 1381, paragraph 3 of the Code of Canon Law.[2] [Such teaching] shall also be given periodically in the form of catechism lessons.

(3) In State intermediary schools, the teaching of religion shall be entrusted to professors, priests or religious and, as an alternative, to lay professors named by the competent civil authority at the suggestion of the diocesan Ordinary.

At this point the student of Spanish Catholicism must pause and take stock. Through Article 6 of the *Fuero,* incorporated into its Final Protocol, the Concordat bans any "external manifestation" of dissident beliefs. In like manner, through Articles 26 and 27 it forbids the education of non-Catholic children in the faith of their elders. Whence, then, religious liberty?

Despite Monsignor Guerra Campos' argument in *Ya,* "note 39" of the Council's Schema—"there is nothing in the doctrine of religious liberty which wars in any way against the contemporary practice of the Concordats"—breaks down completely in the Spanish case.[2a] The "contemporary practice of the Concordat" in Spain is the very antithesis of freedom of worship, and by their vote for the Declaration the Council Fathers in effect con-

[2] This measure reads: "Likewise they [the Ordinaries] shall have the right to pass on professors and books of religion; and, for motives of religion or doctrine, to demand that books as well as professors be removed."

[2a] I could not find this note in the English text of the Schema. Monsignor Guerra, Secretary to the Spanish Episcopate, made the statement in *Ya,* November 24, 1965.

travened the Church's own law in the Iberian Peninsula. For the facts of the matter are clear: while the Concordat remains in vigor, the measures envisioned by the Schema on Religious Liberty *cannot legally be enacted in Spain.* The Schema upholds every civil liberty the Concordat condemns, and the Concordat condemns every civil liberty the Schema upholds.

In a brief study published in 1964, Jurist Angel F. Carrillo de Albornoz, the distinguished ex-Jesuit who is today a Research Associate for the Study on Religious Liberty at the World Council of Churches, addresses himself to this problem:

The specific problem in Spain is mainly of legal character; firstly, because the Constitution, in accord with the Concordat of August 29, 1953, does not recognize religious liberty, but only tolerance of *private* worship and the guarantee of nondiscrimination of the citizens on grounds of their religious convictions; and secondly, because there are no legal complementary provisions for the practical execution of the constitutional principles. The Spanish Foreign Minister himself has recently recognized this gap in the Spanish law. In his opinion this is due to the necessity of the state having, as is imperative under the conditions of the Concordat with the Holy See, to take the advice of the Roman Catholic Church on the matter. In a recent article (in *Rivista Romana,* December 4–12, 1963) Mr. Castiella explains the governmental position concerning freedom of religion: "The state," he writes, "has the duty to guarantee freedom of religious profession and of worship, public and private, to all religious confessions, within the limits demanded by morals and by the common good, as Pope John XXIII demanded in the Encyclical PACEM IN TERRIS" (*ibid.*, p. 19). Mr. Castiella expresses the hope "that the Roman Catholic Church will show Spain the right way for the principles established in the above cited Encyclical to become reality in Spain." [3]

Unless the Church "shows the way" out of the quandary posed by a Concordat and a Schema which are mutually exclusive, religious liberty will not and cannot be a reality in Spain.

The first case—the test case—in the matter of education came

[3] Angel F. Carrillo de Albornoz, *Religious Liberty: A General Review of the Present Situation in the World* (Geneva: World Council of Churches, 1964), pp. 5–6.

up before the Church-State in the winter of 1965. A Protestant group had opened a school the year before, only to see it closed down by the civil authorities. When the *evangélicos* made their last appeal on the closure of this school, the Schema on Religious Liberty had already passed in the Vatican, and the right of all parents to educate their children according to their own convictions had been solemnly ratified at the Basilica of St. Peter's. But where did their appeal get Zaragoza's Seventh-day Adventists? Nowhere. In one of the most lucid expositions of its divine commitments—the document has a strong edge of irony—the Government could only remind appellants that the Law of Rome was still supreme in the land.

I spent two days in Zaragoza with the protagonists of the school case: Señor Félix Pagés Puigdemont, pastor of the church, Señor Manuel Adán Zapater, director of the now-underground school, and his wife Rosalía Rovira de Adán, one of the teachers. All are Seventh-day Adventists. In Madrid I had met Señor Angel Codejón Velayos, president of their church and also a veteran of the Zaragoza scene.

To judge by the calm with which they speak of their past and present difficulties, and the optimism with which they plan for the future, Adventists, for all their Fundamentalism, would seem to be one of the most irenic-minded of all evangelical groups. Señor Codejón, as well as Señores Pagés and Adán, had nothing but praise for the new atmosphere which surrounds their work, the cordiality of today's civil authorities, and the touching, almost apologetical courtesy of policemen and other officials when the school was ordered closed.

The Adventists' very presence in Zaragoza, where they constitute the largest Protestant body, is certainly a test of their serenity. In the city which Mary graced with her presence "in mortal flesh," [4] the sojourn of nonbelievers has not always been

---

[4] The Pillar is a phenomenon unique in the Western world: neither Fatima nor Lourdes can touch its poetic irrationality. According to this central belief of Spanish Catholicism, in the first year of the Christian era, and during Mary's lifetime, a host of angels flew her from Jerusalem to Zaragoza, where she appeared to St. James on a pillar of marble before the

a cause for Catholic joy. During his days as pastor in Zaragoza, Señor Codejón was both trailed and visited by the police, who asked after his activities and inquired if he had been distributing any "proselytist" material—meaning pamphlets or any other evangelical literature. "They would get us mixed up with the Jehovah's Witnesses," he says. But he adds that he had no trouble on this account; every time he stated that there was no connection between his church and the Witnesses, the police seemed satisfied.

(Be it said in passing that the Witnesses have done their bit to muddle the cause of Protestantism in Spain. The average Spaniard, even today abysmally ignorant of the tenets and realities of Protestantism, lumps Witnesses and "Protestants" together into that one word which is the object of his scorn: "sects." To him a Witness, a Lutheran and an Episcopalian are all heretics, all sectarians, and all corrupt; one is hard put to convince him that, although entitled to exercise their ministry in any open society, the Witnesses are not in any way connected with Protestantism, and have in fact been repudiated by Protestants time and again, both in Spain and abroad.)

Señor Codejón speaks of his Zaragoza days without visible bitterness. There is one anecdote which I heard from his successors

---

return trip (also via angels) to her Jerusalem home. The heavenly host, according to the ancient codex which tells the story, were the very same "thousands upon thousands" of angels who appeared "at the hour when Mary conceived Christ, to safeguard her, to accompany her continuously, and to keep her Son safe." The book from which I've taken the quotation, written by a Jesuit, points out that the codex was issued many years after the apparition and hence may be open to some objections; but that "as regards its essence and substance, the authenticity [of the narration] cannot be doubted, proved by a faithful and constant tradition, confirmed by the supreme authority of the Church [Pope Clement XII] and by the exact fulfillment of the prophecies made by the Queen of Heaven to the Apostle James." "Among all the nations of Europe," adds Father Garzón, S.J., "Spain has been the only one which has received the visit of Mary in mortal flesh. . . . " (F. Garzón, S.J., *La Santísima Virgen, en España* [Madrid: Apostolado de la Prensa, 1953], pp. 11, 12, 18.) Today, the magic pillar where Mary "rested her sacred feet" (*ibid.*, p. 13) is venerated literally around the clock in the immense basilica of that name.

in the city and later checked with him in Madrid and which bears retelling. During the time when he was watched by the police, one plainclothesman called regularly at Señor Codejón's house on his investigative rounds, asked the routine questions, and left. Came one day when Señora de Codejón, in the park with her children, met the cop with *his* children. He smiled, she smiled, he greeted her, she answered, he broke down and acknowledged his calling and they became good friends. "He was," says Señor Codejón, "a very nice man."

The story of this ecumenical Scobie again points to the presence of compassionate men in the hate-ridden police. When the dark angel of "unity" is not upon him, the Spaniard faces vital issues with an instinctive, unusually developed "sense of man" (it is Madariaga's phrase) which makes him one of the warmest, kindest humans on earth. Glassy-eyed cop-patriots bent on the destruction of Protestant "treachery" will exist while there is no freedom of religion or expression; but there will also be men under their command who limit themselves to carrying out orders. One *evangélico* in Barcelona told me of going to a police station to notify the officer in charge that his chapel was moving from one place to another, and that the papers authorizing the transfer were expected any minute. "I've no intention of bothering you," the man answered. "As far as I'm concerned you can move wherever you want and build your church wherever you please. Unless a priest comes over and complains, I will not trouble you in any way."

The absence of friction in the Zaragoza school case is indicative of the growing humanization of the law-enforcement bodies. On November 24, 1964, Señor Adán Zapater, thirty-three, made out a report on the proposed school and forwarded same to the Most Excellent Director General of Primary Instruction at the Ministry of National Education in Madrid. Adventists, the document stated, felt that the school "came fully under the dispensation provided by Article 27, Paragraph 1, b, of the present Spanish Concordat with the Vatican." ("The children of non-Catholics shall be dispensed from such teaching—i.e., compulsory instruction in the Catholic religion—if their parents or guardians so request.")

Along with this request for authorization, Señor Adán forwarded a certificate of his "religious and moral conduct" issued by Pastor Felix Pagés.

On the strength of this report, and without awaiting a reply, the school was opened. Several days later, on December 7, the Ministry answered denying authorization on several grounds. Among other things, it pointed out that the application lacked the required certificate "from the corresponding parish priest as to the religious and moral conduct of the teacher, which [certificate] can in no wise be supplied by a document from the Pastor of the Evangelical Christian Church of the Seventh Day, Octavio de Toledo Street, No. 7, Zaragoza. . . ."

By virtue of a Ministerial Order of November 15, 1945, every application for the opening of a school must be accompanied by a certificate from the parish priest of the locality. And no priest worth his Spanish-Catholic salt will ever give a pastor a good conduct certificate with which he can set up an "illegal" and "erroneous" school. The hopeful Adventists, by substituting a document from an Evangelical minister, elicited the Government's confirmation that no moral endorsement of Protestantism is possible in the City of God.

As for the appeal to Article 27, Paragraph 1, b, the Ministry stated that "it must be established that this exception refers only to a personal and individual, and not a collective right." The reference to Article 6 of the *Fuero* (also cited by the Adventists) is quashed in strong words: this article, writes the Ministry, "states that no one shall be bothered for his religious beliefs or the private exercise thereof, but makes clear, without any doubt whatsoever, that no ceremonies or external manifestations other than those of the Catholic Religion shall be permitted; that is to say, that said individual liberty, as far as [a person's] conscience is concerned, is subject to precise limitations, and that the use of said liberty *cannot have as a result either ostentation, instruction or example.*" (Italics mine.)

Señor Adán appealed once more, in his own name and that of twenty-four parents whose children attended the school. In this communication he cites the human rights envisioned by Articles

139

1, 3, 5, 17, 22 and 23 of the *Fuero,* as well as the rights of parents or guardians to the free education of their children contained in Articles 2, 4, 27 and 56 of the Law of Primary Education. His appeal was of course idle in Spain, where the Protestant is deprived of all civil rights by virtue of the Concordat; but the first session of the Vatican Council had shown promise of the Church's rehabilitation of man *qua* man, and the recognition of laws other than "divine" ones in the regulation of human conduct. No member of the Northern European or American churches, un-Catholic, un-Roman and "un-spiritual" in their respect for man, can realize the implications of the Council's discovery of human rights in divinely governed Spain.

The answer to the second appeal came on February 1, 1965. By order of the Civil Government of Zaragoza, and "given the illegal character of the educational activities which are being carried out in said institution," the Civil Guard appeared at the school and, with all courtesy and consideration (the raid was carried out at seven in the evening, when the children were already home), they sealed up the premises.

The Adventists' efforts to reopen the case gave rise to the last, conclusive document issued by the Government. It is dated November 24, 1965, one month after the declaration of religious liberty had been solemnly proclaimed at the Vatican. And it is worth quoting at length. In it the Ministry of National Education wearily washes its hands of the matter and, between the lines, makes clear that only an act of God can alter the *status quo.*

Spanish legalese, like any other, is highly technical and abstruse; it also tends towards an endless piling of clause upon clause. Even granting these characteristics, however, the Ministry's document of November 24 has an exceptional ring. One must read it through only once to realize that it is an outright pastiche.

The excerpt below constitutes a three-paragraph, 467-word sentence in the Spanish original. Out of consideration for the reader the translated text is broken down, somewhat arbitrarily, into smaller units of thought:

In view of the Laws of Primary Education of July 17, 1945, of Administrative Process of July 17, 1958, of the *Fuero de los Españoles,* the Code of the Teaching Profession, Ministerial Orders of November 15, 1945, December 3, 1957, July 8, 1958, the Concordat signed between the Spanish Government and the Holy See on August 27, 1953, and other pertinent measures;

CONSIDERING that the reasons adduced in the present appeal do not annul those which constitute the foundation of the Ministerial Order in question, since it is a general principle proclaimed in the matter of instruction that such instruction be carried out under the aegis of Catholic dogma, as set forth in Article 5 of the Law of Primary Education of July 17, 1945, made concrete in Article 26 of the Concordat with the Holy See,

Therefore, this being the mainstay of education, and in spite of the argument raised by appellant to the effect that Article 2 of the above-mentioned Law has a relative value, one must keep in mind that the right granted under this same measure to families as regards the choice of persons or centers which shall impart an education to their children, is conditioned to the exigencies of the common good as stated in the Laws of the Spanish State, which stand for the absolute value of the Catholic confession;

and, this being the juridico-positive doctrine as regards the matter of instruction, to admit the opening of a School of the Christian Adventist Community of the Seventh Day would be the equivalent of contravening the [doctrine's] expressed statement of rights, which [rights] are not in this case of a subjective nature, but constitutional principles crystallized in our legal institutions and inspired in the national Catholic tradition;

then, [the school's opening] would war against the very constitutional norm, for, although free will is the determining force in a person's spiritual and religious formation, the public projection of nonlaicized but, in effect, non-Catholic instruction would provoke a fissure in the religious dogmaticism which presides the confessionality of the Spanish State; therefore,

for reasons of the above-mentioned principles, the Ministerial Order in question remains in vigor, as it conforms to our juridico-traditional and [juridico-] positive frame of reference, and the present appeal is consequently denied; furthermore,

CONSIDERING that, independently of the arguments expressed above, and as regards the formal basis of the problem posed, the nonfulfillment of the conditions demanded for the installation of an Institution of Primary Instruction as set forth in the Ministerial Order of November 15, 1945, render impossible the approval of the administrative

certificate in the absence of the required report from the competent authority of the Catholic Church,
THIS MINISTRY has resolved to deny the present appeal.

Señor Pagés Puigdemont is a tall, very soft-spoken man with an easy smile and a quick sense of humor. He is a Catalán, and a first-generation *evangélico*. So is Señor Adán Zapater, the school's director. They met me at the station along with Señora de Adán when I arrived from Madrid by rail.

The trip, just under five hours long, is made a delight by the Talgo—a Spanish train, and one of Europe's finest—and the changing scenery. Just outside Madrid a hard-blowing snowstorm began to deck countryside and villages in white. Sigüenza, neatly clustered about its eleventh-century cathedral (surely it is one of Spain's most magnificent medieval cities) was an unforgettable sight in the winter landscape.

When I arrived the Adventists took note of my traveler's instincts (I did not know Zaragoza) and obligingly whisked me on a tour of the downtown section, the Basilica of the Pillar and the superb cathedral church known as *La Seo:* Señor Adán, solidly grounded in Spanish and Aragonese history, made an excellent cicerone.

Next day I visited the Adventists' installations. The forbidden school, like a handful of others, has gone underground: four groups of children are now taught at three different addresses. I saw the chapel at No. 7 Octavio de Toledo Street, and another place of worship on the outskirts of town which is being demolished to make room for a big new church. Permission to raise this important, four-story building was obtained from the civil authorities within the past two years; it is not the least of the blessings for which the Adventists are extraordinarily grateful.

The abandoned school is at No. 5 Rusiñol Street. It is a pleasant building which stands out from its neighbors by the fresh coat of paint on its façade. Inside, though the walls are also neat, the smell of mustiness is already apparent. With Señores Pagés and Adán I walked through the first and second stories, saw the modern kitchen and lavatories, the hallways and other installations—everything except the classrooms. All three of these (two upstairs, one downstairs) had been sealed with bands of tape four or five inches wide, in the middle of which was the emblem of the Dirección General de Seguridad.

The patio behind the building was the school's playground. It is a small, cloisterlike plot that still exudes an air of games and fun. A narrow cement walk borders the high-walled enclosure. On the far end is a tile-roofed shed; there are one large and two small trees in the playing area, which is completely covered with smooth, whitish pebbles. Señor Adán pointed out a sooty ledge which runs along the left wall. It was the place where each child had kept his own plant—an herb or a flowering species—labeled with his own name, and which he tended daily as part of the curriculum.

Few places are as conducive to meditation as the deserted backyard of No. 5 Rusiñol Street, Zaragoza, Spain. Standing on the school porch and looking over the empty playground, one can't help but remember the plea circulated abroad in September, 1965, by which time the small institution had been closed for seven months.

The object of the Church, it stated, is

to revindicate the holy right of each man to his own responsible liberty, above all in the basic field of conscience and religion.
The intention of the ancient and modern persecutors is identical. With physical violence and with the weight of a legal, judicial or administrative apparatus they wish to impose "their truth" and suffocate all contrary expressions of thought and its honest manifestations.
. . . Attempts are made today to strangle the free religious life of the people and of the individual. . . . Gradually the possibilities of renewing the ranks of the clergy, already decimated, are obstructed.
. . . All means are monopolized by the totalitarian organization, the means of the press and of cultural, scholastic, educational and recreational life, in order to take the young people away from the church. . . .

The last sentence ends: ". . . and impose on them the Marxist doctrine." It was Pope Paul VI complaining of the oppression of Catholics behind the Iron Curtain.

II

To sketch the history of the Protestant Bible in Spain one must dwell, if only briefly, on its sixteenth-century origins.

When Francisco de Enzinas presented his translation of the New Testament to Louvain's theologians in 1543, the holy men were not exactly sympathetic:

> they said that they did not understand Spanish and were not able to judge the accuracy of the text, but that they doubted the usefulness of translating the Bible into vulgar tongues, since that had proved the source of heresy in Germany and the Low Countries, as it gave simple and idiotic people a chance to indulge in false interpretations and dreams [sic], rejecting the canons and decrees of the Church.[5]

The Battle of the Bible, as fought by Catholicism since Luther's time, has ever been the struggle of the common man—the "simple and idiotic" John Doe—against the intellectual ascendancy of the clergy. It was not a single battle, of course, nor even a series of skirmishes: it was a slow, evolutionary process which culminated in the Reformation. In his study of Vives, Ortega describes the metamorphosis of the "Dantesque, medieval" world of the fourteenth century into the "Cartesian, modern" world which came into being in the seventeenth. In Dante's time, he writes, man not only *started* from God, but lived *facing* God, with his back to the world. In the transition centuries, man still started from God, but no longer faced Him. "Life has made a 180-degree turn: starting from God, one no longer looks at God, but at the world, at the terrestrial." Then came the sixteenth century with its commercial expansion, its cultural boom, its increasing secularization.

In the sixteenth century all that hierarchical, ecclesiastical, scholarly, theological religion becomes democratized. The relation of man to God itself becomes democratized; a piety without wisdom or complications comes into being, a religion of "poor men." A century and a half earlier the "poor one of Assisi" had walked the world as a

[5] Menéndez Pelayo, *op. cit.,* I, 957.

precursor of this [piety], himself inflamed with it. Now all religion becomes resolutely "vulgarized," it becomes a more intimate experience between God and Everyman, between God and the illiterate— he whom Cardinal Cusano called the "idiot," i.e., he who is not a clergyman, nor who has any position in the ecclesiastical hierarchy.[6]

In Spain the upsurge of scholarship in the fourteenth and fifteenth centuries, and the shock waves of Erasmism in the sixteenth, pointed the way to a moral and intellectual revolution which might have signaled a Reformation after the Northern pattern. Distinguished Spanish physicians, geographers, jurists and mathematicians had turned their backs on an abstract God to find Him in the concrete realities of His world. Men of science were already poring through Scripture with both critical and creative eyes. In 1517 the Polyglot Bible, one of the most significant achievements of Renaissance scholarship, had come from the University of Alcalá de Henares. This colossal work (in Hebrew, Chaldaic, Greek and Latin) had been the dream of Cardinal Cisneros, who, as Menéndez Pelayo says, "Without having been a great literary figure himself, was thoroughly a man of his century: enamored of wisdom and letters, wise in choosing his men, most ardent in his projects and tenacious in their execution."[7] The men he chose (among them Nebrija and Vergara) formed a team of linguists and scholars no nation of the North could have matched; the project he saw to its conclusion was a milestone in Biblical research.

If the Erasmists had prevailed in Spain, the Polyglot would have been one gigantic step towards that spiritual victory which Luther claimed forever: the respectful and uncondescending presentation of the Bible to the common man. By the 1520's Erasmus was already writing to Luis Núñez Coronel and urging upon him "the convenience of laymen reading Scripture in the vulgar tongue."[8] By the 1530's Juan de Valdés was translating the Psalms and the Epistle of St. Paul to the Romans into "beautiful

---

[6] Ortega y Gasset, *op. cit.*, pp. 54, 55.
[7] Menéndez Pelayo, *op. cit.*, I, 777.
[8] *Ibid*, p. 793.

Castilian." [9] And by 1543 Enzinas was hopefully presenting his Spanish New Testament to an Emperor who, unfortunately, was already committed to the forces of intellectual constraint.

Enzinas ended in jail. So did Carranza, who, having written his *Catechism* in Spanish, found that the first accusation made against it by Melchor Cano was: "That it gave unlearned people, in the vulgar tongue, things which were difficult and perplexing." [10]

But the Spaniard who presented his fellow countrymen with all the "difficult and perplexing" treasures of the Bible did not suffer for it. He was Casiodoro de la Reina, whom Menéndez Pelayo identifies as a man born in Granada of Moorish blood. De la Reina, a priest, embraced the Lutheran doctrine and fled Seville at the height of the *autos de fe* of 1559. After a sojourn in London (where, says the author of *Heterodoxos,* he was a paid spy of Queen Elizabeth), he moved to Antwerp and published a catechism there. In 1567 he was living in Strassburg, already engaged in the twelve-year task of translating all of Holy Writ into Castilian.

The first edition of his *Santa Biblia* appeared in Basel in 1569. It was revised and annotated by Cipriano de Valera, another Spanish refugee, in 1602. The de la Reina–de Valera version is the "Protestant Bible" of Spain—the "desecrated Bible" *My Parish* warns readers against. It is the book used for study and worship by all of Spain's and Latin America's *evangélicos,* and the volume which the British and Foreign Bible Society has indefatigably distributed among Spanish-speaking people since the middle of the nineteenth century.

De la Reina's translation has survived bannings, burnings and confiscations. After an interdiction of more than two decades, it surfaced again in Madrid in 1963, barely two years before Catholicism sanctioned the use of the vernacular in most of the Mass.

The new headquarters of the British and Foreign Bible Society at Garcia Morato Street in Madrid are spacious, modern ground-

[9] *Ibid.,* II, 111.
[10] *Ibid.,* p. 26.

floor offices with a big sign across the building's façade. Thus far Señor José Flores, the director, has cautiously refrained from putting Bibles in the window, but the sign is itself proof of the Spanish government's conciliatory attitude towards the Protestant Bible since the spring of 1963.

The Society's official activities in Spain began with the arrival of George Borrow at the town of Elvas, on the Portuguese frontier, one day in January, 1836:

Arrived at the gate of Elvas, an officer came out of a kind of guardhouse, and having asked me some questions, despatched a soldier with me to the police office, that my passport might be viséed, as upon the frontier they are much more particular with respect to passports than in other parts.[11]

Borrow, soon to be known as Don Jorgito, spent four years distributing Bibles and New Testaments across the length and breadth of the Peninsula. His volume of reminiscences, *The Bible in Spain,* has become a classic in travel literature. The Everyman's Library edition of the book bears an introduction by Hispanist Walter Starkie, who draws a delightful sketch of his fellow countryman and the bizarre mission he was set upon:

Before reaching Madrid and beginning his work as biblical agent he spent a fortnight with the gypsy tribes in Extremadura, attended a gypsy wedding at Mérida, collected a list of gypsy oaths, which he duly sent to the Bible Society in London, borrowed a horse from a gypsy and rode with an escort of Romanichals as far as the Castilian frontier.[12]

Of Borrow's singular book Starkie adds:

. . . *The Bible in Spain* makes the greatest appeal to the true wanderer in Spain, who longs for hardship, provided he can meet with adventures at every turn of the road. Anyone with pretensions to be a Romany Rye will cast away any other literature and pack George

[11] George Borrow, *The Bible in Spain,* with an Introduction by Walter Starkie (London: J. M. Dent & Sons, Ltd., 1961; New York: E. P. Dutton & Co., Inc., 1961 [Everyman's Library No. 151]), p. 68.
[12] *Ibid.,* p. vii.

Borrow in his rucksack, for even today he will find that Don Jorgito El Inglés is a legend in various parts of Spain.[13]

He was already a legend in Menéndez Pelayo's time. The grand old man of Catholic history finds Borrow a "simple" soul, "of very scarce culture," and states that his book "is capable of producing inextinguishable laughter in the most melancholy reader." [14] On this last account he was right. One need not share Menéndez Pelayo's arrogance to be amused by Don Jorgito's narrative, set down in a straight-faced style which might have been sired by the early Henry James out of Mark Twain. Here is Borrow dealing with a suspicious guard on his way to Madrid:

I remembered having read that the best way to win a Spaniard's heart is to treat him with ceremonious civility. I therefore dismounted, and taking off my hat, made a bow to the constitutional soldier, saying, "Señor nacional, you must know that I am an English gentleman, travelling in this country for my pleasure; I bear a passport, which, on inspecting, you will find to be perfectly regular; it was given me by the great Lord Palmerston, minister of England, whom you of course have heard of here; at the bottom you will see his own handwriting; look at it and rejoice; perhaps you will never have another opportunity. As I put unbounded confidence in the honour of every gentleman, I leave the passport in your hands whilst I repair to the posada to refresh myself. When you have inspected it, you will perhaps oblige me so far as to bring it to me. Cavalier, I kiss your hands.[15]

The guard not only let him by, but offered him an escort and, before parting, begged to be shown the signature of "Caballero Balmestorn" [sic] once more.

I showed him the signature, which he looked upon with profound reverence, uncovering his head for a moment; we then embraced and parted.[16]

---

[13] *Ibid.*, p. xi.
[14] Menéndez Pelayo, *op. cit.*, II, 1021.
[15] Borrow, *op. cit.*, pp. 95–96.
[16] *Ibid.*, p. 97.

In Madrid Borrow obtained the assistance of the British Ambassador and, in 1837, printed five thousand copies of the New Testament. During his stay in the city he was also received, and politely rebuffed, by the Duque de Rivas, by Rivas' Secretary—a man enamored of the Council of Trent, and one of the book's most comic figures—and by Prime Minister Mendizábal.

Don Jorge's now-famous interview with Mendizábal took place at the Royal Palace:

he was a huge athletic man, somewhat taller than myself, who measure six foot two without my shoes; his complexion was florid, his features fine and regular, his nose quite aquiline, and his teeth splendidly white; though scarcely fifty years of age, his hair was remarkably grey; he was dressed in a rich morning gown, with a gold chain round his neck, and morocco slippers on his feet.[17]

When Borrow stated his intention of printing the Scriptures in Spain, the Prime Minister proved most unco-operative.

". . . What a strange infatuation is this which drives you [the English] over lands and waters with Bibles in your hands. My good sir, it is not Bibles we want, but guns and gunpowder, to put the rebels down with, and, above all, money, that we may pay the troops; whenever you come with these three things you shall have a hearty welcome; if not, we really can dispense with your visits, however great the honour." [18]

The "rebels" the Prime Minister spoke of were the Carlist insurrectionists. Mendizábal had assumed office during the regency of Queen María Cristina de Borbón, widow of Ferdinand VII and mother of the still-infant Isabel II. Upon the death of Ferdinand, who left no sons, his brother Don Carlos had renewed his claims to the throne citing, this time, a document signed by Philip V in 1713 to the effect that a male heir would always have precedence in the line of succession. The strife between *carlistas* and *cristinos* soon crystallized into a struggle between Revolution and Tradition. María Cristina, a Neapolitan by birth, had no qualms in installing

17 *Ibid.*, p. 114.
18 *Ibid.*, pp. 114–15.

liberal elements in her government, while Don Carlos' followers, aided and abetted by the Church, sought a return to the absolute dominion of the "traditional" values of the past.[19] The pendulum of the Spanish temper, having swung to the left, was only gathering momentum for its coming slide to the right—Madariaga's "familiar rhythm" at work.

Mendizábal's most decisive move in his eight-month premiership was a move against the Church. Like the Republican authorities in 1931, María Cristina's first dignitary could see only one way to attack the mighty and troublesome forces of Catholicism: economic warfare. By a decree of October 11, 1835, he suppressed all religious communities except those engaged in the teaching and nursing of the poor; the lands and buildings confiscated passed to Government and private hands. Today, a history text read by all Spanish school children describes the Carlist leader Zumalacárregui and the Queen's Premier in the following terms:

> The man of the Carlist reaction was a hero who, at the time of his death, did not even have money for his own funeral: Zumalacárregui. The man of the liberal revolution was a Jew who had amassed a great personal fortune: Mendizábal.[20]

Between 1836 and 1840, Borrow distributed some 14,000 copies of the Scriptures—a substantial figure when one considers the hazards of traveling in a nation torn by civil war. It is hard to say how much of the seed fell on good ground: briers and tares were certainly not lacking. Barely four years after Borrow had left Spain, Pope Gregory XVI issued an encyclical (May 8, 1844) condemning the Biblical societies. Almost immediately Jaime Balmes, the Spanish Church's indomitable apologist, charged head

---

[19] Carlists and their colorful, red-bereted troops, the *requetés* (named after the nineteenth-century Traditionalist soldiers), are still in evidence, especially around Navarre. Their cause attracted world-wide attention a few years ago when Don Hugo Carlos of Bourbon-Parma, son of the present Carlist Pretender, Don Javier, married Princess Irene of the Netherlands.
[20] José María Pemán, *La historia de España contada con sencillez* (Madrid: Escelicer, S.A., 1958), p. 332. Mendizábal was in fact a banker by profession. His real name was Méndez and he was said to be of Jewish blood.

on against Protestantism. In an article dated September 7, 1844 (*La Sociedad,* Vol. II, p. 474), he states:

Only by resorting to the contradictions of the human spirit, and to the blindness produced by the dominion of the passions or by fanatical sectarianism, can one maintain that it is useful and wholesome to put the Bible in everyone's hands. . . . One need only take a look at the Prophets, the Psalms, the Apocalypse, to realize that their import is only partially intelligible to those who have a great wealth of instruction and who, furthermore, have fixed precepts in view, which [precepts] can only spring from an infallible authority, the preserver of ancient tradition, enlightened by God Himself, which is the Catholic Church.

In spite of the grave harm inherent in [their] system, Protestants have not only refused to turn back from the abysses to which they have led their sects, but they have organized the Bible Societies . . . and try to divulge the Bible throughout the whole world so that it should reach even the lowest classes, thus converting those pages sent by Heaven for the light of intellects and the sanctification of souls into the seeds of error and corruption. . . . Whoever trusts those books [i.e., Protestant Bibles] can no longer adduce any arguments: it is he whom Christ himself has charged with watching over [this] sheep [i.e., the Pope] who now warns us that the grass is poisonous.[21]

The Concordat of 1851 was in the offing. By virtue of this agreement between Spain and Pope Pius IX (whose *Syllabus of Errors* called Protestants "the enemies of the Cross of Christ") Catholicism was proclaimed supreme in the land and compensation for the property confiscated by Mendizábal was made to the Church. Madariaga sums up this one-step-forward-two-steps-backwards ploy in a few lines:

Though dissolved and expelled a few years earlier, orders of all kinds soon invaded the country again, a fact less harmful than is sometimes imagined; but what was harmful was that these orders, through their inveterate policy of acquiring and accumulating wealth, rapidly succeeded in nullifying themselves as spiritual forces, while interfering with the sound economic and political development of the nation.[22]

[21] Jaime Balmes, *Obras completas* (Madrid: Biblioteca de Autores Cristianos, 1949), V, 235–36, 238.
[22] Madariaga, *op. cit.,* p. 161.

151

Thin but insistent, the voice of reason was to be heard again. In 1868 Generals Serrano and Prim led a successful revolution, routed Isabel II and set up a provisional government which decreed universal suffrage, freedom of religion, of the press, of education and of assembly. A new Constitution was drawn up and considered by the Constitutional *Cortes.* "The most discussed article," says an authoritative history of Spain, "was that which established freedom of worship. More than nine thousand sheets with three million signatures were presented requesting that the Catholic religion be the only one tolerated." [23] Against this overwhelming vote for bigotry, religious liberty was proclaimed in 1869.

Thirty-six pages and seven years later, the same author uses almost the same words in referring to the Constitution of 1876, which turned the tables once more: "Article 11 [of this Constitution] was the most debated. It recognizes that the Catholic religion is the official religion of the State. It affirms that no one in Spanish territory shall be molested because of his beliefs, although no ceremonies shall be permitted other than those of the State religion." [24] Together with the Concordat of 1851, the 1876 Constitution was to be the model for today's *Fuero de los Españoles.*

The vicissitudes encountered by colporteurs who followed Borrow were many, not the least of them the open hostility of townspeople who received them with sticks and stones; in the nineteenth century, as today, unyielding religious hate was often concentrated in rural districts. But the Society continued to function through and up to the end of the twentieth-century Crusade. In 1939 it sent the following report to its London headquarters:

Civil war raged in Spain throughout the whole of the year under review, but in spite of that no fewer than 47,000 volumes of the Scriptures were distributed. Of the nine colporteurs employed by the Society, five worked more or less regularly, but it is pitiful to recall how war conditions restricted their activities. They continued to travel as long as possible, but gradually, as food became scarcer, inns closed

[23] Pedro Aguado Bleye and Cayetano Alcázar Molina, *Manual de historia de España* (Madrid: Espasa-Calpe, S.A., 1964), III, 711.
[24] *Ibid.,* p. 747.

down, and it became impossible to obtain accommodations. They were then obliged to confine themselves to the cities where they lived. Señor Adolfo Araujo remained at his post in Madrid, and a sale of 13,000 books was effected at the Depot.[25]

In March, 1939, the Franco forces took Madrid. Eight months later General Magariños, one of the Franco officers, addressed a letter to the Sociedad Bíblica y Extranjera's Director. The document is still on file at the Society's headquarters. It bears the letterhead of the Ministry of the Government, Subsecretariat of Censorship, and it reads as follows:

Dear Sir:
On the 8th and 14th of November, 1939, permission was granted for the free circulation in Spanish territory of the Holy Bible and excerpts of the same, published by the Sociedad Bíblica y Extranjera located at No. 8 Federico Balart Street, Madrid.
For God, For Spain and her National Syndicalist Revolution.
November 20, 1939

Year of victory
THE SECRETARY GENERAL OF CENSORSHIP
[signed] Magariños

The communications General Magariños refers to are also extant: they are written authorizations for the Society to continue its work. After the original permission for the circulation of the Scriptures issued on November 8, a second letter, dated the 14th, specifically states that the version of Holy Writ authorized is that of Casiodoro de la Reina and Cipriano de Valera.

The Church Fathers were to override Magariños' approval and proceed against the Society as first step of that ruthless persecution of "heresy" in which they would soon enlist the Government's support. But Magariños' good will served the cause of the Bible Society for over a year. Today, when Church and State in Spain have taken diverging positions on the issue of religious liberty, with an attendant rift which has been patent even abroad, it is well to remember this liberal gesture from the person of a *franquista* gen-

[25] *God's Word for a New Age* [pamphlet] (Madrid: Sociedad Bíblica y Extranjera, 1964), pp. 31–32.

eral. As far back as 1940 the political right was ready to inch towards the center, however imperceptibly: the ecclesiastical right was not.

On August 7, 1940, the Church struck. Police arrived at the Society's headquarters on Flor Alta Street and took possession of 110,000 Bibles.[26] Señor Flores, the present Director, still remembers the day. So did the late Bernard Malley, honorary attaché and legal adviser to the British Embassy in Madrid, a Catholic who, in twenty-six years of diplomatic service in Spain, had always been, as he modestly described himself, "a friend of Protestants." I spoke to Mr. Malley at the Embassy, two months before his death. He recalled the day vividly, and even the words he addressed in his perfect Spanish to the men who carried out the raid.

"I asked the men who were carting the books away, 'Do you know what you are doing with the word of God?' They didn't seem to know what I was talking about. 'Do you know that is the word of God you have in your hands?' I asked. Finally they understood, and one of them said, 'We have no choice but to obey.' ['*No tenemos más remedio que obedecer.*']"

The Bibles were loaded onto a truck which Mr. Malley followed in his car. "It was a very large lorry which went to the Southern Station. The books were placed on a train and from there taken to a pulp factory."

All 110,000 copies of the Word of God were reduced to pulp, and the pulp in turn used in the manufacture of newsprint for the Government paper. The Church tasted victory; the State, whose conscience could still smart, compensated the Society for the material loss.

Thereafter the Protestant Bible circulated clandestinely. In 1952, two thousand New Testaments were confiscated. In 1956, coincidentally with the closing of the Madrid Theological Seminary, forty thousand Bibles were hauled away in two trucks. Not until the spring of 1963 was the Government able to grant to the

[26] Orders were also given for the confiscation of all the Society's Bibles in all parts of Spain. Books were impounded as far away as the Canary Islands.

Society permission for importing a fixed number of books. This agreement, negotiated by Foreign Minister Castiella, provides for an annual quota of 2,070 Bibles and 4,169 New Testaments a year. Protestant authorities found the quantities too small to meet the requirements of a growing evangelical population; but the authorization represented a juridical victory which would be matched in importance only by the proposed Statute legalizing Protestantism.

9

The suppression of the "desecrated" Bible is only one phase of a larger problem which affects all Spaniards regardless of personal belief; the intellectual and moral ravages of State-imposed, Church-controlled censorship.

Few people abroad realize the extent of the ideological "orientation" Spain has been toiling under. In the twenty-five years following the Crusade, the Spanish Church-State has inspected and passed upon *all* printed matter which circulated in the country. Newspapers and periodicals came under a Press Law; books, pamphlets, and all pictorial matter were controlled by two separate measures.

I

The Press Law of April 22, 1938, states:

Article 1. The State shall organize, watch over and control the national institution of the journalistic press. The Minister in charge of the National Press Service shall have the power of regulating same.
Article 2. In the exercise of the function mentioned above, the State shall:
  1. Regulate the number and diffusion of journalistic publications;
  2. Intervene in the nomination of editors;

156

3. Issue norms for the journalistic profession;
4. Watch over the activities of the Press;
5. [Impose] censorship until such time as it is abrogated;
6. Be empowered with any other faculties deriving from the provisions of Article 1 of this Law.

The only glimmer of hope in 1938 was the slim but significant appendage to the fifth point under Article 2: Censorship would be imposed *"until such time as it is abrogated."* Issued in reconquered National territory while the Crusade was still raging, the law thus posited censorship in its classic wartime sense. But the promise of this small phrase, like the generosity implied in General Magariños' gesture towards the Bible Society, came to naught in the postwar period. Indeed, as the Church gained ascendancy over the Regime, the Press Law, implemented by two other measures in 1938 and 1944, respectively, was to subject Spaniards to a diet of "authorized" ideas for twenty-five years.

As the postwar days rolled on and Spain's "enemies" north of the Pyrenees and west of the Atlantic pointed the finger at her press system, elaborate defenses manufactured by both Church and State circulated over the land. Where "inorganic" democracy was denounced as corrupting and evil, "liberty of the press" was exposed as a gigantic hoax. The classic syllogism, put forward with all solemnity in the forties and fifties, went as follows: in materialistic countries, newspapers are the property of millionaires; but these millionaires have bought the journals so they can foist their own ideas on the unsuspecting reader; *ergo,* when he thinks he is purchasing "free" information, the reader of the so-called "free" press is only getting the millionaire's point of view.

The concept is not novel—Jaime Balmes was voicing a similar one in the nineteenth century (cf. *El criterio,* Chapter IX, "Newspapers"). Today it is mostly relegated to hate sheets such as *Que Pasa,* with a heavy circulation in the Carlist North and a marked tendency towards diatribes on the "Jewish press of New York." But it is so deeply embedded in the Spanish mentality that it can also be voiced by young and forward-looking officials such as Manuel Fraga Iribarne, Minister of Information and Tourism.

Señor Fraga, one of the Regime's new men and the architect of the second, more liberal Press Law, saw fit to echo the traditional line in a speech in Bilbao in December, 1965. The résumé of the address in *ABC* (December 14) states:

[Señor Fraga] referred to liberty of the press as a juridical concept par excellence which is contained within the structures of the society it guides. He pointed out, however, that absolute freedom of the press does not and cannot exist, adding that the State is not the foremost [entity] to tamper with it, since the control of the Press by high finance, foreign, ideological or political groups, whimsical [*sic*] individuals or powerful families is well known. That is why—he added —liberty of information was never greater in the past than it is now.

The "past" Señor Fraga referred to was presumably the Republican era, when, along with other "anti-Spanish" policies such as religious liberty, a free and open press came into being. In spite of his pious explanation, freedom of information was wider in the past, at least in the early days of the Republic, before that Regime fell victim to leftist compulsion. It was freedom of hate which was never greater. Having brought the dignity of human rights to the nation, having established man's freedom to worship according to his conscience (thirty-odd years before Pope John), and having fomented both universal suffrage and a free press, the Republic, too, gave way to Spanish irrationality. No serious apologist for this tragic experiment in democracy fails to censure the large-scale killings of priests and nuns and the burnings of churches by frenzied mobs (of nominal Catholics, let us remember) drunk with the hate of centuries. By the same token, no apologist for the Church-State can or should deny that every bit of this hate was given back in wartime and in peace, bullet for bullet, curse for curse. In the third decade of this century the "familiar rhythm" was ticking away more ominously than ever before.

"No wonder Fascism grew," says Madariaga of the turbulent days of 1936.[1] And no wonder the victorious Crusaders, having reconquered the modern Jerusalem, delivered it in safekeeping to

[1] Madariaga, *op. cit.*, p. 457.

an absolute power pledged to the tenets of absolute Truth. Nothing but the Truth was allowed in the nation henceforth.

As will be seen from the six points under Article 2, censorship was only one of the controls to which the Press was subjected. Equally important was the Regime's policing of journalists through (1) its intervention in the selection of editors, and (2) its prior approval of an individual's right to practice journalism.

The latter provision was—and still is—enforced through the *Registro de periodistas,* a list of all authorized newspapermen which is kept at the Ministry of Information and Tourism. Save for exceptions allowed by the Ministry itself, only individuals bearing an official, numbered *carnet de periodista* can register at the Ministry and exercise their profession in Spanish territory. And to obtain a *carnet,* and thus gain the right to register, the candidate must have normally been graduated from a Government-run school called the Escuela Oficial de Periodismo.[2]

At the Escuela, founded in Madrid in 1941, the future journalist is trained in the technical aspects of his profession and simultaneously given politico-historical orientation on such topics as "The World Today," "Contemporary Spain," and "The Contemporary Historical Picture." The curriculum of the three-year course has "basic" and "complementary" courses. In the second

[2] The new Statute of the Journalistic Profession approved by Decree 1408/64 of May 6, 1964, states in its Article 12: "To perform in any of the capacities mentioned in the article above [editor, associate and managing editor, department head, reporter] in newspapers, journals, general information magazines, news services of radio and television stations, or television newsreels, inscription in the *Registro oficial de periodismo* shall be inexcusably required. The same requirement shall hold for those wishing to perform the work of permanent or temporary correspondents abroad or, within Spain, in cities which do not have a general daily newspaper. The manager of the above communications media shall be obliged to fill all the above-mentioned posts with journalists inscribed in the *Registro oficial.*" An Annex to the statute entitled "General Principles of the Journalistic Profession" declares: "Article 1. In the exercise of his mission the newspaperman shall observe the norms of Christian morals and keep faithfully the Principles of the National Movement and the Fundamental Laws of the State." Cf. *Anuario de la prensa española* (Madrid: Dirección General de Prensa, 1965), pp. 1423, 1426.

year, students take a basic course entitled "Dogma and Morals"; that same year there is a complementary course on "Catholic Social Doctrine." [3]

The requirement that a journalist be a graduate of the Government's official school admits of two important exceptions. By virtue of a resolution approved by the Council of Ministers on July 22, 1960, and in line with Article 31 of the Concordat, graduates of the Church's own official school are admitted to the profession after taking an examination given by the Ministry. The same privilege was extended to the Journalism Institute of the Church University of Pamplona (Universidad de la Iglesia de Pamplona), a school run by Opus Dei, the new militant order of laymen. The document extending this university official recognition is Decree No. 2296 of September 3, 1962, drawn up "in accordance with Canon 1376 of the Code of Canon Law." [4]

The paradox inherent in the Church's domination of the Spanish communications media is that this domination fails to satisfy her. Having infiltrated all civil organisms, having established Catholic dogma and morals as the criteria for national censorship, having even set up her own news agency (the *Agencia Logos*), the Church is now envisioning the creation of "specifically religious" newspapers somewhat in the manner of the Catholic, Protestant and Jewish organs of lay states. In January, 1965, in preparation for the annual Church Press and Information Day, a group of priests met newspaper reporters in Madrid and outlined plans for the observance. *ABC* reported on statements made by Don Jesús González Prado, director of the Archdiocesan Press and Information Office. As Father González explained:

The old concepts of a "good press" and a "Catholic Press" have been surpassed and no longer hold in a country which is officially Catholic, where newspapermen are responsive to them and to the beliefs they

[3] The entire curriculum may be found in the *Anuario de la prensa española*, p. 1503.

[4] Canon 1376, Paragraph 1, reads: "The Holy See shall have the exclusive right to the canonical establishment of Catholic Universities or Colleges."

The texts of the documents mentioned above can be found in the *Anuario de la prensa española*, pp. 1507, 1509.

imply. These concepts are definitions for times past. What we are trying [to promote] through the celebration of this day and the collections [taken up] is a specifically religious press belonging to the Church itself. The Church needs to have its own private means of communication, independent of the others, however loyal [*afectos*] these may be to dogma and to the ecclesiastical hierarchy.

It is difficult not to agree with Father González. When the limits between the civil and religious press have disappeared the time is certainly ripe for the Church to create her "own" newspapers. Once the clergy and laity are served with these, that doctrinal saturation which is the *sine qua non* of Catholic unity will have reached its highest point.

The Church's sphere of influence extends to other media. A few days before the above-mentioned press conference—on January 14—*Ya*, the Church-run daily, had announced that a Church school of radio broadcasting would begin operations during the academic year 1965–66. But the school is only a complement to the Church's already established control of the air: by 1959 (also according to *Ya*) there were more than one hundred Church stations beaming Catholic dogma and doctrine throughout the country. Grouped into a Church network called the *Cadena de ondas populares españolas* (Network of Popular Spanish Airwaves), the transmitters span the nation from north to south, east to west. (Television, officially obedient to Catholic dogma and morals, is still too costly for "direct" apostolate; it may be some time before the Church has her own T.V. station.)

Books have come under a separate code enforced through two interlocking Government Orders. The first was passed on April 29, 1938:

BOOKS, PREVIOUS AUTHORIZATION FOR PUBLICATION
Article 1. Independently of the norms to which the journalistic press is submitted, the commercial production and circulation of books, pamphlets and all kinds of printed and graphic matter, both Spanish and foreign, is hereby subjected to the requisite of previous authorization from the Minister in charge of the Press and Propaganda Services. . . .
Article 2. The submission of originals [i.e., manuscripts], so that their

printing may be authorized in Spain, shall be indefectibly made before such printing is carried out, under the solidary responsibility of authors and publishers. The office in charge of censorship shall have the right to deny [authorization for] the publication of printed matter not only for doctrinal reasons, but also in the case of works which, not being strictly necessary, may contribute, in the present conditions of the paper industry, to hinder the publication of other material which may have priority [over them]. . . .

Article 4. The sale and circulation in national territory of books, pamphlets and other printed matter produced abroad, in any language whatsoever, is forbidden without authorization of this Ministry. Editors, booksellers and dealers who desire to put these works on sale or circulate them shall send two copies to the censorship office.[4a]

The heavy hand of the Church was to be felt in the second book regulation, a Circular dated March 25, 1944, and entitled "Censorship." Its preamble refers to the Order of April 29, 1938 and states:

The present policy regarding books has pointed to the convenience of establishing greater flexibility in the application of norms of censorship. . . .

The "greater flexibility" is nothing short of amazing. Articles 1 and 2 of the circular must be read in their entirety to savor the truly poetic nature of a vertical structure of ideas:

Article 1. Censorship of the following publications is hereby waived:
  (a) Those of a liturgical character, as well as the Latin texts used by the Catholic Church;
  (b) Those of Spanish literature prior to 1800;
  (c) Those which are exclusively musical and those which, having lyrics, antedate 1900;
  (d) Those of technical and scientific nature.
Article 2. The publications mentioned in the above article may be published by submitting to the National Delegation for Propaganda the [proper] application form, and the sample copies required, which shall be accompanied, respectively, by:

[4a] Estanislao de Aranzadi, ed., *Repertorio cronológico de legislación, 1938* (Pamplona: Editorial Aranzadi, n.d.), p. 431.

(a) Those in section (a), a covering letter from the Ordinary of the locality from which they originate;

(b) Those in section (b), by a report from the Royal Academy of the Language;

(c) Those in section (c), by a report from the Royal Academy of Fine Arts;

(d) Those in section (d), when published by the Royal Academies, the Council of Scientific Research, approved State and Church Universities, Special Schools or other official centers of higher learning or research, by a letter from the Director or Rector of the respective institution, with the data required for publication as well as a report on the book;

(e) Those in section (d), when published by [private] firms, by a report from the corresponding branch of the Council of Scientific Research or any of its Delegations or Deans, or from the University Faculties or the Directorate of Special Schools in the locality of the firm in question.[5]

The picture of Church-State censorship of books is thus complete: since all official institutions of learning were servants of the official religion, each and every one of them had a hand in the suppression of politico-religious "error" and the diffusion of politico-religious "truth." From 1938 until 1965, Spanish Catholics had little, if any, chance to see, hear or taste any "corrupted" European or American thought. And during this same period Spanish *evangélicos* went them one better: they braved the wrath of the Theological State by importing and circulating materials which, in and of themselves, were subversive and criminal.

II

It is impossible to say how much money Spanish Protestants have paid into the coffers of the Spanish State for the crime of circulating evangelical literature. The number of days they have spent in jail is likewise difficult to ascertain: the files at No. 32 Trafalgar Street, Madrid, date mostly from the creation of the

[5] *Repertorio cronológico de legislación, 1944*, p. 533.

Evangelical Defense Commission in 1958. Limited as they are, however, the documents at the Commission's office present a harrowing picture of the methods employed by the Sacral State's police in the defense of "truth" and persecution of "error." Anyone with a knowledge of Spanish can apply to Señor Cardona at Trafalgar Street (Tel. 2–57–36–66) and read through his neat, extensive dossiers. Our study will center on Barcelona, Spain's most highly developed region, where Protestantism is more vigorous than in any other part of the country.

In May, 1965, for the first time in the history of the current Church-State, a Protestant bookstore opened legally in national territory. The Librería Evangélica is located at No. 92 Alegre de Dalt Street in Barcelona. Like the rehabilitation of the Bible Society and the movement towards religious liberty, its opening was one more sign of Madrid's new, conciliatory policy towards the nation's religious aliens.

The Librería's manager is Mr. Harold J. Kregel, an American who, during his years of service as missionary to Spain's Baptists, has on repeated occasions felt the back of the Establishment's hand. I met him and Señor José Grau, a Protestant writer, at the small, spanking-new store full of evangelical books and pamphlets produced for the most part in Switzerland, Mexico, Argentina and Costa Rica.

As we talked, Mr. Kregel brought out two Government forms. I was familiar with one of them—the application sent to the "Bibliographic Orientation" section of the Ministry with all book manuscripts submitted for approval. The second was a blank for listing those foreign books which a bookseller must forward to the Ministry (one copy on lots of less than fifty, two copies on lots of more than fifty) in the hopes of obtaining an import license; the license will not be granted without a document from the Ministry authorizing the books, title by title. All Spanish dealers must send this form to the "Book Inspection" section of the Ministry.

Mr. Kregel showed me the Ministry's document dated May 5, 1965, authorizing all the books on an attached list except one: *La borrasca*, by F. Ordóñez. "It's a novel of Protestant life in Colombia," Mr. Kregel explained. "If I'd remembered this, I'd have taken it out."

His statement surprised me: it was the perfect expression of that peculiar caution the Spanish writer or journalist exercises over his work and which he calls *autocensura*. I didn't expect it from an American. But Mr. Kregel hadn't arrived in Spain the week before. He was as inured to the ways of censorship, and as sold on the virtue of prudence, as any Spaniard under similar circumstances. He had had his own schooling in the matter.

Mr. Kregel started collecting his merit badge of fines back in 1954. He was in Murcia, showing a motion picture in a private house, when police broke in and arrested him. The film—*God and Creation*—is a scientific-cultural exposition of the creation of the world and aims at proving the existence of God. It has been shown all over the world and even, as Mr. Kregel points out, in Catholic seminaries. But the world matters not in Murcia. The Police Inspector informed Mr. Kregel that he had been passing out "Communist propaganda" and gave him until nightfall to get out of town.

The worst blow dealt to Mr. Kregel and his Spanish friends came in 1960. Around that time the motion picture *The Ten Commandments* was being shown in Barcelona. A group of *evangélicos* took exception to this American film and passed a pamphlet of the same title in the movie houses where it was showing. The pamphlet is printed by the *Evangelische Europa-Mission* in Winterthur, Switzerland. It is a simple, almost innocuous plea for the Decalogue, with only one jarring note for the orthodox reader: a reminder of the interdiction against the worship of images. Under the heading "A Mutilated Decalogue," the text states:

It has been said that in many countries the Second and Ninth Commandments would seem to have been wiped from the Decalogue, so little heed is paid to the divine prohibition of venerating statues and lying. Haven't you heard many people make excuses for something they consider a little lie, calling it a "pious lie" without realizing that both terms (lying and piety) are mutually exclusive?

Returning immediately to the theme of statues the pamphlet cites the text (Exod. 20:4, 5) which, as it claims, lays down the law against them.

Anywhere else in the Western world, the leaflet would have aroused no speculation. Protestants have no need to reread the twentieth chapter of Exodus; and Catholics have long been applying its message through a liturgical reform that is decreasing the emphasis upon statues in their places of worship. In Spain, however, such ultra-Pyrenean considerations do not hold: the passing of the leaflet was lese majesty and an attempt upon the City of God.

On Holy Thursday night, 1960, the authorities raided the house where *The Ten Commandments* leaflets were stored. Among other publications, the police bagged 1,880 copies each of *Your Christian Life* and *What Is Truth?* both printed in Switzerland. The first is a 210-page book by José M. Martínez, a young Barcelona pastor; the second is a 73-page pamphlet of Señor Grau's. Altogether, seventy-two thousand pieces of literature were confiscated, taken to police headquarters and, as far as the Protestants have been able to determine, destroyed completely.

A second great raid took place in June, 1961. This time the accuser was a Catholic (anonymous, of course) into whose hands fell a copy of Señor Grau's pamphlet, *The Christian, This Unknown*. The man or woman denounced the publication to the police; the police descended on the shop of Salvador Salvadó, a Protestant printer who had undertaken the work, and there sealed the doors of the room where the material was stored. The cache included:

1,100 copies of *The Christian, This Unknown*
  800 copies of *What Is Truth?*
2,800 copies of birth announcement cards used by Baptist parents
  200 copies of advertisements for a correspondence course on the Bible
  200 copies of *Hymns for Children*
   50 cuts and engravings

In December, 1961, Señores Grau and Salvadó were processed and found guilty of distributing clandestine literature. Bond was fixed at 3,000 pesetas; subsequently both men drew one month and one day in jail. Since it was their first offense, and the penalty was less than two months' imprisonment, the sentence (as it is customary in such cases) was suspended and they were released on probation.

Señor Grau in no way modified his intention of continuing to write for and on behalf of Spanish Protestants. An earnest, bespectacled man of thirty-three, he converted to the Baptist faith as a youth and decided to make writing his career. Though his works have seen the light in Switzerland and circulated as far as the United States, in Spain his plight is typical of the "unperson" who is accorded no right of expression.

There is only one Protestant "newspaperman" in Spain and he is none other than Señor José Cardona. In 1965, by virtue of his position as Executive Secretary of the Evangelical Defense Commission, and in view of the public relations and foreign newspaper work this implies, the Ministry of Information and Tourism awarded him a *carnet de periodista*. It was an accolade which surprised few people, since over the years Cardona has won the respect and, what is even more significant, the signal collaboration of certain Government officials. But in terms of Protestant journalists in general, the gesture meant nothing. When Señor Grau, a bona fide writer, sought entrance to the Escuela Oficial de Periodismo, he was told by the Barcelona authorities who passed on such requests that, being an *evangélico,* he needn't even bother to apply. And the authorities' reaction was colored, one must admit, by a fierce Spanish logic: a press completely soaked in the combustible stuff of Catholic doctrine can ill afford a Protestant spark.

In 1960 Grau attempted to gain authorization from the Ministry of Information and Tourism for the publication of *What Is Truth?* He filled out the proper forms and made the necessary application. On July 15 of that year the Ministry answered:

Having received your application dated 21/4/60 with reference to the file cited in the margin,
This General Directorate of Information, at the behest of the corresponding Service, has decided:
To resolve such application according to the indications on the attached sheet.
God keep you many years.
Madrid, July 15, 1940
[*signed*] The Director General of Information
by C. Piernavieja

The "attached sheet" is a stretch of white paper bearing no letterhead, no signature, no date, no names, no reference or citations: only an order. Two-thirds of the way down, the first of the three typed lines appears:

For authorization, the ECCLESIASTICAL LICENSE of the Archbishopric of Barcelona must be presented.

Thus, anonymous and supreme, the Spanish Church issued the order by which the Ministry was ruled. The two documents, side by side, reveal more clearly than any history text the firm hand of the hierarchy inside the Government's glove.

Nevertheless Señor Grau was to see *What Is Truth?* and a few other evangelical publications actually authorized by the Government. Permission for their appearance was obtained through the Commission and Señor Cardona in 1964, when the winds of change had begun to blow from Rome. *The Ten Commandments* and a handful of leaflets are still forbidden, but *What Is Truth?* now bears Official Registry No. 3047–64, *The Christian, This Unknown,* has No. 3049–64, *Your Christian Life* circulates under No. 1640–64, while *Belief . . . and Then?,* a brief tract translated from the French of E. Aebi by Pastor Martínez, carries on the back page this bizarre mixture of advertising and advertence:

Two books which will be powerful helps in
your spiritual life:
"Your Christian Life"
by José M. Martínez
and
"The Bible Says"
by the same author

EVANGELICAL CHRISTIAN LITERATURE
authorized by the Ministry of Information and Tourism
Legal Deposit: B. 13709–64
Registry No.: 1641–64

Salvadó Press — Villarana, 60 — Barcelona 6

What was proselytism in 1960 had been suddenly sanctioned by the guardians of spiritual unity. Why? Perhaps in partial commitment to the Second Vatican Council, where the issue of religious liberty was still unresolved; perhaps as a small tribute to the lingering shadow of Pope John. Whatever the reason, it was an evangelical victory of sorts.

But Protestants knew better than to rejoice: one swallow does not make a summer. The issue of proselytism—invoked against evangelical "bribes" as well as "external manifestations," from the singing of hymns to the holding of conversations, the placing of identifying signs on churches or the passing of literature—was still far from resolved. In 1966, as the Statute on Religious Liberty lay dormant in the hands of the hierarchy, this single word remained the greatest obstacle to the full integration of *evangélicos* into the civil, social and intellectual life of the country.

III

What is "proselytism"? In its earliest and classic sense, the word was used to describe a Gentile convert to Judaism. Liddel & Scott's Greek-English Lexicon defines it thus:

προσήλυτος, ον (προσήλυθον) come to, arrived at; —as Subst., προσήλυτος, ὁ, a new comer, stranger, Lat. *advena:* hence, one who has come over to Judaism, a convert, proselyte.

The Oxford Dictionary alludes to this connotation after spelling out the modern one:

PROSELYTE, n. & v.t. 1. Convert from one opinion, creed or party to another, *as made many* ——ES; Gentile convert to Jewish faith, ——E *of the gate* (not submitting to circumcision, etc.). 2. v.t. (now rare). Make a ——E of (person, or abs.). Hence ——ISM (1, 2), ——IZER, n., ——IZE (2), v.t. (often abs.). [ME, f. LL., f. Gk. PROS(*ēlutos* f. st. *eluth*—come) one who has come, convert.]

Upon consulting the Royal Spanish Academy Dictionary, one is struck by its backward leap to the original usage. In another remarkable bit of Semitic transference, the Hebrew sense is encased in a Catholic meaning:

PROSELYTE, m.[masc.] A Gentile, Mohammedan or sectarian converted to the Catholic religion. fig.[uratively], a partisan gained for a faction, an opinion or a doctrine.

The Academy's definition is a ten-word testimony to Américo Castro's thesis that Spanish Christians absorbed the spiritual attitudes of Judaism lock, stock and barrel, positing themselves as God's Chosen People until the consummation of time. Not incidentally, it also offers the best and most accurate yardstick for interpreting the term "proselytism" in its modern Spanish context.

First of all, the lawyer or layman must bear in mind that, in the eyes of the Spanish Church-State, the right to indulge in the spiritual and intellectual polemics implied by "proselytism" belongs exclusively to the Chosen People, i.e., to "truth." Since "truth" is Catholicism, we come directly to the basic point on which the interpretation of the word hangs: *Only the Catholic Church has the right to make proselytes.*

The saturation of the Spanish communications media with the tenets and dogmas of Catholicism makes this obvious. As anyone who has lived in Spain can vouch, the national press and radio are organs which, within and without their informative mission, exist to praise, exalt and glorify the Church.[6] But proselytism implies more than a positive approach: it implies skillful refutation and attack as well. Now Spanish Protestants are on the one hand denied the right to any "external manifestations" of their faith while, on the other, they are summarily imprisoned for any attack on the Catholic Church. But, by the same token, the Church can assail Protestantism with impunity, safe in the knowledge that it is serving "truth." The widespread campaigns defaming Protestants as sexual degenerates (see Appendix, pp. 350-54) answer to this criteria.

[6] Article 29 of the Concordat reads: "The State shall see to it that institutions and services of public opinion, in particular radio and television programs, give due place to the exposition and defense of religious truth through priests and religious designated in accordance with the respective Ordinary."

Having decreed soon after the Crusade that non-Catholic proselytism was illegal, Spanish Catholicism proceeded to work for its destruction. Here is a call to physical combat issued, not in the sixteenth century, but in a pious magazine in 1948:

Is it allowed to enter chapels or other meeting places of the Protestants or any other propagators of false doctrines, with the intention of spreading disorder and breaking objects?

It is to be understood that the goal in disturbing the religious service and breaking the objects used in worship is merely to render the work of these churches ineffective, and thus force the preachers to go elsewhere. We can answer this question by saying that it is entirely permissible to enter such places for the sole purpose of stopping the service and thus preventing the Protestants from making converts.

These persons do a great deal of harm with their propagandizing. Some human laws may tolerate it, in the interest of preserving the peace; divine law, in any case, is opposed to it, for it threatens the fundamental rights of men. Primary among these is the right to be enlightened by the truth in matters of religion. It is our duty to protect men from the dangers that menace their bodies and souls, by doing everything possible to prevent the infiltration of injustice and evil.

Those who have no other means of counteracting the harm done by these false preachers may therefore create disorder in the churches, without harming people. Indeed, if this method were sure to produce the desired results, and if the difficulties and inconveniences connected with it were not so numerous, it would not only be a duty, but a veritable moral obligation.

As concerns the destruction of furniture or other objects, we must make the distinction between those objects with an heretical value— such as Protestant Bibles, prayer books, books of religious propaganda, pictures that are hostile to the true religion, tables, chairs, robes and all other objects used in their sacrilegious services—and those objects of common usage such as personal effects. The former should be destroyed, and the reason for doing so is evident. Is it not an elementary charitable duty to protect the innocent from the brigand? It is also a duty, then, to destroy the instruments which the brigand uses to do evil. As for the second category of objects, it would not be right to destroy them, for they are private possessions, not used for the services. False doctors have the right to live even if they do harm. Therefore the items placed second, which are personal items, should be preserved.[6a]

Lest this example seem dated, below is a notice posted by a parish priest in his church in Asturias during the month of January, 1963:

TO THE FAITHFUL OF FIOS AND NEVARES,
ON PROTESTANTISM

Dearly beloved: The Holy Bible is the sacred book of Christians, inspired by God, dictated by Him to the holy men who wrote it.

The Church is a society of Christians united among themselves by the same profession of faith, by the same participation in the sacraments, under the direction of His Holiness the Pope. The Church, says the Holy Bible, was founded by God Our Lord Jesus Christ in the year 30, when he said to Saint Peter: "You are Peter and upon this rock I shall build my church, and the gates of hell shall not prevail against her." "Tend my sheep." The Popes are the successors of St. Peter, who was the first [of them].

The principal differences between Catholics and Protestants are:

1. Catholics believe in the entire Bible. Protestants do not believe in the entire Bible.

2. Catholics love God Our Lord Jesus Christ very much. Protestants interpret this love as each of them pleases.

3. Catholics love and believe in the only, Holy, Catholic and Apostolic Church. Protestants neither believe in nor love the holy Catholic Church.

4. Catholics have seven sacraments. Protestants have nothing of the kind.

5. Catholics love and venerate the Most Holy Virgin Mary, who is the mother of Jesus Christ. Protestants do not love or venerate the Most Holy Virgin.

6. Catholics love and venerate holy persons who are in Heaven. Protestants do not love or venerate holy persons.

7. Catholics remember their dead. The Bible says: "It is holy and wholesome to pray for the dead." Protestants do not remember their dead.

[6a] *El Iris de Paz,* January 1, 1948, quoted in Delpech, *op. cit.,* pp. 65–66. I have checked this, and all of Delpech's press texts, at Madrid's Periodical Library (Hemerotoca Nacional).

A SNAKE IN EDEN

8. Catholics love God through the Holy Mass, prayer and good works. The Holy Bible says that God Our Lord in the last supper celebrated his first Mass, taking in his hands a piece of bread which he consecrated saying: "This is my body." After this he took a chalice and consecrated it saying, "This is the chalice of my blood." Then he said to his disciples: "Do this in memory of me." Protestants have nothing of this kind.

9. Catholics have good priests who offer their celibate lives freely to God. Protestants do not offer God anything.

10. Catholics feel sorrow for their sins and confess. Protestants feel no sorrow for their sins, and do not confess.

11. Catholics are always united. Protestants are more disunited every day.

12. Catholicism was founded by Jesus Christ in the year 30. Protestantism was founded by Luther and Calvin, proud, disobedient, lewd [deshonestos] men, in the year 1517.

13. Catholics have their cemeteries. Protestants cannot be buried in Catholic cemeteries.

14. Catholics cannot marry Protestants. Protestants marry many times, whomever they please, and [obtain] divorces.

15. Catholics are inside the true Church. Protestants are outside her.

16. Catholics have all things. Protestants have only a part.

There are other differences, but they are not important.

The Bible says in another passage: "Beware of false prophets who come to you dressed as sheep, but who are ferocious wolves inside."

With a greeting in the Lord,
Your Parish Priest
Fios and Nevares, Feast of St. Anthony Abbot (January 17, 1963)

The reverse of such religious instruction is the policing of all Protestant ideas, facts or feelings which transcend the privacy of authorized places of worship. It is in this sense that "proselytism" is commonly used in the legal language of Spain and invoked against Protestants who by word or deed infringe the "spiritual unity" of the country. The Barcelona raids we have described come under this heading. So do a multitude of other sanctions. In July, 1954, Liborio Cruz Martínez of Madrid was fined 500 pesetas for "holding meetings for Baptist worship in his house and indulging in external manifestations by singing on the terrace of the building." In this case the hymns were the channel, so to speak, of Protestant error. Martínez paid. A recent pamphlet-passing incident occurred in the Canary Islands in October, 1965, when José Cabrera Gil, a worker newly returned from Germany, attended the funeral of a Catholic friend and gave out a small pamphlet describing the beliefs of the Evangelical Christian Church. Cabrera was denounced, processed, and given his choice of a 2000-peseta fine or five days in jail. He went to jail.

An interesting case took place in Elda, Alicante, in 1956. This time it was a Protestant's factual remark to a friend during the course of a conversation which brought about the punishment. On November 30 of that year, Isabel Pérez Guijarro was fined 1,000 pesetas for "proferring disrespectful phrases towards Authority in public, with the [attendant] impairment of the corresponding principle." This was her misdemeanor: When asked by a friendly clerk in a bakery store why a Protestant funeral a few days before had been attended by only two people, she answered that the authorities had forbidden the participation of more than two mourners. (Funeral processions, as we shall see in the next chapter, are considered "external manifestations" of Protestantism.) This information, conveyed as simple news, was the extent of the lady's remarks. No one knows who denounced her, but the fine came swiftly. A full declaration and appeal to Madrid proved useless.

Should Protestants be rash enough to circulate tracts, pamphlets or books which contain direct or indirect contradictions of Catholic doctrine, prosecution is inescapable. The passage from Exodus quoted in *The Ten Commandments* is a case in point: until Vatican II, any mention of the worship of images was an insult to the Catholic Church. Where Mary is concerned, the problem assumes gigantic proportions: any reference to the fact that in the Reformed doctrine Mary is not sinless, not thaumaturgical and not resurrected, is an outrage (*un ultraje*) visited upon the Virgin. And any allusion to the Church's wealth and its estrangement from the masses is likewise subversive and punishable by law.

Now the fact that liturgical, Marian and pastoral questions were openly discussed at the Vatican, with the vigorous collaboration of the Northern European and American churches, is something else entirely in the eyes of the Spanish hierarchy. Though privately criticized as tainted with "materialism," the Northern prelates are still regarded as Bishops of the True Church. Furthermore, by speaking through and on behalf of Catholicism, the Council could not err in its judgment; hence all intramural calls for reform were to be heeded, willingly or not. Which brings us to the second point in the interpretation of the word "proselytism" vis-à-vis the Protestant community: *Only the Catholic Church has the right to criticize itself.*

Proselytism thus remains the crux of the Spanish Protestant problem. More than forty years ago, during the reign of Alfonso XIII and the dictatorship of Miguel Primo de Rivera, a prominent Catholic layman had defined it in all its magnitude. He was Dr. José Torrubiano Ripoll, distinguished jurist and Professor of Canon Law at the University of Madrid, a steadfast friend of native Protestants and chastiser of the ecclesiastical tyranny (in 1925 he was excommunicated for exposing the wealth of the hierarchy in Madrid as contrasted with the starvation wages and living conditions of country priests). In a letter to the Reverend Fernando Cabrera of the Reformed (Episcopalian) Church dated September, 1924, Dr. Torrubiano pleaded with the *evangélicos:*

You [Protestants] cannot afford to live in isolation as if sequestered; you should cultivate personal relationships with outstanding men in politics in all the liberal parties, become familiar to the cultured public in the academies and colleges, come out into the collective life in open and frank intercourse with all social circles. *Spain does not know you,* and steps must be taken so that the traditional prejudice that you Protestants are plague-stricken may disappear.[7]

The prejudice did not disappear, but the Republic, with its promise of human dignity, did in fact give Protestants a chance to participate in Spanish society to the measure envisioned by the late Dr. Torrubiano. Unfortunately, the Republic also bore the seeds of its own destruction; Dr. Torrubiano lived to see its end

[7] Quoted in Araujo García and Grubb, *op. cit.,* p. 84.

and the collapse of the solid achievements attained by Protestants during its brief lifetime. He also lived to see the Crusade, the rise of the New Jerusalem and the triumph of the racial faith.

Today the future of "Protestant" ideas—and the term includes all doctrines contrary to the racial faith, whatever their origin— depends on two phenomena. One is the slow but tangible liberalization of the country's "fundamental structures," with special reference to the press. The other is the nature of the proposed statute emancipating the country's *evangélicos.*

As the Council drew to an end, the *Cortes* had before it the bill of a modified Press Law which maintained the requirement of "depositing" sample copies of all printed matter at the Ministry of Information but, among other things, did away with the mechanics of direct censorship. Months before the bill reached Parliament there was a noticeable relaxation of censorship in the domestic press (foreign newspapers continued to be closely scrutinized). With the coming of Pope John XXIII and the onset of the Council, the Church had begun to be criticized—covertly and discreetly at first, openly by mid-1965. The publication of a reactionary editorial on religious freedom endorsing the Spanish Bishop's reactionary stand in Rome (Appendix, pp. 357–60) stirred up the embers of "anti-Spain" and brought on a deluge of almost vituperative letters upon the weekly news magazine *SP.* Rodrigo Royo, *SP*'s editor and author of the controversial piece, had the moral courage—and the enterprise—to publish some of his readers' most strongly worded attacks. Five years before none of these letters would have seen light. In September, 1965, they somehow got through the priest-censors at the big white building on Avenida del Generalísimo.

Meantime, the statute emancipating the Protestant minority went into its third year as a State secret. Drafted by Foreign Minister Castiella in 1963, the document had been shelved pending resolution of the doctrinal question at the Vatican. Though no one outside of its drafters had any knowledge of the text, there were rumors in Protestant circles that Article 18 dealt with proselytism.

How the Article broaches that problem remains to be seen. The Council Fathers returned from Rome in a spirit of *acatamiento* shot through with misgivings. Though paying homage to the Council and its directives, they made clear that religious liberty is subject to limitations imposed by society, and that the civil authority, as the guardian thereof, must act against any abuses of the newly proclaimed "liberty." On January 5, 1966, the Cardinal Archbishop of Tarragona granted an interview to the newspaper *Diario Español* in which he was asked about the issue of religious liberty. He referred to a meeting between "some Protestant pastors and Spanish bishops," presumably at the Vatican:

Before the Council had reached a definite accord on the issue, and without going into the theological depths of the matter, I replied to one question which was put to me by saying merely that, insofar as possible, we could not permit liberty of propaganda, as this would mean forsaking our faithful, many of whom are not prepared to answer some of the arguments presented by people who make a career out of propagandizing. My interlocutor answered, "Then, no proselytism . . ." And I said, Exactly. But he added, "Then the [matter of] witness . . ." Naturally, I replied, I cannot upbraid you if, by means of an exemplary conduct, you show the sincerity of your beliefs.[8]

Cardinal Arriba y Castro may well have defined the future of "proselytism" by defining its past. A mute Protestant witness, made solely through "exemplary conduct," is acceptable to the True Church; but any expression of the ideas which inform Protestantism, be it written or oral, will quite likely continue to be an offense against the Church-State, punishable by law.

There was no doubt that the nightmare of Protestant advance, unchecked by the traditional measures against proselytism, loomed heavily over the Council Fathers as they returned to their homeland. "Those who belong to the Roman Catholic Church," they proclaimed in their joint message, "have never any reason to abandon it."

No one knows how many would have "abandoned" it if Protestant ideas had circulated freely throughout the country; the

---

[8] Quoted in *Ya,* January 6, 1966.

evangélicos' sixfold growth in twenty-five years of open persecution speaks for itself. Yet the issue of numbers is itself irrelevant: in the "materialistic" world outside Spain, where human betterment is the only goal of a free society, the aim of the Catholic-Protestant dialogue is neither conversion nor betrayal but mutual enrichment. Unfortunately in Spain—where all Western ideas are suspect—this one is most suspect of all. The concept of "dialogue" sits particularly ill on the typical Spanish Catholic who, temperamentally unable to accept anything but a militant, crusading mission for his everlasting "truth," is still wielding the sword against "error."

"Error" is a New Testament printed in Winterthur. "Error" is a pamphlet entitled *Imitation of Mary* which describes the first woman of Christendom as blessed but human, and which any self-respecting subject of the Church-State will turn over to the police. "Error" is a congregation of Brethren at worship in stark simplicity and heartfelt piety, which the Catholic can join only on pain of mortal sin. And "error" is the Christian witness of Manuel Gutiérrez Marín, whom the average Spaniard has never heard about.

Few things are as heartening to the wanderer in the world of medieval Catholicism as the discovery of this man. Born of Protestant parents in the Province of Seville in 1906, Dr. Gutiérrez Marín entered the University of Madrid in 1923, then traveled to Germany for theological and philosophical studies at the Universities of Greifswald, Berlin and Halle. In 1951, already a Protestant scholar of international reputation, he was named President of the Iglesia Evangélica Española, in which capacity he served until 1954. He has lectured on Dialectical Theology in Germany, Switzerland, Holland, India, the United States and Latin America —especially Mexico and Puerto Rico. Between theological works, translations, volumes of poetry and art criticism, he has produced over twenty books. He is a contributor to two of the best-known reference works on German Protestantism, *Die Religion in der Geschichte und der Gegenwart* and the *Evangelische Kirchenlexikon.* His articles appear in Buenos Aires' *Cuadernos teo-*

lógicos and Germany's *Kirche in der Welt.* He lives in Barcelona. Mention his name to the well-read Spanish Catholic and the reaction is one of utter, bewildered blankness. Since Gutiérrez Marín's work comes full-square under the heading of "proselytism," all of it—except his poetry and essays on art, which have seen the light in Cataluña—has been banned in his homeland. Only in 1964, by the embers of Pope John's charity, was one of his theological works authorized. It is *Faith and Action: Existentialist Christian Ethics,* which bears Registry No. 7175/64, and which I obtained at Barcelona's Librería Evangélica. A check of Madrid bookstores proved useless.

Gutiérrez Marín's *God Has Spoken: Studies on Kierkegaard, Brunner and Barth,* appeared in Buenos Aires in 1960. *God and Us, An Introduction to Dialectical Theology,* came out in Lisbon in 1964. A partial list of his translations, all published in Buenos Aires, reads like a veritable catalogue of "erroneous" Western spirituality:

The Character of Protestantism, Karl Heim, 1939
Justification by Faith, Philip Melanchthon, 1943
Christian Liberty, Martin Luther, 1943
The Schmalkald Articles, Luther, 1944
Major Catechism, Luther, 1944
The Our Father, Luther, 1946
An Outline of Dogmatics, Karl Barth, 1959
Our Faith, Emil Brunner, 1959
The Heidelberg Catechism, Classical Works of the Reformation,
Vol. XIX, 1963

To say that Gutiérrez Marín is a ghost in his native land is to place him in the distinguished company he belongs. Karl Barth is known only to a handful of experts with access to forbidden translations.[9] The name of Paul Tillich, spoken before cultured

[9] German-language editions of Barth may be found at Buchholz, Madrid's excellent German bookstore. A check of the Spanish equivalent of *Books in Print* for 1964 reveals only Gutiérrez Marín's translation of the *Outline,* published by a Protestant house in Argentina and of course unavailable in Spain.

people, evokes the classic blankness. No one has heard of Dietrich Bonhöffer and his Christlike testimony before the Nazi tyranny. Niemöller rings no bells, ecumenical or mnemonic. . . .

In August, 1965, the Civil Governor sent word to Barcelona's Librería Evangélica that all books should be removed from its windows, since they constituted an offense against Catholic passers-by. Today the bookstore's external displays feature only stationery and school supplies; but the Catholic inclined to perversion has only to peer past the glass which encloses these objects to perceive, inside the premises, a roomful of sin and error.

10

The last of the Spanish Protestant's indignities awaits him in death. His body cannot be brought to church for a funeral service; no cortege can accompany it to the cemetery; no hymns may be sung or prayers said en route to interment and only a brief, hushed message can be read at the graveside. Any infraction of these rules—as the collection of fines on file at the Defense Commission will attest—brings swift and inexorable punishment.

Heartless, self-righteous and militant, the funeral policy of the True Church simply gives back a hundredfold the injury visited upon her by Article 27 of the Republic's Constitution. Seeking to wipe out even the most nominal vestiges of the Church's influence, the Republic had decreed that *all* cemeteries "be submitted exclusively to civil jurisdiction." Madariaga describes both the cause and the unhappy results of this wanton discrimination:

This spirit of petty, almost vindictive anticlericalism reached its climax in a matter as theoretical and unimportant as that of burials. The Church had always kept a close watch on burials. Efforts—not always dignified—were often made to bury with religious rites persons of note who had left clear instructions to the contrary. In every town, the *Cementerio Civil* was set aside for the obdurate who refused to pass the Gates in the prescribed style. Then came the Republic, and some of us thought that this tug of war would at least respect the bones of the dead. But the bigots and priests of the Holy

Anti-clerical Church were watching, and when so many things, and so urgent, were still undone, the new rulers of Spain found time to decree that all cemeteries should be secularized, while religious burial was prohibited unless provided for in the will of the deceased—which, in a country in which nine out of ten persons die without troubling to put on paper their last decisions, was little short of oppressive.[1]

The victims of the Church's counterpolicy on burials have quite naturally been the Protestants, for suicides and public sinners are buried outside the Church as a matter of course, riteless and officially unmourned. Where a Protestant is concerned, however, "error" again wins out. There is the matter of a forbidden public rite, there is the matter of heretical mourners worshiping outside their private enclosure and, what is worse, there is the danger that an "external manifestation" will be perpetrated before the eyes of the faithful. Hence, in the interest of spiritual unity, all non-Catholic funeral rites are summarily forbidden except those taking place in strict privacy at the home of the deceased, and quiet graveside prayers (excluding hymns).

When put into practice, this ruling has given rise to situations which range from the ludicrous to the guignolesque. In some remote communities Protestant bodies may only be buried at dawn or dusk. As late as November, 1965, measures were still being taken to avoid the danger of "external manifestations." In that month of that year, in the Province of Valencia, permission was obtained to bring a Protestant's body to church; but the authorization was given only on condition that the procession wind its way to the private, unmarked chapel through a circuitous route, traversing only remote side streets.

Jacques Delpech devotes four pages of his small book to the problems of burying a Protestant body.

Once, in the province of Alicante, the hearse was accompanied only by a sergeant, two corporals, and seven civil guards, under orders to keep a procession from forming; it was in the presence of these men that the Protestant pastor gave the Scriptural message at the cemetery.

At times a pastor may even be forbidden to conduct a service at

[1] Madariaga, *op. cit.*, pp. 406–07.

the cemetery, on the grounds that it might be overheard by passers-by. This was the case at Valdepeñas on March 10, 1953. When the funeral procession arrived at the civil cemetery, an agent of the local authorities forbade any religious service whatsoever. The next day the mayor confirmed this prohibition, stating that, because the civil cemetery was not the property of the Evangelical Church, a religious service there was an "outward demonstration"; moreover, at the time of an earlier burial, the Protestant service with its hymns had given rise to complaints from persons who happened to be in the adjacent Catholic cemetery.[2]

Few cases expose the heartlessness of the Church as starkly as the one whose Defense Commission file begins:

On the 29th of January of the current year [1952] appellant had the misfortune of losing an eight-year-old daughter . . .

The document is signed by Vicente Argentés Francés, of the town of Alcántara del Júcar in the Province of Valencia. The fine he was appealing came to 10,000 pesetas. (Per capita income in 1952 was 8,048 pesetas a year, a figure which was close to the actual earnings of villagers and unskilled workers.)

Upon his daughter's death, Señor Argentés solicited permission from the civil authorities to conduct the burial and received it forthwith. Then, in the company of Alcántara del Júcar's judge, Don Vicente Alventosa, he repaired to the priest's house to solicit ecclesiastical approval. As in matters of education, marriage or dissident worship, in funeral cases the priest's word is the law.

The priest refused to receive Señor Argentés but sent word that he could bury his daughter's body. However, shortly before the funeral was to take place, Señor Argentés was called to the Town Hall. There,

in the presence of the Mayor, the priest, the Corporal and two members of the Civil Guard, at the very moment at which the funeral was scheduled to begin, [appellant] was informed that the permit and authorization previously granted had been revoked, and that he would only be permitted to have one person accompany the body to the cemetery.

[2] Delpech, *op. cit.*, pp. 76–77,

From Bernanos to Torrubiano Ripoll, the apologists for the country clergy have spoken up for holy, self-sacrificing men whose lives are spent in poverty and privation. In the course of a trip through the north of Spain in the company of Mr. James Michener, I had occasion to meet a village priest full of fraternal, ecumenical spirit (p. 341). But all exceptions mentioned—and honored—the fact remains that few people can harbor as much rancor in their hearts as some of the parish priests of rural communities in Spain. Ignorance and superstition, those two great bellows of religious hate, work full time in the greater part of Spanish *pueblos*. Thus, at Alcántara del Júcar the heretical father, in his bereavement, was forbidden by the priest—instigator of the countermand—from having more than *one person* see his child's body to its final resting place.

Señor Argentés and his brother Miguel pleaded with both the civil and divine authorities. They explained that all they wanted was "to accompany the body to the cemetery and thus render a last homage of love to the dead child." After the assembled officials were convinced that no ceremonies would take place, they agreed that the body could be accompanied by any number of mourners. The Civil Guard was "invited" to go along and guarantee that the "no-ceremonies" promise would be kept.

Like some pagan deity of old, the Spanish God can never slake His thirst for vengeance. The child's funeral procession, accompanied by the corporal and two men of the Civil Guard, wound its way to the cemetery without a prayer or a hymn. The number of mourners, though silent, was considerable: on hearing of the case, practically the entire town followed the small bier to its grave. All would have seemed to be in order . . . except the size of the crowd.

The townspeople's sympathy triggered the holy vendetta. On April 2, 1952, Señores Vicente and Miguel Argentés were served with fines of 5,000 pesetas each. The citation in the Civil Governor's document, Proceedings No. 392, reads as follows:

For having caused the celebration of an act in Alcántara del Júcar *which could have* degenerated into a disturbance of the peace, and which had been previously forbidden by this Civil Governor. [*Italics mine.*]

An appeal was denied. Señores Argentés paid 10,000 pesetas for the crime of burying a child who, to the scandal of the True Church, had found her Protestant peace.

Where the deceased is deemed an apostate, the situation goes from the funereal to the farcical. In the days before the Republic, as Madariaga points out, the Church was already making "efforts—not always dignified—" to give Catholic burial to people who had specifically requested the contrary. After the Crusade the efforts increased—and often turned into runaway successes. In the spring of 1965 I made a trip to Puertollano to visit a community of Protestant miners and their minister. I had heard of their school case and wished to interview both the pastor and the parish priest involved. But as it turned out the closing of the school was not half as interesting as the activities on another antiecumenical front: body snatching.

I arrived in Ciudad Real on Friday, March 19, the Feast of St. Joseph and a national holiday. I had meant to have lunch there and then continue to Puertollano, but at the hotel I found that the train I'd just left (which went on to Badajoz) was the last one to the mining town that day, and that there were no buses running. Unless I could hire a car—also difficult on a holiday— I would have to wait until morning to resume the trip.

After lunch I took a walk around town and visited the cathedral, an unprepossessing church with a good sixteenth-century reredos; the house of warrior-writer Hernán Pérez del Pulgar (1451–1531), a finely kept mansion of its period; the Church of St. Peter's, which has a Romanesque façade but, as far as I could see in the dimmest of lights, very little of interest inside; and the porticoed Plaza Mayor, whose stone columns have been painted silver, giving it the curious look of an old square staked out in aluminum.

At four o'clock I returned to the hotel. I noticed that the movie house across the street had opened and, hoping to kill a couple of hours, I bought a ticket to *El señor de la Salle,* a Spanish production starring Mel Ferrer.

It was a *sesión familiar,* or matinee, and the theater was swarming with children. After the newsreel, trailers, commercials and intermission, the film finally got underway.

By the end of the first reel it was clear that Señor Luis César Amadori, the director, was not aiming for an Academy Award: a fifth-grader's book of saints might have offered a more nuanced biography of Jean Baptiste de la Salle, founder of the Christian Brothers. Ferrer's talent was pitifully squandered. The script was one long rosary of saccharine thoughts while the sets and costumes—no one who has seen the film is likely to forget Señor de la Salle's sister's wig—seemed lifted from a third-class stock company.

But the children evidently loved it. Though one baby cried halfway through the film and had to be taken out for a spell, the rest of the youngsters were glued to their seats. I was debating whether I should go back to the hotel and continue reading *Religion in the Republic of Spain,* which I had brought with me, when suddenly Señor de la Salle's fortunes changed and the film took on a new but familiar dimension:

Sent into exile by his enemies in Paris, Jean Baptiste, incognito, heads for the South of France. A kind man offers him a ride in his horse-drawn cart. They are passing through a forest when they come upon six or eight bodies strung up on the trees. The kind man explains that the grisly scene is the work of a gang who roam the countryside, robbing and murdering as they go.

Jean Baptiste looks at him in horror. "But who are these men?" he asks. "Bandits?"

"They're Protestants," answers the man in a tone reeking contempt. "You see, these people were given freedom of religion some time ago."

"Yes, I know," Jean Baptiste cuts in. "The Edict of Nantes."

"Exactly. And since then they've declared war on the Catholic Church and the State. They're called camisardos. *They wear red shirts."*

The camera turns sharply on Jean Baptiste's face. He looks pained. Will he say something? Yes. "I have pledged myself to fight evil wherever I find it."

History is everywhere in Spain. The least I had expected to find in Ciudad Real was an echo of the religious wars of France— slanted and reworked for a Spanish audience. The *camisards,* bands of guerrillas who roamed the Cévennes in the early eighteenth century, did not emerge upon the proclamation of the Edict of Nantes, but rather in protest against its revocation. They were an offshoot of the Albigenses and, as such, heretics; but neither their lawlessness nor their religious practices (which came near to witchcraft) reflected the worship or doctrines of French Protestants.

Yet here, in literary Spain, that venerable figure of speech called synecdoche—the taking of a part for the whole—was being used in the 1960's to identify Protestants as thugs. History was also refashioned to present religious liberty as the source of crime —an idea which was expressed before me by a priest the very next day. To complete the cinematic portrait of the Enemy, the *camisardos,* whose name derived simply from the shirts they wore, were clad in *red* garments.

No sooner is the explanation out than a band of camisardos, *duly red-shirted, swoops down on the cart. The kind man unbuttons his tunic and points to a crimson shirt he is wearing underneath. The* camisardos *ride away. The man, now aware of his passenger's identity, speeds him to the next town as he explains that he is forced to wear the red shirt for protection.*

Before the end of the film the camisardos *come into the story once more. A mournful young woman, the wife of one of Jean Baptiste's old friends from the slums, comes up to him with a boy, her son, whom she is offering up to his teaching order.*

Jean Baptiste asks about her husband. Her eyes brim with tears.

"The camisardos?*" he asks.*

She nods.[3]

. . .

[3] Six months later, while doing research at the *ABC* Library, I came across a story, dated November 13, 1964, on the showing of *El señor de la Salle* in Rome. The film, with an English sound track, was presented before

Next morning I sat down with Don Salvador González, the pastor of the Protestant miners at Puertollano, in a small office adjoining his church. Don Salvador is short, stocky, with hair that is barely graying, bright slanted eyes and the air of a man who will march up to the cannon's mouth.

He was born in 1892 in Sabiote, a town in the Province of Jaén. Both his parents were Protestants; in fact they were the first couple to contract a civil marriage in the history of the town. Since there was no infant baptism in the church his parents belonged to, the child Salvador was known in town as *el morito*—or the little Moor—this being the vulgar term for a child who has not been christened. At the age of eight he was forcibly baptized in the Catholic Church.

(Forced baptism is not a thing of the past; today it remains one of the saddest, though not the most common, of the Church's offensives against "error." Delpech makes a brief mention of it in his book [p. 70]: "All hospitals in Spain are under Catholic control. A Protestant mother giving birth in a hospital must generally fight to prevent the baptism of her child as a Catholic. Women who remain firm are sometimes sent home early." He probably goes no further because he could find no documentary proof; neither could I. But his statement is correct, as the oral testimony of various ministers makes clear.)

Though he was never ordained, Don Salvador studied at the Bible mission in Valdepeñas run by an independent evangelical group. When the Civil War was over, having voiced his support of the Republic ("because they were for freedom"), he was imprisoned for eighty-one days in the Puertollano jail. His aged mother also served a term in the South.

As he told me his life's story, his hostility towards Catholicism would rise, uncontained, only to subside into a personal apology. "I tell you, Señorita Carmen, Catholics in Spain are bad. They are bad." (Pause.) "But I don't want to hurt you."

When I pressed him for details of his difficulties with the Catholic authorities of the town, he balked. I told him I was American,

_____

an audience of Council Fathers, laymen, priests and members of the Spanish Embassies in Rome and the Vatican.

and in no way shared the traditional views of the Spanish Church; he was not impressed. Someone, he said, had come to him recently purporting to be the relation of a fallen-away priest but actually seeking information with which to prosecute him. I offered to bring him my passport as soon as I got it back from the police station where, as they told me in the hotel, it had been taken for checking.

When Don Salvador was convinced of my intentions (sans passport), we got down to business. He opened a cupboard in a corner of the room and brought out a sheaf of papers covered with that fine layer of coal dust which seems to coat everything in Puertollano. He apologized for the absence of any files: he had to do everything in the church, and had no time to keep his records in order.

The papers went back as much as fifteen years. Some dealt with the classical marriage cases: permission to marry applied for, permission not forthcoming, appeal made again, etc. One document, signed by Don José María Gómez, the town's parish priest, threatened all witnesses to a Protestant marriage with excommunication *"ad ingressu ecclesia,* with the prohibitions of Canon 2277." Another excommunicated all the members of a wedding: the bride and groom, the witnesses and Don Salvador himself. Yet another was a copy of a letter sent by Don Salvador to the town's only radio station, the Emisora Parroquial y Catequista de Puertollano, owned and operated by the Church as part of its nationwide network. Dated at the end of 1953, the letter complained of a program entitled *Estampas Protestantes* (Protestant Sketches) in which some actors, playing men in a tavern, discussed Protestantism in "untrue," "unjust" and "illogical" terms.

What had brought me to Puertollano was its school case. I had seen the file in Madrid, including the latest document, dated October 15, 1962:

Considering that in order to grant the authorization requested [i.e., permission to reopen the school], it is necessary to submit a certificate issued by the parish priest, vouching for the religious conduct of the interested party, as set forth by Ministerial Order of November 15,

1945 . . . this Directorate has resolved to deny the appeal in reference. . . .

Don Salvador said he didn't have any of the papers at hand but that my understanding was correct: the parish priest had had the school closed. But he, Don Salvador, still taught a handful of children in a classroom upstairs. Clandestinely, of course. Since 1962 there had been no developments in the school case, but if I cared to talk about funerals . . .

The more one gets into the subject of Protestant funerals the more the conviction grows that, tragic as they are, they could provide enough "sick" humor for a dozen films à la Berlanga or Summers. And Puertollano in the fifties might have made the sickest setting of all. Between May 16, 1950, and July 23, 1952, four bodies were snatched from evangelical families there and—in a remarkable variation on the Inquisition practice of exhuming and burning heretics' remains—buried by force in the Catholic cemetery.

The two middle cases—April 21 and May 22, 1952—concerned the bodies of Doña Gregoria Calero Castellanos and Doña Francisca Avellaneda Robles, respectively. Doña Gregoria had been a Protestant since 1928; Doña Francisca since 1925. Both ladies had made and filed their last will and testament indicating their wishes to be buried in the civil cemetery. Don Salvador's letter of June 6, 1952, to the Most Excellent Civil Governor of the Province—who paid no attention to it—cites these facts and goes on to relate how the bodies were forcibly transported to the Catholic cemetery. In the first case, Don Salvador states that "through the intervention of the parish priest, the permit [to hold the funeral] was abrogated and said lady [Doña Gregoria], was buried according to the rites of the Catholic Church, though she had never confessed or received Communion in same." Doña Francisca's remains suffered the same fate:

when the Protestant funeral service was being held at the house of the deceased, two Police agents appeared, interrupted the ceremony, called aside the pastor who subscribes this document, and informed him that the Chief of Police had given a counterorder and commanded that the deceased be given Catholic burial. Then the parish priest appeared and, in the presence of the four policemen, took charge of the body, giving it Catholic burial against the wishes of the deceased and her family.

The procedure was in all cases the same: as the family sat around the body and the preacher read his prayers, a knock on the door turned out to be the secret police, who, as they said, "had come for the deceased." Though at first glance the thinking behind the Church's maneuver defies analysis, it answers to the logic of the True Faith. Once baptized, as we have seen in the marriage cases, a Catholic is, by the magic nature of the Sacrament of Baptism, inexorably bound to the Catholic Church. It is not unreasonable to assume that both Doña Gregoria and Doña Francisca had once been baptized in the Church. Their subsequent conversion to Protestantism mattered not, nor the fact that they had not "confessed or received Communion." Once baptized in the Church, there was no escape: until Vatican II, Divine Law reigned supreme in divinely inspired States.

The last body-snatching case involved Don Salvador's own nephew, Martín Reyes Ruzafa, who was electrocuted in an accident in one of the mines. His widow requested that the remains be brought home from the hospital; as the family and friends were gathered about it, there came the knock on the door. The violent scene that followed—it began in the house and continued on the street, as the body was taken away—was witnessed by neighbors and passers-by. So deep was their shock, and so great the scandal, that Señor Reyes Ruzafa was the last Protestant to be given Catholic burial. (In his futile complaint to the Civil Governor over the snatching of his nephew's body, Don Salvador, the Protestant, makes a vehement appeal to Canons 1240 and 2339 of the Catholic Code of Canon Law which, as he reminds His Excellency, forbid the burial of heathens or heretics on consecrated grounds.)

If body snatching came to an end, however, the harassment was far from over. The Tuesday before my visit (i.e., on March 16, 1965), a lady of Don Salvador's parish died. He obtained permission from a friendly cop to deliver the traditional Spanish eulogy, known as the *despedida del duelo,* in a small square tucked between two streets, where the handful of Protestants were not likely to attract much attention. They were ready to proceed there when the owner of the hearse objected on the ground that such a ceremony was illegal. After an appeal to the cop, a compromise was reached and the mourners gathered and held their *despedida* some ten meters from the house of the deceased.

It was at the civil cemetery that the trouble awaited. The caretaker had new orders from Don José María, the parish priest, not to bury anyone without his consent. If they did not bring Don José María's consent, he would not let them in. Don Salvador and mourners, led by the owner of the funeral parlor, who had taken charge, headed back to town. The dead lady was left in the parked hearse, in the broiling sun (it was a very warm March), to await the pleasure of the Catholic authorities before being admitted to the civil (or, as it is called in some places, the suicides') cemetery.

A visit to Don José María's rectory proved fruitless. The owner of the *funeraria* went in the building, seemed to stay there a long time, and finally came back with word that they would have to ask permission from another priest, Don Gaspar, in another church. The band of bodyless mourners went to Don Gaspar, and Don Gaspar granted authorization for the burial; then they headed back to the cemetery to claim the dead lady parked in the sun. The only problem now was getting the coffin down to the cemetery gate.

That afternoon, as I stood by the civil cemetery, the hazards of getting a casket inside became clear.

The cemetery is an extension of the Catholic burial ground, joined to it by the same front wall. Both enclosures lie along a highway which leads out of town past the Calvo Sotelo Industrial Complex with its factories and workers' homes. The Catholic gate was open; one could see long rows of well-tended graves set amid shrubbery and trees. A man was weeding the manicured entrance which led in from a driveway.

As one went past the Catholic wall and reached the Protestant end of the cemetery, one was struck by the fact that there was no access to the latter. A narrow, rotting wooden gate did keep guard on all the civil dead; but to get to it was impossible without slipping and sliding all the way down and quite likely ending up on hands and knees, as an embankment twelve or fourteen feet deep fell away from the highway at that point. Not only was there no path to the cemetery entrance, but the earth, uncontained, had tumbled to the bottom and piled against the door.

Those bearing a body had two alternatives: to leave the highway at the Catholic end, where the embankment is much shallower, and then, hugging the front wall, make for the civil gate. Or they could go along to the far wall of the civil enclosure (which borders on an empty lot) and turn left. Both approaches present the problem of stepping down steadily descending ground, over mounds of rubble and stones.

I climbed on the running board of Don Salvador's ancient Ford to look over the wall at the two cemeteries. Seen from above, the vertical division between them seemed like a boundary between light and darkness. On the Catholic side all was dazzling marble and landscaped greenness; the Protestant graves were a dismal row of tombstones, separated from each other by the dark dry earth, with barely three or four shrubs growing haphazardly in the entire lot.

The mayor was a kind and friendly man and had offered to help with the cemetery, said Don Salvador; but the mayor could do nothing. Don José María was boss.

Don José María's rectory is at No. 10 Calle de la Soledad, at right angles to another structure which looked much more imposing. The rectory itself is a modest but pleasant house with a stucco façade painted dark rose.

When I first called I had been told to return at nine thirty that evening. It was barely nine thirty-five when Don José María came out to meet me.

We went into his study and sat down. Don José María might have been in his late sixties. His hair was gray and he had a sharp jaw, firm mouth and dark circles under his eyes. His cassock was piped in purple and its buttons covered the same color, and I remembered having read in the Puertollano *Guidebook* that he had been recently promoted to archpriest.

I thanked him for receiving me and said I had come to talk about Puertollano's Protestants.

His face went stony. "They are anarchists, leftists, enemies of the State," he answered.

They were his very first words, and they caught me off guard. I said I had met a number of Spanish Protestants in Madrid and none of them answered that description.

He said that could be in Madrid, "In Puertollano," he repeated, "they are all leftists, enemies of the State."

I asked him what made him say so, and as he answered his face was set in anger and his words came tumbling out without a pause. Protestants, he said, were *all* enemies of Spain. Protestantism had always conspired against Spain. In the sixteenth century Spain ruled the world. Then Protestantism arose and Spain's decline set in. They, the Protestants, had brought it on.

I mentioned Joaquín Calvo Sotelo's play on Archbishop Carranza, which dealt with the tragedy of the Spanish sixteenth century and tried to examine it in a new light. It was produced in Madrid in 1963. Had he heard of it?

No, he hadn't.

Did he ever see any of the ecumenical magazines, like *Cuadernos para el diálogo* and *El ciervo*?

No, he didn't.

I said that in Madrid, the year before, I had sat in a mixed Catholic-Protestant congregation which was worshiping together in an evangelical chapel.

At this, Don José María glared. He said that could be in Madrid, but never in Puertollano. Puertollano Protestants were leftists. Their very pastor had been in jail.

Then he didn't think freedom of religion was a possibility?

"If Protestants are given freedom of religion," he said quickly, "the very next day they'll start burning Catholic churches and killing priests and nuns."

I demurred and he insisted: they were all leftists, Communists.

How about the feeling of brotherhood engendered by Pope John? I asked. Would that have any effect in Spain?

"The Pope is waiting for them with outstretched arms," he replied. "He has been waiting for years, and the Protestants refuse to come."

I said there had already been great gestures of friendship and brotherhood between the two faiths.

It wasn't brotherhood that counted, he pointed out, it was doctrinal unity.

But wasn't brotherhood love? And wasn't God love?

"Yes, God is love, but God is also Christ driving the merchants from the temple in holy fury. And God is justice. If I die in mortal sin, nothing, absolutely nothing, can save me from hell, because God is not just love, but justice too."

Did he know relations between the faiths were rather different in Europe?

They might be different in Europe, he said, but they should never be different in Spain. And besides, Europe defamed Spain. All of Europe. Just recently a French Catholic group had defamed them. And the English defamed Spain. The English, who were just now freeing their African colonies, while Spain had civilized a whole new world. (He did not specify what "French group" had done the defaming. Across Spain *Informations Catholiques* has earned the undying hatred of conservatives for its articles on the Spanish situation; pious Catholics openly call it a "Communist" magazine. But I had no way of knowing whether this French publication had ever roamed as far as Puertollano.)

"But why should all of Europe defame Spain, Father?" I asked him. "What is the reason behind it?"

"The fact that Spain is the spiritual treasure of Europe," he replied. "That is why they attack her. Because we have all the spiritual values here."

Suddenly he seemed to remember Puertollano's Protestants again. "We've given these people freedom!" he cried. "But what do they do? They hold services with the doors wide open, so anyone passing by on the sidewalk can see them and walk in! I gave them permission for a funeral the other day and what did they do? They held a public manifestation!"

I tried America. I told him about our Cardinal Cushing preaching in Protestant churches.

"That could be in America, but it would never do in Spain. And in America," he added, "all the news agencies are in the hands of Masons. And Masons of the Thirty-third Degree have to stamp on the Sacred Form as part of their initiation ritual."

Our conversation, I realized, was turning into a string of *non sequiturs,* each more baffling than the last. I was asking him just how the Masons got themselves a Sacred Form to stamp on when a young priest came in the room. He had detached himself from a group of clerics who had evidently been meeting in another part of the house, and now he came up to us.

He was very young, dark, with high cheekbones and an upturned nose. He wore a look so grave that it bordered on melancholy.

"This señorita has come to talk about the Protestants," said Don José María.

The young priest raised both eyebrows and looked even sadder. "Nothing can be done with them," he said. "Nothing."

He had told me as much, said Don José María. He had told me they were enemies of the State, leftists.

It seemed pointless to continue. We would always come back to the leftists. The young priest did not seem at all inclined to talk. I rose.

All three of us moved towards the door. As we stood there for a second I thought I'd try the young priest. One heard the New Clergy was waking up everywhere, facing up to the world, reading more widely. I asked him if he thought as I did, that the country was more liberal now—in the arts, in literature. As, for example, in paying homage to Unamuno the year before . . . ?

It was Don José María who answered. "As a Catholic I can never accept Unamuno. He and that other one, that other one . . ."

"Ortega," said the young priest.

"Yes, Ortega," Don José María continued. "He and Ortega paved the way for the Civil War."

I turned to the young priest again. "But what do you think of him as a writer?"

He made a face like an old, old man resigned to a cruel fate.

"Yes, Ortega is a good writer," he admitted. "That is just the trouble. He does all the more harm for being such a good writer."

I tried him on Calvo Sotelo's Carranza play. No, said the young man, he did not know of it.

"But the Inquisition was a secular tribunal," Don José María contributed. "It had nothing at all to do with the Church."

Once more his companion agreed. "Yes, it was a secular tribunal. The trouble in those days was that there was too much union between Church and State. That wasn't such a good thing."

"Do you think it's a good thing now?"

The young priest did not answer. He did not move a muscle; he kept his hands crossed over his cassock, his eyes on the floor.

The English attacked the Inquisition, Don José María started again. And the people who attacked the Inquisition were the ones "who took children and sucked off their blood."

I had half turned, ready to step into the hall, when the last sentence rang behind me. I stopped cold. Who were these people? Who were the children? I asked.

But Don José María went back to the Masonic agencies. "All of the news agencies in America are in the hands of Masons," he insisted. "Distorting the truth . . ."

I shook hands with him and said that as a Catholic I only hoped there might be freedom of conscience in Spain some day.

"If the Pope orders it," said Don José María, "all Spaniards would obey. Blindly [a rajatabla]. They would conquer their inclinations and do what the Pope said, because the Pope's word is the law. But not before. One million Spaniards had died for Spain and the faith. One million Spaniards could not be wrong. If you want to know about Protestants you can come over here to my library and read the *History of the Crusade*" (he pointed to a collection of beige paper-bound books with that title on a low shelf).

I took my leave of him and his friend and went back to the hotel. Only there did I remember that I had not asked about the body snatchings.

After a very late dinner I sat in the lobby and watched T.V. *The European Festival of Song* was coming in from Naples. A little

197

blonde from Luxembourg sang a "yé-yé" song about a wax doll and won first prize.

Next morning, Sunday, the nine o'clock Mass had already started when I arrived at the Church of the Assumption. Don José María faced the congregation from an altar set up only a few feet from the front pews. As far as I could make out, only a man and a boy were singing in the choir loft, and very badly indeed; the Communion hymn was a special trial.

Around Don José María's altar, four figures were arranged in military formation. A woman and a little girl stood guard on the left; a young man and a boy on the right. All four held flags of satin with some kind of legend embroidered on them. When Mass was over, the loud-speakers which dotted the nave whirred on and a recorded hymn with a martial beat came through, very shrill, the words almost unintelligible.

It was the recessional. The young man and the boy led the way. Don José María followed, looking grim. The woman and the little girl, their flags on high, brought up the rear.

The church emptied slowly. It was almost a quarter to ten. I thought the next Mass would start in fifteen minutes but I was mistaken; there was no other until ten thirty.

I consulted the little guidebook I had obtained for five pesetas. It spoke of the church as "the most sumptuous and strongest of the Field of Calatrava," and I remembered again that I was in the bosom of Fighting Catholicism. The Castle had risen no more than twenty kilometers away, while the Field extended over the whole region.

Blood flowed as freely here as in any other part of Spain during the Reconquest. The Castle of Calatrava, from which the Field took its name, had been given by Alfonso VII to the Templars in 1147. Sensing the magnitude of the Moslem counterattack, the Templars turned it over to Sancho III, who offered it as heritage to anyone willing to defend it. But there were no takers. Then Raimundo, Abbot of the Cistercian Monastery of Santa Maria de Fitero, rose in holy zeal. He gathered money and arms through his preaching, while the Archbishop of Toledo offered absolution of all sins to those who joined the campaign. The order of Calatrava was born.

After Raimundo's death, when the Knights began to chafe under monkish control, the Cistercians obligingly stepped aside and left the reins of Calatrava to its lay members. But the first *maestre,* García, was not content to lead a band of simple warriors. He asked the monks to promote his Knights from *familiares,* or lay assistants, to full-fledged members in the Cistercian Order. The monks agreed, even if it meant altering the Rule of St. Benedict to allow the newcomers to bear arms. The Knights, in turn, took the triple vow of poverty, chastity and obedience, plus the Cistercian habit.

The Castle which had given the Order its name passed back and forth between Moors and Christians until, in 1216, the fortress of Calatrava la Nueva was built by the eighth *maestre.* Thereafter the Order declined, although its end was not as ignominious as the Templars'. Internal dissension took its toll and when the Catholic sovereigns assumed control of all military orders, Calatrava lost its independence.

I walked around the church, which was almost empty now. The sunlight filtering through the windows gave it a pleasant, airy look. Statues lined the nave, statues stood inside and outside the Communion rail, statues took up side chapels, niches and bits of the wall.

On the topmost niche of the reredos which rose above the main altar stood a statue I could not identify—either Our Lord or a male saint; it certainly didn't look like Our Lady of the Assumption. On the lower level three other figures appeared: a Virgin in the middle, St. Anthony of Padua holding the Infant on her right, and a teaching saint (St. Vincent de Paul? St. John Bosco?) on her left. I could not tell which, but, like all teaching saints, he had a child by his side.

Flanking the altar stood a twin set of life-size images, each on its own pedestal. One was the Sacred Heart, the other a Virgin; identical rays of light of identical size and color issued from the middle of their backs and formed an aureole around their bodies.

A side altar, still inside the Communion rail, was presided over by a saint in what appeared to be a Franciscan habit.

Outside the rail, to the right of the main altar, stood the Virgin of the Pillar, guarded by two large angels and covered by a canopy of cherubs. Looking down the nave past a large side chapel with another Virgin, one found Our Lady of Mt. Carmel between a Holy King (right) and an unidentified nun (St. Margaret Mary?) holding a human heart in her hand (left). Directly across was a large crucifix; a Holy Infant, arms outstretched, stood beneath it. They in turn were flanked by two Virgins, one with a rosary and Child, the other the familiar Miraculous Image with rays of light falling from her hands. Further back, on the left, was another Virgin, with a large golden crown, who looked very much like Our Lady of Fatima. Across the nave appeared Our Lady of Perpetual Help. A Risen Christ on a small pedestal looked rather forlorn against a bare stretch of the back left wall. Opposite him was a large altar to St. Joseph, with statue. In the back stood a Descent from the Cross, while a side chapel with a baptismal font held yet another Virgin. This one was a large Sorrowing image in a real, all-white gown, her tearful eyes fixed on the crown of thorns she held in her left hand. In the right she clutched a lace handkerchief.

The pews had begun to fill with children. They came in twos and threes, some of the girls holding hands, some leading little ones who were barely toddlers. The boys sat mostly on the left and found it hard to keep from fidgeting. But when the church was full it was clear that they were a disciplined lot; a head moved here or there, a whisper passed between two others, but on the whole the youngsters waited for Mass with as much composure as a group of adults.

They ran the gamut of national types. A freckled strawberry blond in a stocking cap sat with a dark-haired charmer whose profile was sharp and almost adult, as it so often is among children of heavily Moorish regions. The boys were sunburnt and wiry, with hair cut shorter than I had ever seen on a Spanish child; under the deep tans, even this far south, there was a handful of blue-eyed blonds, while here and there one saw the promise of that long, sallow, intellectual face one meets so often in Castile.

I wondered how they would grow up in their bleak town, amid the bleak hills which passed for its countryside, so far removed from all natural beauty. A phrase of Elaine de La Souchère's crossed my mind: "It is the Castilian peasant who outstrips all others in his enmity of Nature." [4] Surely "enmity" was too strong a word for these children, but in all likelihood a love of nature would never touch their young lives. There was simply no "nature" that they could give their young hearts to. Not for them a hike through the woods, a picnic by a lake, a moment's compassion for an animal in pain. The woods and the lake were just not there, and the animal "did not count." Instead, to a degree perhaps unknown anywhere else in the Western world, they would revel—even as children—in all that was human: dignity and decorum, courtesy, pride.

But the Mass was about to start. The young priest I had met the night before had entered the sanctuary, vested, followed by Don José María. The latter climbed to the pulpit. Under his direction the children read off the responses to the Mass in Spanish while the young priest, looking even sadder than the night before, moved solemnly, heavily, with slow-motion gestures from one side of the altar to the other.

I had to leave right after the Gospel of the dumb man from whom Jesus cast out a devil. Pointing out that speech was a way of communicating with God, Don José María urged the children to read the responses to the Mass clearly, loudly. I could hear them complying with his request as I reached the main door and went out into the plaza.

There was no sign of life around the other church. After I knocked on the door a woman stuck out her head and asked dryly: "What do you want?" I said I wanted to attend the service.

At that moment Don Salvador came out to meet me and together we entered the building, which was more than two-thirds full. Though I would have preferred to sit in the back and take

[4] Elaine de La Souchère, *An Explanation of Spain* (New York: Random House, 1964), p. 19.

an accurate count of the house, Don Salvador escorted me to a front pew.

He climbed the dais at the front of the church and delivered the invocation. Then he stepped down to a small harmonium which was directly in front of my pew. Hymn 478 rang out while his thick, stubby fingers picked out the accompaniment. (A policeman, he told me later, had once ordered him to put cotton batting over the cracks in the door, because the singing could be heard outside.)

The hymn over, Don Salvador climbed back to the dais, bade me welcome in the name of the congregation and announced that the theme of his sermon would be the obedience man owed to God. As his text he would use the account of Abraham's near-sacrifice of Isaac.

He made his points simply, with homespun examples. Obedience, he said, was at the heart of all love of God; if a boy kissed his father affectionately every day and then disobeyed him, the day would come when his father would reject the kiss as insincere.

I followed the sermon intermittently as I tried to count the house. In my pew sat a pretty teen-ager and a little girl; the teen-ager shared her hymnal and Bible with me. We were to the left of the aisle. Save for a couple in the second row of the right-hand side, the women sat on the left, the men on the right. Across the narrow passage I could see some of the miners in their dark suits—men between twenty and fifty, grave and attentive, their eyes persistently front. If I turned my head a black blur swam into view: it was the women in their black dresses, black kerchiefs, black shawls. Mercedes, Don Salvador's white-haired housekeeper, would smile when she caught my eye.

Where Don José María's church was fairly bursting with statues, Don Salvador's was awash in scriptural texts. From the dais hung a small cloth with "God Is Love" embroidered on it. On the left side of the front wall one could read: "It is not ourselves we preach; we preach Jesus Christ the Lord." Matching it, on the right: ". . . and the blood of Jesus Christ, his Son, cleanses us of all sin." Across the choir, in the back. "Because God so loved the world, that he gave his only begotten Son, so all who believe in him may be saved, and have life everlasting."

The side walls contained six other texts, one of which, to my right, reminded me of Pastor Núñez's Baptist church in Madrid: "For the wages of sin is death, but the gift of God is life eternal in Christ Jesus our Lord."

Don Salvador had turned to the Acts of the Apostles, Chapter 4, Verses 1–4. My companion found the place quickly. I read on from Verse 4 and found:

Seeing the boldness of Peter and John and discovering they were simple men, without learning, they were astonished and recognized them as having been in Jesus' company.

It was a text to take away with me, a gift of the miners, their pastor, and their humblest of churches.

Don Salvador asked if anyone had a hymn to request. A young man rose and asked for Hymn 438. Again Don Salvador moved down to the harmonium; again the voices rose. It was nearly eleven forty.

A pause followed. Then a woman rose and while the rest of the congregation bowed their heads, she closed her eyes and prayed aloud. "We thank thee, Lord, that you have given us this opportunity of worshiping you today. We beg thee, Lord, to keep us on the right path." The clear, guttural Castilian lent a sharp beauty to her words. This is the language in which, as someone has remarked, there are no class accents: a duchess speaks like a flower girl, and a flower girl like a duchess. In Spain, says Madariaga, "illiterates speak like Seneca, sing like Blake." And here in Puertollano—which is in La Mancha, Don Quixote country—this simple woman dressed in black grew eloquent in her prayer. One by one, three others followed her. ("I ask thee, Lord, to watch over my grandson in the Army, to let him see Your light.") Then came the men's turn; three rose to offer extempore prayers, as the women had done.

It was the Quaker vein, still alive after four hundred years, and it made one wonder. What might have happened in Spain if the Erasmists had seen through their Reform? If Valdés had not been forced abroad? If the Castilian heretics had put down roots and built a thoroughly Spanish and thoroughly Protestant creed, a link to the modern world of the North?

There were no answers in the Puertollano chapel. After another hymn the service was over, and Don Salvador walked outside to shake hands with his congregation. Then the women came up and, one by one, kissed me.

After lunch I had a little time before my train to Madrid, and Don Salvador took me out to see the mines. They were ugly, somber, deserted coal mines. In the shafts the cages stood empty and in one of the engine rooms which an obliging guard showed us, the French-made machinery was silent.

We went back to the road and Don Salvador pointed out Puertollano in the distance. The incredibly arid town covered the twin humps of one mountain, with a shallow pass (the *puerto llano*) between them. Towards the left, large and forbidding even from that distance, rose the Church of the Assumption.

III

Towards "So-called Civilization"

11

By the 1960's the world was knocking on Spain's door. In an editorial in February, 1965, the New York *Times* noted:

Spain is changing, mainly because of the irresistible thrust of economic improvement and a breach in the historic walls of isolation. Millions of tourists bring the outer world—the new, exciting world of the 1960's—in with them. Many thousands of Spanish workers go to France and West Germany and see how workmen live in a free, highly developed and prosperous society. The Catholic Church in Spain, once the last redoubt of medievalism, is responding to the progressivism of Pope John XXIII and Pope Paul VI.[1]

Spain's response to the Popes will certainly be one of the most important factors in her rapprochement to nonsacral Europe. Open in spite of itself to the winds of change, her Catholicism may be the spur which will hasten the transformation of Spanish society; then again, ever heeding the call of bigotry and absolutism, it may be the fly in the ointment of her newly acquired, proudly won and highly cherished economic progress.

The Popes have been two, and so have the responses. While Pope John XXIII lived, and until the summer of 1965, the issue of religious liberty was gingerly but respectfully handled by the Church-State press. When the Council adjourned in 1964 without

[1] New York *Times,* February 26, 1965, p. 28. The issue was banned.

207

having come to a decision on the Schema, the Spanish Fathers vehemently denied having been a party to the postponement. In December of the same year Franco issued the historical call for religious freedom. Interfaith contacts in the larger cities of the nation grew. The phrase "separated brethren" took currency and, in some quarters, substantial meaning.

Then, on July 9, 1965, the truce was over and a fanfare blew calling the troops back to battle. The rest is history: the Spanish Fathers' desperate, last-ditch stand at St. Peter's; the sour echo of their ideas in the world press; Pope Paul's hesitation and his final resolution of the matter; the proclamation of the Schema and the difficulties—psychological no less than legal—which its enforcement presented for the orthodox hierarchy of Spain.

Integrismo—the Spanish name for traditionalism—had lived through harrowing days before showing its true colors at the Vatican in the autumn of 1965.[2] Now it was faced with the monstrous task of going back on its own convictions. The new Pope heartened the orthodox with his steadfast support of conservative causes; but the new Schema, proclaimed to the ends of the earth, demanded at least lip service to the newly discovered principles of "human rights."

As one young Protestant minister put it with a smile: "Who's going to bell the cat?"

Between 1963 and 1965, the issue of religious liberty traced a parabola in the civic and spiritual life of Spain. After a wobbly send-off it reached a peak of cautious but firm support in mid-1964, only to be laid low again by the hierarchy in the second half of 1965. The history of the nation had come full circle once more. "Every time that Spain, eager for spiritual renovation, opens herself to foreign influence, this *unconquerable* land delegates one or several of her sons to say 'no' to the invader."

Her sons had their initial misgivings when the Council first took up the Schema on ecumenism in November, 1963. Mon-

[2] The Royal Spanish Academy's Dictionary fixes the word in its historical perspective: "*Integrismo:* A Spanish political party founded at the end of the nineteenth century to safeguard the integrity of Spanish tradition."

signor Morcillo, then Archbishop of Zaragoza, took a mild but "truth-oriented" approach:

It is possible to make progress on the road to union, although a portion of the separated brethren reject the invitation to return [to Catholicism] since they believe they are already incorporated into the Church of Christ. Dialogue is possible. On the methodological level, it is convenient, above all, to bear in mind the necessity of being faithful to the truth, which is not ours, but Christ's, the Gospel's, the Church's. We must be deferent towards the separated brethren and recognize their sincere ecclesiastical conscience.[3]

On November 18, Cardinal Arriba y Castro, Archbishop of Tarragona, had seen danger ahead:

The Church has always considered the ecumenical movement with caution, and rightly; it is a dangerous thing; it can lead the faithful to indifferentism when they see that the Church uses such polite words [*palabras tan gentiles*] in referring to non-Catholics, as if the grace of the Holy Spirit was present in all confessions. . . . Indeed, the text emphasizes the fact that the grace and the interior gifts of the Holy Spirit exist outside the Church. This is true, but not inasmuch as these Christians are separated from the Church, but inasmuch as they remain so in good faith.[4]

Looking over *Ecclesia* one is struck by the statement that follows, issued by Cardinal Ritter of St. Louis. The prelate from a land of materialism and human values, of separation between Church and State, of religious freedom and the attendant diffusion of "nontruth" lays waste the very notion of the City of God:

But let it be noted that, in order to be worthy of the Council, the declaration should not only be founded on principles of mere practical convenience, but on solid theological reasons. That is why one must speak, above all, of the absolute liberty demanded by the act of faith, of the dignity of the human person and his inviolable conscience, and one must also speak of the total incompetence of civil government when it comes to judging the Gospel of Christ or taking decisions on its interpretation. By the same token, this declaration

[3] *Ecclesia,* November 30, 1963, p. 23.
[4] *Ibid.,* November 23, 1963, pp. 28, 29.

should reaffirm the complete independence of the Church from all civil governments in the fulfillment of her mission.[5]

When the next session of the Council opened in 1964, the counterattack was not long in coming. On September 24 the Bishop of Orense went into battle and, as reported in *ABC,* paid homage to Señor Américo Castro:

Monsignor Temino, Bishop of Orense, proved that the text makes all religions equal, whereas the First Vatican Council made it clear that the believer who belongs to the Catholic Church is not in the same condition as he who does not [belong to it], and whereas, in the Old Testament, Yahwe showed the absolute and exclusive right of his people.[6]

On the same day, according to the evening paper *Informaciones,* Monsignor López Ortiz, Bishop of Tuy,

requested the removal of the paragraph declaring that the State is incompetent to judge truth in the matter of religion, since, when a State declares itself Catholic, it is not judging religious matters, but declaring itself obedient to the divine mandate.[7]

Meanwhile, Yahwe's People opened their papers every day to find one, two or more references to the doctrine being discussed at the Vatican. The news stories, most of them datelined Rome, were of a positive nature. On September 26, 1964, a dispatch in *ABC* stated that the Spanish episcopate had met to consider the bill of a statute extending juridical recognition to non-Catholic confessions in Spain. On September 27, through an article in *Ya,* Dr. Morcillo, Archbishop of Madrid, explained that the discussion in the Council Hall had been "wide, profound and serene," praised the proposed law but reminded one and all that "proselytism" would continue to be forbidden. On the 1st of October (also in *Ya*) the Archbishop of Zaragoza, Monsignor Cantero, stated that a declaration on religious liberty was not only convenient, "but necessary." In a T.V. interview, Cardinal Bueno Mon-

[5] *Ibid.,* p. 29.
[6] *ABC*, September 25, 1964.
[7] *Informaciones,* September 25, 1964.

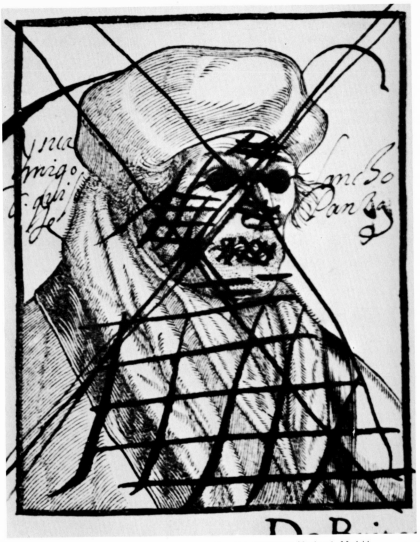

Courtesy Biblioteca Nacional, Madrid

The defacement of this portrait of Erasmus of Rotterdam, from
the 1550 Basel edition of Sebastian Munster's *Cosmographia*, is
one result of the zeal of the Spanish Inquisition.

B

MINISTERIO DE JUSTICIA

SUBSECRETARIA

Comisión de Rehabilitación
y Penas Accesorias

Exp. núm. 58.489

(CITESE ESTE NUMERO)

M.C.-33

Visto el expediente incoado por la Comisión de Rehabilitación y Penas Accesorias a instancia de D. GREGORIO JOSE NUÑEZ MORENO con domicilio en C/ Ros de Olano nº 10, Madrid que solicita la cancelación de la nota de condena de 2 meses de arresto y múlta de mil ptas.

de Madrid impuesta por la Audiencia en fecha 7 octubre 1959

en sumario número 365/51 procedente del Juzgado de Madrid nº 17

por el delito de desobediencia

Habiéndose estimado cumplidos los requisitos legales, este Ministerio ha tenido a bien disponer la cancelación del referido antecedente penal.

Lo que de Orden comunicada, traslado a V. para su conocimiento y demás efectos.

Dios guarde a V. muchos años.

Madrid, 13 de enero de 196 5

S. D. Gregorio José Nuñez Moreno.-

Five years and three months after his sentencing, the Ministry of Justice canceled Pastor José Nuñez's "criminal antecedent" for the crime of "disobedience."

Barcelona's Librería Evangélica shortly after its opening in May, 1965

The bookstore three months later, after the Civil Governor's verbal order to remove the window displays for the protection of Catholic passers-by

Expediente N.° I.- 493-65

(Déjese en blanco)

RELACION DE OBRAS PARA VISADO

JOSE CARDONA GREGORI

VIEIDE.

N.° de Orden	N.° de Reg.	N.° de Ej.	AUTOR	TITULO	EDITORES
1	Sin nºR.	20	A.Canolini	SE CASARON Y FUERON UTILES	J.B.Publ/.
2	"	20	P.S.Rees.	PRIMERA EPISTOLA DE PEDRO.	J.B.Publ/.
3	"	20	D.L.Moody	LA VIDA VERDEDERA.	Moody
4	"	20	C.A.Reno	¿ES UN HECHO LA EVOLUSION?	id
5	"	20	L.T.Lyall	CONTRA VIENTO Y MAREA.	id
6	"	20	W.L.Wilson	EXPERIENCIAS DE UN MEDICO	id
7	"	20	A.Canolini	ONESIMO.	id
8	"	20	P.W.Stoner	LA CIENCIA HABLA	id
9	"	20	N.A.Ironside	GRANDES PALABRAS DEL EVANGELIO	
10	"	20	K.H.Friederichsen	LA PALABRA DE DIOS AL ALCANCE	" id
11	"	20	A.S.Rodriguez	HIMNOS FAMOSOS.	C.B.Publi/
12	"	20	id	JUAN BUNYAN.	id
13	"	20	H.L.Dana	EL MUNDO DEL NUEVO TESTAMENTO	id
14	"	20	Campbell	JUGUEMOS	id.
15	"	20	S.Culross	GUILLERMO CAREY	id.
16	"	20	C.M.Sheldom	EN SUS PASOS ¿Qué haría Jesus?	Aurora
17	"	20	W.J.Schnell	ESCLAVO POR TREINTA AÑOS EN LA T.V.	B.B.Hous
18	"	20	D y N Brichez	BARBADOC Y OTROS CUENTOS.	Alianza
19	"	20	Anonimo.	CANTICOS DE SALVACION. Num 1.	Mexico
20	"	20	N.Grubb	AVIVAMIENTO CONTINUO	C.L.Cruzade
21		20	Romanenghi	MAS COSAS QUE SE CUENTAN	Llamacecer
22		20	F.Ordoñez	LA BORRASCA	Publ. Juvent/
23	Sin nºº	20	Y.C.Weiss	EL CRISTIANO VERDADERO	Mexico
24	"	20	Anonimo	CANTOS DE SALVACION Num 2	Mexico
25	"	20	Billi Graham	MI RESPUESTA.	L.V.

Observaciones:

An application submitted to censorship authorities for the importation of books

MINISTERIO DE INFORMACION Y TURISMO
DIRECCION GENERAL DE INFORMACION
INSPECCION DE LIBROS
fm.

Exp. n.º   I.- 493-65

(Cítese en la correspondencia)

Vista su instancia de fecha 22-4-65. y examinadas las obras que la acompañan, esta Dirección General ha dispuesto lo siguiente:

Se AUTORIZAN las obras n.º 1 a la 21 y 23 a la 25 inclusive sin nº de Registro.

~~Cuyo número de Registro se hará constar de la relación adjunta.~~

SE DENIEGAN las obras n.º 22

que deberán ser devueltas al país de procedencia, en virtud de la Orden Ministerial de fecha 16-VII-45 (Boletín Oficial 28-VII-45).

Madrid, 5 de mayo de 1965.

Dios guarde a Vd. muchos años.

El Director General de Información,

Sr. D. JOSE CARDONA GREGORI.- M A D R I D.-

The Government's reply. All books on the list are "Authorized" except one, No. 22, a novel of Protestant life in Colombia.

The cover of *The Ten Commandments,* a pamphlet whose distribution brought on the confiscation of 72,000 pieces of Protestant literature

A Baptist birth announcement card, 2,800 copies of which were seized in the great Barcelona raid

The premises of a Barcelona school raided on Holy Thursday night, 1960. Tape on door bears the seal of the Dirección General Seguridad.

A U T O. —Barcelona,   **diez**   de   **junio**   de mil nove-
cientos **sesenta** y uno.= **Dada cuenta; y**

    RESULTANDO: que **de lo actuado aparece que JOSÉ GRAU BALCELLS,
representante en España de la Editorial "Ediciones Evangélicas
Europeas" encargó a SALVADOR SALVADÓ COTS, dueño del taller
imprenta titulado "Impresos y Ediciones Salvadó" sito en la
calle Vallirana número sesenta, planta baja, la impresión de
diversos libros, folletos y hojas para uso de todas las iglesias evangélicas radicantes en España, habiendo así editado
"El Cristiano, ese desconocido" y " "Qué es la verdad?" de los
que es autor el propio José Grau, "Himnos para niños", folle-
to invitación para presentar a los recién nacidos en la Iglesia
Evangélica,yhoja circular de propaganda conteniendo al dorso
versículos bíblicos, todo lo cual fué publicado careciendo de
autorización oficial y sin el pié de imprenta reglamentario, ya
que en los dos primeros libros aparece como pie de imprenta ima
ginario el de "Ediciones Evangélicas Europeas-Winterthur,4 Sui-
za", habiendo sido ocupados en la imprenta del citado Salvadó
diversos ejemplares de tales publicaciones.=**

    CONSIDERANDO: que los hechos que se acaban de relatar pueden ser constitutivos
de **un** delito **de publicación clandestina**

previsto y penado en **los** artículo **s 165 nº 1ª**
del Código Penal vigente **y Ley de Imprenta de 26 de julio de 1883**
y que de las actuaciones sumariales aparecen méritos bastantes para reputar responsable
criminalmente de **1** mismo a **los** acusado **s JOSÉ GRAU BALCELLS y SALVADOR
SALVADÓ COTS,**

a **los** que procede declarar procesado **s**, a tenor de lo dispuesto en el artículo 384 de la Ley
de Enjuiciamiento Criminal; y atendidas, la penalidad a **1** mismo señalada y las cir-
cunstancias concurrentes en **los** inculpado **s**, a tenor de lo previsto en los artículos **libertad** 503,
504 y 529 de la antedicha Ley Procesal, procede también decretar la _____
de **los** acusado **s en la forma que se dirá.=**

    CONSIDERANDO: que el responsable criminalmente, lo es también civilmente.

Señores Grau and Salvadó's sentence for the crime of "clandestine publication."

SE DECLARA PROCESADOS por razón de esta causa a **JOSÉ GRAU BALCELLS y SALVADOR SALVADÓ COTS,**

con quien **se** entiendan las sucesivas diligencias en el modo y forma que determina la Ley de Enjuiciamiento Criminal.

Se decreta la **libertad** provisional de **los** referido **procesado mediante que presten obligación apud-acta de comparecer ante este Juzgado o Tribunal que conozca de la causa, los días uno y quince de cada mes y siempre que se les llame,**

hágasele **s** saber este auto enterándole **s** de los derechos y recursos que pueda **n** ejercitar póngase en conocimiento del Ministerio Fiscal.

y fórmese pieza separada respecto del particular.

Recíbase indagatoria **los** procesado **s citándolos de comparecencia ante este Juzgado**

apórtense sus antecedentes penales, acta de nacimiento o bautismo e informe de conducta a cuyo fin se expidan los oportunos despachos.

Requiérase a **los** indicado **s** procesado para que a las resultas de la causa, preste fianza en cantidad de **TRES MIL** pesetas **cada uno,** y no verificándolo dentro de las veinticuatro horas siguientes, embárguensele bienes bastantes a cubrir dicha suma, acreditandose caso de no poseerlos, su insolvencia legalmente y fórmese pieza separada respecto del particular **.-**

Lo mandó y firma el Sr. D. **José Cacho Castrillo, Magistrado,** Juez de Instrucción del Juzgado número CINCO, **de esta ciudad;** doy fe.

E.

Notificado en 17-6-61

DILIGENCIA.—Seguidamente se puso el anterior auto en conocimiento del Ministerio Fiscal, se formaron las piezas separadas doy fe.

They are free on conditional liberty with bail set at 3,000 pesetas ($50.00) each.

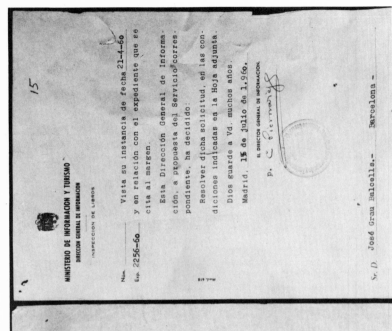

15

MINISTERIO DE INFORMACION Y TURISMO
DIRECCION GENERAL DE INFORMACION

INSPECCION DE LIBROS

Núm.
Exp. 2256-60

Vista su instancia de fecha 21-4-60 y en relación con el expediente que se cita al margen.

Esta Dirección General de Informa-ción, a propuesta del Servicio corres-pondiente, ha decidido:

Resolver dicha solicitud, en las con-diciones indicadas en la Hoja adjunta.

Dios guarde a Vd. muchos años.

Madrid, 15 de julio de 1.960.

EL DIRECTOR GENERAL DE INFORMACION

p. *Pierrarie*

Sr. D. José Grau Balcells.- Barcelona -

Para su autorización deberá ser presentada LICENCIA ECLESIASTICA del Arzobispado de Barcelona.

The answer to Señor Grau's request for authorization to publish *What Is Truth?* To the right, the State's official notice: it defers to the conditions set forth "on the attached sheet." To the left, anonymously, the Church lays down the law.

A los fieles de Fíos y Nevares

SOBRE EL PROTESTANTISMO

Queridos hermanos: La Sagrada Biblia es el libro sagrado de los cristianos que Dios dictó, inspiró, a los santos hombres que la escribieron.

La Iglesia es una sociedad de cristianos unidos entre sí por una misma profesión de fe, por una misma participación de sacramentos, bajo la dirección de Su Santidad el Papa. La Iglesia, dice la Sagrada Biblia, la fundó Dios Nuestro Señor Jesucristo el año 30, cuando dijo a S. Pedro: «Tu eres Pedro y sobre esta piedra edificaré mi Iglesia y las puertas del infierno no prevalecerán contra ella». «Apacienta mis ovejas». Los Papas son los sucesores de S. Pedro, que fue el primero.

Las principales diferencias entre católicos y protestantes son:

1.ª Los católicos creen en toda Biblia. Los protestantes no creen en toda la Biblia.

2.ª Los católicos aman mucho a Dios Nuestro Señor Jesucristo. Los protestantes entienden este amor al gusto de cada uno.

3.ª Los católicos creen y aman a la Iglesia única, santa, católica y apostólica. Los protestantes no creen ni aman la santa Iglesia católica.

4.ª Los católicos tienen siete sacramentos. Los protestantes nada tienen.

5.ª Los católicos aman y veneran a la Santísima Virgen María, que es la madre de Jesucristo. Los protestantes no aman, no veneran a la Santísima Virgen.

6.ª Los católicos aman y veneran a las personas santas que están en Cielo. Los protestantes no aman, no veneran a las personas santas.

7.ª Los católicos se acuerdan de sus difuntos. La Biblia dice: «Santo y saludable es orar por los difuntos». Los protestantes no se acuerdan de sus difuntos.

8.ª Los católicos aman a Dios por medio de la Santa Misa, la oración y las buenas obras. La Sagrada Biblia dice que Dios Nuestro Señor Jesucristo en la última cena celebró su primera Misa, tomando en sus manos un poco de pan lo consagró diciendo: «Este es mi cuerpo». Luego cogió un cáliz y lo consagró diciendo: «Este es el cáliz de mi sangre». Después les dijo a sus discípulos: «Haced esto en mi memoria». Los protestantes nada tienen de esto.

9.ª Los católicos tienen buenos sacerdotes que ofrecen a Dios libremente el ser solteros. Los protestantes no ofrecen nada a Dios.

10.ª Los católicos tienen dolor de sus pecados y se confiesan. Los protestantes no tienen dolor de sus pecados, no se confiesan.

11.ª Los católicos están siempre unidos. Los protestantes están cada vez más desunidos.

12.ª El catolicismo lo fundó Jesucristo el año 30. El protestantismo lo fundaron Lutero y Calvino, hombres soberbios, desobedientes y deshonestos, el año 1517.

13.ª Los católicos tienen sus cementerios. Los protestantes no se pueden enterrar en los cementerios católicos.

14.ª Los católicos no se pueden casar con los protestantes. Los protestantes se casan muchas veces con cualquiera, se divorcian.

15.ª Los católicos están dentro de la verdadera Iglesia. Los protestantes están fuera de ella.

16.ª Los católicos tienen el todo. Los protestantes tienen una parte.

Hay otras diferencias, pero no tienen tanta importancia.

Dice la Biblia en otra parte: «Guardaos de los falsos profetas que vienen a vosotros vestidos de ovejas, por dentro son lobos voraces».

Os saluda en el Señor,

Nuestro Párroco,

Fíos y Nevares, día de S. Antonio Abad (17-1-63).

A public notice "On Protestantism" posted by a parish priest in Asturias

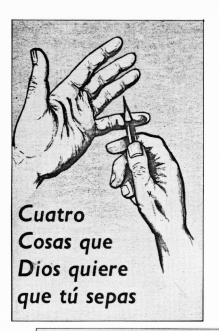

Cuatro Cosas que Dios quiere que tú sepas

 Que tú necesitas ser salvo.

Por cuanto todos pecaron, y están destituídos de la gloria de Dios. **Romanos 3 : 23.**

Engañoso es el corazón más que todas las cosas, y perverso; ¿ quién lo conocerá ? **Jeremías 17 : 9.**

Todos nosotros somos como suciedad, y todas nuestras justicias como trapo de inmundicia. **Isaías 64 : 6.**

Todos nosotros nos descarriamos como ovejas, cada cual se apartó por su camino. **Isaías 53 : 6.**

El que no naciere otra vez, no puede ver el reino de Dios. **Juan 3 : 3.**

 Que tú no puedes salvarte a ti mismo.

Hay camino que al hombre parece derecho; empero su fin son caminos de muerte. **Proverbios 14 : 12.**

Porque cualquiera que hubiere guardado toda la ley, y ofendiere en un punto, es hecho culpado de todo. **Santiago 2 : 10.**

Por las obras de la ley ninguna carne será justificada. **Gálatas 2 : 16.**

Jesús . . . dice: Yo soy el camino, y la verdad, y la vida: nadie viene al Padre, sino por Mí. **Juan 14 : 6.**

Y en ningún otro hay salud; porque no hay otro nombre debajo del cielo, dado a los hombres, en que podamos ser salvos. **Hechos 4 : 12.**

 El Señor Jesús ha provisto para tu salvación.

Porque de tal manera amó Dios al mundo, que ha dado a Su Hijo unigénito, para que todo aquel que en El cree, no se pierda, mas tenga vida eterna. **Juan 3 : 16.**

Todos nosotros nos descarriamos como ovejas, cada cual se apartó por su camino: mas el Señor cargó en El el pecado de todos nosotros. **Isaías 53 : 6.**

Al que no conoció pecado (a Cristo Jesús), hizo (Dios) pecado por nosotros, para que nosotros fuésemos hechos justicia de Dios en El. **2 Corintios 5 : 21.**

Porque también Cristo padeció una vez por los pecados, el justo por los injustos, para llevarnos a Dios. **1 Pedro 3 : 18.**

One of two pamphlets given out by José Cabrera Gil at the funeral of a Catholic friend in October, 1965

The Cabrera Gil aftermath.

Pastor Manuel González Calvín (hands behind back) awaits Cabrera's release at the end of his five-day jail sentence. The legend above the doorway reads: "If the penal establishments of other countries were visited and their systems compared with ours, I can assure you without shadow of a doubt that one would not find anywhere a program as just, Catholic and humane as that established for our inmates since [the inception] of our movement. Francisco Franco."

Centro ecuménico de Barcelona

/la Layetana, 32 - 34, despacho, 101 - Tel. 231 63 92 - BARCELONA - 3

C i r c u l a r   nº   11   J u l i o–Septiembre 1965

        Tal como habíamos anunciado ya en el último número de
la Circular, al preparar el programa del próximo curso, hemos procurado dar una unidad a los temas de las reuniones
mensuales, de tal modo que, al mismo tiempo, pudiéramos sa-
tisfacer el deseo repetidamente expresado por numerosos
miembros del Centro, de dar una información tan completa y
objetiva como fuera posible sobre el protestantismo español. Por esta razón hemos decidido colocar todas estas reu
niones - que abarcan desde el mes de octubre hasta el de
junio - bajo el tema global de LAS CONFESIONES CRISTIANAS
Y LA UNIDAD. Hablará en cada una de ellas un miembro de
una de las confesiones actualmente representadas en Barcelona, a saber :

    Asambleas de Dios (Pentecostales)
    Asambleas de Hermanos
    Adventistas
    Federación de Iglesias Evangélicas Independientes de Es -
       paña
    Iglesia Católica Romana
    Iglesia Española Reformada Episcopal
    Iglesia Evangélica Española
    Unión Evangélica Bautista Española

        El curso concluirá con una reunión en la que tomarán
parte todos los conferenciantes en una mesa redonda.

        Lamentamos no poder facilitar aún el programa detalla-
do con el orden correspondiente a cada mes, dado que tres
de los conferenciantes previstos no han confirmado todavía
su participación; esperamos poder hacerlo en el próximo número de la Circular, en el cual será convocada ya la primera de estas reuniones.

                        - 1 -

The Centro Ecuménico de Barcelona's Circular for July–September, 1965. In the list of churches to be represented by speakers
the following season, the Iglesia Católica Romana appears, as one
more denomination, in the fourth line from the bottom.

tende contraer matrimonio civil, tan pronto el impedimento que le afecta de ordenado "in sacris" -
sea dispensado en la legislación civil española.—

4.— que para contraer matrimonio civil no le al-
canza ningún otro impedimento. Y en conciencia con
sidera que el Derecho Natural prima sobre el Derecho legal en la institución matrimonial; y en tan-
to el impedimento de "ordenado in sacris" le prive
iniciar el expediente legal correspondiente, prome
te a la señorita Guillermina Crespo Vega, recibir-
la como esposa y asumir hacia ella todas las obli-
gaciones que el estado matrimonial implican ante -
Dios y la Sociedad. ———————————————

5.— Y en su día cumplir todos los requisitos y—
exigencias que la Ley determine, para que este matrimonio natural, adquiera la plena validez legal-
en España. ——————————————————

II.— La señorita Guillermina Crespo Vega manifies

The marriage affidavit signed by
Enrique García and Guillermina
Crespo in Madrid, a document
bereft of all legal significance under
Church-State marriage laws.
Paragraph 4 reads: "That [Enrique
García] holds in conscience that
natural right has primacy over legal
right in the institution of marriage;
and that, as long as the impediment
of a party 'ordained *in sacris*'
prevents him from undertaking the
proper legal action, he promises
Señorita Guillermina Crespa Vega
to receive her as his wife and to
assume toward her all the obligations that the married state implies
before God and society."

"De Wartburg," Dutch
"ex-priesterrefugium"
at No. 11 Boulevar, Velp,
near Arnhem

The new Iglesia de Jesús
(building in the center),
at No. 25 Calatrava Street
in the heart of Old Madrid

Alberto Araujo,
pastor of the Iglesia de Jesús,
preaching

real, President of the Spanish Commission at the Council, pointed out:

Religious liberty, which is a didactic evolution of modern human thought, regards individual liberty as indispensable, especially as it is [manifested] in that inner, most personal, transcendental sanctuary of the conscience. When man enters into a relationship with God, no human power should interfere. Therefore, as the Church wishes for herself the liberty to preach, and to manifest and exercise her Christian religion in order to fulfill her divine mandate, so also, recognizing the dignity of the human person, and the respect due the consciences of all men, the Church wishes that all men be free in the profession, exercise and promulgation [*anuncio*] of their respective religions.[8]

When the Council shelved the declaration and adjourned in silence in the autumn of 1964, the Church-State made haste to scotch all rumors that the Spanish Fathers had engineered the delay. Dr. Enrique Tarancón, Bishop of Oviedo, declared in *Ya* (November 25) that only twenty-five of the eighty Spanish Fathers had been in favor of postponing the declaration. In *ABC,* on December 6, the auxiliary Bishop of Seville, Monsignor Cirarda, echoed Dr. Tarancón's sentiments.

In the meantime the Government, convinced that religious freedom was a feather in its cap, issued a booklet entitled *The Spanish Hierarchy and Religious Liberty* which reprinted newspaper stories on the Council Fathers' pronouncements, the more liberal passages underlined in red. (The most positive statement it contains is that of Cardinal Quiroga Palacios, Archbishop of Santiago, who declared himself openly and without reservations for religious freedom over television on the 27th of November. In his statement, reprinted in *Ya* on December 2, the Cardinal even tossed in a positive and hopeful reference to birth control.) When, as the climax of this drive, Franco issued his call for religious liberty in his end-of-year address for 1964, the Government, again through the Office of Diplomatic Information, put together a collection of more than seventy foreign news stories which praised the *Caudillo*'s speech.

[8] *ABC,* November 11, 1964.

Cuadernos para el diálogo and *El ciervo,* the nation's two most liberal magazines, continued to press for a reformation of the Church and the transformation of Spanish society. (For samples of their contents, see Appendix, pp. 362–68.) Bold, independent, checked only by the strictures of Church-State censorship (*Cuadernos* especially has had its trouble in this connection), they must unfortunately be overlooked in a study of the Establishment's position vis-à-vis religious liberty. To put together their remarkable issues, *El ciervo* and *Cuadernos* draw on the finest writers, theologians, liturgists, lawyers, sociologists, economists and statisticians of the new Spain; to instruct the masses through its controlled press, the Establishment, like Boston's Cabots, speaks only to God.

Within the Establishment itself, however, there were men who teetered on the edge of a dialogue with the world. At the end of 1964 and beginning of 1965 a series of articles by Señor César Vaca appeared in *Ya* under such titles as "Truth and Right," "The Right to Be Wrong," "From Liberty of Conscience to Religious Liberty." Señor Vaca is a liberal shackled by orthodoxy. He defends man's right to worship according to his beliefs, he has words of caution for those who would condemn a Catholic who left the Church, but he toes the party line when it comes to the defense of divine revelation, i.e., the proscription of proselytism. On April 20, 1965, Señor Vaca stated that "Three stages of liberty are linked in a logical sequence: interior liberty of conscience; liberty to make religious practices external; and liberty to propagate one's convictions." He addresses himself to the last in the following terms:

In the measure to which religious beliefs may have a more important role to play in the social life [of the nation], public authority will find itself more involved with them, and will therefore intervene to regulate the use and consequences of the liberty granted to a group of citizens. Public authority is not concerned, in its own right, with religion; but its role as guardian of the common good compels it to adopt the pertinent measures to guarantee the religious freedom of all, and to avoid the harm [*daño*] which can follow from the above-mentioned use [of liberty].

Señor Vaca's is the classic statement on the defense of truth. As repeated *ad nauseam* in the Church-State press, the argument, and the lexicon, is always the same: when the propagation of non-truth can harm (*dañar*) those in the possession of truth, then the religious liberty of the latter has been infringed, and civil authority, as the guardian of the common good (itself based on the absolute value of truth), can and should interfere to safeguard the integrity of the supreme freedom granted, by divine mandate, to the possessors of truth.

It was this heady argument which, along with two other factors of great importance, brought on the debacle of 1965.

Most of the Council Fathers' positive statements on religious freedom in the autumn and winter of 1964 had been riddled with "buts," and the most significant "buts" concerned the safeguarding of truth. Inevitably, as the wave of reservations on "proselytism" grew, the tide of bigotry swelled again. Then, after the Council resumed on September 14, 1965, a new phenomenon sowed consternation in Spanish religious circles: the "distortion" of the Council by elements of the foreign press—or, in the language of the City of God, the intrusion of the secular upon the sacrosanct.

By that time Eternal Spain had shown her ashen face once more: between Franco's speech at the end of the previous year and the autumn session of the Council, the native hue of resolution had lost all its bloom. Ever conscious of how the Roman wind is blowing, the hierarchy had found inspiration and solace in Pope Paul's manifest support of the orthodox wing of the Church.

A documentary study of the three factors—the specter of proselytism, the encroachment of the outside world, and the consolation of Pope Paul—is imperative.

The first rings out like a leitmotiv in most of the statements on religious freedom made in 1964. During an interview in Rome on September 26 (published in *Ya* the following day), Monsignor Morcillo, Archbishop of Madrid, was asked, "But will they [the

Spanish Protestants] be permitted to indulge in proselytism?" His answer:

The proposed law, in accordance with the spirit of the Council and the principles of ecumenism, forbids non-Catholics to engage in proselytism and all kinds of proselytist propaganda, [i.e.,] that which uses coercive means, or [means] opposed to decency. In this sense, the law falls squarely within the orientations which doubtless will be forthcoming from the Council in the near future.

On October 1, in *Ya,* Dr. Cantero, Archbishop of Zaragoza, singled out the so-called "sociological" and "historical" reasons which make Spain a special case when it comes to applying the principles of religious liberty.

When a declaration results in trends which will affect more or less directly the historico-religious future of a country, the exigencies of the common good acquire an importance which warrants serious reflection, since these trends are not envisioned for abstract entities, but for actual men whose cultural level, history, tradition and mentality are different. Those countries which have been living within the spirit and norms of the Edict of Nantes differ in their conditions from others like Spain, where religious liberty and toleration were first discussed on the occasion of the 1869 Constitution.

By far the most important statement was issued by Dr. Alonso Muñoyerro, Vicar of the Armed Forces and Archbishop of Zion (a title which is not altogether irrelevant). In an interview conducted by journalist Luis de Armiñán for *ABC* and published on December 17, 1964, the prelate was sounded out on the dangerous new trends.

ARMIÑÁN: Though it is a very delicate point, I can hardly refrain from mentioning to Your Excellency that in Spain [people] dislike any discussion of the possibility that religious freedom may be established as a general norm.

MUÑOYERRO: I am aware of that dislike, and I understand it. The fear of an invasion of Protestant error in a nation where the immense majority of the citizens are Catholic justifies this dislike. But we must bear in mind that a reasonable liberty for those who profess a religion different from ours is not incompatible with a Catholic unity recognized by the State. An elaboration of this would fill a book. I can say that today, thanks be to God and our rulers, there can be no fear that the reasonable limits set to liberty will be exceeded. Liberty is understood in the sense that no one can be compelled to practice a religious creed. The private exercise [of a non-Catholic religion] is also recognized. Liberty begins to take on limitations when it comes to projection of the [non-Catholic] conscience in the social environment. I have already said that the rights of a human being are susceptible of limitation in the measure demanded by the rights of others, by public order and the common good. The Council will deal with this in its next session. Let Catholics be at peace: neither at the Council nor in Spain are there any signs that our Catholic unity is in danger of disappearing. It would be convenient, however, to be on guard always so that we may know how to defend it from what the future may bring.

ARMIÑÁN: Excellency, under the pretext of the Spanish Episcopate's alleged attitude in regards to religious liberty, the foreign press, or at least some newspapers, have felt free to defame Spain.

MUÑOYERRO: That is true, and not surprising. The Black Legend, far from having disappeared, has grown since our War of Liberation. What's more, certain organs of world opinion appear to suffer from a phobia towards Spain. It is not rash to believe that all this hubbub to establish almost absolute liberty obeys designs to make Catholic unity disappear from our Motherland. Take a look at what one of the most important English-language papers has to say, after mentioning the Counter Reformation, which it regards as having begun in Spain, the Inquisition, etc., etc. It reads like this: "If Pope Paul opens the doors of liberalism so wide that the winds of change can reach Spain, the Second Vatican Council will be credited with another great historic feat."

It is clear that the thoughts of these and other organs of opinion are fixed on Spain when they speak of religious liberty. This should be a lesson for Catholics in the entire world if they can read and if they do not want to be deceived, and much more so for Spanish Catholics. Those who wish to emulate the leaders of the all-out Liberty chorus should consider that they are undoing a heritage which comes to us from Saint Leander and Recaredo, a religious heritage which made us powerful before the Half-Moon, which defended Catholicism in other regions, which left its mark on the Council of Trent, which shaped, with the principles of the Gospel, the Hispanic nationality of

215

America and the Philippines, and which, finally, liberated Europe from Communism with the defeat Spain inflicted on it in our Crusade of Liberation.

These historical realities, and the actual reality of Spain, compel us to be circumspect and not to echo those champions of liberty for whom the success of the Second Vatican Council hangs upon the enslavement of the conscience of Catholic nations, among them Spain.

That was the end of the interview and the beginning of the newspaper neurosis. Three months later, as an echo to a series of articles by the Jesuit counterreform (one of them the story quoted on p. 235 on the Jews and deicide), *ABC* ran two editorials entitled "Storm Warning for Catholics." The first, dated February 10, began thus:

The press of the entire free world has devoted great space to the deliberations of the Second Vatican Council, especially during the last three sessions. In this [activity] certain newspapers of France, Germany and the United States have been prominent, [papers] which do not by any means belong in the all-purpose category known as the "Catholic press," but which are in the main large organs of information with an agnostic orientation, linked closely to some circles of Jewish capitalism.

This preamble introduced the Establishment's agitation over the reporting being done from the halls of St. Peter's. It was not the references to Spain, as such, that rankled: it was the general principle of treating the Council *as an assembly of men* deliberating in human fashion. The very thought of "disunity" at the Church assembly made the Spanish hierarchs pale. The very mention of factions, majorities and minorities, with its echo of "inorganic" systems, was deemed a scandal. The first "Storm Warning" states:

Without doubt the international commentaries take advantage of certain equivocal and confusing expressions such as "the climate of the Council." Applied to something as complex and rich in nuances, what does the word "climate" mean? . . . Does it refer to the number of speeches, the tone of voice in which each of them was made, the humor which enlivened them, the striking quality of some expressions, the boldness of the criteria? Who has measured, counted, valued all that?

216

Next day, the second "Storm Warning" was hoisted.

It is not too hazardous to affirm that one of the most typical of these [controversial issues at the Council] is that of birth control, that of the legality or illegality, before the Christian conscience, of using certain chemical or physical means for artificially controlling the conception of children. Because, as everyone knows, this moral preoccupation among Catholics has coincided with sensational abortion and birth control campaigns—as the ones unleashed in Japan and in the Island of Puerto Rico, under an administration associated with the United States; [furthermore] the entire phenomenon answers to the present population "boom" [sic] in the world. Without doubt, the consequences of the accelerated growth [in population] have been a series of economic difficulties, forced migrations, social alterations, etc., which constitute a great world problem. BUT IT IS NECESSARY, NAY URGENT, TO WARN CATHOLICS THAT THE COUNCIL HAS NOT PRONOUNCED ITSELF YET ON THIS DELICATE PROBLEM.

The Council had barely resumed before the Church-State press had the culprit at bay. In an editorial entitled "Distortions" on September 18, 1965, *Ya* referred to the gravely distorted vision of the Council offered in the "non-Catholic Western press."

An example of this distortion is offered by an informational article published a few days ago in the New York *Times*. For the author, the dynamics of Council deliberations are reduced, time and again, to the repeated clash between "the progressive majority of the world's prelates" and "the archconservative administration of the Roman Curia." The first, adds the article in its preposterous urge to synthesize, have the votes; the second controls the procedure and "the machinery of the Council."

As can be easily deduced, the author's vision makes him focus on the Council as if it were purely and simply a deliberative organ, completely similar to any national or supranational political entity. In addition to this, it is extremely curious to note the enthusiasm which the "more conservative" organs of the international press and politics feel for the Catholic sectors which they dub "progressive."

And there is more to it. The columns of the New York *Times* which we refer to add that the Pontifical interventions at the third session of the Council have modified the sense of certain Council documents or braked the spontaneous movement of the deliberations.

Such statements do not surprise us. We know the *political and ideological context* within which they fall. [*Italics mine.*] But we must rebut them. . . .

The Council's deliberations, *Ya* pointed out,

do not proceed along the normal channels and with the instruments of a simple political assembly restricted to concrete, temporal problems and ends.

The Council is, above all, [and] in its plenitude, the interpreter and guardian of the "depositum fidei" [deposit of faith] of Christian revelation, which it cannot modify, but rather maintain in its fullest integrity. At the Council, as in any other "corpus" or deliberating body, there are majorities and minorities. But the fact of a numerical majority in the purely deliberative phase is not, in itself, a convincing argument of fidelity to the "depositum fidei." It is not the number, but the weight of the arguments that is decisive.

The date of *Ya*'s editorial must be marked well. In September, 1965, there was hope that the Declaration would pass the Council only on Spain's terms: as a limited "civil" measure, without theological foundations and therefore susceptible to any modifications demanded by the defense of "objective truth." The inroads of the outside world—with its relative morality, its religious pluralism, its defense of human over "divine" values— were thus a serious cause for alarm.

Five days after the appearance of the editorial, on September 23, Archbishop Morcillo of Madrid joined the Council discussion on Schema XIII ("The Church and the Modern World"). His words recalled the days when Spain was the self-appointed "Third Power" in the sinful world of Communism and Capitalism:

The Schema, generally worthy of praise, should include the Church's judgment on the new ways of life introduced by technology and by so-called civilization or mass society. . . . The Schema errs in its exposition of family and economico-social life, since it considers these almost exclusively within the capitalist system in force in most countries. . . .[9]

[9] *Ecclesia*, October 2, 1965, p. 30. On September 27, Bishop Antonio Pildain of the Canary Islands stated that "The cause of there still being so

Archbishop Morcillo had put the entire issue in its proper frame. The question in those tense days before approval of the Declaration on Religious Liberty was clear: Would Spain continue to be the only nation in the possession of truth, and as such responsible only to God in matters of religious and political freedom, or would she join "so-called civilization"? There was no hiding the issue now. Her reluctant honeymoon with the Johannine concept of liberty was over: for almost a year she had been harking back to the eternal verities on which she stood, confident that no one would take them away from her.

And her confidence was not unfounded. There had been signs all along that the new Pope looked with favor on a deepening of the Church's traditional outlook. On January 21, 1965, *Ya* had published a dispatch from its Rome correspondent quoting a speech made by Pope Paul VI the previous morning to a general audience of "faithful and pilgrims," among them a group of students from the Madrid University Law School. Here, verbatim, is the bulk of the news story:

THE UNION OF CHRISTIANS CANNOT BE BOUGHT WITH THE MODIFICATION OF TRUTH

"For those who are only superficially acquainted with the problem of the reunion of all Christians," says the Pope, "its resolution seems very easy and to be acted upon quickly. But those who are acquainted with the historical, psychological and doctrinal points of the same are aware of the great and multiple difficulties it presents, to the point where some [people] despair of ever solving it, while others consider that it may need much time and a special, almost prodigious intervention from the grace of God."

After this premise, the Pope added that he did not want to speak of these difficulties, but to call [the audience's] attention "to a temptation which could easily present itself in good souls and originate a bad attitude." This temptation, added His Holiness Pope Paul VI,

---

much poverty in the world is liberal capitalism, which, by abusing [its] wealth, opens enormous chasms between men and nations. The Council should solemnly condemn liberal capitalism and take for its own Cardinal Suchard's motto: "No proletarians: all proprietors." *Ecclesia,* October 9, 1965, p. 34.

consists "in removing points of controversy, in hiding, weakening, modifying, annulling and if need be denying those teachings of the Catholic Church which are not accepted today by the separated brethren." "We say that this temptation is easy [to come by]," insisted His Holiness, "because it may seem an unimportant thing to minimize, to put aside certain truths, certain dogmas which are the object of controversy in order to reach without effort the desired union, whereas Christianity is a divine truth we cannot modify, but accept for our salvation."

THE INTENTION IS GOOD, THE METHOD IS NOT

But the importance of the Pope's words shines out, above all, when he goes on to warn that "this calculation does not deceive only those who are wanting in knowledge of theological matters, but it insinuates itself on those who are experts, and who are often seeking, in good faith, a way to clear the path for a meeting with the separated brethren. "The intention is good," states the Pope, "the method is not."

Elaborating on his admonition against a misunderstood Ecumenism, His Holiness Pope Paul VI affirmed that, "if Catholics wish to acknowledge the good elements within the heritage of the separated Christian churches and confessions, that is well. If they wish to present Catholic doctrine in its authentic aspects, doing without the debatable and nonessential points, that is well. . . . This is fraternal patience, this is good apologetics, this is charity at the service of truth.

A DISSERVICE

"But," added His Holiness Pope Paul VI, evidently alluding to those Catholic elements which grope blindly along the road to Ecumenism, "to attempt the removal of doctrinal truths by disauthorizing, underrating or forgetting affirmations which the Teaching Church has declared firm and definitive is a disservice to the cause of union, because it creates mistrust among the separated brethren [and] the suspicion that they are being deceived; or it engenders the proclamation of fallacious possibilities and introduces into the Church the fear that union will be sought at the price of truths that are not debatable; and [it] raises fears that the dialogue will result in an impairment of sincerity, of faithfulness and of truth."

As will be seen, Pope Paul's misgivings about "method" were a repetition of Archbishop Morcillo's objections on "methodology" at the first session of the Council in November, 1963. On the other hand, the Spanish Fathers' criticism of "positivist" and "naturalist" tendencies in Schema XIII had been scooped, so to speak, by the Pope himself during the previous summer. On July 7, 1965, as reported in next day's *Ya,* Paul made clear that *"aggiornamento"* was not what it was made out to be.

A spirit of criticism, of disobedience and of rebellion places in danger the sacrosanct norms of Christian life, of ecclesiastical behavior and of religious perfection.
There is talk of "liberalization," man is made the center of all worship, naturalist criteria are employed, the conscience is deprived of the light of moral principles, obedience is impugned, certain forms and tastes of action, of thought and of entertainment are accepted, [none of] which make the Christian the strong and austere disciple of Jesus Christ. . . .

The Schema passed with a gigantic rider on the duty of all men to "seek . . . and embrace" the "true Religion." In the world of capitalist or lay states the dictum is meaningless; in Spain, unfortunately, it will provide the basis for the Church-State definition of "the common good" and the police measures taken to defend it.

Nonetheless, error is not likely to disappear from the face of Spain. The small band of *evangélicos* who have so long symbolized it are dwarfed by the European influences at work in the country today. Intellectually, politically, socially and spiritually Spain is discovering "so-called civilization." The tensions and countertensions of this discovery (*evangélicos* themselves, as we shall see, offer strong opposition to some "modern" ideas) will determine the future configuration of Spanish society and its accession to the basic civil liberties of the West.

12

In the New York *Times* for November 29, 1965, Herbert L. Matthews spoke of an organization which is the most striking symbol of Spain's continued engagement in the Holy War for Christ: Opus Dei. Opus brandishes an olive branch, not a sword; it works through the peaceful and intelligent infiltration of all social structures, not through the clumsy suppression of "evil" or "erroneous" ideas; it smiles, it never frowns. But like all Catholic roads, Opus' *Camino* leads to Rome.

In its sophistication (the word, vulgar and hackneyed, is the only possible one) Opus stands in sharp contrast to another, more modest society also engaged in the Holy War—the Jesuit entity known as Fe Católica, from whose headquarters have come the most acrid statements against religious liberty in general and Protestantism in particular. Before turning to the positive achievements of the past few years in the field of ecumenism and interfaith contacts, a brief look at both Opus and Fe Católica is in order.

In his *Times* piece, Mr. Matthews states that Opus Dei, which was approved by the Holy See in 1950 as a "secular institute," had recently and "without any publicity" been downgraded to "an association of Catholic faithful." The information is correct. The reasons behind it remain secret. Word went about in 1965 that the Vatican, increasingly concerned over its inability to control Opus' vast finances, had removed it from the category of "secular institute" (the lay equivalent of religious order) and recast it as a private spiritual association. The counterrumor held that Opus, ever more concerned for its work in and through the laity, was de-emphasizing celibacy as a means of perfection and had changed labels accordingly. Both theories, as most referring to Opus, are conjecture.[1]

Whatever is official description of its status before Vatican authorities, Opus Dei ("The Work of God") is today one of the most powerful forces within the Catholic Church. In Spain, where it was born, it exudes a strong air of traditionalism-in-modern-dress. Mr. Matthews does not fall wide of the mark when he calls it "a sort of *haute bourgeoisie* of brains and money": there is a strong flavor of Victorian respectability behind Opus' sparkling bookstores, its plush residences and pious schools.

The best suggestion of its background is to be found in a biography of its founder written by one of the most distinguished Opus men in Spain: Florentino Pérez-Embid, Professor at the University of Madrid and a historian and writer of stature.

The author states that Josemaría Escrivá de Balaguer was born in 1902, in the town of Barbastro, "on the south side of the Aragonese Pyrenees." "The baptismal font where he was received into the faith," he writes, "was destroyed later, in the assault and looting of the church during the Marxist domination." [2] Young Josemaría studied law at the University of Zaragoza, entered the Seminary of San Carlos in the same city, and "received his clerical tonsure from Cardinal Soldevila, the famous Archbishop of that diocese who, a short time later, was assassinated by an anarchist." [3]

Ordained in 1925, Father Escrivá was soon in Madrid where, in 1928, he founded the Work of God. Professor Pérez-Embid ap-

---

[1] In actual fact, Opus members who aspire to the highest degree of perfection still take all three monastic vows and live a life of "apostolic celibacy" in Opus residences. They remain "in the world," however, and wear no clerical garb.

[2] Florentino Pérez-Embid, ed., *Forjadores del mundo contemporáneo* (Barcelona: Editorial Planeta, 2d. ed., 1963), IV, 618.

[3] *Ibid.*, p. 619.

pends a vivid description of the milieu in which the young priest and his newly founded society took their first apostolic steps:

In the suburbs of Madrid, particularly in the working-class quarters, there were growing signs of Marxist revolutionary ferment, of Masonic influence and hatred towards the Church.[4]

In this atmosphere Opus' first Students' Residence opened in 1934. It was destroyed shortly thereafter "when the Marxist militia attacked the nearby *cuartel de la Montaña*. They were tragic hours," adds Pérez-Embid, "the beginning of a series of hazardous maneuvers under the Communist persecution." [5] (Among the most hazardous was Father Escrivá's escape to Andorra with a small band of Opus followers, "on foot, in the winter nights, across the Rialp mountains." [6] Today one of Opus' largest publishing houses bears the name "Rialp.")

The Crusade over, Opus began its apostolic task anew. According to Professor Pérez-Embid it was instrumental in establishing the Colegio Mayor system in its present modality (*colegios mayores* are the student residences attached to all Spanish universities)—a task which,

as we have seen, was the continuation of the mission it began before the War, in the midst of the adverse environment [created] by the Republic's legislation, which persecuted the liberty of the Church and of Catholics, particularly in the field of education. [Opus] also took part in the creation of new institutions of scientific research and in the doctrinal and moral renewal of many University Departments and Schools, of technical professions, of journalism and similar activities, with the attendant influence on the rebirth of Catholic science in Spain.[7]

In 1946 Monsignor Escrivá moved to Rome and in 1947 the Holy See approved the Work of God as a model institution of its kind: *"clare patuit Opus Dei prae se ferre exemplar germani Instituti Secularis,"* read Rome's document ("it was patent that Opus Dei was the model among secular institutes").[8] Final approval came, as Mr. Matthews correctly states, in 1950.

[4] *Ibid.*
[5] *Ibid.,* p. 620.
[6] *Ibid.*
[7] *Ibid.,* p. 621.
[8] *Ibid.,* p. 623.

Born of reaction, nourished by the spiritual backlash of the Church-State, Opus grew and prospered. "Its aim," writes Pérez-Embid, "can be synthesized in a brief formula: to place Christ at the head of all human activities." [9] Its machinery can be described just as succinctly: Opus' gears are oiled by the ascetic practices, the doctrines and the dogmas of the traditional Church. And its *modus operandi* is simple infiltration.

Opus' transformation into an "Association of Faithful" in 1965 did not subtract one cubit from its awesome stature. In thirty-nine years the little band of apostles who crossed into Andorra has grown into a dynamic phalanx of God's Workers throughout the world. Opus does not give out statistics, but Professor Pérez-Embid notes that it now has members of "one hundred and four nationalities in five continents." [10] Father Escrivá's volume of ascetic counsel, *Camino* ("The Road" or "The Way"), has been translated into nine languages; eleven more foreign versions are now under preparation.

The ghostly but formidable presence of Opus Dei in modern Spanish society has been adequately described by Mr. Matthews:

Almost all its work is done by members acting as individuals, so that the association as such can disclaim direct involvement. The Government ministries are believed to be honeycombed with members and *simpatizantes* (English-speaking Spaniards call them fellow travelers).

A great many of the top banking and businessmen are Opus Dei. So are many high military officers. So are the rectors of some major Spanish universities and a great many professors. Opus Dei has its own university in Pamplona, which is rated as far and away the best in the country. They are always seeking men high up in the professions. Many Monarchists belong to Opus Dei, which is reputed to favor Don Juan's son, Prince Juan Carlos, for the throne. There is a women's branch which does a great deal of worthy work in social fields. Opus Dei controls newspapers, magazines, radio stations, movies and advertising agencies.

It is forward-looking in economics and finance and paternalistic in social fields. Politically it is very conservative—and this is what many Spaniards consider its dangerous side—it is linked to the Church and

[9] *Ibid.*, p. 624.
[10] *Ibid.*

firmly opposes separation of Church and State or the weakening of the Church's powerful role in education.

A good example of an Opus-inspired initiative in the publishing field is the four-volume collection of biographies entitled *Hewers of the Contemporary World* (*Forjadores del mundo contemporáneo*). Edited by Professor Pérez-Embid—who also contributed the piece on Father Escrivá we have quoted above—the books contain almost two hundred and fifty brief lives. In the fourth volume, along with the founder of Opus Dei, the biographies range from Diaghilev to St. Thérèse of Lisieux, Chaplin to Frank Lloyd Wright, Kafka to Heidegger. There are thoroughly balanced and well-written pieces on a variety of scientists, musicians, artists and writers. But when religion or politics rears its head, so does the Spanish Right.

Professor Pérez-Embid entrusted Señor Pedro Gómez Aparicio, Professor at the Official School of Journalism and President of the Madrid Press Association, with the biographies of Hitler and Mussolini. Here are the words Señor Gómez Aparicio uses to describe the child Adolf as he plays by his home, "in the small Austrian town of Braunau, by the river Inn, on the Bavarian border."

The frontier did not ever constitute a barrier to his childish pranks: on both sides the landscape was the same, the language the same, the customs and mentality the same, the children with whom he played the same. . . . What meaning did [the frontier] have, then . . . ? The primary impressions which acted on the soul of that child would open deep and indelible furrows in the soul of the man, where they would germinate into a personal concept of Fatherland and Nation: the Nation and the Fatherland are not limited by frontiers, but are defined as an identity of spirit, of race, language and purpose.[11]

With this air of patient understanding Señor Gómez Aparicio expounds Hitler's entire life—his successes, his mistakes, his glory, his ultimate failure. In Vienna, as a young man, Adolf reacts with distaste to the society around him:

[11] *Ibid.*, p. 527.

He searched for the reasons for that degraded situation [i.e., the state of Viennese society] and thought he found them in the monstrous "promiscuity of peoples" of the Austro-Hungarian Empire, in the corruption of social and political customs introduced by Judaism into the nation in order to dominate it, in the lack of an effective "national" conscience which would propel and perfect all kinds of solidarities. And he thought that the remedy could lie with an exaltation of Germanism which would unify, purify, and galvanize the German nationality, make it the master of its own destinies and capable of a Universal enterprise.[12]

This mention of Judaism, along with a statement (p. 530) on the racial standards for German citizenship put forth in 1920, are, curiously, the only references to Jewry in the 13-page sketch. The Nazi measures taken to "unify" and "purify" the German nationality merit not the slightest mention in this biography of the German leader. One reaches its end to find a conclusion which strains one's credulity even further:

Had he triumphed, Hitler would have been a universal hero; in defeat, he became in the eyes of many one of the greatest criminals in History. A man of immense achievements and unspeakable errors, Hitler was probably neither a villain nor a madman: perhaps it would be fairer to say that he betrayed his own destiny, [that] through tactical errors or through the intrusion of unforeseen events which he could not or did not know how to cope with, he brought down over Europe the very tempest for which he had wanted to be the lightning rod.[13]

Mussolini's biography runs along the same lines. It ends with a quote from Signora Rachele, Il Duce's widow: "I always thought whoever killed Benito could not have looked him in the eye. If he had done so, I am sure he would have dropped the weapon." Señor Gómez Aparicio ends:

He would have dropped it had he been a man.
But he was only a Communist.[14]

Though no Spanish *evangélico* belongs to Opus, the Work of God has no bias against non-Catholics; indeed, it numbers both Protestants and Jews among its "co-operators" abroad. Fe Cató-

[12] *Ibid.*, p. 528. [13] *Ibid.*, p. 539. [14] *Ibid.*, p. 434.

227

lica, on the other hand, constitutes the very heart of the age-old battle against the "evil" of Protestantism. It is a Jesuit organization, directed by a Jesuit and with headquarters in a Jesuit house.

I called on its director, Father Sánchez de León, at No. 1 Maldonado Street, Madrid, the organization's headquarters. When I told him that I was writing a book on Spanish Protestantism, Father Sánchez de León took a deep breath, cast down his eyes and said, very evenly: "You must know that Spanish Protestants are not like Protestants abroad. They are uncultured and lewd [*deshonestos*]. In Germany, in England, there can be dialogue. Not in Spain."

For a few seconds I was back in Puertollano, hearing—in that same flat, final tone of voice which laid all arguments to rest—that all Protestants were Communists. It did not seem politic, just yet, to counter with the information that I had been in contact with Spanish Protestants—cultured and uncultured—for a year and a half. I asked Father Sánchez de León if, in view of the new Council directives, his organization had taken any new stand on the matter of religious liberty.

He answered affirmatively. Fe Católica was now engaged in the "formation" and "education" of Catholics so they could resist the onslaught of proselytist propaganda, such as that engaged in by Jehovah's Witnesses.

"But Jehovah's Witnesses are not Protestants," I said.

"They are Protestants."

"Protestants don't consider them thus."

"It makes no difference how they consider them," he answered with a fixed smile. "They work from the same principles of the free interpretation [of Scripture]."

"But Protestants have repudiated them. Here and abroad."

"And I tell you that that repudiation is worthless. They stand on the principle of free interpretation, and therefore they are Protestants."

Mention of the Bible made me recall the Council once more, and the new, more liberal pronouncement on Scripture among both Catholics and Protestants. I mentioned the American Presbyterians' new confession of faith, which regarded the Bible as a fallible, human account containing an ethical message, and the Council directives which echoed the view of Scripture as a document of its time. "The Council has not said that," Fray Sánchez de León said sternly.

I did not have the Council text at hand—his admonition was so sharp, in fact, that I was inclined to believe he was right and I had misread the Schema. I asked if he thought there would be a new outlook on inflexible dogma ("It must be inflexible," he said), or an evolution towards a more open interpretation of doctrines, somewhat like Protestantism's.

"But Protestants have dogmas too," he replied.

"I think not, Father."

"Look up the articles of belief drawn up by the World Council of Churches. It's all there."

I said that within the Protestant denominations there was a wide gamut of belief. As an example I mentioned Bishop Pike of the American Episcopalian Church and his challenge of the Virgin Birth.

"Yes, there is that tendency," he agreed, adding that it existed among the Anglicans too. Then there was a pause. "Have you heard of the Wolfenden business?" he asked.

For a moment I was at a complete loss. Then I wondered, aloud, if he meant the Wolfenden report on homosexuality.

"Exactly. That is what happens when you have no dogma."

Our discussion veered to the Report, to the concept of disease and the concept of vice, to public morality and finally to psychopathic behavior. We had gone from Protestantism to Krafft-Ebing in less than twenty minutes.

I asked again about Fe Católica, its history and aims.

The organization was founded in 1950, said Father Sánchez de León, to combat Protestant propaganda in the country. "Indecent propaganda, like the one passed by the Jehovah's Witnesses. There was a little girl in Vallecas [a working-class suburb of Madrid] saying the Virgin was not a virgin, that Jesus had brothers and sisters."

"I've heard of that problem before," I said. "I believe it's a semantic difficulty—"

"I can show you the Scriptural passage and explain it to you," he offered.

I told him I was acquainted with the controversy over the word "brethren" as used in the New Testament. "But why couldn't Mary have had children in a normal way after the birth of Jesus?" I asked.

"Because Scripture says that she didn't." Father Sánchez de León rose and fetched a copy of the Bible from a nearby desk. "Let us read Luke's account—he is the only non-Semite." He read me Luke 1:28–35 and explained that, having conceived Christ in a miraculous way Mary was not to conceive in a human way afterwards.

"But it is all the same to me," I told him, "whether or not Mary had more children after Christ."

"It is not to me," he said very vehemently, but smiling still.

Our interview concluded with a brief mention of the dogma of the Immaculate Conception—one of the tenets whose contradiction may land a Protestant in jail. I had read Jean Guitton's admirable, and most orthodox, book *The Virgin Mary* (banned years ago by the late Cardinal Segura). In its exposition of the various Marian dogmas it makes reference to St. Thomas' and St. Bernard's objections to the Immaculate Conception. The latter held Mary couldn't have been Immaculate because she was born in the normal, concupiscent way of ordinary sex. I couldn't, however, recall Aquinas' objection.

The difficulty, explained Father Sánchez de León, revolved in all cases around the principle of Mary's having to be redeemed just like anyone else. She did have to be redeemed. One could explain the seeming contradiction thus: "People can be rescued from jail, or they can be pardoned from going there."

I thought it was a reasonable simile to illustrate the nature of Mary's sinlessness, and I so told him. Then we parted and I went home to study the literature on Fe Católica which he had given me on the way out.

The very mention of Fe Católica makes Spanish Protestants pale: upon its establishment in 1950 the organization took on, singlehandedly, the task of providing the Spanish police with the material for the prosecution of "proselytism."

As told in one of its pamphlets, the organization was born in 1950 as Defensio Fidei ("Defense of the Faith"). "A group of young university students, sodalists of Our Lady, had been deeply impressed by the propaganda of the sects [i.e., the Protestants]. In this youthful environment was born the idea of repulsing the attack against the Faith of the Church among God's poor people." According to another leaflet, the students brought their aspirations to their spiritual director, Father Sánchez de León, S.J. "Their initial purpose was to oppose the false Protestant ideas which, based on an erroneous interpretation of Biblical texts, tried to insinuate themselves into their environment. And for the moment, they thought of making available to the competent authorities [i.e., the police] all possible information in this field, and to collaborate with them in any initiative taken under the existing legislation, soon to be made official through the Concordat."

For nearly ten years, Fe Católica kept the Spanish police archives on all Protestant activities in Spain—in other words, during that time the Society of Jesus was an arm of the Spanish F.B.I. The police acted on the evidence furnished by Fe Católica; Fe Católica in turn kept the criminal dossiers on all "proselytists" and their activities in the country.

The police files have been removed from No. 1 Maldonado Street, but a reminder of the organization's late mission occasionally comes up in its press campaigns. On July 4, 1964, Father Francisco Peiró, S.J., one of its more fierce collaborators, recalled some statistics in *ABC*. In an article entitled "Spanish Protestantism, an Artificial Problem" (and illustrated with pictures of a Jesuit church burning during the anarchical thirties) Father Peiró states: "According to the Offices of Fe Católica, a center of religious information and orientation located at No. 1 Maldonado [Street], there are 250 Protestant chapels in Spain, with some 150 pastors or ministers for the twenty or thirty thousand Protestants who live here. That is to say, there is a church for each 150 individuals and a minister for each 200 affiliates. . . ."

But Fe Católica's offensive against religious liberty in the press

231

represents only half of its work. The other part consists in (1) a direct-mail operation through which 100,000 Spaniards receive an intensive course on the Bible and its use in the refutation of Protestant doctrines, and (2) the recruitment and mobilization of shock troops known as "Christ's Witnesses."

It was, of course, inevitable: The Witnesses Fe Católica so despises, and in whose name it fights the entire malediction of Protestantism, have in turn inspired the counterattack. Christ's men are out to outrun Jehovah's and, given the nature and zeal of their organization, the former may yet win the race.

According to a descriptive pamphlet, *Los testigos de Cristo* are divided into four categories:

CHRIST'S WITNESSES—TRAINED

When a layman, in the priest's opinion, is sufficiently trained, he is given a locale where he may operate—the crypt of a church, a comfortable sitting room in any center, etc. Through a well-directed propaganda, efforts are made to attract an audience for him.

This group of men and women of all social conditions [i.e., the audience which has been attracted] meets for one hour on a given day of the week. The result is a true Cenacle, enlivened by the Word of Christ. . . .

CHRIST'S WITNESSES—AUXILIARIES

Their role [Auxiliaries work in conjunction with Trained Witnesses] is to teach the handling of the Bible, to enter in direct contact with each person in the group, to take their addresses, to try to be helpful; in a word, to fraternize with all and work towards the formation of a brotherly atmosphere. . . .

CHRIST'S WITNESSES—SPECIALISTS

are those who give instruction on the controversies against Catholicism which are propagated by the more extremist sects. There will often be Catholic families pursued by heterodox propaganda and in need of help. To their aid come the Witnesses, whom we familiarly call the "Firemen." After their first appearance, when they solve the controversies against the Faith, comes the visit of the normal Witnesses of Christ, Trained or Readers, who carry out, without controversy, the exposition of Catholic truth using our habitual [teaching] methods. . . .

CHRIST'S WITNESSES—READERS

Experience has amply proved the efficacy of this plan. These Witnesses act only in small familiar groups, in private homes. The essential thing is that Christ's Word be actualized, no matter how elemental the form in which it appears; and that it be so [actualized] by a living member of the Mystical Body of Christ before other brethren who are weak in their Faith or who do not know the Mystery of the Kingdom. . . .

The Witnesses' foot soldiers are covered by the heavy guns of Fe Católica's Jesuit collaborators. Between 1964 and 1965, no less than seven articles inveighing against religious liberty appeared in *ABC,* all by-lined by colleagues of Father Sánchez de León. Coming at the height of the Council, the Jesuits' stories were the dismal counterpoint to a press coverage which, as we have noted, tried to present the issue of freedom of worship in a positive light.

Fe Católica's campaign reached its own nadir on October 29, 1964, when Father E. Guerrero, S.J., gave out with a sexual simile which may have no equal in the history of the modern world. Spaniards opened their most distinguished newspaper that morning to find a large photograph of Pope John XXIII and to read:

Addressing Catholic nations with non-Catholic minorities, they [Popes Pius XII and John XXIII] exhorted their rulers to keep watch over Catholic unity, and taught them that tolerance of dissidents could be permitted in order to prevent greater evils. They did not proclaim the rights of these [dissidents], but those of the true religion and of the country to, on the one hand, keep its Catholic religious unity, and, on the other, to be rid of evils which would no longer be tolerated. . . . Just as they never spoke of the rights of citizens to frequent houses of prostitution, but of the convenience of tolerating them at times in order to prevent greater disorders against decency.

Father Francisco Peiró had already played on the sexual theme on June 27 of the same year. On that occasion the mud was slung against Protestant women in the course of a tirade on proselytism. To get the full impact of Father Peiró's reasoning one must read the paragraph from the beginning:

It is useless to argue that proselytism would be forbidden, as stated in an article published in *America,* a magazine of the Jesuit Fathers of

233

the United States and Canada, on August 24, 1963, and signed by a person who knows the ground he's treading on. [*The author was Spanish Foreign Minister Castiella.*] Because this prohibition can be impaired if, as the very article implies and as some Spanish magazines have stated, the non-Catholic associations, once legally registered, can celebrate their meetings in previously approved places of worship. Because then they would not need to carry on their proselytism out in the streets. Although naturally they will continue to do so, as they always have. Only a few days ago some señoritas (pardon me for calling them that) approached three priests who were walking towards their home, which is an authorized and recognized College in the outskirts of Madrid, and, without the slightest apology, handed them Protestant propaganda.

On April 6, 1965, Father Guerrero took up the cudgel again with an article entitled "A Just and Well Understood Religious Liberty," illustrated with a full-page photograph of a mitered Pope Paul VI. The Jesuit sought to warn *ABC* readers against a false interpretation of the Schema on religious freedom, which the Council still had on its agenda:

But, "salve meliori judicio," I understand that an egalitarian statute for all religions in a given country, or in the entire world, should be considered by all Catholics who are in communion with the teachings of the Popes and oriented towards a wholesome theology as a rule of tolerance: the "permission" [*sic*] of an evil, the evil of the profession of false religions, for there is only one true one: the Catholic; the "concession" to the dissident of the right not to be molested in the profession of his false belief, but not the recognition of an objective natural right, much less a supernatural one, which he may have to profess [*sic*] and diffuse his religious errors. Hence such an egalitarian statute could not be correctly called a statute of liberty, but of tolerance. There is no true right to error and evil and, where no right exists, neither can liberty, as the legal recognition thereof.

One last text is germane. It is also Father Guerrero's, and it appeared in *ABC* on February 6, 1965, under the title "Council Directives." "We are often exhorted," it begins, "to follow Council Directives; but many people understand as such the opinions aired by participants during the Council debates, as well as everything written about them in a certain Press favorable to the progressive movement." Father Guerrero zeroes in on his target, in his tortuous style, only two paragraphs later:

Thus, according to the Press, one prelate held that the Jews could not have been deicides since, as God could not die, they could not have slain him. And another one asserted that, since the Jews did not know Jesus Christ was God, but took him for a mere man—a bad man, an impostor, as one possessed, and a blasphemer—they couldn't have committed the sin of deicide by killing him. Forgetting that the Incarnate Word died on the cross because of the Sanhedrin and the populace it manipulated, and that if they [the Jews] did not acknowledge him as God and the Son of God, the divine Legate and the Messiah, it was through their own fault, as the Lord himself affirmed, and as Saint Peter and Saint Paul taught and as the Church has always reiterated.

Whither the Society of Jesus? To those who have known Jesuits abroad, the existence of priests such as Fathers Sánchez de León, Guerrero and Peiró comes as something of a shock. But fortunately "anti-Spain" functions in the Society too: there are a few men in Ignatius' ranks whose hearts and minds are attuned to the "unspiritual" world beyond the Pyrenees.

The consensus of those who know the Order well is that liberal Jesuits tend to cluster in Barcelona, while the *integristas* function in Madrid and the North. Yet every rule has its exception: the Madrid Province counts among its priests Father José María de Llanos, a man whose wide-open Christianity has manifested itself in fraternal contacts with Protestants, whose articles in *El ciervo* have been one of the most luminous pages of Spanish ecumenism, and whose pastoral work in one of Madrid's worst slums is known throughout the country. It is only one short step from him to Father Josep Cardus, whom I met in Barcelona.

Reader, you have a delicate book in your hands. A Catholic priest presents it to you in faith, hope and love. Do not be surprised.

Its author, Juan Estruch, a Christian of the Reformed Episcopalian Church of Barcelona, has experienced it in grief, in expectation, in hope, in prayer, in tears—before setting it down in writing.

You stand informed, then. The author is a pious Protestant. I am a Catholic priest. We are friends, good friends. I tell you this immediately, though you will soon discover it for yourself. Besides, I have no reason to hide it. Our friendship is of some years' standing. It has been progressive, dynamic, intense. Both of us consider it a blessing from God. . . .

In the autumn of 1965, in Cataluña, I met the secular priest who wrote the words quoted above and the author of the book to which they refer. The priest is Father Josep Cardus; the author is twenty-two-year-old Juan Estruch. I had the pleasure of talking with them and with Heide Axmacher, Estruch's German fiancée, and Pastor José Luis Lana (also an Episcopalian) at Barcelona's Ecumenical Center, a small office on the top floor of 32–34 Via Layetana.

Coming from Castile, where ecumenism is the exotic hobby of a few bold "progressives," the existence and the atmosphere of the Barcelona institution were a healthy shock. Five minutes after the introductions I was fully conscious that Father Cardus was bound to the Protestants—and they to him—in something that went far beyond public relations. There was unmistakable affection in the air.

"Do the Church authorities know about your organization?" I asked Father Cardus.

"They know it exists," he answered. "That's about all."

I was under the impression that the Center had come into being in the wake of the great thaw effected by Pope John's warmth. Estruch set me right. "The first meetings took place twelve or fourteen years ago," he said. "A few Catholics and Protestants, of the clergy and laity both, decided to get together for discussions. Four years or so ago the Center began to grow. Now we have a meeting once a month. We pick a topic for discussion for an entire season—for example, 'Christian Confessions and Unity'—and a member of each faith talks about it each month. Then there are special meetings for the Center's directors, the editors of the Circular, etc."

He brought me the latest copy of the Circular, which bore the date July–September, 1965. It was a small mimeographed booklet of twenty-four pages with a variety of articles and Ecumenical news. On page two it listed Catholic-Protestant lectures in Barcelona and vicinity, including one given before thirty Salesian priests by "J. Estruch, protestante," and "J. Desumbila, católico"; Señor Desumbila is a layman who has distinguished himself in interfaith work in Cataluña and who is the author of *El ecumenismo en España,* the first authoritative work on the subject ever written by a Spaniard. On page three the Circular transcribed a letter sent by a Catholic layman—a member of the Center—to Radio Nacional de España complaining of its "truly offensive" treatment of Luther in a cultural program. On page four appeared an announcement of a Liturgical Congress at the Benedictine Abbey of Montserrat, followed by "Notes" for its "Ecumenical Evaluation." On page seven was printed a report on Colombian Catholicism by a Catalan priest—and thus brief items and longer articles succeeded each other until page twenty-four, which was taken up by the last section of an interfaith bibliography.

This small but unusual booklet goes to a mailing list of five hundred—two hundred and fifty copies in Spanish, two hundred and fifty in Catalan.

In answer to my question, Father Cardus and Pastor Lana told me the Center was indeed unique. It is the only interconfessional association in Spain, they explained; the Pope John XXIII Institute of the Pontifical University of Salamanca, a similar body, is run strictly by Catholics. (Unfortunately I had no time to visit this organization, whose reputation for open, fraternal dialogue is growing; the Salamanca Institute admits Protestants as members and, in 1965, was host to the Pax Romana Congress on Religious Liberty.) As for sponsorship, the Barcelona Center owes much of its support to the Episcopalian and evangelical churches (Iglesia Reformada Española and Iglesia Evangélica Española), the most ecumenical-minded of Spanish Protestant denominations.

When speaking of ecumenism among Spanish Protestants one can, however, speak only of bitter division. In general terms, there are two camps: on one side stands the Episcopalian-I.E.E. faction, open to dialogue, intellectually conditioned and more or less willing to forgive and forget the injuries of Spanish Catholics; on the other loom the so-called "Fundamentalist" denominations —Baptists, Plymouth Brethren, Adventists and Pentecostals— whose orientation is basically negative where interfaith contacts are concerned. Within this spectrum, further nuances obtain. Episcopalians of "the Estruch persuasion," as a learned Protestant abroad has described them, seek union with Catholicism on a theological, quasi-mystical plane, minimizing the legal and traditional barriers that separate the two faiths. In his book, *Ecumenism, A Spiritual Attitude: Contribution and Witness of a Spanish Protestant,* Estruch takes his stand for a mystical, truly evangelical union. Here is a beautiful and thoroughly idealistic passage:

At the same time, the twentieth century has witnessed the renewal of the Church's vision of herself as a *tent* rather than a *temple.* Christ came to the world and became incarnate; St. John says that "he became flesh, *and set up his tent among us"* (John 1:14). Although most versions of the New Testament translate the passage as "he dwelt," or "resided among us," the original text makes use of a metaphor which had profound significance to a nation acquainted with the nomadic life and its long marches across the desert. But this expression of a *tent* set up among men also makes sense among us today. For the Church is a nation on pilgrimage . . . on its way to Christ, [a nation] which cannot stop to raise permanent *temples,* but only *tents* that are easy to move and carry. This is the sense of the Church's pilgrimage . . . of her members' expectation of the coming of Christ; and this is a possible explanation of her *renewal.*[15]

While Estruch does make mention of the walls of prejudice and misunderstanding which plague Spanish Catholics where Protestants are concerned, he looks forward to a rapprochement through mutual "renewal" and good faith. Many of his fellow Protestants in the two "ecumenical" churches take exception to his idealism. His desire to meet the Catholic Church on the plane of spiritual renewal, they feel, crashes against the realities of the Spanish situa-

[15] Juan Estruch, *Ecumenismo, actitud espiritual: aportación y testimonio de un protestante español* (Barcelona: Editorial Nova Terra, 1965), p. 27.

tion. In their view, an ecumenical dialogue such as Germany's or the United States' is impossible in a nation where one party to the conversation stands theologically condemned before he opens his mouth. Their moderate stand, to give it its just name, consists in a firm, unflinching battle for the emancipation of Protestant citizens and ideas without excluding, at any moment, those personal and fraternal contacts which will bring the two faiths together in mutual love and forbearance. The moderates are mostly within the Iglesia Evangélica Española (I.E.E.), a body which has inherited the spirituality of the Lutherans, Methodists and Presbyterians which united to form it.

Nonetheless, it is difficult not to admire Estruch's forward-looking spirit. His thought is perfectly attuned to those European currents which have indeed brought the two faiths closer together since the end of World War II. Estruch will build on the foundations his elders are raising; and he himself is lending a hand with the trowel. In 1967 he will complete his doctoral thesis at the University of Barcelona, a study of Spanish Protestantism with special reference to that city. It will be the first detailed sociological study on the subject, based mostly on personal interviews with *evangélicos* of the area. After completing his studies—interrupted by his military service in 1966—Juan and Heide (who is from Cologne) will register at Louvain for further work on Religious Sociology.

Below the Episcopalians and the I.E.E., very little Protestant-Catholic contact is possible in Spain. The more Fundamentalist the church, the greater its aversion to dialogue. Estruch smiles when he tells how the Fundamentalists stay away from the Center in droves and criticize its Protestant members as *"los sectarios ecuménicos"* ("the ecumenical sectarians"). He told me how, during the Protestant Congress in Madrid in 1965, one man accused members of the Center of "running blithely after the so-called Catholic brethren when they should have been attending their own prayer meetings." "When I told this to one of the Catholic priests who were there as observers," says Estruch, "he said that was exactly what had happened with him; when we invited him to the Congress he dropped the Nocturnal Adoration and came running." [16]

With few exceptions, Fundamentalists are heirs to centuries of bitterness compounded by the exigencies of Protestant triumphalism—a peculiar form of religious pride quite similar, if not sister, to the Catholics' worship of truth. "I call them the Protestant *integristas,*" a young minister of the I.E.E. said to me on one occasion when we were discussing the peculiar dogmaticism of some Fundamentalists. A few days later a layman agreed. "Fundamentalism and integrism are cousins—extremes touch, you know," said Enrique Miret Magdalena, the Catholic layman who is single-handedly propelling the vindication of Protestants in the Spanish ambiance.

And surely, both *integristas* and Fundamentalists start from the same premises and reach the same conclusion: truth is a permanent temple where each resides (to echo young Estruch), not a tent to knock down and carry on the Christian trek.

A prime example of evangelical self-righteousness is to be found in *Cuadernos de Orientación Bíblica* (No. 2, 1964), organ of the Spanish Evangelical Alliance. This issue of the magazine prints (pp. 19–20) extracts from a motion "voted by the Synod of the French Reformed Church at Orthez in 1963, on the theme "Proselytism and Evangelization"":

Evangelization is the transition from joy discovered to joy shared; it has always impelled the Christian towards humility. It is not carried on through self-assertion, but rather in an open dialogue in which the Christian has as much to give as to receive.

It also opposes proselytism based on a spirit of conquest and rigid truth to which man must submit while ignoring the existence of his fellow man as a free and original person.

The French manifesto is an admirable definition of open Christianity. It is followed, in the Spanish magazine, by the crushing "reply" of a triumphalist which reads, in part, as follows:

[16] The best report on this important Congress was published by *Herder Correspondence,* the German Catholic periodical. It is included in the Appendix. Dutch television also took films of the *evangélicos'* meetings, which took place in several Madrid churches.

Evangelization definitely implies a well-defined Gospel. Though this be called "rigid" truth, though it be said that man must bow before it, we cannot elude the fact that Scriptures proclaim the *"exigencies"* of the Gospel and that, from the very beginning, Christian evangelization stressed the absolutely unique and decisive nature of the name of Jesus (Acts 4:12).

Let us recognize that this is where we come up against the "stumbling stone" (Acts 4:11). We must face the truth that the Gospel does not only reconcile; it also divides. Let us remember that our forefathers in the faith, whose heirs we are, refused to soften the edge of their message by substituting a vague religiosity.

The reply was contributed by Leighton Ford, Billy Graham's brother-in-law and assistant. From *L'Illustré Protestant* the text evidently passed to *Pour la verité,* organ of the Federation of Free Evangelical Churches of France, from which the Spaniards in turn took it.

Such well-traveled notions could well be the undoing of all ecumenical progress, especially in Spain where they crash against another solid wall of "truth." Fortunately the tide has turned. In the wake of Pope John's revolutionary pontificate, men of good will have let down their personal—if not their theological —barriers and begun to know each other by name and face.

The meeting, in Spain, has been poignant and dramatic.

When I say dramatic I think of the inside of the I.E.E. Church at Noviciado Street in Madrid on the opening of the Church Unity Octave for 1965. I arrived ten minutes before the service was due to start and for a moment I stood at the door, aghast. Finally I ventured down the middle corridor and found a small place at the end of a pew near the back. By five to eight there was a double row of standees along the center aisle and a solid wall of people, three or four deep, at the rear of the Church.

The remarkable thing was that the press had given no advance word of the Octave. The Sunday before, at Mass, I had heard the announcement of a "special time of prayer" for the cause of ecumenism. It was, said the Carmelite priest in the church by my house, "an Octave for the union of Chr— Catholics." The good Father's slip of the tongue stayed with me; I wondered if he had "Catholics" in the printed text and unwittingly started to say "Christians," or whether he had "Christians" in the text and knowingly substituted "Catholics." At any rate his semantic distinction was to strike me later as the epitome of the Church's feelings in the matter. The Octave was for Catholics, not for "Christians": in its horror of any personal contact between the faithful and the *evangélicos,* the Church did not allow a single word of the interfaith services to appear in print until they were over. I found out about them through a Protestant friend; the other Catholics, I gathered, had word through a private grapevine.

For somehow, there they were—a solid phalanx of Spanish Catholics—priests, nuns, businessmen and black-mantillaed ladies—rubbing shoulders with Protestants whose faces I remembered from various evangelical churches around town. In a front pew sat Pastor Núñez of the Ros de Olano church; scattered here and there were people from the I.E.E. church at Calatrava Street. Pastor Benito Corvillón of Noviciado, host for the evening, came out at the stroke of eight, accompanied by two priests, to conduct the service.

I met the same crowd at the different churches the following nights. The nuns were a good many; I remember especially a group of Little Sisters of Jesus in their humble serge dresses and sandals. After the third night the Octave moved to the Oriental Rite Chapel of the Jesuit Fathers of Serrano Street—a locale so small that the overflow filled halls and stairs until it was settled in a large auditorium connected with the chapel by loudspeaker. The final service took place in a large Catholic Church in Princesa Street where the only jarring note was struck: the "ecumenical" service included Benediction of the Blessed Sacrament and a sermon—preached by an auxiliary bishop of Madrid—on the text "The Prodigal Son."

The 1966 observance once more attracted overflow crowds. And on January 19, at the Iglesia de Jesús on Calatrava Street, a church of the I.E.E., Enrique Miret Magdalena climbed to the pulpit to address an audience which—like thousands of people across Spain—knew him already as the most outspoken Catholic in the country.

It is as difficult as it is unjust to mention Miret briefly in any book on Spanish Protestantism. The man is worth a book of his own. He began to come into national prominence with a series of articles on the Council in the Madrid illustrated weekly *Triunfo*. Reading one of these pieces one admired the author's enlightened Christianity. Reading two, one began to wonder how he got his stuff in print. Reading three, one inevitably began to ask: Who could this man be whose theological soundness was matched only by his courage?

He is a layman. I was introduced to him at the 1965 Protestant Congress—a powerfully built man with burning dark eyes and a straightforward manner who seemed to know practically every pastor in attendance. He invited me to chat with him at his office, and there I found him a couple of weeks later, after his return from a visit to the Council.

Miret has a doctor's degree in chemistry from the University of Madrid. He is associated with his father, Enrique Miret Espoy, a manufacturer of insulating materials and industrial plastics. He looks as if he might just have turned forty; he is fifty-two, married, the father of seven children.

"I never attended a Catholic school," he told me when I asked where he had received what Spaniards call "moral formation." "Which I consider a distinct advantage," he added. From the French *Lycée* he went to the university; then in the late forties, and on his own, he began to read theology.

His reading was deep, critical, but made immensely difficult by the censorship at the time. "There were no good books in Spain then. None at all. I had to get them from abroad." His interest in theology led him to the field of lay spirituality, and he began to write on the subject in a small magazine of that name. (The first issue of this now defunct periodical, dated May, 1953, bears an article by Miret whose title was prophetic of the path he was to blaze in Spain: "Must the Christian 'Become as Nothing'? ")

A short time later the newspaper *Informaciones* invited him to write a weekly column called "Catholicism in the Modern

243

World"—news and comment from the world outside. "Those were the days when one couldn't say much. I did the column until the paper changed hands and it became evident that my liberty would be even more limited. I quit then."

When the Council opened, *Triunfo* asked him for a few articles of general ecumenical information to appear weekly. "The first one, which came out in 1963, didn't cause much of a stir," says Miret. But as the issue of religious liberty began to be discussed in the country, *Triunfo* began to pass from hand to hand and the name Miret Magdalena to attract the most venomous attacks in the various hate sheets which circulate in the country.

In one double-page spread, in 1963, Miret ticked off the names of the Spanish Protestant churches, their beliefs and organization, and spoke of their Christian integrity before God and society. Such a story had never—*never*—been seen before in the Church-State. Week in and week out he commented on the Council discussions in a tone which was not evident anywhere else in the Spanish press. In November, 1965, he lashed out against "Catholics Who Are Not Christians" through a defense of Luther, his doctrine and his rebellion:

On the 31st of October of 1517 [the day Luther nailed his 95 theses to the Church door at Wittenberg] Luther acted as any other Catholic who had the same authority as he, a doctor in theology. His was not a subversive gesture, as has been erroneously said at times, but a call, within Catholicism, to bring to the attention of cultured men (clerics and students) certain excesses which many knew existed in the Church. Whether or not his message was correctly drafted is something else entirely; the fact is that he did not feel himself outside the Catholic Church by virtue of it, nor did anyone else think him so [separated] at the time. There have been other examples across the centuries, of Catholic personalities who have been upbraided by the Church and then vindicated by her; we have the recent cases of Fathers Congar, O.P., Lubac, S.J., and K. Rahner, S.J., who have labored under so much suspicion until recently.

On July 3 of that year he had come through with "The End of Clericalism." ("For years we laymen were hurled, like cannon fodder, in the defense of certain rights of the Church which were sometimes only the privileges—the most unevangelical privileges —of a comfortable, routine-bound clergy.") On January 22, 1966, the explosion at Spanish newsstands bore the title "The Religious Culture of the Clergy. ("As for *morals,* on the other hand, [in seminaries] their practice is explained like a penal code; or, at most, like a list of sinful actions which is bereft of positive orientations and which overlooks the most important aspects of human existence. Wasn't it Unamuno who said that he felt need of confessing things which do not appear in any prayer book's catalogue of sins?")

Meanwhile Miret Magdalena had become active in lay movements. Today he is National President of the Graduates of Catholic Action, Secretary General of the National Association of the Lay Apostolate, and Member of the Council of Directors of the Pastoral Institute at Salamanca's Pontifical University. The last title is perhaps the most significant: it marks the first time a layman has ever sat in an ecclesiastical institute.

"Yes, I'm in great demand as a speaker," Miret told me, "and it's a curious thing: it's priests that they want me to speak to. I just delivered a series of fourteen lectures on the theology of the laity to a group of newly ordained men." When he took the pulpit to speak at the Calatrava church on January 19, 1966, he was hoarse: he had delivered five lectures that day to "priests, nuns, seminarians and religious." At Calatrava he spoke for over an hour. He called for a theology which "will overcome pure polemics, which will be more concrete, which will go deeper into the history of salvation." Catholics in Spain, he stated, "are in a state of invincible ignorance where Protestantism is concerned." He assailed the distortions taught at seminaries, in schools, found in books. "I have here a little book written by a famous Catholic theologian in the last century and which was reprinted fifteen years ago. It is full of statements on the morals, history and doctrines of Protestants which should make us Catholics blush for shame. Such as, 'Among Protestants there can be no faith, that is clear.' And, 'They care nothing for religion. . . .' " "Dialogue," he concluded, "will not be possible until we realize that the man we are facing is not *across* from us, but *beside* us, because he is our brother."

Miret *was* painfully hoarse. Six lectures and a failing voice attested to his unique mission. "There is no other like him—not even in his own circles," say his Protestant friends. "But today I don't feel lonely," he protests. "In the fifties I did; I felt immensely alone then. Today there are many other people who share my views."

The industrial chemist who is leading the Church by the hand is, in a sense, entirely right. He is not a Spaniard any longer, he is a universal figure: the layman-come-of-age. His articles, with their stirring views on everything from justification to birth control, are the voice of the cannon fodder of old, now graduated from Officer Candidates' School.

Slowly, cautiously, other Spanish voices are rising around him. The layman, long the serf of the Church-State, is awakening to the spiritual, political and economic realities of the sixties.

13

With their victory in 1939, the Crusaders decreed the death of sinful, or "erroneous," sex. In the wake of truth, inevitably, came the rebirth of a moral order in which the male-female relation was totally committed to divine authority. "For Catholic nations," Franco had told the *Cortes* at the time of the Concordat's ratification, "matters of Faith assume a foremost place among the affairs of State. The salvation or the loss of souls . . . are capital problems before which [the State] cannot be indifferent." And so, for twenty-six years the Government has given ninety-nine per cent of all Spaniards (the nation's Catholic population) a clear-cut choice in the delicate matter of "morals": they could have marriage in the Church, or no marriage at all.

The legal complications in the case of ex-Catholics who have embraced Protestantism are, as we have seen, many and onerous. As Spain entered into the new, European phase of her life in the late fifties and early sixties, its marriage law brought new troubles: in the wake of the migration of workers to Northern Europe, a mounting number of "illegal" unions began to plague Spanish authorities. Since the Church-State cannot follow the workers abroad, conduct the required investigation of each marriage case, and give the judicial approval for the performance of a non-Catholic—or civil—ceremony, the following situation obtains:

(1) A Spanish Protestant who marries another Spanish Prot-

247

estant in a Protestant church in Germany (or Holland, or France, or Switzerland, or any other country where he may have temporarily migrated) is not married in Spain. (2) A Spanish Protestant who marries another Spanish Protestant in a civil ceremony in Germany, etc., is not married in Spain. (3) A Spanish Protestant who marries a foreign Protestant in a civil or non-Catholic ceremony in Germany, etc., is not married in Spain. (4) A Spanish Protestant who marries a Spanish Catholic in a civil or non-Catholic ceremony in Germany, etc., is not married in Spain. (5) A Spanish Catholic who marries a Spanish Catholic in a civil ceremony in Germany, etc., is not married in Spain.

There were signs, by the mid-sixties, that Spaniards were yearning for release from their theological Shangri-La with its "spiritual" marriage laws. Writing in the *Information Bulletin of the Ministry of Justice* for May 5, 1965, Antonio Cano Mata, Judge of the District Court of Pina de Ebro, takes exception to the current "administrative exegesis" of Article 42 of the Civil Code as a "juridical absurdity."

Some will argue that the Spanish situation is different from that of [other] countries, on the one hand because . . . our country did not endure the Protestant Reformation, and on the other because of the privileged situation the Catholic Religion enjoys above all the rest.

These or any similar arguments are not convincing.

In the first place because, while it is true that in Spain there is a more or less sizable group of people who, not having been baptized, or having apostatized "formally and materially," may enter into a civil union, it is no less certain that there are also many people who once received the Sacrament of Baptism but later lost their faith and their religious beliefs. Since the latter cannot qualify for civil marriage in the light of Article 42 of the Civil Code, and especially of its administrative exegesis (Circular of the General Directorate of Registries of April 2, 1957) [*see p. 121*] they are compelled to receive a Sacrament in which they do not believe—which is in divine terms useless, and in human terms a monstrous compulsion in the sphere of liberty of conscience, among other things.[1]

[1] Antonio Cano Mata, "Necesidad de un cambio en el sistema matrimonial español," *Boletín de Información del Ministerio de Información,* Year XIX, No. 661 (May 5, 1965), pp. 5–6.

That same month, *Cuadernos para el diálogo,* in a special issue dedicated to women, considered the plight of the female who had succeeded in obtaining a canonical separation from her husband and was left "a shadow of a woman," "neither married, widowed, or single." Ten years ago none of these articles would have seen light; today each is a faint but unmistakable sign that Spain might eventually shed her archaic, quasi-Oriental sexual code and adopt the "erroneous" mores of the West.

Those mores are, in Spanish eyes, Protestant and/or pagan. The introduction of foreign ideas in the sixties may make way for their eventual acceptance. But as in the matter of religious freedom, the change will not come overnight. The relativization of the sexual function, the emancipation of women, the disestablishment of *machismo* and the repeal of the Natural Law present almost insurmountable problems to the male Spaniard. Absolutist and despotic by nature, unpragmatic in his *Weltanschauung,* fiercely committed—in sex above all—to a series of abstractions, the Iberian would seem to be totally unfitted for life in a pluralistic, post-Freudian world. As in the matter of freedom of worship, the investigator can only weigh the new, "progressive" currents against the culture and legal factors which inform the Spanish moral code.

Beginning with the cult of the Mother God.

Every Spanish woman—Catholic, Protestant, agnostic and atheist—is traditionally cast from birth in the image of the Virgin Mother. Until recently, a "decent" woman's relationship to man had no other meaning than the "spiritual" joy of motherhood; in other words, for all legal, psychic and moral purposes, her existence was inseparable from maternity. Untrained in any profession, abysmally unintellectual, unschooled in any but the "genteel" arts (if she was of the social class where they were deemed an ornament), when she chose a husband the Spanish woman took the first and last step of her adult life. Thereafter she was inexorably bound to an indissoluble marriage and—if she considered herself "virtuous"—subject to the biological ebb and flow of the Natural Law.

The phenomenon of the Virgin Mother is of course not peculiar to Spain. It is a truism in the entire Mediterranean, in the southern half of the American Hemisphere and in certain societies outside the West. In its Latin context it springs from a racial worship of sexlessness which, at the beginning of the Christian era, found its most dazzling expression in the cult of the Maiden who gave birth to the Messiah. As such Mariology is one of the most Roman aspects of Catholicism, and, it must be said in passing, one of the most misunderstood in Northern societies. Protestants who accuse Catholics of deifying Mary have been barking up the wrong tree for more than four hundred years. What the Southern Catholic has deified (and, through him, the entire Romanized Church) is the state of virginity itself. Mary's sexlessness is, in actual fact, the pedestal from which her sanctity rises.

In its blind and passionate defense of Mary's "purity" (and its theological derivatives), Spanish Catholicism is again a racial faith, miles apart from the Catholicism of the West. The rational, measured, commonsensical approach to Mariology evinced by Northern prelates at the Second Vatican Council was described by young Father Juan Arias, the most liberal and dynamic Spanish reporter at the great assembly, in the following words:

The Council has also taken up the problem of the Virgin. Marian devotion is characteristic of Catholicism, but within it there are two currents: the maximalist and the minimalist. Latin countries generally tend to Marian inflation while (with the exception of Poland) other peoples—especially Germans and Anglo-Saxons, tend to adopt a more severe and measured devotion. . . . [Dogmatic theologians] believe that the Virgin is better respected by proclaiming the bare truth than by indulging in exaggerations and inexact expressions which at times confuse the laity and almost always confuse the Protestants.[2]

But Father Arias was very much alone. On September 17 the Church daily, *Ya,* had run a story entitled "The Council Studies the Schema of the Virgin" in which the following passages appeared:

THE SHADOW OF PROTESTANT THEOLOGY

Spain is a nation that makes recommendations: all of us know the practical value of knowing the mother of a powerful individual, even

[2] *Pueblo,* October 3, 1964.

if we are close to him. The convenience of appealing to Mary as an intermediary before God, especially in the most difficult problems, has ever been heard in Spanish pulpits and confessionals.

Due to a certain puritanism of a practical order joined to a rigid loyalty to theological concepts, Protestantism, born in the more Northern countries, frowns on the "exaggerations" of this alleged interference of the Mother of God. They [Protestants] accuse us of theological error and of vicious practices in the matter of Marian mediation.

"Exaggeration," it will be noted, bears quotes. A little further on, the story broaches the subject of the "geographical" differences in Marian thought and predicts that, in the final draft of the Schema, "Those who are in closest contact with Protestantism and paganism [sic] may emphasize prudence in the use of the titles and expressions which *do not lead to error* or scandal in the practices of Christian people, but which startle strangers." (Italics mine.)

To a Catholic or Protestant "stranger," the most startling expression of the cult of Mary in Spain is the status of Spanish woman. This, in turn, is one of the props of the sexual code which makes Spain a Catholic island in the West.

Writing in the special issue of *Cuadernos para el diálogo* mentioned above, Lawyer María Luisa Suárez states, "In our country, the legal situation of the married woman may be compared to that of a minor." [3] And with this statement Señorita Suárez defines the issue: since time immemorial the Spanish woman has been a legal child who bore children.

At the heart of her problem is her astonishing lack of education—a word which comes from the Latin *educere*: to lead forth, and which bears no relation to the static "moral formation" which is woman's lot in Spain. With honorable exceptions (there is the group of distinguished women novelists who have emerged since the Crusade), the Spanish girl has not been led forth into that world of ideas, of the mind, of the psyche, where a normal woman finds her sexual stimuli. On the contrary, from childhood she has

[3] María Luisa Suárez, *"Condición jurídica y realidad social—la discriminación de la mujer casada ante el trabajo,"* Cuadernos para el diálogo (Extraordinario), Diciembre, 1965, pp. 23-24.

been led back into the twin fortresses of "spiritual values" and "moral truths" where she remains—childish, passive and serene—throughout her adult life. As Madariaga writes: "The story of Eve and the apple—the fruit, be it remembered, of the tree of knowledge—is a marvelous basis for a crusade against education, and in a country in which husbands do not trifle with feminine slips, the Church is bound to find many an ally—avowed and unavowed—in its efforts to keep Eve away from apples and serpents." [4]

The extent to which the Church-State has succeeded in keeping Eve away from temptation is evident from the figures of her employment and higher education. Both are available in the issue of *Cuadernos* mentioned above. In an article by María Rosa de Madariaga (the historian's granddaughter), Rosario de la Iglesia and Valentina Fernández, the ratio of Spanish working women is given as 18.84 per cent of the total female population—the lowest in all Europe. And when this figure is broken down into fields of endeavor, it becomes more appalling still: of this percentage, the greater majority are domestics untrained in any calling. The full figures are as follows:

Domestic service	33.8 %
Farm work	23.9 %
Artisans and day laborers	24.7 %
Sales clerks	3.19%
Clerical workers	7.0 %
Professionals	6.69%

As for higher education, Señorita Amalia Arana, in her article, "The Social Conditioning of Feminine Education" (in the same issue of the magazine), gives the figures for male university students during the 1963–64 academic year as 82,862 and that for women as 19,884: i.e., girls comprise just under one-fourth of Spanish college attendance.

The Spanish woman's intellectual nonexistence, added to her moral quietism, in turn spell the death of her sexuality. Premarital

[4] Madariaga, *op. cit.*, pp. 159–60.

sex is, quite simply, prostitution: a psychosexual relation free of the Natural Law is considered degenerate even in marriage (see reference to the Bishop of Sigüenza-Guadalajara below). But where agnostic couples may resort to birth control with impunity, premarital sex will automatically brand a woman a strumpet. Reading Betty Friedan's *La mística de la feminidad*, published in 1965 in an excellent translation by poet Carlos Dampierre, the non-Spanish reader is struck by the statement: "In former times, woman was divided into two types: the good, pure woman who was put on a pedestal, and the prostitute of carnal desires."

Miss Friedan's "former times" are modern times in Spain. The physical repugnance or moral hatred which the Spaniard feels for the sexually responsive woman who surrenders herself before marriage was admirably expressed in an *ABC* article on December 8, 1965 (perhaps by coincidence, the Feast of the Immaculate Conception). It bore the simple title *"Erotización."* The author, Ricardo Cobos, began the story by mentioning a lecture given a short time before by Professor Juan José López Ibor, the most renowned psychiatrist in Spain and a stalwart defender of the moral *status quo*.

The famous professor . . . adduced in his lecture the impressive fact that 47 per cent of women of a certain powerful country are not unedified when they reach marriage. Which nearly means that when they arrive at [marriage] they are erotized (in some of the meanings of the word); but let us not forget, in passing, that this percentage is perhaps topped in some Northern European countries.

Señor Cobos' notion of the "unedited" woman may be the most striking expression of *machismo* in the Spanish language: it is refined, intellectual, and unspeakably base. It sums up, in one mordant concept, the entire Latin sexual code from flamboyant Italy to sober Spain.

These are, schematically, some of the cultural factors surrounding the plight of the Spanish woman. A glance at the legislation which keeps her "in her place" is a glance at Catholicism in action, since Spanish laws in this field, as in all others, embody the traditional doctrine of the Church.

253

Señorita Suárez's article provides the best tour of the disaster area which is the juridical status of the married woman in Spain. One of the disabilities that draws her ire is the humiliation known as "marital leave" or "marital license." Under Article 5 of the Law of July 22, 1961, she reports, a Spanish woman must obtain her husband's consent "to elect or practice a trade or profession," "to go into business," "sign to a work contract" or even "dispose of her own property." Señorita Suárez delves into the recent legislative history of this measure:

In the statement of Motives at the last reform of the Civil Code on April 24, 1958 . . . the following arguments were given to justify woman's submission and her juridical incapacity: "organic differences . . . ; inasmuch as the *exigencies of the unity of marriage* require the exercise of leadership, which *nature, religion* and *history* attribute to the husband. . . ." [*Italics hers.*]

It is Article 57 of the Civil Code, says Señorita Suárez, which "sets forth the principle of 'subordination' by saying that woman must obey her husband and the husband must protect his wife." From the provisions of this sexual paternalism derives another, and far more bitter, limitation of woman's life; the fact that the husband "has custody of the children, to the absolute exclusion of the wife, who shall assume such custody only in the absence of the husband, i.e., when he is incompetent or deceased." Though Señorita Suárez does not go into it, in both letter and spirit the law also demands that a woman who leaves her husband will, if he should so determine, be deprived of her children in punishment for the crime of insubordination or disobedience.

Marriage, like all other Spanish institutions, is "inorganic" through and through. When "inorganic elections" are called (such as those for City Councilors held in Madrid in the winter of 1963), "heads of families" constitute one of the qualified categories of voters. A "head of family" is the husband and, only if he is dead or incompetent, the wife. Where the man is living and competent, neither the wife nor adult children can vote. When the man is dead or incompetent, only the wife can vote, and not adult children. In Franco's words, "he who creates a family, he who supports it and presides over it is he who should speak, and not those who depend on him." This address of the *Caudillo*'s in 1957 was echoed by another in 1960 in which his speech writer took him further into the logic of inorganic government. On March 23 of that year, on the celebration of the twenty-fifth anniversary of the Falangist newspaper *Arriba, el Caudillo* declared:

Why do the old political systems of nations fly from the most clear and direct expression of democracy, which is the referendum? Ah! because they do not want democracy to be sincere, because what the parties want is a deceitful democracy, an entirely false interpretation of democracy, that of establishing it through political parties; thus one comes to the bizarre case of the father of a family, who supports a family, whose opinion should have weight in the Motherland, and who sees [this opinion] belied by that of his wife or children.[4a]

Before going on to a last indictment brought by Señorita Suárez against the Ruling Fathers, it is well to look at the antecedents of female subjection in the tradition of the Church. In his widely discussed book, *Apostolic Promotion of the Religious Woman in the World Today*—a book whose importance transcends convent walls—León Cardinal Suenens speaks of Canon Law as a code which was set down by man "in the spirit of an age which treated woman as a minor and defended her against herself. Canon Law is still cast in this masculine mentality. . . . It is a tradition of long standing, and there is no reason not to call it antifeminist." [5]

Cardinal Suenens traces the antifeminist vein in Canon Law to Tertullian, then cites two decrees of the twelfth-century monk Gratian which contain, as he states, some rather "strong" remarks on the subject:

"Woman has not been made in the image of God. This explains why the law wishes women to be subject to men and that wives be almost the serfs of their husbands."

[4a] *Discursos y mansajes del Jefe del Estado, 1960–1963* (Madrid: Dirección General de Información, 1964), p. 11.
[5] León José Cardenal Suenens, *Promoción apostólica de la religiosa en el mundo de hoy* (Bilbao: Desclée de Brouwer, 1965), p. 61.

And (this one should be marked well):

"It is evident that woman is under the domination of man and does not enjoy any authority; she cannot teach, nor act as witness, nor judge."

But by far the most interesting quotation adduced by the Belgian prelate to prove his point is taken from Aquinas, the phoenix of the Latin Church:

"With relation to her particular nature, woman is something deficient and accidental. . . . If what is born is a girl, this is due to weakness in the generating principle, or to an imperfection of preexisting matter, or also to a transformation provoked from the outside, as, for example, by the noontime winds laden with humidity, as Aristotle says." [6]

Back in Madrid, eight hundred years after Gratian, Señorita Suárez charges with Iberian indignation against another provision of the Law of 1961—which was, ironically, drawn up as a reform measure in the field of women's rights. In her own words:

The Legislator proves himself cautious once more when he establishes some professional limitations which have no scientific basis—such as, among others, the exclusion of women from the administration of justice, from the positions of Magistrate, Judge and District Attorney (Article 3, Paragraph c), although the article adds: "except in juvenile and labor courts." But the latter exemption . . . is meaningless in actual practice, since the woman who is bold enough to apply for such posts will find herself caught in a web of thousands upon thousands of delicate strands woven by the functionaries; hence, in fact, she is also excluded from them.

Thus is the spirit of Gratian—the medieval Italian who has been called the Father of Canon Law—alive in the Spanish Civil Code of the twentieth century: "she cannot . . . judge," he decreed in the 1100's, and in Spain she still can't.

The matter taken up in *Cuadernos* for January, 1966, might have rested there if the *Cortes* hadn't met and, barely a month

[6] *Ibid.,* p. 62.

later, considered a project to lift the ban on women judges. The motion—perhaps a tribute to Señorita Suárez's spirited protest—was presented by Deputy Hernández Navarro and roused a veritable storm. One member of Parliament who rose to defend the proposal (Señor Reyes Morales) reminded the assembly that a woman—Indira Gandhi—was Prime Minister of her nation in 1966. Other voices were heard pro and con, among the latter that of Deputy Señor Codón, who, according to *Ya* (February 24), stated that "woman's destiny is marriage" and that "one cannot conceive of a Magistrate who has to look after the house, the children and the Tribunal," and who ended, as reported in *Pueblo,* by declaring that "to open doors for women is to establish a matriarchate, which seems to me a return to barbarousness."

The cult of the Virgin Mother, with its annihilation of all factors which might condition, alter, or in any way relativize the sexual function, is mirrored in two equally "spiritual" absolutes: the prohibition of divorce and the condemnation of birth control. Spanish *evangélicos* are solidly behind the Catholic Church—her "unavowed allies," as Madariaga would say—in the matter of divorce. But they take a divergent stand on birth control.

Few things brought home to me the ghetto in which Spanish Protestants live as did the statement of a young Catholic in Madrid upon hearing that there were *evangélicos* in a remote southern province. He looked puzzled and shocked, but he didn't have to think more than two seconds to find the reason for the catastrophe. "Tell people they can get divorces and they'll come running to join the Protestants!"

As a Spanish Catholic he associated divorce with Protestantism, and Protestantism with sexual degeneracy; it followed, in logic, that the children of Luther were heirs to his promiscuousness in Spain, too. His thinking is not uncommon in the jungle of ignorance that surrounds Protestantism in Spain. It is ironic as well: the Thirty Thousand, not one of whose doctrines or beliefs have been allowed to circulate in the Church-State, stand accused, in Spanish eyes, of a practice they formally condemn.

Divorce came to Spain in 1931 and disappeared after the

Crusade. Madariaga believes the Republic itself hastened its death:

The divorce law . . . was demanded by the spirit of the times, and so much overdue that there was a long line of ill-assorted couples waiting for the day when the courts would at last be empowered to grant them their longed-for liberty. Even here, the Republic went from one extreme to the other, and made the country pass from a marriage which only death could dissolve to one which the two conjoints might dissolve by mutual consent after a paltry two years of conjugal experience. The Church was of course indignant. It should be added that, at the time, a brisk business in dissolution of marriages had been set up by the Diocese of Paris, to which—the Church being universal—Spanish couples with French francs to spare could apply. Still, these are temporal infirmities which a spiritual power can outlive with dignity; and the fact remains that even in this matter of divorce, in which the Republic stood on strong ground, it might have acted with more moderation.[7]

The "strong ground" the Republic stood on was a composite of those human and psychological values which inform sex and marriage in pluralistic societies, and which are only now making a dent in the doctrine of the traditional Church. One of the most significant motions made at the Second Vatican Council took place on September 29, 1965, when Elias Zoghby, a Patriarch of the Orthodox Church, spoke up for the "innocent spouse abandoned immediately after marriage . . . condemned . . . to a loneliness for the rest of its life." "Couldn't the Church," asked the prelate, "dispense the innocent party in such cases from the bond of marriage, as is done traditionally in various Oriental Churches?" [8]

He received his answer next day when Charles Cardinal Journet of Switzerland pronounced the most accurate summary of the Church's thinking in this matter—and by extension in other sexual matters:

Some Oriental Churches admitted divorce in cases of adultery and allowed the innocent party to contract marriage anew. But this happened, in view of the relations between Church and State at the time,

[7] Madariaga, *op. cit.,* pp. 405–06.
[8] *Ecclesia,* October 9, 1965, p. 45.

under the influence of a civil law which decreed the legitimacy of divorce and remarriage. . . . To justify this practice, these Oriental churches cited the clause in St. Matthew regarding divorce in cases of adultery. But since these Churches admit other causes for divorce, aside from the one already mentioned, it is clear that in this matter they acted in a fashion which was more human than evangelical.[9]

The dichotomy human/evangelical is indeed at the heart of all sexual problems affecting the Church today—from the growing number of marriages annulled on special or specious grounds, to the issue of birth control and the increasing defection of priests who, in breaking away from celibacy, have made their agonizing choice between evangelical annihilation (or Catholic virtue) and human fulfillment (or Catholic sin).

In the Special *Cuadernos* for December, 1965, layman Antonio Menchaca echoed Patriarch Zoghby's plea for the "innocent party." He spoke on behalf of the Spanish woman "whose marital life has become impossible" and who applies for the only solution offered her by the Spanish Civil Code—a legal separation:

Pressed by circumstances, besieged, the Spanish woman—who as a rule has a large dose of patience—reaches the point where she cannot stand her hell on earth any longer, both on her account and on her children's. She then invokes the help of society, [and] of the State, and after a thousand maneuvers obtains a hybrid situation, defined in the Civil Code as separation from marriage, which converts her into a shadow of a woman—neither single, nor married, nor widowed, tied to the guilty husband and unable to remake her life. . . .

Now this shadow of a woman, if she should wish to avoid a situation in which the man will emerge in total triumph and she in total defeat, can request a canonical annulment of her marriage. But this is a costly process, inaccessible to many; moreover, considering the nature of the Sacrament, if the marriage was in fact valid, she will have to do violence to her conscience to represent as flawed something which had full efficacy.

This situation . . . cannot continue indefinitely. We do not know when the remedies will be forthcoming, but we do know they will come, among other reasons because woman is becoming a sociological being capable of generating [her own] positive law. . . . The Church, alert in modern times to the importance of deep human problems . . .

[9] *Ibid.,* October 16, 1965, p. 17.

could perhaps, without abandoning the inalterable and permanent values of the Sacrament, extend to all social classes what seems to be today, in actual practice, the privilege of a few. . . .[10]

Señor Menchaca's piece ends with a plea similar to Señor Cano's: that couples be given their choice of canonical or Church marriage "regardless of their confessional circumstances." Though he apologizes for the brevity of his piece (it is a two-column box) he touches on the main aspects of the tragic situation of Spaniards whose marriages have gone wrong and, most importantly, on the bitter fact that an annulment, in present-day Spain, is the prerogative of the rich.

If and when the shadow of the Virgin Mother recedes from the Civil Code and Spanish woman succeeds to the rights of a human being, the marriage question may ease somewhat. One of the most surprising statements on the matter was issued by Cardinal Bueno Monreal of Seville shortly after the Council was over. In an interview printed in *La vanguardia española* (Barcelona) on January 2, 1966, he was asked: "In view of the dangers presented by the generalization of divorce, which some codes already admit, is there a probability that the Church will eventually accept it?"

His answer is four paragraphs long, and ranges over the traditional thinking of the Church on the matter. But it ends as follows:

A valid marriage (sacrament) which has been consummated continues to be indissoluble in Church law. Could the day come when the Pope exempts [people] from this bond by making use of his power as Vicar of Christ, as he exempts [them] from the bond of nonconsummated marriage? This very day, one cannot see that probability. But I would not make bold to exclude the possibility with absolute certainty. On the other hand, there is the strong testimony of twenty centuries during which this power has not been invoked other than in the Church's application and interpretation of the "Pauline privilege." [11]

[10] Antonio Menchaca, "Ni soltera, ni casada, ni viuda," *Cuadernos para el diálogo* (Extraordinario), Diciembre, 1965, p. 25.
[11] The "privilege" makes it possible for an unbaptized person, on becoming a member of the Catholic Church, to leave his former unbaptized spouse and remarry a Catholic, if the other party impedes the convert's practice of religion.

Spanish Protestants' objections to divorce are as theological as their Catholic brethren's—and colored by the same temperamental repugnance to the establishment of empiric or pragmatic standards in measuring sexual relations. "The lifelong character of marriage, as demanded by the Christian faith," writes Manuel Gutiérrez Marín, "is based upon the [human] will and upon God's command." [12] The feelings of the distinguished theologian—who transcribes them with reference to N. H. Soe's *Christliche Ethik*—are shared by all Spanish Protestants. The very mention of the fact that ninety per cent of the Reformed Churches outside of Spain accept divorce brings a troubled look to the face of the *evangélico*. It is the exact look that steals over the faces of traditionalist Catholics when they hear of their Church's progressive tendencies abroad: the same Spanish shock at the hubris committed by co-religionists in the outside world.

And yet, curiously, in the matter of birth control the Protestant is firmly aligned behind the Reformed tradition. "We adhere to the Protestant principle of freedom," a Baptist minister told me. "We think of birth control as something to be decided in the privacy of the individual's conscience, something to be settled between himself and God, with no interference from the outside."

The *evangélico*'s position on the matter—the reverse of his stand on divorce—is the fruit of a cultural attitude which, in spite of a hostile ambiance and a total ban on all education and literature, he has somehow achieved. The breach between him and the Catholic on this issue can be gauged by the fact that the Spanish Civil Code considers birth control an attempt upon human life, and chastises it as such. A book entitled *Crimes, Penalties and Prisons in Spain* (*Delitos, penas y prisiones en España*), published by the Ministry of Justice in 1963, speaks on page fifteen of the "juridical values protected by the Civil Code" and lists, as the first one, "life and corporal integrity." "In accordance with Christian morals," it explains, "the Spanish Code punishes him who induces or helps another to commit suicide. It also sanctions, with care and meticulousness, the crime of abor-

[12] Manuel Gutiérrez Marín, *Fe y Acción: ética cristiana existencial* (Madrid: Editorial Irmayol, 1965), p. 229.

tion and all those who participate in it even by circulating birth control propaganda."

Suicide, abortion and birth control are thus leveled before a "Christian" interpretation of the Fifth Commandment. And "Christian," in this case, again stands for Roman or absolutist. One of the leitmotivs in Madariaga's *Modern History* is the almost total coincidence of the Roman-Catholic tradition (the hyphen should be mandatory after the Second Vatican Council) and the Spanish temper:

The synthetic and spontaneous nature of Spanish thought, for instance, is readily attracted by the doctrine of a revealed dogma, and there are obvious lines of sympathy between the transcendental pessimism of the Catholic and the experimental pessimism of the stoic— stoicism being at bottom the natural attitude of the Spanish soul. Such an attitude places the subject in the mood of a contemplative spectator who sees the world as drama, a point again on which the stoic Spaniard can find himself at home in the Roman faith. Add the Spanish tendency to lay stress on synthetic human standards rather than on ethical values, and we shall see how deeply the Catholic roots have struck ready earth in the Spanish race.[13]

But "stoicism," "pessimism," and its end result, passivity, have been conditioned, in the Spanish temper, by another and far more important factor: the worship of personality or self. The Spaniard's difficulty, says Madariaga, is "too much stress on the person; not enough stress on the thing." When faced with a "materialistic" doctrine in which the generation of a human being is made dependent on, if not subject to, a variety of "things," the Spaniard instinctively balks. The economic realities of life do not worry him, for his values are abstract and not concrete: "Every child," says a blithe old Spanish adage, "brings his own loaf of bread under his arm." The sociological problems of overpopulation have not been brought to his attention; he is conditioned to an individualistic way of life in which the "horizontal" tendencies are nonexistent or at best dormant. And the promotion or supervaluation of sexual pleasure is thoroughly incompatible with the

[13] Madariaga, *op. cit.*, pp. 157–58.

moral education he has received. "Sanctified" sex is functional, institutional and, as the Latin Council Fathers repeatedly stated, "heroic."

"Matrimonial chastity exists," said Ernesto Cardinal Ruffini on September 29, 1965. "The Schema [The Church in the Modern World] should make this evident; it should not forget, but rather exalt . . . the value and superiority of virginity and of perfect chastity chosen for love of God." [14] The theme of "perfect chastity" or, in the case of married Catholics, self-immolation before the Natural Law, was taken up next day by Ignacio de Orbegozo, a Peruvian prelate who was alarmed by "the manner in which the Schema says the couple should determine the number of children." "The text, as it stands, can give rise to many doubts and lead couples to a 'minimalist' or casuistic interpretation, which is precisely the one that should be rejected, as it is not desirable that laymen should live within the bounds of the licit, but rather that they be pushed to perfection." [15]

Now the Spaniard has never needed that push; he seeks "perfection" (i.e., self-denial) wholly by instinct. To dwell on sex for its own sake, in the Western manner, is repugnant to his ascetic, do-or-die, black-or-white moral code. In his penetrating study of Don Juan and donjuanism Marañón explodes the myth that the philanderer of world literature is a Spanish figure. "In Spain donjuanesque love is an exotic import, without national roots and without tradition." The sexual athlete, he explains, reached the peak of both his real and legendary development in Renaissance Europe, and from there passed to Spain.

If Don Juan had his literary birth in Spain, and not in France or Italy, it was due to a circumstance which we can easily determine today.
It is the following: since Don Juan is a rebel before the social and religious orthodoxy of his environment, evidently his rebellion is more heroic, more showy in Spain than anywhere else, for among us the powers against which he rose—God and the State—were stronger than anywhere else.
In no other country of Europe could Don Juan's rebellion have had

[14] *Ecclesia,* October 9, 1965, p. 43.
[15] *Ibid.,* October 16, 1965, p. 21.

the dramatic impact than in a State whose external and internal norms were as rigorous as ours. In sum, nowhere else as in Spain could Don Juan be a hero.[16]

On the other hand,

The purely national modality of Spanish love is, and was then above all, that of the Castilian home, monogamous, austere to the point of mysticism, the home of numerous offspring conceived almost without sin in a bedchamber which had the dignified plainness of a monastic cell.[16a]

As usual, Marañón makes his point with telling scholarship and insight. And no one who has lived in Spain will dare contradict him. The Spaniard, as philoprogenitive as the Chinese, mates for the purpose of having children and builds his "inorganic" marriage around them. Where the European derives very few children from his unsublimated pleasure, the Spaniard derives his highly sublimated pleasure from an abundance of children. An American friend who visited Spain some years ago told me, in both amazement and admiration, of having seen a man addressing a one-sided but perfectly serious conversation to a three- or four-month-old baby he was carrying in his arms. In Spain no one would have wondered. The child is the center of all attention, the highest good in life. Spanish children are in turn far more quick-witted than their Western counterparts and—some Dr. Spock should study the phenomenon—among the world's earliest talkers.

In sum, the Spaniard is larger than life. He is the monarch of all that he surveys, unconcerned with the accidentals of day-to-day living, enamored only of his very existence and its triumphant assertion in the world around him. He has little feeling for nature, which is simply the frame—or the foil—for his own supremacy. He has no sense of the practical; he must be helped, says Madariaga "to develop co-operation, continuity, technique, method . . ." In his *Existentialist Christian Ethics* Gutiérrez Marín deals with the "Ethical Values of the Iberian-Latin World" (Chap-

[16] Gregorio Marañón, *Don Juan: ensayos sobre el origen de su leyenda* (10th ed.; Madrid: Espasa Calpe, S.A., 1964), pp. 97–98.
[16a] *Ibid.*, pp. 87–88.

ter 7) and speaks of the Spaniard's personality as a mixture of the theocentric tendencies of Greek thought superimposed on the anthropocentric tendencies of Christianity.

The Iberian is "the measure of all things" praised by the Greeks, but in actual fact controlled dogmatically by the Church. From this springs his aloofness towards Nature, be it vegetable (his horror of the tree) or animal (his lack of compassion for beasts), and his indifference before death: man is superior to all that surrounds him, even to all *contingency*.[17]

The very idea of birth control—a moral code based primarily on sexual, psychic and economic contingency—is hence repugnant to the traditionalist Spaniard. But here, too, cultural attitudes are giving way before the infiltration of "materialism." In its December, 1964, issue, *El ciervo* published an article by Father José María de Llanos, S.J., which may be one of the frankest pieces on the subject of birth control ever written by a Catholic priest (Appendix, pp. 363–68). Father de Llanos' comments, based on his pastoral experience in one of Madrid's slums (*El pozo del tío Raimundo*—"Uncle Raymond's Well"), will have meaning for all sociologists and moralists engaged in the fight against poverty and its bitter fruits. But it is in assailing the Spanish Natality Prizes that the Jesuit has gone furthest in his attack on the Church-State blessing upon "indiscriminate production of offspring." (As in Russia, the Spanish State offers cash prizes to couples who produce the greatest number of children. The idea, grotesque in itself, becomes macabre with the division of the prizes into two separate categories: "Children Living" and "Children Had." The 1965 National Champions for "Children Living"—there are also provincial contests—were Francisco Crespo Martin and his wife, who received their prize from Franco himself; in three marriages, Señor Crespo has sired twenty children, all living. The National "Children Had" Award went to Domingo Rivero Alvarez and his wife; in two marriages Señor Rivero produced twenty-four offspring, eighteen living and six dead.)

Father de Llanos had company in his birth-control stand. Writ-

---

[17] Gutiérrez Marín, *op. cit.*, p. 176. Italics mine.

ing from the Council, Father Arias of *Pueblo* had consistently expressed the hope that the Church would modify its traditional outlook. But this remarkable priest let wishful thinking get the better of him. On November 17, 1965, he jumped the gun. Under the headline, "Schema XIII Virtually Approved; Number of Children Left to Conscience of Couples," Father Arias wrote that the Council "had accepted responsible parenthood and definitely left the number of children to the conscience of the married couple." It was one of the last stories he wrote as regular correspondent for *Pueblo*. Before the Council was over he was removed from his job and promoted to Secretary General of his Order (the Missionaries of the Sacred Heart), a post which will keep him permanently in Rome.

Pueblo was undaunted—the working-man's paper is the spunkiest and most liberal of all Spain. On November 24, 1965, it published a report entitled, "A Spanish Question: More Children?" The page-long piece was based on capsule interviews with Spanish women.

M.C.C. Age twenty-six. Married seven years. Two daughters. "I've been using the pill for two years. . . . I feel, in conscience, that I should. Childbirth has been very painful for me and, sociologically, I can see no principles which would compel me to have more children than I want."

A mother of three children. "My opinion is just like [Pope] Paul VI's [*It wasn't, of course, as Pope Paul had not yet pronounced himself definitely on the matter*]. The main thing in marriage is that husband and wife love each other. One doesn't think of children when one marries, one thinks of the man. One has a right to space pregnancies."

The attack was coming at the Church from all sides. Women, liberated from their "spiritual" existence, were finding their way to sexual maturity. Members of the enlightened clergy were granting approval to the much-discussed pill. ("I know other Catholic women who take it," said M.C.C. "They have obtained their confessor's permission.") And articles in newspapers and magazines from all Europe left no doubt as to the Catholic stand throughout the Continent.

It was, as ever, a *casus belli,* and the Church, rallied by Pope Paul's U.N. speech and his subsequent encouragement to the orthodox camp, doubled its warnings and caveats on the new morality. The September 29, 1965, International Edition of the New York *Times,* detailing Mexican Bishop Sergio Mendez's defense of Freud and psychoanalysis, was confiscated on arrival and never reached Spanish newsstands. The October 7 edition of the same paper, with its headline, "Council Debates Problem of Birth Control; Bishop from India Disputes Teaching on Natural Law and Contraception," was also banned by Church-State censors.

In the meantime members of the hierarchy aired their views in the press. On February 10, 1966, the Bishop of Sigüenza-Guadalajara went further than any other prelate and, in a lecture on "The Christian Family According to the Council," stated in Madrid:

In spite of the efforts of an intelligent and audacious minority, the traditional doctrine of the Church has been reaffirmed thanks to the perseverance of another minority, no less intelligent and with more theological depth.

If, on the one hand, the Council has strengthened and valued the convenience of conjugal love, on the other hand it has avoided supervaluating it by putting it above *or on the same plane* as procreation. To have done so would have meant an immense doctrinal rectification, with dismal practical consequences.[18]

Against the Church's frantic campaign, birth control—that "Protestant" and "pagan" idea—seems to be making serious inroads in the country. Deprived as they are of any voice in Spanish society, *evangélicos* can take no credit for its acceptance. Their name, however, comes up repeatedly in relation with another form of "degeneracy": the marriage of their ministers—initiated by "lewd" Luther with a "lewd" nun—and the attendant manifestation of sex as a help and not a hindrance to a man of the cloth.

Paradoxically, apostolic celibacy—the living refutation of Protestant doctrine—is claiming its victims in Spain as it is everywhere

18 *ABC*, February 11, 1966. Italics mine.

else. But if the situation abroad is alarming, in Spain it is tragic. The lot of the ex-priest in the Church-State is fraught with anxiety and even terror: he is a social, sexual and, above all, a professional pariah who has literally nowhere to go.

Only those who have known an ex-priest in Spain (or abroad, if he has managed to forge his papers and escape) can grasp the psychic and spiritual journey his desertion implies. Many, guilt-ridden and disoriented, are lost for life before they depart over the clerical threshold. Others survive through an elementary will to live. In Madrid I met a man whose struggle did not end with his abandonment of Holy Orders; he fought, just as boldly and tenaciously, to remake his own life and to support and nurture the family he had always yearned for. He has totally succeeded. Today he is joyfully married, the father of four children, a Catholic still.

I also traveled to Holland to visit the refuge opened by an ex-priest who is now a minister of the Dutch Reformed Church. Some sixty men, twenty of them Spaniards, have passed through this house on their way to rehabilitation—and Protestantism. And many more will follow.

In the middle of the twentieth century, the human and the evangelical are locked in a deadly struggle.

14

A story in *Newsweek* for February 14, 1966, cites "a provocative article prepared for *The Lamp,* a Catholic family magazine," by theologian Charles Curran of the Catholic University of America. According to *Newsweek,* the article "suggests that the widespread use of contraceptives by Catholic married couples may be as theologically decisive in the birth-control debate as the church's complex theological tradition."

Father Curran's cause-and-effect thesis has a parallel in the amazing breakdown of priestly celibacy. The layman's rebellion against the evangelical is marching hand in hand with the cleric's —and, amazingly, producing the same results. "Release from celibacy," that modern, stopgap solution to the problem of priestly "purity," has been a victory won by ex-priests in fear and anguish. By the same token, the ultimate rejection of Natural Law will be effected solely through the courage—and the inner torment—of married Catholics who have challenged the authority of the Church. Only fourteen years elapsed between Pope Pius XII's address to the Italian Association of Catholic Midwives in October, 1951, and the revolutionary sessions of the Second Vatican Council in which Northern prelates stood firm in their defense of conjugal love as a good in and of itself. But in those fourteen years Catholics had traveled a long way. From a fearful acceptance of the quasi-ascetic rhythm method (all but sacrificed by Pope Pius on the altar of the "primary purpose") they had passed to a mature, scruple-free confrontation with their psychic and sexual needs.

I

Birth control and the marriage of priests revolve around a single issue: the meaning of sexuality and its place in the Christian ethic. From time immemorial the Christian Church regarded sex as an occasion of sin cleansed and made holy by the conception of a child. Procreation was not only the primary purpose of the sexual function; it was *its saving grace*. Simultaneously, as the monastic tradition grew and took root, so did the notion of sex as an obstacle to Christian perfection. The cult of sexual denial which was to reign over the Church until the twentieth century was full-blown by the late Middle Ages; one will meet it even in *The Little Flowers of St. Francis of Assisi*, the gentle book inspired by the gentle saint who honored Creation.

Our frail and miserable human flesh is like to the swine, that loves to wallow in the mire, and find its delight therein. Our flesh is the devil's knight; for it resists and fights against all those things which are pleasing to God and profitable to our salvation. A certain friar said to Brother Giles: "Father, teach me how to preserve myself from sins of the flesh." And Brother Giles answered him: ". . . It is impossible for a man to attain any spiritual grace, so long as he is inclined to carnal concupiscence; and therefore, whithersoever thou turn thyself, thou shalt never be able to attain spiritual grace until thou canst master all the vice of the flesh. Wherefore, fight valiantly against thy frail and sensual flesh, thine own worst enemy, which wages war against thee day and night. . . ."[1]

[1] *The Little Flowers of St. Francis of Assisi* (New York: Catholic Book Publishing Co., 1946), pp. 347, 348. Seven hundred years after the *Little Flowers,* this sad tradition is still in bloom. In writing *Camino,* the vade mecum of Opus Dei members (it has been called a second Kempis), Father Escrivá has produced an ascetic's handbook straight out of the Middle Ages. Its numbered maxims take the reader—or the disciple—through a way of physical and moral punishment which will aid him in gaining salvation. Here is *Camino* on the treachery of the flesh:

The war raged on with no truce in sight. The three enemies of the Christian were ever the world, the flesh and the devil, and the greatest of these was the flesh. In his *Mercury and Charon,* whose second part is an allegory of the souls which gain salvation, Alfonso de Valdés finds that only two merit heaven: a married man and a friar—because (as Valdés himself says) "in the opinion of some people the married state is outside Christian perfection, and in our century that of the friars is in danger of being calumnied." [2] Like all Erasmists, the Emperor's secretary sought

---

28. Marriage is for the rank and file, not for Christ's general staff. If eating is an exigency for each individual, engendering is an exigency only for the species, and singular people can take no notice of it.

You thirst for children? Then, children, many children, and we shall leave behind us an indelible trail of light by sacrificing the selfishness of the flesh. . . .

122. Many live like angels in the midst of the world. Why not you? . . .

124. You wrote me, apostolic physician: "We all know by experience that we can be chaste if we live in vigilance, if we frequent the Sacraments, if we put out the first sparks of passion before the bonfire begins to rage. This is precisely why the most integral men in all respects are numbered among the chaste. And among the lewd are counted the timid, the selfish, the deceitful and cruel—the characteristics of little virility. . . .

175. No ideal can become a reality without sacrifice. Deny yourself. It is so beautiful to be a victim!

220. Don't you get a bad taste in your mouth at that wish for physiological well-being—"God give you health, brother"—uttered by some beggars when they receive or require alms?

226. Treat your body with charity, but not with more charity than is due a treacherous enemy.

493. Love the Lady. And she will obtain for you grace enough to triumph in that daily struggle. And the damned one shall not avail himself of those perverse things which rise and rise, seething, within you, until they would drown in their fine-smelling putrefaction the great ideals, the sublime commandments which Christ himself has put in your heart. *"Serviam!"*

677. Gold, silver, jewels—dirt, heaps of manure. Enjoyment, sensual pleasure, satisfaction of the appetites—like a beast, like a mule, like a pig, like a cock, like a bull.

2 Menéndez Pelayo, *op. cit.,* I, 885.

to salvage what was salvageable in both camps; his *via media* was deemed heretical "contagion." Erasmus' own influence in Spain died with his followers'. Menéndez Pelayo attributes the Dutchman's antipathy for the monastic life to the fact that, as an illegitimate child placed in a monastery, he had been ill-used by the friars. "A man who judged everything by his personal or, as they say now, *subjective* impressions, he condemned the vows because he did not know how to keep them." [3] On the other hand, Cipriano de Valera, "fearful of the rigors of the Inquisition, sought asylum abroad and married in London, following the evangelical pattern of so many lustful, apostate friars and clerics who swelled the army of the Reformation." [4] Menéndez Pelayo's spleen is vented on every Spanish ex-priest down to the nineteenth century when, in speaking of Blanco-White, an Irish-Spaniard who passed to Protestantism in the early 1800's, he echoes the classic phrase of the universal bigot: "There are always skirts mixed up in this heretical business!" [5]

Across the centuries the mixture of heresy and skirts remained a fetid affair, to be kept from the eyes of the faithful and dealt with—as all sexual matters—in the secrecy of the theological caucus. It was a Spanish bishop, Abilio del Campo of Calahorra, who on October 30, 1964, stated at St. Peter's that marriage was "such a delicate subject that it would have been better not to treat it in the Council Hall, but in a secret commission, so as to avoid possible disorientations for our faithful and inopportune public comment." [6]

On the subject of marriage (and every other religious issue) Bishop del Campo had a shackled national press behind him. But on the subject of celibacy Pope Paul VI was faced with the "unspiritual" and unsympathetic journalism of the West. His problem was agonizing, his solution equivocal. While he did not close the door on the topic, Pope Paul ordered the Council Fathers to make their opinions known to him in writing, and, therefore, in

[3] Menéndez Pelayo, *Ibid.*, p. 767. Italics his.
[4] *Ibid.*, II, 138.
[5] *Ibid.*, p. 919.
[6] *Ecclesia,* November 7, 1964, p. 36.

confidence: open discussion remained forbidden by the tradition of the Church.

In Spain all was obedient silence. News that the issue had come up in the Council was duly given but no background studies appeared anywhere in the press. On the other hand, there was both triumph and joy in the dispatches from Spanish correspondents in Rome the day Pope Paul banned public discussion of the problem and assembled Council Fathers "burst into applause."

If there was any applause in the West, it had been drowned out by a storm of inopportune public comment. Newspapers in Europe and America had echoed the rumor that the Council held in its hands ten thousand requests from priests seeking reduction to the lay state and release from celibacy. *Time* supplemented the information on February 18, 1966, with the statement, "Around the world about 60,000 priests have left the ministry and many of them have married." While Vatican II was still in session René Laurentin, a French priest in attendance, produced a series of articles on Dom Grégoire Lemercier's introduction of psychoanalysis among the unordained novices of his religious foundation in Cuernavaca, Mexico.[7] It was on the KLM flight to Amsterdam—on my way to

[7] Bishop Sergio Méndez of Cuernavaca had spoken up for Freud and psychoanalysis at the Council Hall on September 28, 1965, with the attendant Spanish ban of next morning's New York *Times*. A month later, the small publication of the Center of Intercultural Documentation—a Catholic organization in Cuernavaca—published a report by Dom Grégoire himself on the uses of psychoanalysis at the monastery of St. Mary of the Resurrection. Here are two excerpts therefrom:

> Statistics provide some idea of our experience. Some sixty members of the community have undergone, or are undergoing, analysis. Only twenty of the original sixty are still here, and the majority of the twenty are still undergoing analysis. Among those who have left the monastery (forty), there are some who took full advantage of analysis and realized that their vocation oriented them toward matrimony. Nevertheless, more than half of the forty who are no longer with us left after less than one year of analysis. They refused to allow the interior "surrender" to take place. This is the one thing necessary if a man is to confront his own essence. In other words, they left the monastery not *due* to psychoanalysis, but because they lacked further analysis. It must be added that these young men left during the first

the Protestant "priests' refuge" at Arnhem—that the stewardess brought me *Le Figaro* with Father Laurentin's story, "Monastery in Analysis—the Tragic Origins of an Experience."

This open, straightforward man [Dom Grégoire] revealed, cards on the table, and without explaining confidential findings, the number of failures registered [during psychoanalysis]. Such frankness contradicts tradition, which hides failures for fear of causing scandal or of driving the men who fail further away [from the Church], the assumption being that they left for reasons of health. According to certain statistics, 3,000 ex-priests have taken refuge in the vast anonymity of Paris. I know of no abbey, no diocese, no country which reveals the number of failures, whether they consist of vocations abandoned in major or minor seminaries, or of sacrilegious ruptures with the priesthood; revealing the number of these ruptures (known only approximately) would be considered unforgivable. Doubtless there are motives for this policy of silence. But it also has its drawbacks: it hides the gravity of certain problems and keeps alive the causes which feed these secret and dramatic hemorrhages.

In Spain, the microcosm of the Romanized Church, the term "hemorrhage" is the perfect description for the stream of sexually warped, maladjusted, useless men who leave the priesthood only to find themselves juridically nonexistent in "the perfect society"

---

two years of the psychoanalytical program. At that time the monastery was simply not prepared to give them the support they needed while undergoing analysis. Many of those who left have expressed a desire to return to the monastery and continue analysis.

To pursue the religious spirit into the remotest depths of the human personality, and to discover it behind the most primitive masks and disguises, no taboos can be allowed. Freud's main argument, which traces all life and love to sexual roots, could not allow us to become squeamish when confronted with sexual motivation. This was especially important in view of the fact that the patients undergoing analysis were monks whose religious sentiments include the rejection of sex in its biological reality. This consideration led us to choose a woman as the analyst for the new candidates, especially during their first sessions. This placed them before the "unknown" from the very beginning. [*CID Reports,* Vol. IV, No. 20, October 16, 1965, pp. 152, 153–54.]

and, as such, (1) unable to marry, (2) unable to work, and (3) unless they can get past the police, unable to leave the country and seek human fulfillment abroad.

Only God knows their number. At the end of the article mentioned above, Father Laurentin speaks of "a certain nation where there are 10,000 priests who have broken with the Church." The figure is high. It could be Spain's, but there are no statistics. The ex-priest, say those who have known him, is a man wearing dark-tinted glasses who proffers a card reading "John Doe, Professor of Greek and Latin."

There would seem to be enough "professors" to fill hundreds of Classical Language Departments in universities around the world.

II

I first met Eusebio Goicoechea-Arrondo in a café on Madrid's Puerta del Sol, downstairs from the struggling firm that now employs him. Goicoechea was a leading composer of liturgical music and one of Spain's youngest authorities on Gregorian chant; today he is a salesman in plastic gewgaws. A man whose world was bound by the priesthood, by his passion for the liturgy and his devotion to the Church, today he travels in candy containers, costume jewelry- and watch-cases, toys and "Souvenir-of-Madrid" novelties.

We had just found a table in the crowded Café de Levante when a child approached us and jiggled a *Domund* container under our noses. It was the annual observance of the *Domingo mundial para las misiones* (abbreviated *"Domund"*)—the time when the Spanish Church, through swarms of schoolchildren, solicits contributions for its foreign missions. Having made a beeline for our table, the boy stood poised before us, plastic bank thrust eagerly forward. "We made those for them," said Goicoechea with a smile and a nod towards the child's container. The youngster went away, jiggling for the infidels abroad.

I explained to Goicoechea the nature of my curiosity, the purpose of my interview, the theme of my book. "But I am not a Protestant," he warned, looking steadily at me, his voice rising on the last word. It was the first statement of his hard-core loyalty to the Church; it was firm and challenging, and, for a fellow Catholic, curiously edifying.

But at the Café de Levante nondoctrinal rapport carried the day: there is in Goicoechea that quality Spaniards call *llaneza,* from the adjective *llano,* defined by Appleton's dictionary as "honest, openly rough, simple, unadorned." He is a sturdy man with dark, Semitic features, an intense look and an air of unquenchable energy. I had to do very little asking; he seemed unable to hold back a single detail of his remarkable odyssey, and when our time at the café was up, he invited me to call on him at his home and continue my interrogation there.

Goicoechea was born in Argentina in 1925, the son of immigrant parents who returned to Spain with him when he was two years old. His mother, like many women of the Carlist North, had made a vow to offer her first son to God. The boy duly entered the Minor Seminary of the Redemptorist Order at El Espino, Burgos, at the age of twelve. It was 1937; outside, the Crusade was raging.

As the door of El Espino closed behind him, Eusebio began his spiritual apprenticeship. Every class, every prayer, every sermon at the Seminary was designed to bend the children's will to their irrenounceable vocation. They had been "chosen" by God; if they defected they would end up in hell. "We were told that anyone who left the Seminary would quite simply be damned for all eternity," he explained. "We used to file into our dormitory at night, fingering our rosaries, and we would literally shake when we went past the priest who kept watch there, sitting in the corridor. If this man called any of us out of the rank, it was to notify us we would have to leave."

Spring and summer, autumn and winter, the child ascetics remained behind the Seminary wall, completely cut off from their families and the world. Eusebio's incarceration lasted fourteen years in two institutions. At Christmas, relatives came to visit. He was also allowed to see his mother in summer—for the space of two, or at most three, days. "She would get off the train at the town station and walk twelve kilometers in the sun, loaded with baskets of grapes. I never saw the grapes after she left, either," he adds with a wry smile. The isolation was so complete that death had no power against it. "I remember the case of a boy named Jalón. Yes, that was his name, Jalón. He fell seriously ill. His family came, but they didn't get to see him. They were not allowed to see him when he was dying in the infirmary, and they were not allowed to see him after he was dead. And mind you, the Seminary was not under papal clausure" (i.e., cloistered, like convents and monasteries of contemplative orders).

Young Jalón was buried in the Seminary graveyard. "His family was not allowed to attend the interment either," Goicoechea continued. "Then after Jalón died, another child had a nervous breakdown and had to be sent home. Next day, in chapel, the preacher offered us the two examples to ponder: one boy, the dead one, was in heaven; the other one had 'picked up his passport to hell.' Which is a favorite phrase of Ligouri's."

(The "passport to hell" notion, which Goicoechea remembers as the steady counterpoint to his childhood and adolescence in religion, sent me on a reading tour of the *Ascetical Works* of St. Alfonso Maria de' Ligouri, founder of the Redemptorists. My search was, in this sense, fruitless: the phrase, as Goicoechea told me later, occurs in one of the Circular Letters the saint wrote to the Superiors of the Order. But a study of Ligouri is a trip through the darkest zones of the mind. A Doctor of the Church—and a talented musician—this eighteenth-century Neapolitan is the prototype of the man (or woman) for whom "purity" opens all doors on heaven and earth. A thorough, scientific analysis of his *Ascetical Works* is imperative in the post-Roman phase of Universal Catholicism if his spirituality, and that of a host of clinical cases canonized by the Church, is to be seen in its proper frame of reference.)

During his years as an apprentice celibate, Goicoechea was, very exceptionally, granted permission to leave the training house only once. "That was the day I went to the railroad station to say goodbye to a sister who was entering a convent. And when I came

277

back I got a very severe reprimand. I had kissed her and, they told me, given scandal to all those around me. And I told them that she was my sister and that if I had to, I'd do it again."

Goicoechea was too young to realize it then, but the Way of St. Alfonso, like that of most ascetics, lies through a valley of sexual darkness. When, on April 20, 1950, Pope Pius XII proclaimed the Neapolitan the "Celestial Patron of all Confessors and Moralists," he struck a blow for "purity" from which the Church has yet to recover, morally and theologically. To pore over Ligouri's *Ascetical Works for the Clergy* is to find the doctrine of the Eucharist—the pivot of priestly dignity and power—perfectly crystallized around the lucubrations of a minatory sexual obsessive. The physical contact between the flesh of Christ and the flesh of the unworthy (or sexual) priest adds up to a sacrilege to which the "Celestial Patron" devotes upwards of three hundred quotation-filled pages.[8] St. Augustine, St. Peter, the Evangelists, Doctors of the Church, visionary nuns, hermits, Early Fathers— all contribute to the Gothic splendor of Ligouri's prose.

"The hand that touches the sacrosanct flesh of Jesus Christ, the tongue that reddens with his divine blood," says Chrysostom, "should be purer than the rays of the sun." And he adds in another passage that "the priest who goes up to the altar should be so holy that he could take his place among the angels." What horror, then, these angels must feel when they see the priest who is the enemy of God extend his sacrilegious hand to touch and to feed on the immaculate Lamb! . . . God turns his eyes away so as not to behold such infamy. . . . Then says the Lord, to proclaim the nausea these sacrilegious priests provoke in him, "And I will spread dung upon your face, the dung of your solemn festivities." (Mal. 2:3.) [9]

The physical immolation of Christ at the hands of the Jews is brought to play via St. Augustine:

[8] I speak of Volume II of the abridged Biblioteca de Autores Cristianos edition of Ligouri's work. The Neapolitan ascetic wrote thirty-eight books for the clergy, thirty-four for religious, and thirty for laymen.
[9] *Obras ascéticas de San Alfonso M. de Ligorio* (Madrid: Biblioteca de Autores Cristianos, 1954), II, 123.

"One thing," says Peter Damian, "is to break the laws of the prince, and another to strike him with one's own hands, which is what a priest does when he celebrates in mortal sin." Such was the sin of the Jews who dared lay hands on the person of Jesus Christ; but St. Augustine adds that "the sin of priests who celebrate [Mass] unworthily is much more serious." The Jews did not know the Redeemer as priests know him; besides, as Tertullian says, "they had the audacity to lay their hands on Jesus Christ only once, while priests are bold enough to repeat their offense frequently." [10]

Dung and damnation, physical and moral degeneracy are the themes with which Ligouri builds his doctrinal edifice. The effusions of overimaginative minds (unfortunately including St. Teresa of Avila) provide the arabesques for his grotesque monument to priestly "purity." One Sister Mary of the Crucified had, in Sicily, on "a certain day of the year 1688," a vision of a Mass celebrated in sin:

She first heard the funereal sound of a trumpet which announced to the whole world: "Vengeance, punishment and pain!" Next she saw many sacrilegious clerics who were singing in a disorderly manner. She saw one of them rise to celebrate Mass; while he was vesting, darkness began to cover the church. He approached the altar, and as he said, *Introibo ad altare Dei*, the trumpet sounded again, repeating "Vengeance, punishment and pain!" and the altar was covered with flames. . . . When the monster [i.e., the priest] reached the Consecration, several explosions were heard among the flames, which were nothing but [the priest's] fears and remorse. . . . When he pronounced the words of Consecration, the servant of God [Sister Mary of the Crucified] heard a universal earthquake which made heaven and earth and hell tremble. Once the Consecration was over, the scene changed [*sic*] and she saw Jesus Christ, in the form of a meek little lamb which allowed itself to be mauled in the claws of a

[10] *Ibid.*, pp. 124–25. Conversely, the physical conception of Christ is a cause of priestly joy. "Mary conceived Jesus Christ only once; but the priest, in the Consecration, conceives him, so to speak, as many times as he pleases; so that if the person of the Redeemer had not remained in the world, the priest, by pronouncing the words of Consecration, would produce the sublime person of the Man-God." (*Ibid.*, p. 61.)

wolf. . . . And the author of [Sister Mary's] *Life* tells that in the year 1688 an extraordinary earthquake occurred that lay waste Naples and surroundings; from which can be deduced that this punishment was effected by that sacrilegious mass.[11]

Ligouri counsels his priests to avoid all contacts with women by keeping watch over their conversations, their eyes, their touch. "A willful and prolonged look at the face of a young girl will be the infernal spark which will ruin the soul." "And if, to keep chastity, it is necessary to abstain from looking at women, it is more necessary still to flee from their conversation." His warning against commerce with spiritual and devout women ("for the more spiritual and devout, the more they will seduce and attract you") is laced with quotations from St. Augustine, St. Thomas and other holy men who knew the way of the devil in such matters. In his chapter on "Mortification" the saint enjoins his children in religion:

As far as touch is concerned, one must abstain from all familiarity with women, even if they are relatives. "But they are my sisters and my nieces . . ." "Still, they are women." Prudent confessors will do the right thing if they forbid their penitents to kiss [such women's] hands.[12]

Having unwittingly (but remorselessly) broken this rule of the Founder's on his one and only sortie, Goicoechea returned to the Seminary. Except for the communal walks in adjacent woods and mountains which were the children's only form of recreation, he was not to set foot outside of it again. In 1943, when they had completed the required six courses, his entire class was moved from El Espino to the Valladolid Novitiate by train—in a special wagon, with all shades drawn.

A year later it came time for Eusebio to profess. He was nineteen. Except for the trip to the railroad station to bid his sister

[11] *Ibid.,* pp. 127–28.
[12] *Ibid.,* p. 298. In his *Useful Reflections for Bishops* Ligouri counsels seminary prefects "To take special care that Seminarians do not touch each other, even playfully; that they have no familiarities or speak to one another alone. . . ."

goodbye, he had not set eyes on the world since he was twelve. But he wanted to leave. He was told that it was quite impossible. "Juridically, they said to me, vows were not binding after three years. But morally they held, because anyone who had a religious vocation and abandoned it would be damned." The a priori conviction of his superiors that he, like all other seminarians, had an unrenounceable vocation, was to follow him for the rest of his life in the Order.

He had his second misgivings the day preceding his ordination. "The Superior told me he knew my family, and that it was a good family. Therefore I couldn't leave. 'But what if I am making a mistake?' I asked him. He said that no one who acts under obedience ever makes a mistake—this being another of St. Alfonso's maxims."

At that time another priest of the Order also spoke to Eusebio. "He was a good priest, a holy priest. He persuaded me to stay and said he'd pray for me. He has told me he is ready to testify on my behalf now," adds Goicoechea, whose application for release from celibacy is one of the alleged ten thousand currently before the Vatican.

Upon his ordination in 1950, Eusebio expressed his desire to serve God through his one ruling passion: music. In his childhood home his father had played the violin, while he himself had started solfeggio lessons at seven. During his theological studies he had been allowed to take a correspondence course in harmony and had composed some songs. "I even persuaded the Superior to allow the celebration of a High Mass with a small orchestra—unheard of in the house!"

Now, as a young priest of twenty-six, he longed to continue his musical studies.

But the Order brought him up short. "The general idea was mortification. In other words, you should do the opposite of what you wanted, you should go completely against your grain. So, to mortify my bent for music, they announced I was being sent to Rome to study theology."

Through a last minute change of orders, another man got the Rome assignment while Goicoechea was dispatched to the Redemptorists' newly opened training house at Santafé, Granada. "It was at Santafé that I first had *serious* doubts," says Goicoechea. The doubts were provoked by an internal battle in the new community. The Superiors of the congregation had wanted to establish the institution as both a Major and a Minor Seminary; but a certain faction in the Order opposed the training of children in Granada. "Andalusians, they said, were no good for the priesthood. In their opinion the house should exist only for the training of philosophers [older students, age twenty to twenty-one]." As a reflection of the ideological struggle the children of the Minor Seminary—entrusted to Goicoechea—were openly discriminated against.

Eusebio was to teach his young charges all subjects, including music. And teaching them Gregorian, he saw immediately, presented grave problems. "In the first place they had no hymnals. The philosophers had all the books. I tried to teach the children the Latin texts by heart, but it was no good. They couldn't get the hang of it. They wouldn't learn."

Thus Goicoechea began what he soon considered his lifework: the translation and adaptation of Gregorian to the Spanish literary and musical idiom. "There were two great walls around the problem of liturgical music. First, the use of Latin, which no one understood. Second, the complexities of monastery Gregorian, which over the centuries evolved as music for trained voices and ears—a musicians' Gregorian, more polished, with more style than the original."

Alone, against the unceasing hostility of his superiors ("They called me a heretic because I clamored for the use of Spanish; you can't imagine my satisfaction when Pope John XXIII brought in the vernacular"), Goicoechea began to devote every minute of his spare time to simultaneous study of (a), Gregorian and (b), the incredibly rich folk music of Spain. "I pored over hundreds of songs. Literally hundreds. I was looking for the basis of the Gregorian accent in Spanish popular music."

As an ordained priest, Eusebio could now visit with his kinfolk and travel with some freedom when his duties permitted. On his vacations from his teaching chores at Santafé he took liturgical courses at Salamanca and did research at the monasteries of Escorial, Silos, Montserrat and even Solesmes, France, world capital of Gregorian studies.

We were speaking of Gregorian chant and of his days as a liturgist in his small apartment in a low-rent housing project near Madrid. In his wife's absence (she was at the hairdresser's, and expected shortly), Eusebio had fetched four-month-old Juan Carlos, warmed his bottle, fed him and put him back to sleep. He handled the baby with unconcealed joy: the only son was evidently the apple of his eye. His youngest girl, Gloria, age two, then burst in briefly in the company of the eldest, Catherine (born in France and given a French name); Ana María, the middle one, was playing outside.

"Papa, I want a duro for a *chupa-chus*," announced Gloria. (A *chupa-chus,* also known to cognoscenti as a *chupa-chupa* and a *chupa-chup,* is a sticky, one-peseta sucker.)

Eusebio picked her up and put her on his knee. "All right, but no chewing gum," he said, reaching for a coin. "You're not to have chewing gum."

"No, it's *not* for chewing gum," said Gloria with exquisite condescension. Of all the children, she is the one with that inner grace Spaniards call "salt." "What I want" (pause, sigh) "is a *chupa-chus.*"

Eusebio teased her gently, utterly taken with her sassiness. After another assurance that gum would not be bought—a line delivered just as haughtily, through flashing dark eyes—Gloria ran off with the coin followed by Catherine, who had watched the scene with the patience of her seven years.

We went back to Goicoechea's days in religion. The young priest's research into Spanish popular songs led him to a comparative study of French and Italian sources. "In Spanish," Goicoechea explained, "most words are accented on the penultimate vowel. In French the accent is almost always on the last one. Italian skips along, with the accent on the penultimate—this is why Gregorian chants taken from the Greek translate better into Spanish than into Latin."

He continued to teach the children at Granada, taking special care about their musical training. "I remember once I taught them a two-part *Tantum Ergo* of my own during a walk in the country. By the time they returned to the house they knew it perfectly." From Santafé Eusebio was transferred to El Espino. There he took charge of the Order's youngsters in the same classrooms where he had studied as a child. (At Santafé Goicoechea had already fought for the children's right to spend their summer vacation at home—a privilege which, yielding to mounting pressure from young priests, the congregation eventually granted its embryonic celibates.)

At long last, after his teaching stint at El Espino, Goicoechea-Arrondo was allowed by the Order to go to Paris for musical and liturgical studies at the Centre de Pastorale Liturgique.

It was in Paris that he underwent the moral crisis which led to his break with the priesthood; it was in Paris that he first knew a Protestant and it was there that he met his wife.

The *Misa Comunitaria,* in whose literary texts another Redemptorist, Father A. Danoz, had collaborated, had been the fruit of Eusebio's burning desire to render Gregorian into Spanish both linguistically and musically. Though he could not guess it then, his work was to be an overwhelming success. Today the Mass is sung in parishes throughout Spain and Latin America. At the large Jesuit church in Madrid's Serrano Street, where a group of three or four boys take the solo parts, it may be heard every Sunday. There is no choir; the music springs from the children to the congregation in antiphonal form—a true dialogue with music.

Technically, the Mass is "popular" through and through; emotionally, it is unmistakably Iberian. Intervals larger than a sixth, rare in Spanish folk pieces, are almost nonexistent. On the other hand, its eleven cantos unfold in that free, asymmetrical pattern that is at the heart of the Spanish musical idiom (perhaps the most beautiful, and quintessentially national, is the Communion chant, "As the hart panteth for clear waters," with words by a third Redemptorist, Nicanor Moriones).

"The hardest part of the Mass was that first page of the booklet," says Goicoechea. He referred to a small pamphlet, which is sold with the recorded version, in whose first page there is a schematic breakdown of the ceremonies: I, Entrance Rite; II, Liturgy of the Word; III, Liturgy of the Sacrifice; IV, Concluding Rite. "I wanted to go back to the tradition of the early centuries, to the celebration of the Mass as a re-enactment of the Last Supper. Above all, I wanted the people to feel that the Mass was really and truly a joyous banquet. First they enter, then they greet their Host, they listen to what He says, they offer their gifts, they sit down to table and express their thanks, they say goodbye. . . ."

Had Pope John XXIII already reached the Vatican, Goicoechea would have had no trouble. But it was 1956, and, in Spain, his ideas were heresy. Not only was the use of Spanish suspect, but the division of the Mass into such "untraditional" parts was not to be countenanced. Goicoechea, who like every reformer had gone back to the Primitive Church for inspiration, found the solid, baroque edifice of Latinity blocking his path. "I could not speak of the 'Liturgy of the Word,' for example. That was Protestantism. I could not work openly. Everything I did had to be done in a roundabout way."

At the time he left for Paris the Mass was still unfinished. There remained some technical difficulties which Eusebio hoped to work out at the Centre, where he plunged into his studies with enthusiasm. "Abbé Jounel" (the Centre's Secretary) "told me they had better Entrance Chants, better Glorias, better Creeds, but that the Mass as a whole was unique: there was nothing like it in France." In Paris he also met Father Gélineau, S.J., whose famous Psalms he adapted for use in Spanish churches, adding antiphons of his own in the ancient Spanish modes. ("There was one he liked an awful lot," Eusebio recalls. "He said it sounded completely Moorish.") Alone, unaware of what was being done abroad, Goicoechea had pioneered in Spain what the Frenchman had already raised to an art in Paris. The friendship between them was solid, and to this day Eusebio remembers his French mentor with affection and respect. "He is a wonderful man, a holy priest," he said, fetching an old letter from Gélineau which he let me read with understandable pride.

285

Shortly after his arrival in Paris, Eusebio had received a note from one of his sisters asking him to look up a distant cousin from their home town who had gone to France and was working as a maid with a French family. Her name was Gloria Socarro. "I thought she would be an older person, a married woman," he says. Instead he found she was single, young and attractive.

His meeting with Gloria went unheeded as he worked at his music. When she fell ill he took her to the hospital and saw that she had adequate care; other than that, he had no contact with her.

He had been back in France a short time, however, when he got word that the Order—without asking for his consent or consulting him in any way—had published his unfinished Mass in Madrid.

The accumulated frustrations of the years came to a head when he received the news. "I was stunned. I got into a layman's suit and went to Pigalle, ready to plunge into barbarousness. I walked around and around Pigalle. I did nothing."

Nevertheless, back at the house, Eusebio decided the time had come to make a definite break. "When he arrives at that decision, a priest finds himself facing a double negative. If you stay in the priesthood, you know you will have a tough time of it. If you leave, the prospects are just as dark. What can you do if either alternative is unfeasible *in conscience?*" Goicoechea, for one, began to think his way out. He remembered Gloria and went straight to her. There had been no courtship; there was to be no romance.

"I needed a woman. It was either that or complete dissolution. *One* woman. A wife. A family. All my life I had yearned for a family. So I put it squarely before her. And she refused." Goicoechea leans forward as he tells the story, his eyes shining exactly like little Gloria's. "Had she said yes that first time, I'd have left her flat." Her refusal—she was a practicing Catholic—filled him with encouragement. He talked to her at length, reasoning much as he had with himself. "I fell back on my moral and philosophical training. What I wanted to do—to marry and raise a family—was not *wrong*. But they [the Order] would never let me do it. So I would take justice into my own hands."

In his crisis Eusebio could not stop to assess them, but he had two great advantages over most men in his straits: his Argentine birth and his remarkable mental health. The first, to his surprise, paved the way for his civil marriage in France. The second was to remain with him in the months of indecision that followed, as he faced up to the consequences of the "outrage." "Because what I did was an outrage. It was a terrible mistake. If I had to do it again, I'd have asked for a dispensation and waited. But I was desperate."

What he calls the "outrage" was the common-law marriage he proposed to Gloria. Because of course he could not enter into a legal union. A civil marriage would have required a visit to the Spanish Consulate, and all Spanish Consulates are police agents of the Church by virtue of the Concordat. What he placed before her was a union by mutual consent, to be made legal if and when and as soon as he found a way to get around the Church-State law.

Gloria gave in. "I wanted a child," says Eusebio. "That was the first and main thing I wanted. And we had our first immediately."

But having taken Gloria as a wife and made her pregnant did not ease matters. Torn by doubt, Eusebio remained at the Centre, living in his old rooms in a convent where he served as chaplain's assistant. "It did not occur to me that I could ask for a dispensation directly from Rome. I had no idea that could be done. I thought I would have to go through my Provincial in Spain." And he was loath to do that: the Provincial had befriended him all along and stood up for his work. There were rumors that he would soon be removed, and Eusebio, hoping to spare the man the shock of his desertion, decided to wait until the change had been made. Catherine was born in October, 1958. In December, Eusebio went back to Spain for his Christmas vacation. He said nothing of his life in the past year. The Mass was about to be recorded and he found himself busy with the production of the record and its accompanying booklet. His Superior instructed him to register the composition with the Copyright Office and he did so without quibbling. Then he returned to Paris.

When the Provincial had been removed, Goicoechea decided the time had come to make a clean break. It was 1959. He made two trips to Spain to seek release from his vows; on one of them he faltered. "I told my Superior that if he should so order it, I would return to religion. That is known as remorse," he says emphatically, as if he had invented the word. "It hits us all about a year after we leave. It hit me. You can't undo twenty-five years' conditioning in a few months."

The only proviso he set for his return to the Redemptorists was that Gloria and the child be taken care of. "I told them the girl and the baby had to be looked after. And they told me the Order would do nothing of the kind. 'We had one woman come around here to make a claim recently,' the priest I spoke to said to me, 'and she left thoroughly chastised.' "

That was all the penitent Eusebio needed. He pressed for his release from the Order and traveled to Valladolid. "I went to the Valladolid house because there was an old priest there who knew of my problem from the days he was my confessor at El Espino, when I was a child. He did not approve of what I wanted to do, but I wanted to talk to him because he had the same problem himself. He's still in. He's never been able to bring himself to leave."

After he had obtained his release from the Redemptorists, Eusebio visited a sister in Ciudad Real and then returned to Paris, ready to do anything in order to solve the marriage problem.

In Paris, a Spanish friend told him that, by virtue of his birth near Buenos Aires, quite likely he had dual nationality. Eusebio called at the Argentine Consulate and to his joy was told the friend was right. The Consulate wrote to Buenos Aires, obtained his birth certificate and extended him a passport. On December 19, 1959, as an Argentine citizen, he married the mother of his child before the Justice of the Peace of Eaubonne, Department of Seine-et-Oise, fifteen kilometers from Paris.

But the worst was yet to come: he and Gloria wanted to return to Spain.

As Eusebio found in Madrid, the Spanish ex-priest is as legally nonexistent as his marriage and his offspring. In the "perfect society" priests do *not* leave religion, do *not* marry, do *not* beget children; if they should do any of these things they become, in the

Richard Wright sense, invisible men. Their greatest burden is not their sense of guilt nor even their inability to contract a legal marriage. It is their uselessness.

Eusebio's Argentine nationality was of no help whatsoever. In Spanish eyes he was legally and morally a Spaniard and hence a pariah. Employment in a serious business firm was out of the question. First of all, he had no documents to present. He was bereft of a *cartilla militar* attesting to his military service or legal exemption therefrom, and he did not have a *libro de familia* to present for his wife and child. On the other hand, if he made a clean breast of it, he stood revealed as a sexual degenerate in the eyes of respectable Church-Staters—and respectable Church-Staters control business and finance.

In his despair Eusebio saw an ad for an employment agency run by Caritas, the Catholic Charity organization. At Caritas he met Don Ramón Echarren, who, with two other men—one Protestant, one Catholic—were to come to his moral and material rescue.

Echarren found Eusebio work as a sacristan in the Campamento parish, a church very near the furnished room where he was living with Gloria and little Catherine. The job was his first source of income, and he took it gratefully. He rose early, was at the church before six to open the doors, prepare everything for the first Mass and, if necessary, provide music. At Campamento, Eusebio played the *Misa Comunitaria* and taught it to a group of boy singers without once suggesting he was the composer. (The parish priest, who had been told his identity by Caritas, suffered Eusebio but cut Gloria dead every time he saw her.)

Before long a compassionate priest-friend found Goicoechea an afternoon job. The man, who was (and still is) a Canon at Zaragoza, knew of a small, plastics-manufacturing firm which had just been launched there and which was looking for salesmen. On the strength of his recommendation Eusebio began to peddle the merchandise for nine and ten hours at a stretch. Mornings he worked at the church; afternoons, and late into the night, he went about with his plastic gadgets. "I used to put in sixteen- and eighteen-hour days," he recalls.

Gloria was soon expecting her second child. The Goicoecheas had by then moved to a small apartment in the Campamento section. They had no telephone; there were no taxis. (Campamento, somewhat more populated today, is a remote suburb on the Extremadura Highway.) Gloria was alone in the flat for hours at a time while Eusebio made his sales rounds. Concerned for her, the coming child and the baby Catherine, Alberto Araujo, pastor of the I.E.E. Iglesia de Jesús, and his wife Lilias took all the Goicoecheas into their home. It was from a Protestant household that Gloria was taken to the hospital to have Ana María. She then went back to the Araujos' with the newborn baby—Catherine had been welcomed as a sister by the five Araujo children—and remained there until she could settle in again at the Campamento apartment (itself furnished with pieces taken from the Araujo home).

Araujo the evangelical pastor and Goicoechea the ex-priest have remained close; so have their respective families. The two men's relationship, begun in Eusebio's most trying hour, progressed into a deep theological dialogue and mutual respect. A conversion was never discussed. "Alberto never pressured me, never said a word—he is utterly incapable of that. He helped me. He did nothing but help. I'll tell you the greatest thing that he meant to me. He meant peace of mind."

Today Goicoechea remains a Catholic who stumbled across his first Protestant by a perfect fluke and, through that meeting and the contacts that followed, gained a soul-shaking insight into an "evil" he had been taught to hate and fear. It had all begun in Paris, at the time he was still living at the convent of the Filles de la Croix, at No. 233 Rue Vaugirard, corner of Rue Volontaires. "The Mother Superior was a very intelligent woman. And extremely kind," he recalls. "She used to charge me less for my boarding than had been agreed, so I would have more pocket money. To show her my gratitude I'd do odd jobs for her." As assistant to the chaplain, Eusebio also said Mass, heard the Sisters' confessions and, at times, preached to the community in French.

One day a girl knocked on the convent door. "It turned out she was Spanish and could hardly speak French, so they sent for me. I came down to talk to her and found she had the wrong address. She was looking for an employment agency further up Rue Vaugirard. The intersection there is like this"—he took out a pen and drew a diagram on the margin of his newspaper (a copy of *Pueblo*). It was our third interview and we were sitting in a coffee shop off the Calle Mayor, near a firm where he had paid a business call. He pinpointed a small square to one side of his sketch. "This is the Métro entrance. This is Rue Vaugirard. The girl came out on this side of the Métro and, thinking this was Rue Vaugirard, she crossed over and came to the number she was looking for. Which was the convent's door on the side street."

When she found herself with a priest who spoke her language, the young Spaniard burst into tears. She was alone in Paris, she had been fired from the house where she was working and she did not know where to turn. Eusebio promised to help. He accompanied her to the employment agency, had her register there, and then remembered an institution where girls in her situation were sheltered. "I don't know if someone showed me their ad in the paper or if I first went by the place myself. It was near a liturgical-book-and-record store where I had done some shopping, at any rate. I checked the address of the place again and took the girl there."

After a few words with the Director, Eusebio discovered that he was Spanish—Mañueco by name.[13] The man took the girl in hand and made all arrangements for her. Only when he was bidding Eusebio goodbye did he express some surprise that he, a Catholic priest, should have brought the girl to his institution.

"And then I found that he was a Protestant minister!" Goicoechea explains. "I had never met a Protestant. All my life, in the Seminary, I had been told they were devils. But I had already made my decision to leave, and I was glad to know him. I wanted to talk to him, to enter into a real dialogue—not polemics, mind you, simply dialogue."

[13] Pedro Mañueco was attached to the American Board of Missions at San Sebastián during the Crusade of Liberation, when he was evacuated to France. A member of the Iglesia Evangélica Española, he is still engaged in mission work there.

Mañueco not only talked to him but gave him the names of various Protestants in Madrid, among them Alberto Araujo's. Six months or so after his return to Spain, Eusebio found the young pastor's address among his papers, called him and received the moral and material help which, along with Echarren's, saw him through the worst of his job-hunting days. (If he wants a poignant remembrance of those trying times, Goicoechea has only to read his own scholarly translation of John Calvin's *Reply to Cardinal Sadoletus*. He sold it, through Araujo and with a grateful heart, to the Netherlands' Editorial Foundation for Reformed Literature.)

While Catholics and Protestants were coming to his rescue, however, Goicoechea was tasting the rancor with which the Order, and the Established Church, sought to chastise and "crush" him. He was near starvation in Madrid when he thought of the *Misa Comunitaria* and the records that had been made thereof. On obtaining his release from the Order he had told his Superior that the Mass was theirs to do with as they pleased, asking only that they share part of the earnings with him if he should ever come to them in need. He came to them penniless, with a wife and child to support. The Order denied him a single peseta.

Rescued from his despair by Echarren, Araujo and the Zaragoza Canon who got him the plastics job, Goicoechea forgot about the Mass. But one day when he returned home Gloria handed him a notice which had arrived from the Sociedad General de Autores (the official Spanish writers' and composers' association). Its message was brief: royalty payments for the *Misa Comunitaria,* registered under his name, awaited claiming. Eusebio rushed to the S.G.A. and found that 30,000 pesetas ($500) in accumulated royalties from the record indeed awaited him (the Mass had been one of the biggest hits in the history of the Discoteca Popular Católica, the private firm that had launched it). Overjoyed, he claimed the money and bought himself a motorcycle with which to ply between his sacristan and salesman jobs.

But when he next applied to the S.G.A. for his six-month royalty payment he found that the organization had incurred the

Order's wrath and received instructions to withhold all further disbursements. Once more hoping to settle things amicably, Goicoechea asked the S.G.A. to contact the Redemptorists and let them know he was willing to negotiate the matter and come to an agreement. The S.G.A. complied—and thereupon stirred a veritable hornets' nest. The answer to their offer was an official decree of the Bishopric of Madrid-Alcalá, dated June 5, 1962, ordering the S.G.A. to annul Goicoechea's registry of the Mass and make it over in the name of the Redemptorist Order—inasmuch as he (Goicoechea) had made said copyright registration "prescinding from his condition as a professed religious." "As in the dates mentioned above [i.e., the dates of registry], the aforesaid Father Goicoechea-Arrondo was a professed religious, since he was not reduced to the lay state until May 25, 1960 . . . he could not, in accordance with ecclesiastical laws, validly inscribe under his name any work, as set forth in Canon 580, Paragraph 2: '*Quidquid autem (religiosus professus) industria sua vel intuitu religionis adquirit, religioni adquirit. . . .*' "

Eusebio argued that it was a barefaced lie; that he had inscribed the Mass under obedience, at his Superior's command. The S.G.A. was sympathetic, but it refused to budge. " 'We've come up against the Church,' the official in charge said to me,[14] and I said I didn't care if we had, I'd fight for my rights." Goicoechea appealed to Echarren, who immediately put one of the Caritas lawyers to work on the case. And so, in mid-1963, in Spain, the official charitable agency of the Roman Catholic Church challenged the Vatican-blessed Roman Catholic Establishment in a legal controversy in which the very nature of Catholic temporal power was at stake.

For the religious Order—and the Church—had been quick to adduce the dispositions of Article XXIV, Paragraph 4, of the 1955 Rome-Madrid Concordat. One of the most devastating

---

[14] Echoing Don Quixote's famous aside to his Squire, *"Con la iglesia hemos topado, Sancho,"* a phrase which has entered the Spanish language as the Iberian equivalent of "You can't fight City Hall."

weapons of the "perfect society," the article in effect gives any and all ecclesiastical decrees validity as civil measures in Spanish territory:

4. In general, all sentences, administrative decisions and decrees issued by Ecclesiastical authorities in any matter within their competence, shall also have effect in the civil order after they have been communicated to the competent Authorities, who shall, moreover, lend all necessary help in their execution.

"The idea is to crush the individual," says Goicoechea. "First you render him powerless and then you crush and crush."

Fortunately for him, Caritas took on the fight with spirit. The case was appealed to the Ministry of National Education, upon whom it was incumbent to decide for or against the decree, and for whom Goicoechea's lawyer prepared a brief. On November 13, 1963, the Director General of Archives and Libraries made known his opinion: the matter in question "as stated at the present time, remains between a Moral Person of the Church (the Congregation of the Most Holy Redeemer) and a layman (Sr. Goicoechea); [plaintiff's] document has not examined, nor does the adduced article of the Concordat account for, the juridical effects of Sr. Goicoechea's leaving the religious state upon the work under litigation; all of which bars acceptance of the exclusive and excluding competence, demanded by the aforementioned Article, of the Ecclesiastical Authority in the matter. . . ."

It was a triumph for Don Manual Jiménez de Parga, the Caritas lawyer, and for Goicoechea's perseverance. The Redemptorists and the Church, given their choice of taking the case to the Supreme Court, dropped it altogether.

To date Eusebio has collected over 100,000 pesetas (over $1600) in royalties from the best-selling record of the Mass. His energetic pushing of plastic gadgets has made him sales manager of the small firm which employed him and to which he now devotes his full attention. Every spare minute after his long days in the home office or the field he spends with Gloria and the children. "I'm speaking only of my case," he says, "but I've found happiness in marriage comes *afterwards*. With passing time." He and Gloria, ideally matched, may be proof enough for the theory. The children are healthy, happy, spirited youngsters who are receiving a Catholic education in a nuns' school.

Officially "reduced to the lay state" in 1960, Eusebio is still awaiting release from celibacy in order to marry in the Church—and in Spain. ("Reduction to the lay state" implies a release from priestly vows but not from celibacy; a man so reduced is in the same condition as a divorced Catholic who, living as a layman in the middle of the world, must forgo all sexual contact if he is to "save" his soul.)

Yet Eusebio's Catholicism, enlightened and purged of all casuistry, will remain with him for the rest of his life. "I see no need of becoming a Protestant. The label of what one is and is not is immaterial: remove a few controversial points and Catholics and Protestants will stand united. Let the Catholic Church modify some of its erroneous doctrine—let it preach *charity* in Spain—and let the Protestants understand some of their own errors and we will stand united, Christians all. There is more difference between a Jesuit and a Dominican than between some Catholics and Protestants!"

Eusebio's insistence on marrying in the Church, on the other hand, is cleansed of all sentimentality. "They took away every one of my civil rights; let them give them back to me. They took away my youth. Let them restore what's left of my life." In October, 1965, he showed me a document from the Vatican stating that his case was under study and solution would be forthcoming. Six months later, when Rome had not yet spoken, Eusebio conferred with Echarren, who, once more, is championing his cause.

When the time comes, Eusebio and Gloria will gladly kneel before a priest to receive the Church's benediction. Perhaps on that day Goicoechea will look back over the years and be thankful for the sanity which saw him to his salvation. "All my life I had a vocation to the married state," he says thoughtfully. "What I wanted was a family of my own." But he can be grateful, too, for the lack of bitterness with which he emerged from his ordeal. His passion for liturgical music is undiminished. Indeed, it is difficult to engage Goicoechea the plastics salesman in conversation without soon rousing Arrondo the liturgist (since there were two Goicoecheas in the Order—the other by coincidence also a musician—Eusebio, as is usual in such cases, was familiarly called by his second surname). If he is at home, the ex-liturgist will rise, fetch records, tapes, books, scores, find a psalm or an antiphon, point to a phrase and speak of its basis in Gregorian, sing it out in his clear tenor, tell of the days he was trying it on his young charges in the Seminary . . .

We were sitting in the coffee shop off the Calle Mayor when he made a memorable statement that he was to repeat, and elaborate on, in the days that followed. "I had nothing against the priesthood. Nothing. It was the system, it was the Order that I rebelled against. Had I been a secular priest I can assure you I wouldn't have left. Had I had a friendly hand in Paris—had I known a Don Ramón [Echarren], I'd still be inside."

I wondered again who this man Echarren was, and what made him tick so unusually at the very heart of the Church-State.

A T.V. high up on the wall was blasting the evening's news. The announcer spoke of the radiation scare at Palomares following the loss of an American H-bomb, and the screen lit up with the famous swimming party headed by Ambassador Duke and Minister of Information Fraga. For a second I was distracted and, though the view from our seat was not very good, I caught a glimpse of the seaside activity with Ambassador, Minister, aides and photographers splashing about.

Eusebio spoke again and my attention went back to him; and it was at that moment, unaccountably and curiously, that I first realized he was wearing dark-tinted glasses.

III

My lack of perception on Echarren had been just as great. It was very late in my research when, hoping to get a business address and telephone number, I asked Goicoechea where I could contact the man. "He's very hard to get hold of," Eusebio warned. "But he says Mass every morning in a church between San Bernardo and Quevedo—"

"You mean he's a priest?"

"Of course Don Ramón's a priest," replied Eusebio, himself surprised at the question. "He was an assistant at the Campamento parish when he got me the job there. And he teaches at the Seminary."

When I persisted in my shock, Goicoechea enlightened me further. "Oh, but he's not the typical Spanish priest. Far from it. He was educated in Europe."

Where could I find him? Should I go to that church . . . ?

"You could. Or you could call his office at Caritas and see if you can get him there. But it won't be easy. . . ."

I called and was given an appointment two days away, skirting a Thursday when Echarren would be busy at the Seminary. When I arrived at the Caritas headquarters in downtown Madrid—one of the oldest, seediest buildings imaginable—I was shown to a sparsely furnished sitting room where, after five minutes, Don Ramón's secretary came to fetch me.

The office she led me to was small and crowded with books and papers; the man who came forward to meet me was Don Ramón himself.

My apprehensions vanished. In fact I knew at once that I was really in luck. Echarren is a man in his thirties, of medium height, with close-cropped brown hair, horn-rimmed glasses, a perfectly round, beaming face and a crushing handshake. There is nothing of the religious about him: the cassock hangs on his person like a cheerful idiosyncrasy, cheerfully indulged. As I was to find soon enough, he is not just a young priest. He is the New Priest upon whom the salvation of the Church depends.

He led me to a chair and offered me a cigarette. "It's dark tobacco, though." I said I didn't mind and, after he had given me a light, I told him of my book on the *evangélicos* and Catholic-Protestant relations in Spain. "Anything I can do for the ecumenical movement, I'll do happily," he said. "I am at your disposal."

He did not know what I had come for—beyond taking my name and identity, his secretary had not inquired into the nature of my visit. I explained my interest at the moment was the lot of the ex-priest and the pains he had taken in the Goicoechea-Arrondo case.

297

"Ah, Arrondo?" Father Echarren's moon-face broke again into a smile. "He's so nice! [*Es muy majo!*] And his wife . . . ! Have you met his wife? They're awfully good people."

"How did you first meet Eusebio?"

"It was through a German pastor and the case of a Protestant child from La Carolina. The boy was kidnaped from a Protestant school by a Government agency and placed in a Catholic institution. Utterly shameful. They baptized him, confirmed him, gave him First Communion, everything—the poor child was completely undone. We put a lawyer on the case and returned him to his family."

In checking back with Arrondo, I found Echarren had erred on his dates: he already knew Eusebio—who had applied to the Caritas employment agency—by the time the child's case came up at the Catholic agency. In fact, it was Goicoechea who told Echarren about it. But later, as I pieced together the facts, it struck me that in a nation utterly bereft of human freedoms only the web of circumstance (or the hand of God) could have meshed together the case of the adult Catholic struggling to nurture a family and that of a Protestant boy brutally deprived of his.

The abduction took place at No. 85 Bravo Murillo Street, Madrid, on October 4, 1955. Churches closed, marriage permits denied, funerals forbidden, books and Bibles burned, court-martial celebrated for refusal to kneel before the Host—all pale beside the six-year ordeal of a child plucked from his family for the salvation of his soul.

I had no idea Caritas had intervened in the case; nor, indeed, of the bizarre circumstance that it had come to Eusebio's knowledge after his return to Spain with Gloria and the baby Catherine. Now, as I put together the life of the man who left the priesthood, I found myself reviewing the story of the child who was turned over to a succession of priests for de-Protestantization and utterly lonely access to the kingdom of heaven.

As with all Church-State bigotry, the facts of the case would provide the basis for a novel—or, better still, a harrowing documentary. The child had been born to an evangelical mother in

La Carolina, Jaén, a mining town that has been heavily Protestant since Charles III, its founder, settled it with German workers and engineers in the eighteenth century. Until age nine, no shadows crossed the boy's life, though his birth had been tragic enough: his mother, who was mentally retarded, had been raped by a Catholic (who, having been identified by her shortly thereafter, denied paternity of the child). The girl's mother, helped by her own sister, reared the boy with all love and solicitude; in 1948, when the former's health began to fail, the child's great-aunt, who lived in Valdepeñas, took charge of him.

When the boy was nine the family decided to send him to Don Teodoro Fliedner's school for Protestant children in Madrid. Fliedner is the "German pastor" Father Echarren spoke about: in actual fact, he is the grandson of the first Fliedner, Fritz (Don Federico), a missionary from Kaiserswerth who served at Madrid's Iglesia de Jesús in the late nineteenth century and established a line of pastors which has survived to our days.[15]

Madrid's Protestant school is housed in a massive brick building which, during the Republic, housed one of the *evangélicos'* main educational institutions: El Porvenir. Partly because of its existence prior to the Crusade (one of the talismans of Protestant survival), the police have chosen to overlook its blatantly illegal existence. Under the name "Hogar El Porvenir," or El Porvenir Home, the institution has been allowed to take in children provided—as in marriage cases—that proof of their non-Catholicity is presented to the Church-State.

On October 4, 1955, the President and Secretary of the Madrid Juvenile Court called on the school and demanded the boy from La Carolina. Quite clearly they had the law on their side. In Spain, as in most nations, only a legally constituted family council, through an appointed guardian, can assume custody of an orphan

---

[15] The Fliedners are an integral part of the history of Spanish Protestantism in the last century. Fritz had three sons: Don Teodoro (Sr.), dead after World War II of the effects of Nazi imprisonment; Don Juan, who died in 1964; and Don Jorge, who died in 1966. Today the surviving members of the family are Don Teodoro (director of El Porvenir) and Don Juan's daughter, Irma, also of Madrid.

or a destitute child. No such council had been formed by the boy's kin.

But the civil measure had deeper meaning in the City of God. As the authorities avowed in writ after writ, it was concern for the child's eternal salvation which had brought on his removal from the Protestant school. The Church-State rescuers were not officials of an "erroneous" lay State taking emergency action to safeguard the welfare of a minor. They were agents of the Catholic God bent upon the salvation of an immortal soul.

The child disappeared from sight.

Six months went by before the Church-State made its first statement:

INASMUCH AS corrupting examples are the cause of privation of the right of guardianship and education, one must consider it a supreme corruption to educate a child outside the Catholic Religion, the only true one, which he must profess for his eternal salvation, which Religion is endangered if the child is allowed to grow up, not only ignorant of the dogmas of the Catholic Faith, but in the disdain which the Protestant sects feel towards them.

On October 24 of that year (1956) came the first and only ray of hope: the Juvenile Court had decided to review the case.

But it was only the prelude to the family's long night. On March 23, 1957, the Church-State spoke again:

WHEREAS: Maintaining the doctrine expressed in the previous document . . . and since it would be a supreme corruption for the child, who is already a Catholic, to be educated outside of the Catholic Religion, the only true one, which he must profess for his eternal salvation, he must be separated from those persons who induce or counsel him to separate himself from it.

The child was indeed "already a Catholic." As the Church-State was to allege later, he had himself asked "in writing, to be baptized in the Catholic Religion, the presumed religion of his unknown father [sic]"; and the magic nature of baptism, so useful in marriage cases, is no less handy in a custody case. Since the boy had received "the baptismal waters according to the rite of Holy Mother the Church, it is the inescapable obligation of the State's juvenile organizations to defend the minor from all those who would pluck from his heart the beliefs he has obtained for the good of his soul." (Needless to say, the child had also expressed "a vivid desire to receive the Holy Eucharist.")

The boy's grandmother, in failing health for years, took a turn for the worse. A family council had been duly formed and a friend elected and legally constituted guardian to carry on the fight for her and her sister. But the man in question was Protestant, too, and as such a "corruptive" influence in the eyes of the Church-State. The years went by. As soon as the family got word that the child was in one school, he was transferred to another. Catechized, sacramentalized and Catholicized over a good portion of Spanish territory, in one of these sudden moves he was taken from an institution in Valladolid (the Escuelas de Cristo Rey) and carted across the country to Valencia, where he was handed over to the Jesuit Fathers.

On May 10, 1958, the guardian addressed a plea to the Ecclesiastical Tribunal at Madrid: ". . . almost three years have gone by without the Civil Tribunal having dictated a sentence." The man had presented a medical certificate attesting to the grandmother's serious illness—she was in fact near death—and soliciting permission for the boy "at least to visit her." The answer was "a wall of silence." A personal call by the guardian and the great-aunt to His Grace the Attorney for the Bishopric of Madrid-Alcalá with the plea that the lady "wished only to kiss and bless her grandson for one last time before dying" elicited the information (from His Grace) that the Madrid Juvenile Court had the last word. The Juvenile Court demurred: the Ecclesiastical Court had the last word.

On May 2, 1958, His Grace had pressed into action the heavy artillery of Canon Law. The guardian had questioned the child's baptism; His Grace, after referring to Canons 89 and 1648, Paragraph 3, makes clear that:

As for the effects of Baptism, it is doubtless that, since the boy has reached the age of discretion and can realize well enough, through the enlightenment he has received, that [his] eternal salvation is at

301

stake, natural right also liberates him from parental authority, since the business of one's salvation is strictly personal, and no one can interfere with it, not even parents.

After further appeals to Canon 750, Paragraph 3, and Canon 745, Paragraph 2, His Grace lays down the final law:

3. The condition of perfect society which the Spanish Concordat acknowledges in the Church grants it an exclusive competence in spiritual causes, as set forth expressly in the very Concordat, which, in Article 24, Paragraph 4, decrees that the decisions of Ecclesiastical Authorities "in any matter within their competence" will also have civil effect.

The conclusion, under the Rome-Madrid political and spiritual pact, is inescapable:

In view of all the above . . . the undersigned solicits that Your Honor . . . dictate a sentence to the effect that there is no cause to hand over the child —— to the guardian who claims him for the harm of his soul, and decree that he remain under the custody and guardianship of the Church. . . .

Article 24, Paragraph 4, was the same under which ex-priest Goicoechea had almost seen his royalties case crushed. In 1959, as the "calvary of writs" (so deemed by the child's guardian) continued in Spain, Eusebio was arranging for his marriage, as an Argentine citizen, in France. Though neither party knew it, the two lines of anguish were soon to touch.

But two more years of fighting remained for the child's desperate family. Late in 1959, the guardian presented to the Papal Nuncio in Madrid the three pathetic letters the boy had managed to write during his imprisonment. (Safe in the loving hands of the Catholic God, the child had been told (1) that he had no family, and (2) that his family would have nothing to do with him; but neither lie had had any effect.) Letter No. 1 had been sent one month after his abduction: "Auntie, I remember you very much. Auntie, I am well here. Auntie, come see me soon, it's been so long since I've seen you." Letter No. 2 (*three years and four months* after the abduction): "Auntie, I remember you very much and Rosi and Mother and all the other uncles and aunts and cousins. . . . Please fix everything so that I can be with you again. I am well here and I am grateful for all they have done and are doing for me. But there is nothing like being with my family and I want to go with you. I will continue to be a Catholic, I know there'll be no problem about that; but please fix everything so that I can go back to you. . . ." Letter No. 3 (three months later): "Dear Auntie: . . . I am making out this letter so you will show it to my godfather and he will see I am anxious to go home with you, and so you will give it to the Court and it will know I want to be definitely with you in the coming vacations. Don't forget to show him this letter. . . ."

My collection of documents on the child's and his family's searing ordeal ends with the "sentence" issued by the Church on November 3, 1959. These are the findings of Roman Catholic officialdom, issued through the special resident Curia in Spain:

The Juvenile Court acted legitimately in the fulfillment of its mission when it removed the minor —— from the Protestant school where he was being educated, as he practically lacked for parents, since his mother was incapacitated and the whereabouts of his father are unknown. The Ecclesiastical Attorney assigned to the case by the Ordinary, in accordance with Canon 1651, Par. 2, acted righteously when he sued in order to safeguard the spiritual welfare of said minor, who already belonged to the Catholic Church.

Had the case come to the attention of Spain's "enemies" abroad (as church closings sometimes did), the Establishment might have had to take some face-saving action. But the child's ordeal, like all heretical matters, was cloaked in the deepest secrecy. The press, a slave to Rome and the Regime, could never have been enlisted in the cause. Indeed, *no* means of public expression were open to the "corrupt" Protestants: until the coming of Pope John XXIII, political and religious "truth" meted out its swift, unilateral justice in the assurance it was responsible only to God and to history.

One cannot conjecture how or when the case might have been solved if Caritas had not intervened. But in Paris, in his days of crisis, Goicoechea met a girl in distress whom he attempted to help. Through her he met Mañueco, and through Mañueco, Araujo. It was Araujo who told him of the child's situation; it was Goicoechea who told Echarren, who in turn went into the legal battle with a Caritas lawyer.

Caritas' intervention may not have been decisive in and of itself: it was simply the last and most telling blow against the Church's tyranny. By then the case had been taken to the Vatican's Holy Office, the child's lawyer had submitted a profusion of briefs, and six years had gone by. Caritas might have been the Catholic straw that broke the camel's back.

The boy was returned home. Today he is a young man of twenty-one who has "given his witness" in his family's church (they belong to the Plymouth Brethren) and become a full-fledged *evangélico*. His soul, marked for damnation in the eyes of the Catholic Church, has found the light of his family's faith because they never gave up the battle for him—and quite possibly because a "modern" priest was shocked and revolted by his ordeal.

But I had come to the "modern" priest to speak of Goicoechea. "So Eusebio came to you for help. And then what did you do?"

"At first I got him some private Greek and Latin classes," said Echarren. "And then a job at the Campamento parish."

I told him I knew of Eusebio's work there, and the gratitude with which he took it. Echarren smiled as if he remembered the event with some relish. "That had its risks, you know. I can't give you the exact reference now, but that sort of thing is absolutely forbidden by Canon Law. It could have got us an excommunication."

"Then you're aware of the situation of ex-priests, Father . . ."

"Am I!" he said good-naturedly. "Tell me, would you like another one for your study?" He rose and fetched an address book from which he read me a name, Madrid street number and telephone. "Is he married?" I asked.

"No, this one's single. Give him a ring and you'll see what he's going through."

"Do many of them come to Caritas?"

"I'd say I've seen some twenty pass through here."

"And how do the Church authorities react?"

"Very well. In every case I know of Don Casimiro [Casimiro Morcillo, Archbishop of Madrid] has shown himself one hundred per cent behind them."

I expressed my surprise. Don Casimiro is not known for his liberal turn of mind.

"No, you musn't judge by appearances. Don Casimiro may seem close-minded in theory but he is very open in practice. Just now, while he was at the Council, he fixed up everything so that an ex-priest from Cuenca could get married—a very good man who has several children."

It was the second time Don Ramón had used the word "good" in referring to an ex-priest. He did so without unctuousness; one understood he believed in their goodness.

When I asked how he handled the usual cases which come through Caritas, he answered that his first concern was to get them psychiatric assistance. "Most of them are neurotics by the time they come out of the seminary."

"Do any of them want to embrace Protestantism?"

"Oh yes, some come out clamoring that they're going to join the Protestants. And ninety per cent of *them* are hopeless neurotics. Their personalities were completely distorted by the time they left the Seminary. If they do become Protestants, they'll quite likely end up in one of two extremes. They'll either fall into an out-and-out Puritanism or they'll return to the Church looking for punishment, eager to be chastised." He paused. "And then there are some cases of authentic conversion, like Celso Muñiz's."

It was the second time in our interview that Echarren had touched on a key case in Church-State history.

"I've heard of Muñiz," I said. In fact, I had heard Father Echarren's exact words (an "authentic conversion") applied to the phenomenon by a perceptive Protestant.

"Yes, well you know he was Spiritual Director of the Seminary of Oviedo. The man had lived his entire life in a neuroticizing atmosphere, what I call pseudo-Ignatian Catholicism—a Catholicism of anguish, very much in the Kempis line, centered on asceticism. His very position as Spiritual Director, his devotion to his duty only made his anguish worse. He discovered in Protestantism some values which, for certain schools of thought among us, are typical of Catholicism. He found values which were *contrary* to the neuroticizing environment in which he lived. He found his liberation. I wish I had a letter of his here to show you—I have several."

Father Echarren waxed eloquent on the "neuroticizing" tendencies in seminary education. "I came into the seminary very late," he explains. "I was studying to be an engineer. I came in clean, off the street, from the world of science and mathematics."

The word "clean" struck me. Proponents of training priests from childhood advance the term "purity" in speaking of tender souls who have never been sullied by the world. Yet here was a modern priest free of all pietism, dynamic, bursting with charity, who referred to himself as "clean."

"And you studied abroad?"

"Yes. I did my philosophy at Salamanca, then I went to Rome for theology and Louvain for sociology." He spoke of his open contacts with Protestants while he was a student in Rome and of his enthusiasm for the ecumenical cause. "And I'm a Navarro [i.e., born in the Carlist North]," he added as a laughing boast. "And when I was a child I heard the most frightful things about Protestants."

His secretary had twice poked her head in the door to remind him the twelve o'clock appointment had arrived. "Yes, yes, in a minute," he'd said. We had been speaking for over an hour about ex-priests, the roots of bigotry ("lack of culture, nothing but lack of culture," Echarren insisted), and even politics. Before I left I wanted to touch on one last matter. Did he know—for it is sadly true—that Protestants were often denied Caritas food by the nuns who distributed it in Spain?

"Yes," he said. "It happens. The nun will think she's doing a very good thing. She's been told Protestants are devils, you see" (he used the same word as Goicoechea: *demonios*).

The man who had been waiting in the outer office gave me a sharp look as I emerged with Echarren. Don Ramón and I took our leave; the young priest turned to his next visitor with his open, welcome-to-Caritas smile and motioned him briskly to his office.

As Echarren's secretary escorted me to the ancient, creaky stairs that descend to the Cuesta de Santo Domingo, I apologized for having overextended my stay. "I quite understand," she said. "Really, so few people can get a whole hour with Don Ramón. . . ."

15

The underground railroad of Catholic priests who convert to Protestantism leads directly to Holland. There is an institution run by the French Reformed Church in Montpellier that also shelters them, but it is not as widely known as "De Wartburg," headquarters of the Dutch foundation "In de Rechte Straat" (or "On the Straight Street." The title refers to the vision which moved Ananias to seek out Saul of Tarsus: "And the Lord said to him, Rise up and go to the road called Straight Street; and enquire at the house of Judas for a man of Tarsus, named Saul." Acts 9:11–12).

Among the distinguished alumni of De Wartburg is Celso Muñiz, the "authentic convert" Father Echarren spoke about. The former Spiritual Director and Professor of Ascetical and Mystical Theology at Oviedo now lives in Kampen, the Netherlands, with his wife and infant daughter. He is working towards a doctorate in theology at the Free University of Amsterdam, where Señora Muñiz is professor of Spanish. My visit to Holland, of necessity brief, precluded my meeting the couple; but I called at De Wartburg on a rain-and-shine afternoon in the month of November, 1965.

I had heard of Rechte Straat through two sources: a *Time* news story on June 22, 1962 (the week of De Wartburg's opening), and material given me by Protestant friends in Madrid. *Time* concerned itself mostly with the personality of the organization's founder, Herman Johannes Hegger, minister of the Calvinist Church of the Netherlands:

Doubts About Dogma. A seminary student from the age of twelve, Hegger was ordained as a priest in 1936. Even as a novice, he had doubts about Catholicism's Marian dogmas and about papal infallibility; as a priest, he also came to question the validity of the Mass and confession. Sent to Brazil to teach philosophy, Hegger learned the tenets of Protestantism from a Methodist pastor in Rio; in July, 1948, he formally left the church.

On finding the "pure Gospel," as Hegger calls his conversion in one of Rechte Straat's pamphlets, he also found his unique mission: lending moral and material assistance to ex-priests who were adrift in the world. "They need help," Hegger told *Time.* "They are so much alone."

The "help" extended them by the man who entered the seminary at twelve carries a heavy baggage of anti-Catholicism. One Spanish-language pamphlet issued by Rechte Straat—and available to fallen-away priests through Protestant churches in Spain —sets forth the principles of the Reformed Faith in question-and-answer form. There are thirteen points for would-be converts to ponder: 1. How can you be saved? 2. Faith in the authority of the Bible or in the authority of the Popes? 3. Confession. 4. The cult of Mary. 5. The Mass. 6. You too can be a priest. 7. Purgatory. 8. The exact number of books in the Bible. 9. Celibacy. 10. Unity. 11. Who is the Vicar of Christ on earth? 12. Apostolicity. 13. The apparitions at Lourdes ("Therefore, heeding the word of God, we should attribute these apparitions to the Power of Darkness, and not to the God of Light").

The inside back cover shows a picture of De Wartburg with the words:

The foundation in de Rechte Straat shelters in this house any Roman Catholic priest, without distinction as to nationality, who leaves his Church for reasons of conscience; it helps him morally and financially so he may start a new life as a layman or as a pastor, evangelist, etc., if he has a true, God-given vocation thereto.
For more information write De Wartburg at
11, Boulevar
VELP (Gld.) HOLLAND,
Tel. 08302–4959

THE THIRTY THOUSAND

I

Number 11 Boulevar is a pleasant, mellow house of Dutch brickwork, its red walls, like so many of its style, set off by the sparkling-white window sashes. The taxi ride from Arnhem is brief, and it wasn't quite two o'clock when I was ringing the doorbell.

I had written to Mr. Hegger, who had replied with a cordial invitation to the house. He greeted me in Spanish and summoned a young man whom he introduced in the same language, adding, for his benefit: *"Puede hablar con toda libertad. Es una buena evangélica."* ("You can speak freely. She is a good Protestant.")

"But I am *not* Protestant, Mr. Hegger," I hastened to explain. "I'm a Catholic."

The smile vanished from Mr. Hegger's lips; he narrowed his eyes and fixed them sternly on me. There was a crashing silence. Standing in the vestibule of De Wartburg, I wondered if I had come all the way to Holland only to be turned back.

I found myself explaining I had come on my own behalf, for my own research, and in no way represented any Catholic school of thought. Hegger continued to frown in stony silence. The young Spaniard murmured a word or two on my behalf which I seconded as spiritedly as I could. After two or three minutes of pleading on my part, and another awkward pause, Hegger bade the young man take me upstairs.

We climbed to the top floor, where a girl in a blue smock was busy preparing a meal. The young man introduced her as Guillermina Crespo. I turned to ask his own name (I had not caught it the first time) but he had already disappeared down the stairs.

The room we were in contained a couple of couches, a tape recorder, a stove and sink, a small dining table and a few chairs. Guillermina—a petite, very pretty girl with an expression so earnest it was almost grave—apologized for her smock and her chores and showed me to a seat. A little later we were joined by another young man.

310

The new arrival was short, stocky, with flaming red hair and blue eyes, and at first glance I took him for some Dutch assistant of Mr. Hegger's. But he was a Spanish guest: Esteban Peña, age thirty, from Soria. Presently I engaged him in conversation while Guillermina went back to her work.

I asked him how many Spaniards were in the house at the moment and he said ten: one ex-Jesuit, one man who had gone to a seminary for late vocations, three married couples, a six-month-old baby, and himself.

"And you left the religious life too?"

"I escaped."

When I asked when he had entered religion, Peña replied he had joined an Augustinian monastery at the age of twelve and a half.

"Your parents sent you there?"

"No, I went of my own free will. I had a real vocation. I wanted to be a monk—an Augustinian."

He explained that his mother had died when he was four and that his father (who still lives in Soria) opposed his entering the Order because, as the only son, he should have assumed responsibility for the family. "No, my father and my relatives were not very keen on my going into the religious life. But they loved me and they left me free to do my own will."

Peña professed at eighteen, made perpetual vows at twenty-three, and was ordained at twenty-four. He had a bent for art (which he had studied for a year and a half at Salamanca) and for belles-lettres. After ordination, he was assigned as teacher of Spanish literature in one of the Order's high schools in Logroño.

One day he heard what he refers to as "the call." "I felt psychologically imprisoned. It was a real bondage, it was like being in chains. I was serving my Superior, not God. God asked me to break with all that."

"All that" was the religious-life-cum-Catholicism; Peña, who had been in Holland all of six days, was virulently anti-Catholic. He spoke tonelessly, raising his voice only when he made a point against the Church. After a while it seemed to me that he was in a mild, controlled shock, unable to utter anything but pious Prot-

311

estant clichés. "The religious life is against the Gospel." "For me, anyone who believes in Christ is a priest."

As he elaborated on the first point I expressed some disagreement. The religious life might be for very few, unusual souls, but it couldn't be altogether antievangelical. What about the community of Protestant monks at Taizé?

Taizé was no proof against his argument. He resumed it with vigor, quoting a passage which I later identified as John 17:15–19: "They do not belong to the world, as I, too, do not belong to the world that is truth. Thou hast sent me into the world on thy errands and I have sent them into the world on my errand; and I dedicate myself for their sakes, that they, too, may be dedicated through the truth."

Dialectically conditioned or not, Peña's own irruption into the secular life was as deeply traumatic as any ex-priest's. "What can you do," Eusebio Goicoechea had told me in Madrid, "if either alternative is unfeasible *in conscience?*" Peña put it more briefly: "The first leap is a leap into nothingness."

When he decided to make his break, Peña had his tonsure made afresh in a barbershop "to throw off the police," announced he was going to visit his father (which he did) and then, instead of returning to the Order, changed course for the eastern part of the country.

He spent four months working as a waiter in Peñíscola and a year in Barcelona. In the latter city, where he was first sheltered by a poet friend, he earned his living as a bricklayer and lamplighter ("I lit the lamps at Pedralbes Palace for a month and a half," he recalled). During that time he also applied himself to the greatest problem facing an ex-priest who wishes to leave Spain. In his own words: "I started changing my papers from priest to layman."

The change is an absolute requirement if a man is to leave the country: in the past twenty-five years police regulations have demanded that a priest soliciting a passport present authorization *in scriptis* (in writing) from his bishop for obtaining same. Every ex-priest I met spoke of the rule with ill-contained bitterness. One of them even recalled the days when police authorities, as a double check, phoned bishops and inquired personally into the priest's authorization to go abroad.

"One police official offered to make out a passport for me," says Peña. "At first I accepted but later I changed my mind and told him I'd rather wait a few months than have him lose his job."

When he obtained his new papers and passport he got on the train and came to Arnhem, where, like all of De Wartburg's protégés, he is doing manual labor to support himself. Like all of them, too, his conversion is a *fait accompli*. "I had an infamous [*infame*] idea of Protestants," he says. "I even translated [from the Italian] a poem of Vito Liberio's which had Luther writhing in hell." At the time of my visit with him, Peña had not yet decided whether he would become a Baptist or a Methodist.

I had had a few minutes with Guillermina before Peña came in; and towards the end of my interview with Peña we were joined by Guillermina's husband, Enrique García Vall. After my misgivings downstairs I was grateful for the ungrudging attention all three gave me; especially the girl, who, in her quiet and straightforward way, had broken the ice when I first arrived.

She was small and frail and wore no make-up. "My husband went in when he was eight," she had begun, and her next statement came in the same breath. "He didn't visit with his mother or his family for fourteen years."

When I asked what order her husband had belonged to, she told me he had been a Capuchin at El Pardo (a monastery in suburban Madrid, just outside Franco's palace, famous for a statue of the Dead Christ known and venerated as the "Cristo del Pardo").

She herself was from Vigo, where she had had a normal and happy life and had spent her school days as a boarder in a nuns' *colegio*. From childhood she had studied the piano, traveling to Madrid each year to take the official examinations at the Conservatory until she had completed the entire eight courses required for professional standing. It was not in Madrid, however, but in Vigo, that she met young García Vall—a musician and composer sent there by his Order to direct a choir.

They knew each other seven years. At first, she explained, it

313

was a matter of casual friendship. "We were two people who liked each other, simple friends." When she discovered it was a deep friendship, "then, in conscience, it seemed wrong. I went to Italy, I did not write him, I had no contact with him. I didn't want him to leave the priesthood. I wanted him to be a priest, a good priest, a man given over [entregado] to God."

It was quiet in the attic room as she spoke in her grave and composed manner. "God can't go against what is basic in man. People are born, they marry, they die. . . ."

Peña then came in, and Guillermina went back to work. Apparently almost everyone in the house had already had lunch, but halfway through my talk with Peña another Spaniard arrived and apologized for having to sit down to his meal while I was carrying on the interview. He was the late-vocation man, Manuel de la Torre.

García Vall, thirty-five, turned up just before Peña left for a Dutch class. García is dark, good-looking and as solemnly earnest as his wife. Seen together, they strike one as an unusually attractive and sedate couple.

He corrected Guillermina's statement as to the age of his entrance in religion. "I was ten, not eight," he reminded her. The first seminary he went into was diocesan; from there he passed to the Capuchins. His memories of childhood in the secular training house are a faithful echo of Goicoechea's reminiscences of life at El Espino. "One boy left when he was thirteen," García recalled, "and they said he had damned himself because he had 'taken his hand from the plow and looked back.' He had betrayed his vocation. He would find nothing in life, absolutely nothing."

García was the third sacrificial offering I had met after a tortuous escape. Thinking back to my own convent school days, when we re-enacted a ceremony known as the "Petite Marie" (the order was French), I wondered about the Jewish antecedents of presenting children to God. At Sacred Heart School, a specially chosen girl was dressed as the virginal Mary and acted in her place and stead in a ceremony commemorating the Blessed Mother's internment in the Temple at the age of three. Afterwards, in celebration, we had a brief holiday (congé).

What was a symbolic Jewish ritual in our school is, however, a reality in Spain, and the vigor with which the custom has survived (in 1965 I visited an ancient seminary near Palencia in whose cloisters baby priests of eight and nine were playing tag) may point to another hardy Hebrew strain in the Spanish temper. On the other hand, there is an element of down-to-earth, practical hope in the minds of some parents who "offer their children to God." As in ancient times the priest, in Spain, is a man of letters. In villages across the land he is a combination guru and gray eminence, statesman and scholar. In the past twenty-five years a child from the gigantic lower class had, in the seminary, a chance for higher education unavailable to him anywhere else in the closed, oligarchic system. "I've taught some of these children," says Enrique García, who speaks of the social realities behind the minor seminary system with bluntness. "And believe me, they had to be taught everything. I've had boys of nine who had never seen a toilet."

We had been talking for about half an hour when Guillermina left us and returned with six-month-old José David. She settled him on her lap and began to feed him lunch; García and I spoke to the rhythmic scraping of the spoon against the dish as José David—a beautiful child who has his mother's features and his father's coloring—took his creamed spinach with gusto.

Upon leaving the Order, García worked in Madrid as an insurance salesman and a painter (his father was a sculptor who did the cupola of El Fénix, the art-nouveau headquarters of an insurance company in Madrid's Gran Via). He also did credit ratings for a firm which paid him from eight to ten pesetas (thirteen to sixteen cents) a report. "I used what sources I could, including sometimes the concierge of the party's apartment house. They didn't expect any wonders from eight to ten pesetas a case," he added with one of his rare smiles.

But he was grim when he referred to the life of the ex-priest in Spain. "We have to live under three denials: One, the denial of the right to marry. Two, the denial of a passport to leave the country. And three, the denial to work."

The passport problem, in theory the most formidable of all,.

is in practice quite often solved by collusion: the humane police-man or government official willing to help out will wink at regu-lations and issue new papers. Such was probably the case with García's *carnet de identidad*—his and every ex-priest's first ob-stacle. The *carnet* is a police identification document, renewable every five years, which every adult Spaniard must possess. On its three-by-four-and-a-half-inch surface appear his or her name, ad-dress, parents' names (even if deceased), date of birth, profession, civil state, photograph, one fingerprint each from the right and left hands, and a control number.

García's old *carnet* said "priest." "I went to the identification authorities and told them I had never had one made out. They made me pay a hundred-peseta fine and gave me a new one as a layman." When I asked friends in Madrid I was told the likelihood of the official's not checking his files on García was very slim. Outside of gypsies very few Spaniards, even illiterate or resident in the most remote parts of the country, are without a *carnet*.

The marriage problem that faced Enrique and Guillermina in Madrid (where, as Baptists, they were wed in a Baptist ceremony) revolved around the classic Vatican-inspired nightmare of juridical nonexistence outside the "True Church." Goicoechea had been saved in Paris by his Argentine birth; García, a Spaniard, is com-mitted for life to the stranglehold of the Catholic God. After "changing" every paper besides his *carnet,* obtaining a passport, fleeing to Holland, contracting marriage under Dutch legislation and becoming a father, Enrique attempted to register his new state of life—and legitimize his son—at the Spanish Consulate. The Consul's reply is a testimonial to what Spanish theologians call "the rights of truth":

I hereby acknowledge receipt of your letter of June 25 past, in answer to which I inform you that, in accordance with Paragraph 4, of Article 83 of the Spanish Civil Code, "those who have received holy orders, or those who belong to a [religious] order approved by the Catholic Church and who have a solemn vow of chastity cannot contract marriage if they have not obtained a dispensation from the Church. Save in cases where such dispensation has been granted, their marriage is illegal and therefore the children born of such marriage are illegitimate.

With my deepest respect, I enclose a copy of this letter in the Spanish language, and remain,

Yours truly,

The Consul-General of Spain

[*signed*]   by Miguel Sainz de Llanos

Nor does the "spiritual" blackmail end there. Like most ex-priests, García sought release from celibacy in order to marry in Spain. But the Vatican, only now coming to grudging terms with the "hemorrhage" of fallen-away men, is not willing to let its guard down where Spanish cases are concerned. García brought me a letter sent him by a friend in the Order who is taking charge of his negotiations in Spain. The friend regretfully quoted the reply received from the Vatican, which was an energetic *no:* dispensation from celibacy, it read, would be granted only to those men who remained "in the bosom of the Church" (*"en el seno de la iglesia"*). García's checkmate is thus complete. In order to marry in Spain, he would have to get a dispensation from the Church, and in order to get a dispensation from the Church, he would have to return to the Catholic faith. In the post-Council age, Catholics can merit clemency from the Church-State; Baptists remain subject to the "truth." "In Spain," says García (with the exact note of despair that rises in Protestants' voices when they speak of their indignities), "my son would be like a child born on any street corner." He is remaining in Holland.

But like all converts abroad, he hopes that someday he may be able to return to Spain and preach the Gospel there. "The Lord will open the way." He describes his conversion simply, in a simple statement: "In Spain I found that true Christianity was being preached in the Protestant churches. I belong to the [Baptist] Church at General Lacy Street in Madrid. My pastor in Done José Luis Rodrigo."

García, whose field is music (while a Capuchin he received ex-

317

tensive training in harmony and composition), has recorded some of his works for Rechte Straat and is now an assistant to Mr. Hegger in the latter's missionary endeavors. Before he left for a preaching campaign that afternoon, he mentioned the personal ostracism in which he and Guillermina had found themselves since their marriage. "I was closest to my elder brother; he is precisely the one who will not speak to me." In Guillermina's case it was far worse. "She was the dearest of her family's children. But she doesn't hear from them. They won't even answer her letters."

The strain on Guillermina's face came into focus now. Had I not seen her downstairs a little later, relaxed and happier, I would have remembered her as a girl fighting back tears. Her parents, she explained without losing her composure, did not even know she had had the baby.

I took my leave of her and Mr. Hegger in a spacious room on the rear of the ground floor. My host had come round after his initial disapproval and we chatted about Rechte Straat, its history, the foundation's publications and its plea for funds (among the recent contributions had been one from a Dutch priest in perfectly good standing). Guillermina seemed to have taken on some of the cheeriness of the room, which had a high ceiling, white-painted walls and a half circle of armchairs around a large fireplace faced in Delft tiles. "The Dutch are marvelous people. They live for their homes and their children," she said.

Certainly De Wartburg, named for the Saxon fortress which sheltered Martin Luther, seems committed to hearth and home. Rechte Straat's small magazine, printed in Dutch and circulated to some twenty-five thousand people, carries pictures of ex-priests, their wives and children. Hegger himself lives in the house with his family. At the time of my visit Mrs. Hegger was expecting their seventh child; Guillermina pointed out a large, dark-wood infant's cradle on massive rockers which, in anticipation of the event, had been brought out for airing.

There was something both fierce and tender in the sight of that old-fashoned cradle in the back porch at No. 11 Boulevar, Velp, near Arnhem.

318

II

Don José Luis Rodrigo received me in the small office at his Baptist Church, which is located near Madrid's Atocha Railroad Station. He is a man in his late thirties, married, the father of five children, who ministers to the four hundred and fifty *evangélicos* in the General Lacy congregation.

He told me he had met García at the home of a member of his church. "He [García] had seen in the *evangélicos* a peace and serenity he himself did not have in spite of all his years of study and sacrifice. He wondered why. His own spiritual unquiet roused his interest [in Protestantism]. I talked to him. He had many questions to ask me and I answered them. We prayed together. He was touched, he was impressed by the manner in which we pray. As you know, we pray just as we talk. We talk to a Father, to a personal God, not to someone far away. The simplicity of it all impressed him. We talked further. Then he came to the church and I myself baptized him.

"All this spiritual unquiet coincided with a problem of a social nature. 'Why can't I marry?' 'Why can't I have children?' he would ask. He told me of the young lady he knew in Vigo. She came to Madrid and they were married in my house."

In Holland, García had given me a mimeographed flier in Spanish which he had prepared for circulation among other ex-priests.

It has been one long year since I left the Roman Church and I must confess that Wartburg has been a good experience for me. Let me explain:

I was a Capuchin friar, and when I abandoned my Order and was joined in marriage to the woman I loved, my intention was to break completely with the past. I didn't want to know anything about "all that." . . .

For nine months and a half I lived on my own with my wife, without the least awareness that cassocks and habits had ever existed in this world; nor did I think of the problems of others who had taken the same step as I. At Wartburg, contact with my companions awakened me to reality. . . . Through your letters I have realized one thing: the majority of our dear "exes" are still in anguish.

. . . I speak of anguish. Of lack of peace. Of something very like what I used to feel before, when I was at the Monastery, and which impelled me to leave.

The problem is wholesome, the anguish is not. Adversity makes us bigger and gives us a chance to prove our faith. Anguish cuts us down and shows us we have no true faith.

García's answer to his anguish was having "found Christ." "Have you," he asks his readers, "found that ideal, real Christianity that I know (through my own case) that you yearn for? A Christianity without subterfuge, without things produced from the sleeves of men 'higher up'—THE CHRISTIANITY OF CHRIST'S, OF HIS WORD, THE GOOD KIND . . . THAT ONE . . ."

Through his conversion, García also found social dignity and the right to marry. In contrast to Goicoechea's case, he had fallen in love with Guillermina years before, and she with him. Music, both admit, was their common meeting ground and the basis for their spiritual closeness. When they acknowledged their mutual attraction and surrendered to it, Guillermina (whose family seems solidly musical—the sister with whom she was living in Italy is married to a cellist in the chamber ensemble I Musici) made plans for her return to Spain.

The "marriage" took place before a notary on July 1, 1964; it was not the first so performed for ex-priests who have left the Church, and it will not be the last. "Many ex-priests come through here with tremendous problems," Rodrigo told me. "They say 'We're turning Protestant' and expect us to help them immediately. We will not do so. We are only interested in cases of true conversion. When we see there is sincerity and true repentance for sin, then we help."

The only marriage certificate Enrique and Guillermina have under Spanish law is not a certificate at all. Faced with the tragic situation of ex-priests who convert, Protestant authorities have drawn up an affidavit to be signed and sworn by the contracting parties in which they promise, and swear, to marry whenever the

320

law so allows them. Señor Cardona of the Evangelical Defense Commission, through whose office a steady procession of ex-priests threads its way, has a bulging file of such *actas notariales.*

Only time will humanize the lot of the priest (and therefore, of the ex-priest) in Spain. To date, children continue to be herded into minor seminaries, grown men in many dioceses are forbidden to attend the movies, the theater or any other "shows," and the cassock—that symbol of sexual apartheid—continues to flap about the feet of men given over to God.

The cassock is, in fact, known in Spanish as the *hábito talar,* or "habit which falls to the ankles" (*talones*). One of the most spirited exchanges in the Letters column of *El ciervo* took place in 1965 between two priests who took their ankle-length griev-ances to that courageous publication. The first to write was Father Isaac Morillo of Seville, who in the June issue contributed two columns of spirited infighting against the cassock, alleging reasons of a "pastoral" and a "practical" order. In the letter was a truly burning paragraph:

As I write this (6:00 P.M.) our thermometer marks 90° in the shade (this is no Andalusian whopper); in barely a month we shall reach 100° in the shade and 115° in the sun. Can you, and my brother priests in the North, imagine what this must mean for us who wear a cassock 24 hours a day?

A brother priest in the North took up his cry in September. Meteorologically, Father Alberto Torga Llamedo of Onis, Asturias, and *his* fellow clerics did not come off any better:

I can well realize what a "delight" it must be for my Southern brothers to wear a cassock when the thermometer goes over 100°. But it is no less "appetizing" to wear it on a rainy, blustery day, and such days are as common in our region as sunshine in Andalusia. The lower part of the habit then becomes like a mop with which one has just finished wiping the floor.

Father Torga, whose letter was briefer, ended it with vigor:

To finish, I shall ask a question in case there is someone who can answer it for me: Couldn't the fact that men flee from the priest and

321

the church, while women are more "clerical" and more "church people," have to do with the fact that our habits are, when all is said and done, skirts?

On December 15, 1965, when the tremors of the Declaration of Religious Liberty were shaking the *integristas,* newspaper reporters submitted some questions to the Archbishop of Madrid-Alcalá. As *Ya* had it:

"What truth is there to some rumors about the abolition of the cassock?"

"There is no truth to them. They are a rumor. . . ." [1]

The newspapermen went on to another measure of "decorum" required of Spanish priests: "Is there a regulation prohibiting priests from attending *espectáculos?"* they asked.

There is in fact such a measure, and there has always been in the life of the Church-State: hardly any priests are seen in movies or theaters in Spain. Those that do attend (unless the film or play being shown is religious) do so in flagrant violation of diocesan rules. As Archbishop Morcillo answered through his secretary: "There is a synodal decree to that effect in the Diocese of Madrid. We have upheld, therefore, the diocesan legislation. Maybe it doesn't matter to some, but to others these amusements seem scandalous."

The saddest evidence of the worship of "purity," however, was to be found on September 19, 1965, in a small Sunday newspaper, *Luz y vida,* distributed in all Madrid parishes. Under a headline entitled "One Hundred and Eighty Boys Want to Be Priests" it proclaimed:

What foolishness we men talk when we are speaking of theories! Childhood vocations and adult vocations! As we progress in the dis-

[1] The *sotana* problem is raising semantic difficulties in Spain, where there is no other word to describe ecclesiastical clothing. The English term "clergyman," introduced after the Council, is rapidly coming to mean "clergyman's *garb.*" To the Academicians' all too natural despair, the word has entered the vocabulary much the same as "Christmas," which has come to mean "Christmas card." Thus, after the holidays: "Thank you for the lovely Christmas you sent me"; and, to describe a foreign priest: "He was wearing a clergyman."

cussion, the beautiful words pile up: psychology, evolution, crisis, maturity. Then, suddenly, one comes up against a child or a boy who wants to be a priest and the theory vanishes. . . . I mention all this apropos of two marvelous days among children who wanted to be priests. Our Archbishop had asked for more vocations, and this year 180 have turned up for admission to the Seminary. . . . A group of Capuchin Tertiary Fathers, specialized in psychology, ran after the children with intelligence, sensitivity and personality tests— three fundamental aspects in the first moment of the child's decision. . . . How difficult and amazing it is to discover the small trace left by God's passing!

The war of the human against the evangelical is far from over. Only God knows how many of the 180 baby bonzes who entered the seminary in Madrid will swell the casualty lists. But one thing is sure: the human is winning the day.

In far-away Holland, when José David was born, Enrique García Vall wrote the words and music of a *nana,* or Spanish cradle song, to sing his Dutch son to sleep:

Nana, nana, nanita, suza nina,
Doll of snow, son of my soul,
Nana, nana, nanita, suza nina,
The dawn is breaking through your sleep,
Nana, nana, nanita, suza nina,
And my mouth has breath for your tomorrow.

When you cry
Your tears are like a flake
Of foaming light before me;
When you smile
I am as water held in its course, sparkling, alive;
And smile you or cry,
I feel life itself
In the pupils of your eyes.

In your soul you carry
The dunes of Holland,
The mountains of Spain.
Be kind and good like Joseph,
Like David, strong and brave!
Live and sing out, my son. . . .

Epilogue

When "God opens the way" and young José David García Crespo comes to Spain with his Baptist preacher father, he may have the luck of taking up residence in an open society. If so, his lot in that "unspiritual," "erroneous," "lay" system will be as serene and full of dignity as any Spaniard's—including (if she is still alive) the sheepherder's widow who dispatched a letter to Rome during the Second Vatican Council.

She did not write it, of course; she is illiterate. She dictated it and asked that it be sent to Father Juan Arias, the young champion of the Catholic Left, who wrote about it in the Labor Syndicates' national magazine, *Tiempo Nuevo*.

While in Rome covering the Council, says Father Arias in his article, he received two memorable letters from his homeland. One was from a Spanish labor official wishing him well in his work.

The other letter was dictated in a far corner of Spain by an old woman who cannot write, and who had been through the grief of seeing the body of her husband—a sheepherder, also illiterate—buried in un-consecrated ground.

The man had had a heart attack. Since his wife had called the doctor before she called the priest, the latter, alleging the existence of a family problem, refused to give the man burial in the Catholic cemetery—to the indignation of the entire village who, she says, bore "her Antonio" great love. The wretched woman has not gone back to the Church, but as she tells me, she feels an emptiness in her soul. She says she is willing to forgive everything if—and I quote—"the Pope and Father Arias" can fix it so that "her Antonio" may lie in the Catholic cemetery, because "he was more Christian than anyone else and had his wallet full of saints" [i.e., holy pictures]. I must forgive the poor woman for thinking I have so much authority, but blessed be her ingenuity, which would make Paul VI smile and think! What pains me is that, if she is putting it correctly, the priest should not have treated her with the same benevolence with which he has behaved under similar circumstances with persons who were "better off." [1]

Father Arias gives us a classical cameo of post–Civil War Spain. The protagonist is of such insignificance in the human scale that he borders on irreality: a shepherd is not only illiterate, he is utterly lacking in social or political substance. He is of the anonymous masses, indentured by Catholic tradition to the homage of the Catholic ruling class. And yet when the poor wretch died, his wife, rising above ignorance and superstition, thought of his earthly existence before she thought of his eternal salvation. She summoned the doctor *first*—and thereby damned the husband she sought to keep alive.

The priest, supreme dispenser of God's authority, alleged a "family problem," pointed to the lack of absolution and banished Antonio to the plot known as "The Suicides' " or "The Protestants'." (There is no way of knowing what the "family problem" was. Though it is doubtful, the man may have had a mistress— there are a number of euphemisms to describe the situation—or he may have committed some other infraction of Church law.) An illiterate shepherd—dirt-poor and tattered, if one may judge by his brothers in that benighted calling—Antonio was doomed; his body was cast off with alacrity and, be it said, in full accordance with Canon 1240. With people who are "better off," however, divine justice is more accommodating: service to Catholic *señores* has been, in the past twenty-five years, service to the Catholic God.

Twenty-five years cannot be undone overnight. Neither can

[1] *Tiempo Nuevo,* March, 1966, p. 14.

Spanish Catholicism, with its thirst for prestige and absolute power, surrender meekly before a "horizontal" system it has consistently excoriated in the name of Marxism-Leninism. Describing the Church in the early days of the twentieth century, Madariaga notes:

> The efforts of the clerical faction were . . . most pertinacious in the field of education. The policy of the Church rested on two rules: to seek material power by "cultivating" the rich, thereby obtaining legacies for its institutions and, through political and social influences, to block all state developments in education.[2]

After the Crusade the "cultivating" was resumed more zealously than ever, though the poverty-stricken State proved the most munificent donor of all. According to the semiofficial newspaper *El Español* (January 23, 1965), the Spanish government spent 4,520,240,720 pesetas—or over seventy-five million dollars at the present exchange rate—in the "construction and repair of ecclesiastical buildings" after the war. The gigantic building program, according to *El Español,* was undertaken to afford the Church the "liberty" it had lost under the Republic's anti-Catholic laws, "some of which it is convenient to remember now: the divorce law, the law on civil marriage [i.e., the measure granting Spaniards freedom to marry outside the Church if they so desired], the law of religious orders and congregations, the law dissolving the Society of Jesus."

While Protestant churches were being closed by the dozens as hotbeds of "Communism and Masonry," the temples of the racial (and "the only true") faith were rising at Government expense. Today the greatest difficulty facing the historian of post-Crusade Spain lies not in sifting fact from fiction, truth from propaganda, or indeed in taking a position for or against the Church-State. It is comprehending the magnitude of the Catholic-Fascist coalition between Rome and Madrid: after 1939 it is nearly impossible to tell where Government begins and Catholicism ends, or vice versa. Looking back over the past two decades, perhaps the clearest definition of the medievally inspired partnership was penned by

[2] Madariaga, *op. cit.,* p. 163.

a writer in *Ecclesia* on the occasion of the signing of the 1953 Concordat: "One thing is certain: that Church and State sincerely agree to a common action through which the successive citizens of Motherland and Heaven are seen to their ultimate goal." [3]

At present the Spanish government foots the bill for its citizens' access to their ultimate goal by paying the Catholic Church approximately twenty million dollars a year,[4] a sum divided between priests' salaries; the upkeep of thousands of parish churches; the maintenance of scores of seminaries and special schools and three pontifical universities; the aid to Spanish foreign missions; and the expenses of the Spanish College in Rome, whose new building, according to *El Español,* was financed by eighty million pesetas (over $1,300,000) of State money.

The hard fiscal realities of the Church's existence in Spain are, quite logically, a source of anxiety to Catholic leaders at home and at the Vatican. The twenty-million-dollar-a-year government subsidy is undeniably the basis for the Church's material survival (income from Church services and property is merely added thereto). Were the separation of Church and State ever a reality in the country, the annual stipend would of course have to be supplied—as in nations such as France, Germany, and the United States—by individual communicants among the citizenry. Slicing the figure to fifteen million, and positing the existence of another fifteen million practicing, contributing Catholics (or half the nation's population, a wildly optimistic estimate), the individual cost would come to one million pesetas ($16,666) apiece. Per capita income in 1966 was 35,629 pesetas [5] ($593).

There is no danger of Church and State being separated within the next generation; but the native hierarchy has felt the menace of a Declaration of Religious Liberty, with its corollary of free-

[3] *Ecclesia,* October 31, 1953, p. 44.
[4] Concretely, the 1964 budget of the Spanish State awarded the Church 1,026,978,967 pesetas (over seventeen million dollars), which figure, according to *El Español,* would "soon be raised by virtue of the Law of July 28, 1963." Cf. *El Español,* January 23, 1965.
[5] According to the National Statistical Institute, as published in *La Vanguardia* on April 1, 1966.

dom of expression and the attendant circulation of "anti-Catholic" ideas. Hence, after the first rash of cautious approval the Church girded its loins for the coming battle. During the summer of 1965, while there was still hope the Declaration would not pass the Council on any but Spain's terms, there were rites and pronouncements with an unmistakably reactionary flavor.

On June 25, in one of the most spectacular Church-State ceremonies of recent years, the Monument to the Sacred Heart was reinaugurated on a promontory outside Madrid. Busloads of pilgrims were deposited at the top of the Cerro de los Angeles (Hill of the Angels). Pope Paul VI sent a message. The Government and Diplomatic Corps attended en masse. Thousands stood under the broiling sun to hear Generalísimo Franco consecrate the nation to that most Catholic devotion, using the same formula used for the same purpose by King Alfonso XIII in 1919 (Alfonso's grandson, Prince Juan Carlos, was also present).

It was a timely reminder of the how and why of the Church-State. The $1,283,000 statue of the Sacred Heart and adjacent monastery (built, as stated in *Ya* of June 26, 1965, "in part from public subscription") stands at the site of a similar installation which was destroyed by the "Reds" [i.e., the Republicans]. A band of militiamen "commanded by a woman" (*Ya, supra*) took the Hill on July 23, 1936, shot five monks of the monastery and, one month later, blew the big Christ to bits.

The new gigantic Redeemer, which can be seen kilometers away, is a crushing affirmation of Holy Spain against *all* the enemies of the racial faith. There is not one statue, but several; the central effigy, a Sacred Heart with one arm gently outstretched, towers over four groups of figures kneeling at his feet. Two of them represent the Church Militant and the Church Triumphant. The other two, as described in *Ya*, "are representative of Missionary Spain and Spain, Defender of the Faith."

The first [group] includes Isabella the Catholic; Christopher Columbus; Hernán Cortés; Fray Junípero Serra; and three Indians. In the second are included Osio, Bishop of Córdoba; Don Pelayo; Father Laínez, S.J.; Don Juan de Austria; Father Polanco; and Don Antonio de Ribera,

"The Angel of the Alcázar"—representing Spain's fight against Arianism, Islam, Protestantism, the Turks and Communism.[6]

"We thank thee, Lord," read Franco, "for having singled us out as defenders of your faith and missionaries of your Gospel in the far corners of the world. Let your loving providence help us keep the integrity of our beliefs, the loving thirst for evangelization, and the religious unity of our Motherland."

Fifteen days later, a headline in *Ya* echoed the "unity" plea: "The Statute on Religious Liberty, says Monsignor Morcillo, Should Not Break Catholic Unity." At a lecture in Vich, Cataluña, the day before, Don Casimiro Morcillo, Bishop of Madrid-Alcalá, had sounded the call back to battle.

In Spain Catholic unity is the principal cohesive element of [our] nationality. To break it would be equivalent to breaking off contact with Spanish history, literature and culture; it would be to deprive ourselves of the keystone of our rebirth and prosperity and to open the door to all manner of foreign sedition and influences.

He called on the nation to follow the principles of Balmes in its thinking on religious liberty. And Balmes meant tolerance of the classic Spanish sort. "To tolerate is to suffer something which is evil, but which it is deemed convenient to let go unpunished. Evil and error are tolerated. Balmes already said, in his lifetime, that no one is molested [*sic*] for the profession of his faith and its worship within Spain." "If a person has the right to profess his faith . . . he also has the right to be instructed and educated in the truth and in goodness." "It is hardly possible to extract from Scripture a conclusion favorable to religious liberty."

[6] Osio, Bishop of Córdoba, was a fourth-century warrior against the Arian heresy. Don Pelayo was the eighth-century King of Asturias who defeated the Moors at the crucial battle of Covadonga in 718. Diego Laínez, second General of the Society of Jesus, fought Protestantism at Trent. Don Juan de Austria, bastard son of Charles V, commanded the fleet which won the famous battle of Lepanto against the Turks in 1571. Father Polanco was a Civil War martyr killed in Teruel. Don Antonio de Ribera was a young man who distinguished himself for his valor during the siege of Toledo's. Alcázar in 1936.

The rest is history. In the fall of 1965, the Spanish explosion at the Vatican made headlines around the world.

When a national Statute of Religious Liberty is passed by the *Cortes,* Spain will be able to mount the threshold of a new life. The economic boom of the 1960's, one of the most dazzling in European history, is leading the nation out of the nightmare of vertically oriented wealth and authority and into the social, scientific and intellectual realities of the twentieth century. "Materialism," that archenemy of the lay and ecclesiastical aristocracy, is transforming the lives of millions of Spaniards who a decade ago toiled twelve to fourteen hours a day without the slightest hope of human betterment for themselves or their children. A new, vigorous generation committed to social justice is pouring out of the universities and technical schools. What is perhaps more significant from a political standpoint, the newcomers' revolutionary spirit is shared by a small but growing number of "modern" priests.

Juan Arias of the Congregation of the Sacred Heart, whose gentle boyish face belies the passion of his convictions, states flatly in *Tiempo Nuevo* (*supra*) that the Church has nothing against what he terms "socialization."

Anything except capitalist formulas. If there is anything patently un-Christian, it is capitalism. [Capitalism] is an anti-Christian structure which, whatever its form, is in the end an exploitation of man by man. Much more so if it does not fulfill the conditions the Church demands . . . : [labor's] participation in capital and in management, freedom of assembly, freedom to strike, etc. Until such time as we grasp the fact that there is no such thing as a person condemned to manual labor and a person [raised by] privilege to a liberal profession, we shall not live in a purely Christian structure.

The revolution is at hand. When the new Press Law, weighted with pious caveats, went into effect on April 18, 1966, Western observers voiced their skepticism; but in the days that followed there were major and minor fireworks in most Spanish newspapers. Barcelona's *Telexpress* led off with a long illustrated story on Pablo Casals, a figure confined to oblivion by Church-State

331

censors since the end of the Crusade. *Pueblo* entered the lists with a headlong charge against "the New Spanish Right." *Informaciones* printed the demands of restless workers in Cataluña, while the Monarchist *ABC*, outdoing one and all, made so bold as to print a barely veiled attack on the person of the Chief of State (followed by an abject apology the next day). To foreigners' surprise and Spaniards' delight, freedom of the press was a near reality.[7]

Expansiveness is in the air. On September 20, 1964, the Sunday *Telegraph* noted that "Four Western Powers . . . are engaged in Madrid in one of the toughest trade battles . . . for what is potentially the richest untapped market left in Western Europe." Two years later the dust of battle had not quite settled. French, German, British, Italian and American firms continue to pour into Spain on the wave of the biggest economic boom since the reconstruction of Europe after World War II. Madrid is filling with skyscrapers, department stores, scores upon scores of gigantic apartment houses. In a decade the old city, "the Madrid of the Austrias" with its echoes of Hapsburg splendor, will be encircled by one of the most modern urban developments in the Continent. Nor is the boom confined to the capital city. Across the land communities hum with activity as the Government's economic recovery scheme, or *Plan de Desarrollo,* sets up factories and business establishments throughout the most remote, underdeveloped provinces.

The human awakening is no less prodigious. The problems of educating millions of functional illiterates and their underprivileged children are being discussed openly in government circles. Vested interests—the aristocracy with its immense *latifundios* staffed by hereditary servants, the upper bourgeoisie with its

---

[7] The Government reserves the right to seize any papers that violate the nation's "Fundamental Principles." The new law was invoked for the first time on June 5, 1966, when an entire press run of *Signo,* organ of the Young Catholic Action Movement, was seized in Madrid. Barely a month later, on July 2, a stock of *Madre y Maestra,* published under the leadership of Father Juan Arias, suffered the same fate.

dreams of status, titles and self-righteous wealth—will continue to block every effort to rescue subhuman Spain through suffrage and education. But barring another internecine struggle, the wave of progress will not be contained.

Like the social question, the religious problem revolves around the political issue of "succession": who or what will follow Franco? The small but influential Monarchist faction hopes to assume power and enthrone a male Spaniard of royal blood who will symbolize "traditional" authority and rule in the name of the past. There is a wide gamut of monarchism, from out-and-out opponents of universal suffrage to more enlightened aristocrats who envision a mildly constitutional form of government held in check by an anointed Crown and the life around it. In the spring of 1966, the evening paper *Madrid* asked a number of leading Monarchists to take part in a symposium on the political future of Spain. Alberto Martín Artajo, former Foreign Minister and Father of the 1953 Concordat, put forth the idea of a "Catholic monarchy" wherein— among several other possibilities—the *Cortes* might be freely elected and the head of the government appointed by the king after consultation with a Council of the Realm. In comparison with Monarchist tirades of past and present, his scheme was remarkably progressive.

But the Monarchists' weakness is the monarchy's. The distance between the Spanish noble and the Spanish worker or peasant is so abysmal that only pre-Revolutionary Russia can offer a suitable comparison. As in the Czarist frame of reference, the very thought of educating the aristocracy in social justice is outrageous: the Spanish ruling class carries paternalism in its marrow. However "constitutional" its platform, every Monarchist faction looks to the day when a full-time royal court is again installed in Madrid's Palacio de Oriente, with the country's Graustarkian profusion of titles polarized around it. Such a solution offers little or no hope of progress to the newly awakened masses; yet in the past two decades only the Monarchists have been able to organize, to draw up programs for the future, to voice their ideas cautiously but firmly in the controlled press.

As the nation's economy makes gigantic strides, there is no other political alternative before it. In his defense of the monarchy, Señor Martín Artajo vigorously rejected the idea of a Republic—and he is not alone in stating that a presidential election every six years would mean a revolution every six years. Many solid-citizen Spaniards, inured to strong-man rule and the Catholic-inspired worship of authority, look back on the horrors of the Civil War as the wages of sin. For them the monarchy is a middle-of-the-road solution which admits of some "modern" ideas while retaining the divine-right principle, *sine qua non* of political and social respectability. Indeed, the monarchy, with its dazzling social cachet, finds its greatest supporters among the well-off, firmly entrenched, arch-pious bourgeoisie. Though Opus Dei disclaims any political orientation, many of its leaders are vehement Monarchists, and the Work of God, every day in every way gaining beachheads in commerce, government and the arts, will be an ideological bloc to be reckoned with when the chips are down.

Spain's true hope lies with its younger generation, with its post-Crusade intellectuals, with writers and philosophers and economists who yearn for a European way of life and a democratic, egalitarian future. There are atheists and agnostics and leftist-oriented Catholics among them, all pledged to the common cause of human dignity. Late in 1965 the lot of the Thirty Thousand came under the scrutiny of a young professor of International Law at the University of Madrid. Writing in the *Revista española de derecho internacional,* Julio González Campos examines the international agreements which Spain's religious policy flagrantly violates: on the *regional* plane, Resolution 30 of the Ninth Inter-American Conference of Bogotá in 1948; on the *European* plane, Article 9 of the Rome Convention of November 4, 1950; and on the *universal* plane, the United Nations Declaration on Human Rights. The young jurist devotes special attention to Article 18 of the latter document, whose text is a direct contradiction of the Rome-Madrid Concordat:

Every person has the right to liberty of thought, of conscience and of religion; this right includes liberty to change religion or beliefs, as

334

well as liberty to manifest his or her religion or belief individually and collectively, in public as well as in private, through teaching, practice, worship and observance.[8]

In its scholarly way, González Campos' article speaks for every young Spaniard's awareness of his country's place in the community of nations and her commitment to supranational ethics. As Spain stands on the threshold of new, "unspiritual" glories, the days of religious truth are numbered. The Universal Church, almost totally rid of its Syllabarian obscurantism, is making rapid progress in the "aggiornamento" impelled by Pope John-of-blessed-memory while Catholics abroad are more and more eager for contact with the new Spain.

Their eagerness is clear-eyed and thoroughly political. "The Catholic Popular Party Does Not Want Franco Spain in the European Economic Community," ran a blunt headline in *De Tijd-Maasbode,* Amsterdam's Roman Catholic newspaper, on October 23, 1965. Under that legend was a detailed story of the Party's pronouncement on Spain's admission to the Common Market. Pointing out that membership in the E.E.C. entails not only an economic, but a political commitment, the Katholieke Volkspartij was "of the opinion that Spain must be excluded [therefrom] while Franco is in power and there are no clear signs of a free

[8] "Jurisprudencia española sobre cuestiones de derecho internacional público (III)," in *Revista española de derecho internacional,* Vol. XVII, No. 4, 1965, p. 548. The U.N. Declaration and the political realities it implies have long been viewed with hostility by the Government. On January 27, 1966, the Dirección General de Seguridad forbade "all meetings" of the Madrid UNESCO Club—an organization sponsored directly by UNESCO headquarters in Paris, and devoted to the cultural and scientific education of the working classes. Two months after the order was issued I visited the Club, located in a ramshackle building in Old Madrid (membership: 1,500). The officers had gathered for an "administrative" session while many young people milled about the halls and library. Such meetings, President Rafael Taibo informed me, were permitted by the police; it was the "public ceremonies" which have been banned—the art exhibits and film showings, the experimental theater, lectures and concerts had all ground to a halt. The UNESCO Club, like the Protestants, had been forbidden all "external manifestations."

and democratic way of thinking. . . ." Calling for "exchanges in the fields of culture, science and sports as a means of stimulating in Spain a gradual evolution toward a free and democratic political structure," the K.V.P. flatly states, in *De Tijd*'s words,

> that under the actual Spanish regime, the fundamental rights of man as set forth in the Universal Declaration of Human Rights are not fully respected, and therefore the minimum requirements for the democratic concept are not met.
> The gradual evolution towards a free and democratic political structure in Spain . . . must at the same time promote the emergence of a system in which the Church's position, as well as the relation between Church and State, will coincide with the norms universally accepted today. . . . An important criterion is the implantation of religious liberty and tolerance in consonance with a democratic regime.

The Statute on Religious Liberty, fruit of Prime Minister Castiella's political vision, went into its third year as a State secret in 1966. On April 24 of that year, *Ya* stated that a new draft, drawn up "in accordance with the ecclesiastical hierarchy," would be presented to the Council of Ministers the following summer. "All seems to indicate that the new text is more positive than the former one, and permits greater religious liberty," read the brief item.

Protestant authorities were not hopeful of seeing the bill through the *Cortes* in 1966; the summer of 1967 was, in their opinion, a more realistic estimate.

Whatever the date of its enactment—it may be sooner or later than the experts' predictions—the Statute will mean the promise of liberty for non-Catholic Spaniards and a formal or informal modification of the Concordat. The latter has already been alluded to by several members of the hierarchy. In a post-Council lecture before a Catholic group, Archbishop Morcillo of Madrid-Alcalá stated, as reported in *Ya* for February 25, 1966:

> Our entire episcopate "desires that the right to religious liberty be recognized in the Spanish juridical system"; at the same time, it is aware "that the Spanish State can reach this recognition only by agreement with the Holy See, since one of the fundamental principles of the Concordat signed between the two powers is in question."

Aside from this hopeful note, Monsignor Morcillo's lecture was another appeal to the inflexible principles of warring, racial Catholicism as construed by the Spanish hierarchy. "The declaration does not recognize any objective human right to atheism, nor even to religious indifferentism." "The right to religious liberty can neither be absolute nor unlimited." Among the limits: the defense of the "common good," and of the "just public order, which is a part of the common good"; "the limits imposed by the natural moral order (for example, a religion which established the sacrifice of human lives could not enjoy liberty)"; and the prohibition of proselytism:

All propaganda based on lies, calumny, the fallacious exposition of the religious truths of other confessions, promises or material benefits, the besieging of persons and families, the dazzling effect produced by external signs of abundance and preponderance, and (when not justified by the existence of coreligionists) the penetration with churches and schools into places which have been normally evangelized, all constitute "indecent forms of religious liberty which can and should be suppressed."

The Archbishop concluded by urging Spaniards to implement their religious unity by making their faith "more enlightened and founded on Scripture and tradition," " more personal and more sociological each day."

To accomplish this we must doubtless cover a lot of ground very rapidly. But it is also doubtless that the Spaniards of the late Middle Ages did not slacken their rapid pace to maintain the Catholic unity of Spain while respecting the religious liberty of Moors and Jews. That is why I hold it equally doubtless that Spanish Catholics of the twentieth century, who are not lame, will not relinquish the dynamic apostolicity of their faith.

The Archbishop's evocation of the late Middle Ages was not the first in recent times. After the Declaration of Religious Liberty was proclaimed at the Vatican, allusions to that period began to appear in the press. All were proud and unbending, but all were significant. Caught in the gyves of the new morality, the Establishment was eager to show that in Spain it is really very, very old.

And so it is; ironically, Spain pioneered pluralism in the West. As secular and humanitarian values replace her warring Catholicism, she will look back with growing pride on that remote era when—as Américo Castro so brilliantly describes it—the Spanish soul was as a strong, cohesive plait woven out of three fibers called the Moor, the Christian and the Jew.

The first sacrificial offering to the Catholic God, the Jew, will share modestly in the victory of Pope John XXIII. There are eight thousand Jews in Spain today, twenty-five hundred of them members of the *Comunidad hebrea de Madrid*. They live and worship quietly, almost anonymously, in the land of their Sephardic forbears. The present Madrid synagogue, opened in 1959, has never been closed or threatened with closure. "We obtained a juridical statute for the Community last year," Max Mazin, leader of the Congregation, told me in April, 1966, "therefore the changes produced by the new law will have little effect on our existence." Like almost everyone else in Spain, he was in the dark as to the contents of the new bill. "I know nothing about the proposed law, but as far as proselytism is concerned, it will not affect us either. There is no Jewish proselytism."

But there is a gnawing anxiety at the heart of the Jew in Spain: his desire to eradicate the centuries of prejudice and hatred that remain in the bosom of Spanish society. Mazin, who hopes to raise funds for a Madrid synagogue (his congregation worships in an apartment), personifies this hope and takes an active hand in his own private antidefamation campaigns. His protests against the exuberant anti-Semitism of a famous priest-orator several years ago were direct and effective, while his contacts with the new, ecumenical-minded clergy continue to multiply and bear fruit. On April 4, 1966, he was extended a joint invitation by the Diocesan Seminary of Avila and the Dominican Community of the Monastery of Santo Tomás in that city. The Monastery was Inquisitor Torquemada's, and houses his remains. The program which took place there included a lecture by Mr. Mazin on the tenets of Judaism, another by Father Vicente Serrano, cochairman of Madrid's Association of Jewish-Christian Friendship, and, at 6:00 P.M., a "Representation-celebration of the Jewish Paschal Feast (seder) by a group of seminarians." Mr. Mazin admits he had previously received many invitations from Catholics eager for contacts with Jews. "But not of this category," he says with a broad smile. "Not from . . . Torquemada."

To judge from their policy in the last few years, Mazin has the authorities on his side. Scholarly and poignant studies on the Sephardites in the Balkans were published in both *Ya* and *ABC* in 1964 and 1965, when censorship was still in full bloom, while the Government opened Toledo's famous Sinagoga del Tránsito as a national monument.

Unfortunately anti-Semitism is still virulent among the *integristas* and the ignorant. The hate sheet, *Qué Pasa* (which, with its sister publications *El Cruzado, Juan Pérez, Tradición* and *Montejurra,* caters to fanatics of all persuasions with a special bow at the Carlist faction), carries on almost all of its covers the cut of an ugly, hook-nosed Jew speaking into a Star-of-David-shaped microphone. *Integristas,* however, are not to be confused with the ignorant. And the ignorant are certainly not *integristas.* In the lower levels of the population medieval legends and superstitions account for much anti-Semitism. Centuries-old stories of ritual murder—a subject in which Mr. Mazin is keenly interested—are perhaps the most widespread source of blind, undying hostility.

Education will go a long way in dispelling deep-seated prejudices. But only under a Church-State regime which guarantees full liberty of expression will the Jews, and most especially the Protestants, ever achieve emancipation in Spanish society. The Press Law of 1966, while a milestone in modern Spanish history, remains a Church-State trap for any individual or group who gives public utterance to un-Catholic or anti-Catholic moral concepts. Article 2, Paragraph 2, of the bill as presented to the *Cortes* in January, 1966, stated: "The liberties of expression and information recognized in Article 1 will have no limits other than those imposed by the law of the land. General limitations [to those liberties] shall be respect for morals and truth. . . ."

When the Article came up for discussion, three deputies suggested that the wording be changed to read "Christian morals." Several others proposed "Catholic morals." The Bishop of León stated (*Ya,* January 18, 1966) "that Christian morals are the morals of Christ, which are [the morals] embodied by the Catholic Church." A priest, Father Fermín Izurdiaga, pointed out that "The word 'Christian' is the all-purpose term behind which many enemies of Catholicism take refuge." The last word was had by Señor Fernando Martín Sánchez-Juliá, prominent Catholic layman and member of the Government Commission for Study of the Law. According to *ABC* of the same date:

. . . Sr. Martín Sánchez-Juliá summoned a stenographer to draft the following statement: "Let the following appear in the record: 'All of us deputies here present agree that whichever formula wins out, the morals in which we believe, whether or not [the term is] qualified, are morals as understood by the Catholic Church. Therefore as regards the dogmatic or religious point there is no discrepancy whatsoever.' Are we agreed?"

The deputies assented and the Article passed with the original wording. Coupled with the hierarchy's battle to toughen the antiproselytism measures in the new Statute—see Archbishop Morcillo's statement re "the fallacious exposition of . . . religious truth" *supra*—the new Press Law bids fair to keep all discussions of twentieth-century morality out of the daily press (scholarly journals have somewhat more latitude).

Until such time as Church and State are rent asunder and the mechanics of self-rule replace her "vertical" system, Spain will be a nation in fetters. Today her patience and perseverance are matched by her hope as, one by one, she breaks the chains that bind her to the past.

Three great assets underlie her material and spiritual transformation: her hard-won economic triumphs, her increased awareness of secular values, and the treasures of intelligence and good will which have lain dormant in her people. The Johannine Age has been welcomed by the man in the street—and sometimes by the cleric too. In 1964, on a trip from France to Santiago de Compostela along the route of the medieval pilgrims, Mr. James Michener, two officials from the Ministry of Information and Tourism and I were admiring the façade of the Church of San

EPILOGUE

Martín—a newly restored gem of Romanesque architecture whose foundations date from 1066—when the town's parish priest came out to greet us. It was windy and bitter cold and Mr. Michener, who was wearing a black raincoat, had buttoned it tight over his suit. Our host wondered if perhaps he was a foreign priest? No, said one of the Tourism officials, he was not. Was he a Catholic? Our escort answered negatively again, beginning to look worried. Was he a Protestant? Yes, came the guarded answer.

Then, said the priest, he wished to embrace Mr. Michener, who was his brother, the son of the same Father. Brothers sometimes argued—yes, it happened—but their arguing in no way destroyed the relationship between them. They remained brothers forever.

Mr. Michener was deeply touched.

We had our lunch in the home of Father Miguel Bustillo Pérez, *Párroco arcipreste de Frómista*—a tiny, two-storied house where he lives in near-monastic simplicity with his canary and his greyhound bitch, his work table framed in holy pictures and Christmas cards. I don't know if Father Bustillo had ever talked to a Protestant before, but the day he meets a Spanish *evangélico* his journey of discovery will have truly begun.

Barely two weeks after I saw him I began my own journey into the Spanish Protestant unknown in Pastor Núñez's shacklike little church at Ros de Olano Street. Without Núñez's help, and that of dozens of *evangélicos* who received me, a Catholic, with implicit trust, the materials for this book could never have been unearthed. I am especially indebted to José Cardona and Alberto Araujo. Señor Cardona, the most significant personality in Spanish Protestantism today, is the domestic and foreign spokesman (and unofficial historian) for a minority that has traveled a bitter road since 1939. Ordained a Baptist preacher at eighteen and still engaged in the ministry, he has been responsible for the *evangélicos'* major and minor triumphs in the past seven years. Under his direction the Evangelical Defense Commission has become the clearing house for all legal, social and religious problems of the six Spanish denominations and, with the coming of the Ecumenical Age, for interfaith contacts as well.

Most if not all of the legal victories won by the Evangelical Defense Commission to date can be traced directly to Cardona's steady hand. His knowledge of Spanish law is deep, his energy boundless. As perhaps no other man in Spain, he can grasp the theoretical and practical aspects of a potentially explosive situation and stand firm before the Church-State. But the most remarkable quality about Cardona is his psychic and spiritual balance. His magnificent calm never fails; but neither does his *simpatía* or his humor. Early in my research I began to come across both Spanish and foreign Catholics who were happy to express their admiration and respect for Cardona. When I met him I agreed with Father Arias' opinion as expressed in *Pueblo* on October 9, 1965: "[Cardona] is a man thoroughly schooled in theology, thoughtful, an integral Christian." I worked from the E.D.C. office for a rewarding year.

The other half of my gratitude goes to Alberto Araujo, the thirty-six-year-old pastor of the Iglesia de Jesús in Madrid's Calatrava Street. My debt to Alberto is very difficult to itemize. A great many of the sixteenth-century texts I consulted for this book he made available from his late father's library; he was also my source, or my guide, to much material on the development of Protestantism after the Civil War. But all technicalities, important as they might have been, pale before the fact that he blew life and meaning into my work by exposing me to his own.

A fourth-generation Protestant and the third in a line of ministers, Araujo took over the Iglesia de Jesús upon the death of its pastor, Don Juan Fliedner. At that time the church building had just been inaugurated on the site of a nineteenth-century chapel; as Alberto recalls, when permission was obtained—out of the blue—to raise a new church, the ceiling of the old one was coming down in good-sized chunks.

Though his work would be charged with the same ideal of Christian service if it radiated from a Quonset hut, it seems fitting that Araujo should have inherited the most modern and, perhaps, most beautiful Protestant structure in the country. To hear him preach is to grasp the undying relevance of the Reformed message in Spain; to know him is to understand its flowering. The heritage of the sixteenth-century pioneers—Erasmists, Protestants, mystics—are met in his own. His late father, Don Carlos Araujo, was director of the Religious Tract Society during the Republic. A scholar and educator whose literary work included a translation of *Pilgrim's Progress,* he was twice imprisoned in the "Protestant-Mason-Communist" raids which followed the Crusade. (In the early 1940's the three terms were interchangeable; anyone accused of one stood automatically accused of the other two. The special "Tribunal for the Suppression of Freemasonry and Communism" was abolished in 1963.) His uncle, Don Roberto Araujo, Professor of Mathematics at the University of Valencia, was netted in another raid and thrown in that city's jail. Don Roberto was restored to his chair many years later and died shortly thereafter. In 1965 a secular priest of the Diocese of Madrid, quickened by the spirit of the man named John, dedicated a section of his book, *The Message of the Council,* to the memory of the Protestant who taught him mathematics in his youth (Appendix, p. 371).

Alberto (one of whose sisters is an Anglican nun in Massachusetts) obtained his *Licenciatura* in Philosophy and Letters from the University of Madrid, his B.D. at the Faculty of Divinity at Trinity College in Glasgow, and was ordained a minister in the Iglesia Evangélica Española. Today he lives at Calatrava with his Scottish-born wife and six children, his home and office open to men of all faiths. Our long sessions on theology and ecumenism, literature and the arts were, I soon realized, part of the never-ending dialogue he carries on with his parishioners, his fellow ministers and his Catholic friends.

From Calatrava he serves three far-flung missions—two to the south, one in Asturias. He engages in clandestine educational and beneficent activities among his Madrid flock, which he tends with the dynamism of an intellectual with both feet firmly on the ground. On Sundays his unmarked church is chockablock. After one sermon when he had ranged over the modern currents in European thought, cast back to Kant and Nietzsche, plunged into St. John of the Cross and came back to his scriptural text with breath-taking lucidity, I asked him offhandedly what the educational level of his congregation might be. "Out of three

343

hundred and fifty I don't have more than twelve or fourteen with college degrees. I have ragpickers. I have men who have stalls in *El Rastro* [the Flea Market]. . . ."

The future of the Thirty Thousand is, in a very real sense, the future of their country. Belatedly, traumatically, Spain is learning that in a civilized nation no minority is expendable. After twenty-five years of stupor she is also beginning to realize that oppression devours its own. When truncheon-wielding government troopers attacked a group of nearly one hundred priests in Barcelona in May, 1966, the message of the Church-State—proclaimed in 1939, solemnized in 1953, defended in Rome in 1965—came to its saddest and most significant fulfillment.

The clerics had assembled in peace to deliver a petition against the alleged police treatment accorded a student of the University of Barcelona who had been imprisoned for leading an "unauthorized" manifestation. But the nonviolent nature of their protest went completely unheeded: the very act of protesting was considered lese majesty and—in this instance—lese Catholicism. The police attack followed as swiftly as a raid on an "external manifestation of Protestantism" in the spiritual 1940's and 1950's.

Behind the Barcelona incident was the entire Catalan question with its political, economic and social connotations. A linguistic and cultural unit of its own, European in its way of life, materialistic and highly developed, Cataluña is several light years away from the spirit of its Castilian rulers. Its desire for an independent, federated existence in the manner of a German *Land* (a hope shared by the Basque provinces) is scorned by Madrid as an affront to the "political unity" of the nation.

Inevitably, when Catholic priests—the traditional cogs in the machinery of "unity"—rose up against the system in Cataluña, the hate of decades came to life in Madrid. Between May 10 and May 13, 1966, Radio Nacional de España and Television Española broadcast documentaries and "dramatizations" of the church-burnings of 1931. Radio news of the clerics' protests were followed by long editorials beginning: "Today is the thirty-fifth anniversary of the first burning of a convent during the Republic.

. . ." Survivors of the frenzied mobs of church-burners appeared on television and recounted their experiences. The Madrid press joined the attack with more viciousness than the armed police who had wielded their billies. In an editorial, the Monarchist *ABC* rent its garments at the thought of "priests and religious who take to the streets in the attitude of demagogues and with an air of defiance, protected by a cassock or the Seraphic habit of St. Francis." "Something very serious is amiss in certain clerical circles," it continued, remembering the recent closing of the Seminary of San Sebastián and the Catalans' protests against the nomination of a Castilian auxiliary bishop for Barcelona. "It behooves the ecclesiastical authorities to study the roots of the phenomenon and apply the necessary measures to nip it in the bud, with prudence but without leniency."

Caught in the maelstrom of compulsory "unity" for twenty-five years, Spanish Protestants had unexpected company in 1966. In that company, and in the spirit of Pope John, lay all their hopes. Democracy is nearer every day. So is enlightened Christianity. Slowly but surely the Latin Church is taking apart its monolithic structure. And slowly but surely it is learning the basic tenet of human salvation: unless it is many-faceted, the truth will not catch the Light.

Across the centuries the spirit of the Reformation has made itself felt in the government, the arts, the philosophy and economy and social structure of Western Civilization. Now its influence has come full circle to touch—some say to "Protestantize"—the Catholic Church. As Spain emerges from her political and spiritual shadows and the Universal Church turns bravely to the task of inner renovation, Spanish *evangélicos* may well be coming into their own.

How fully into their own I realized one Sunday in the month of July, 1965, as I sat in the morning service in the I.E.E. Church on Noviciado Street, Madrid. The congregation had been thinned by summer vacations and the church was two-thirds full; there were fifty or sixty Spaniards present, a French couple with two small children, and a young foreigner who turned out to be an Australian evangelist on a visit from his Italian mission.

345

On that warm morning Pastor Benito Corvillón, a dark, intense, bearish man and one of the best preachers in the I.E.E., delivered a sermon to remember. His texts were Isaiah 58:1–12, Matthew 5:27–37, Romans 14:14–23; his message was an open warning to Protestants who feel their worship of "liberty" would in itself make them free. "Let us beware of talking in unison, walking in unison, raising our hands in unison, condemning our brethren in unison." Neither justification nor works, neither slavish devotion to faith nor slavish dependence on rite, he said, would bring men closer to righteousness. Only the spirit which informed their religion—whatever that religion might be—gave it vibrancy and power and validity before God.

After he had preached, Don Benito invited the Australian missionary to address the congregation. The young man was brief; the only message he wished to leave with his Spanish friends was this: faith, and not works, would secure their eternal salvation.

I was willing to make allowances for his limited Spanish, but after Corvillón's sermon I found myself taking a dim view of the visitor's exhortation. In Spain, where the air fairly hums with shibboleths, it sounded like yet another: sweeping, categorical and dull.

I glanced above the young evangelist at the figure of Corvillón, sitting hunched up in his black robes in the raised pulpit which dominates the Lutheran-style meeting house. And I heard his unforgettable words again: "In the common cause of love, let us strive for that variety of expression which our search for God implies."

It was a Spaniard speaking. It was a Protestant.

Appendix

I · SPAIN

HISTORIA DE LOS HETERODOXOS ESPAÑOLES, Preamble to Book Four: *Erasmists and Protestants*

[The antepenultimate paragraph of Menéndez Pelayo's introduction to his study of sixteenth-century Spanish Protestantism (Vol. I, pp. 753–54 in the Biblioteca de Autores Cristianos edition) sums up his hostility towards all manifestations of the Protestant genius as well as his disdain of Northern civilization. The allusion to Rembrandt is altogether remarkable.]

Such are, in sum, the relevant details of the development of the Reformation as a preamble to the history of Spanish Protestants. One need only enumerate their errors to understand the benefit humanity owes Luther and Calvin. In philosophy, the negation of human liberty. In theology, the principle of free examination [of Scripture], absurd from the lips of anyone who accepts revelation, as the truth can only be one and one the authority that interprets it. In the plastic arts, *iconomachy,* which brought art down from the serene height of the religious ideal and reduced it to depicting what is admired in Dutch painting and its most famous exponents: syndics sitting around a table or harquebusiers leaving a shooting gallery, works in which the [artistic] ideal has found refuge in the effects of chiaroscuro. In literature, suffice it to say that eighteenth-century Geneva rejected the theater, and neither Ariosto, nor Tasso, nor Cervantes, nor Lope, nor Calderón, nor Camoëns were Protestants, and it is doubtful that Shakespeare was. How could the artist who has most energetically interpreted the human personality, which has its roots and foundation in liberty, have been engendered by a doctrine that denies free will? As Erasmus said very rightly: *Ubicumque regnat Lutheranismus, ibi litterarum est interitus.* Nor is England's political liberty the work of Protestants, as it had been developing since the

Middle Ages. Nor can the growth of the exact and natural sciences, of population or wealth, of commerce or navigation be attributed to causes so divergent from them, unless one subscribes to the sophism: *post hoc, ergo propter hoc*. Nor does the much touted and relative morality [i.e., civism] of Northern countries, in which climate has had a great influence, have anything to do with Protestantism; rather [this civism] is in conflict with the principles [of Protestantism] which, as they ring in our ears and as they are explained by its doctors, justify every kind of moral aberration. They say that Luther created or defined *the German tongue and the German motherland*. Even if this were true, which it is not, why should we Southerners, who already have a tongue and a motherland, lose ourselves in ecstasy before these creations, or join in the fanatical enthusiasm of the perpetual enemies of our race? [Italics his.]

THE PROTESTANT FARCE

[This booklet was published in 1948 by the Apostolado de la Prensa (The Apostolate of the Press), a Catholic publishing house in Madrid. There is no by-line. The booklet bears the legend, "With ecclesiastical license," and, on the back of the page, the words, "This Booklet Is Distributed Free." Its 46 pages are notable on several counts. The sexual note is repeated obsessively. In its vulgar, street-corner language it echoes the *iconomachy* theme of Menéndez Pelayo's, and in many passages, notably the middle of Chapter II, it provides a near-model for the notice tacked to the church door by the parish priest of Fios and Nevares.]

The other night, at a café where students meet, we heard the following conversation:

"Listen, Pepillo, you've been in England and Germany. Will you please tell us what the devil is this thing called Protestantism?"

"You want me to tell you with all frankness? You won't blush?"

"Students blush? You don't know our kind."

"All right, here it goes. Protestantism is the means devised by a very clever friar, called Luther, to marry a little nun, and to fix it so everybody could believe whatever they want and do whatever they please."

"But that doesn't make sense. If this Luther or whatever he's called was more of a ladies' man than the Order allowed, he still didn't have to devise anything."

"That's true. But since one of his passions was pride and the other one was having a woman, the little priest didn't stop at trifles: he looked for texts and arguments to protect himself from people's criticism.

"Since he was a friar and a priest, anyone who saw him arm in arm with his wife, or rather his concubine, could have said to him: 'But see here, you friar, does religion permit you to live like that? You made a vow to be chaste, and now you go off on a spree like any wild boy? And you speak to us of *reformation* and *faith?* Your faith, and that of all your children, is faith in things . . . feminine.'

"And since he couldn't have offered any arguments in reply, he invented them by saying that Religion was a very good and holy thing, but that sacred texts could be interpreted by each one as they saw fit, and that he had discovered that he could marry; and, of course, protected by this ingenious device, he could not just have a wife, he could have a harem."

. . .

"Then," another one of his listeners replied, "what they say out there about Protestantism being more or less like Catholicism can't be true."

"How can it be true!" exclaimed Pepillo. "It's a most solemn lie. I'll tell you why, if you want, since there's news of this Protestant propaganda being spread here in Madrid, and everywhere, with English money, by a handful of degenerates who'd just as soon believe in Luther as in Mohammed, but who like to live a life of freedom and collect a nice little salary with which to feed their pastoresses, bishopesses, and the rest of the feminine flock. . . ."

"Let him talk! Let him talk!" everyone shouted.

"When the agents of that foreigners' religion run across simple or ignorant or foolish souls, they begin by telling them: 'To be a Protestant or a Catholic is more or less the same thing.' And how can it be the same thing? It is absolutely the contrary. The Catholic religion comes from God, the other, from Satan.

"The Catholic has the teaching of the Church as a rule of faith. The Protestant rejects the Church, scorns its authority, and only knows the Bible, which he interprets in his own way, as he sees fit, making room for his more or less clean passions. . . ."

"You say that on account of the *Pepa* [vulgar for "woman"] who accompanies every renegade priest," someone interrupted.

"Since all those renegades have their corresponding *Pepas,* I say it on account of all of them.

"Let us go on. The Catholic venerates the Pope as the Vicar of Jesus Christ. . . . The Protestant only sees in him an Anti-Christ, a vicar of Satan. . . .

"The Catholic venerates, invokes and loves the Most Holy Mary, Mother of God. The Protestant runs from her in invincible revulsion, and at times even looks on her with scorn and hate. This is why Protestantism bears the mark of reproof."

. . .

Once more we found the indefatigable Pepillo in the café as he spoke day and night against that plague of professional racketeers who, under the name of Protestants, have set up shop in the City of the Bear and the Berry Tree [Madrid] and other cities of Spain. Of course all honest men and men of common sense took his side; but it was inevitable that he should have been contradicted by scoundrels, senseless rationalists and bad Catholics. And of course if there happened to be a *lady* there who led a *non sancta* life, she would join the cause of the children of *chaste* Luther and *sweet* Calvin, since *free examination* goes very well with free love, free thinking and free hands and—long live liberty!

. . .

"I believe, Don Pepe, sir, that one must speak with more respect about that because, whatever it might be, when all is said and done it is a religion."

"What rubbish!" said Pepillo. . . . "That is no religion or

anything like it; it's a masquerade, it's the pretext of a handful of woman-chasing priests to eat, drink, have a good time and above all it serves to corrupt people, to fight Catholicism, which is the true religion, and to plant doubt, impiety and religious indifference everywhere. Are we agreed? . . .

"I repeat that it is no religion nor anything like it, but a religious comedy and nothing more, though you may not like to hear it. Let us examine the matter. Would you be bold enough to call a church a more or less spacious room, more or less comfortable, where nothing is said about God, where there is no altar—and if there were one, it would be useless as they have no sacrifice to offer on it; where there is not a single painting, nor a single statue nor a single bas-relief to excite piety or invite men to the practice of Christian virtues? If this is a church, where is the God who is adored in it? And if it is a church without God, or a *house of God* without God, why don't they call it by the equally beautiful name of ballroom or merchants' exchange? . . ."

. . .

[On pp. 20–21 there is a footnote reference to a book by a "Señor Bon":]

" ' Some libertine who never went to Church; some ignoramus who never took the trouble to seek instruction in religion; some man living in concubinage who has been admonished by his priest; some "traviata" (in Castilian it is better expressed with a four-letter word) who hates confession; some priest who has quarreled with his bishop because the bishop controlled him where he needed it most; some harebrained loafer, etc., etc.' That is the kind of people whom Sr. Bon has seen by the millions in Protestant chapels. (Folio 6 of his book.)"

[The pamphlet continues in this vein to the very end; the last chapter, says a note, is "taken almost in its entirety from Balmes. . . ."]

The Apostolate of the Press, still at the same address, is still engaged in the holy war. A book entitled *El protestantismo,* published in 1956, was displayed in its stand at the 1966 Madrid Book Fair. The 168-page work, authored by "Arturo Fosar Bayarri,

Engineer," is *The Protestant Farce* on a more sober but equally embattled plane.]

THE 1953 CONCORDAT

[A 526-page work published by the University of Madrid Law School in 1956, this volume contains a prologue by the then Foreign Minister, Señor Alberto Martín Artajo, and the texts of fifteen lectures on the Concordat delivered at the Law School during the academic year 1953–54. Below are excerpts from the last dissertation, entitled "Non-Catholic Worship in Spanish Law," and delivered by José Maldonado, Professor of Canon Law. Maldonado looks into the background of the doctrine of tolerance in the Church, from St. Augustine to Pius XII. From his examination of the subtleties of Canon Law as well as the Concordat's language, Maldonado elucidates every one of the civil disabilities visited on Spanish Protestants under the Rome-Madrid agreement.]

We have studied, then, the contents and dispositions of [the doctrine of] tolerance of worship. Canon Law, a spiritualist juridical system, always mindful of human nature, has developed to the utmost, and with an enormous sense of charity, those conventions which endow [the Code] with flexibility . . . : custom, privilege (*ius singulare*), dispensation (*relaxatio legis*), *dissimulatio* (the isolation of an evil surrounding it by a zone of silence), and tolerance *ad maiora mala vitanda* [for the avoidance of greater evils].

· · ·

Above all it must be made clear that we are dealing only with *tolerated,* and not with *authorized,* worship. As has been set forth in the Italian doctrine—which has dealt with this matter so extensively and has so clearly set forth the distinction between the two concepts—tolerated worship implies that the same cannot be practiced in public, nor is there to be liberty of discussion in religious matters or liberty of propaganda or proselytism.

· · ·

The religious minister. There is mention of this concept in Paragraph 1 of the Circular Order of November 12, 1945, as follows: "The directors of these sects or the persons in charge of [their] worship are at liberty to organize religious ceremonies" within the limits already stated; but nothing is said of the requirements or personal conditions which these ministers must meet, either in themselves or in relation to their sect. A warning is in order: their acts in this capacity cannot have official effect in the civil sphere. Hence, for instance, those certificates of non-Catholicity [1] required for a civil marriage which have on occasion been issued by non-Catholic ministers in Spain, cannot be regarded as official documents and must be considered only as a testimonial information.

. . .

A series of concrete applications to the general prohibition of external manifestations must be elucidated. Thus, no newspaper advertisements must be permitted; nor advertisements at the doors of churches; nor will it be possible to broadcast a service over the radio; in fact, quite probably care will have to be taken that [these services] will not be heard on the outside, through the windows, so that they may not thus constitute external manifestations; nor will bells or any other elements of sound be rung, etc. The special problems of burial places will have to be studied in order to determine if non-Catholic worship inside cemeteries can be considered private. The Royal Order of February 28, 1872, so considered them, and it permitted dissident sects, as well as municipalities, to set aside civil cemeteries.

. . .

Protection of [non-Catholic] worship. Article 3 of the Circular Order of November 12, 1945, states expressly: "The Civil Governors will protect the worship hereby authorized and will not interfere with the work of the churches, nor with their private ceremonies."

At first glance it would seem that Article 211 of the Penal Code refers to [the protection of non-Catholic worship], when it states that those guilty of acts that offend "the religious feeling of the

[1] In an obvious misprint, the text reads *"la catolicidad"* instead of *"la acatolicidad."*

355

assembly" in "a religious place"—without specifying that this place be Catholic—are subject to arrest. Nevertheless, one cannot construe it in this manner, since this article is part of Section 111, Chapter II, Book II, of the Penal Code, which comes under the heading "Crimes Against the Catholic Religion," and which therefore makes the above-mentioned Article 211 inapplicable to other religions.

CONCERNING SPANISH PROTESTANTISM

[This article by Joaquín María Alonso, C.M.F., was published in *The City of God,* a scholarly magazine edited at the Monastery of El Escorial, Vol. CLXXIV (1961), pp. 483–522. Father Alonso, one of the most implacable foes of religious liberty, teamed with Father Eustaquio Guerrero, S.J., to produce *Religious Liberty in Spain: Principles, Facts, Problems,* a 250-page book published by Fe Católica in 1962.

Father Alonso begins by referring to a New York *Times* story of May 4, 1959, which stated that the two hundred fifty Protestant chapels functioning in Spain would soon be three hundred. This, points out the Franciscan priest, averages out at thirty-three Protestants for each place of worship.]

For whom are these empty churches? For whom these deserted places of worship? Under what right are buildings evidently destined for religious uses registered as private houses? Why have they been able to multiply under surreptitious or absolutely false permits? Finally, how can Protestants complain when, in all justice, they are ordered to close some of them? Here is the answer. Speaking of one of the most propitious eras for Spanish Protestantism, the years between 1868 and 1874, a well-known Protestant of the time, Carrasco, revealed the true reason for opening chapels; as he said: "One must regret that in those days there weren't enough agents and funds for opening a chapel in each city and town of importance across Spain. If this had been done there would be as many congregations today as there were chapels open to the public." In other words, for Spanish Protestants chapels are not first and foremost places of worship; they are centers of religious proselytism. Hence the [Protestants'] boldness, their audacity in openly defying the law on this one point which is so vital to their purposes. Thus the Pastors' Convention held in Tarrasa [Cataluña] in September, 1954, took the following password, *which would have been enough to bring on a serious civil process:*

"To work indefatigably and by all means towards the opening of new chapels and meeting places, whether they be tolerated or not, for once this is accomplished it will be feasible to obtain the longed-for liberty with the assistance of the United States and England."

Aren't they the first to state that they possess "new locales with old permits," "new locales without permits" [or] "Where there is no official permit, most churches have helped themselves to it"? On May 4, 1959, the New York *Times* was shocked by the fact that the Government had closed all places of worship which had no permits; this would affect—it stated—some two hundred places which in fact did not have any [authorization] and ten others which had it merely verbally, leaving only forty [chapels whose affairs were] perfectly in order.

Before such statistics the conclusion is simple: Protestant chapels in Spain, in their excessive number, do not meet a specifically religious but a proselytist purpose. Moreover, most of them contravene State legislation. Can the State remain passive before such an open transgression of one of the nation's important laws?

[Italics mine. The three quotations, which Father Alonso acknowledges, are from J. David Hughey's *Historia de los bautistas en España.*]

MORE PAPIST THAN THE POPE

[The most famous and widely discussed newspaper article on religious liberty in recent times was written by Rodrigo Royo, editor of the news magazine *SP,* and published on October 1, 1965. In his "Letter to the Reader" column, two months before the Declaration on Religious Liberty passed the Second Vatican Council, Royo voiced the alarm of the orthodox before the untraditional views which, as it seemed, had been put forth by foreign elements at the Council.

The most significant note of Royo's column is his insistence that the religious problem is an "artificial" one in Spain: the sheer non-existence of native Protestantism has been the number-one argument wielded by all enemies of freedom of worship. In fact, in mid-1966 conservative elements continued to remind Spaniards that religious liberty was an issue that affected only "tourists."]

The Kingdom of Spain, for centuries defenders of the Catholic faith, right hand and sword of the Church of Christ on so many occasions, is following the developments at the Vatican Council with attention and worry. . . .

The principal focus of Spain's attention and worry as regards the Council is the debate on religious liberty, whose preliminary schema was approved by an overwhelming majority of the Council Fathers (1,997 to 224) against the judgment of the Spanish hierarchy. If a poll or general consultation were to be taken, I believe it would show that the good Catholic people of Spain support, en masse, the position of their bishops; these simple and open people understand the true spirit of Spain much better than the dozens of sophisticated intellectuals or young snobs who, from the height of their presumptuous and old-fashioned liberalism, pretend to be scandalized before the authentically representative position of the Spanish hierarchy at the Council.

That hierarchy, and the opinion it represents, is doing nothing but interpreting Spain's authentic genius; it is keeping faith with tradition and with the role Spain has played in the universe and will continue to play across the centuries. To renounce that calling, to climb on the victors' chariot or join factions diametrically opposed to those which have limned Spain's profile and physiognomy throughout history, would be the equivalent of ceasing to be Spaniards and becoming another, unidentifiable nation.

What are the master lines that mold Spain's historical and universal physiognomy, that define and identify her as a nation? To me they are clear as day. On the one hand Spain's most salient and vigorous characteristic is that, when necessary, she can be more Papist than the Pope. On the other hand Spain represents, above all, the role of opposition to the world, of opposition to those currents of disintegration and dissolution which, from time

to time, take the driver's seat in human affairs. Spain's fundamental mission lies in acting as a counterweight in the scales of
humanity so the world will not lose its senses. Spain has represented—and must continue to represent, if she wants to be herself—a moderating, leveling, equilibrating force, in other words,
[she must occupy] the other side of the scales against those radical
[currents] that dissolve humanity. The greatness of Spain, protagonist of this drama, resides in this one fact: that she knows no
terror. It makes no difference how great, strong, colossal or crushing the opposing forces might be. She counterweighs them; she
knows no terror.

Being permanently in the long-suffering, thankless, obscure opposition is a beautiful role. As beautiful as it is uncomfortable.
But it has greatness. When faced with the three phenomena of a
universally transforming force in the modern world (Protestantism,
the French Revolution and Marxism), Spain knew how to play
her part with the dignity required of her. Against Luther, she jux-
taposed Trent; against Napoleon, the War of Independence; and
against Karl Marx, the War of Liberation [the Crusade]. Spain is
the only nation that has shed her blood to check the heresy of
Protestantism, the dissolving spirit of the French Revolution, and
the demolishing thought of Marxist socialism. Three dates contain and define the most difficult portion of the universal role
Spain has had to play: 1545, 1808 and 1936. The other signal
date—proof that Spain does not play at opposition systematically,
but that she simply opposes with discernment whatever she, in
her great conscience, deems evil—is 1492, the date when the positive achievements of the Renaissance took root in the Peninsula,
when Spain was launched onto the wide routes of her discoveries
and the founding of twenty nations of her own race.

Because Spain is as she is, we can be sure that the matter at
hand [i.e., the proposed Declaration on Religious Liberty] is a
storm in a teacup. Spain's counterweighing influence will make the
Council Fathers think and help them reach moderate and well-
balanced conclusions. One cannot enact uniform laws for the entire world. Each nation has its own specific problems. Contrary
to what many people believe, Spain leads many of the world's

communities in the solution of those fundamental problems which face all nations. As any other country, Spain has political, economic and social problems which she is trying to solve to the best of her ability. But, thanks be to God, Spain does not have the religious or racial problems which, to their misfortune, exist in many great nations that boast of their progress and think of themselves as superior. Spain solved those two terrible problems five centuries ago.

Spain has no religious problem because she dealt with that problem at the proper time, outdoing other nations by several centuries; in view of this it would be absurd, even foolish, to invent that problem over again, artificially and gratuitously. It would be as foolish as if, considering that there is no racial problem here because we knew how to digest that bitter pill with five centuries' anticipation, somebody would insist in settling five million Negroes in Palencia and force us to deal with the consequences.

If it is true that the people of Spain are on special occasions more Papist than the Pope, it is not because of a whim, or because of ostentation on their part, nor is it due to an irrational spirit of contradiction. The reason for it lies with the categorical demands of their history and their temperament, in both of which the Catholic religion is inseparably blended and fused.

RELIGIOUS LIBERTY DOES NOT DEMAND THE SUPPRESSION OF [THE STATE'S] CONFESSIONALITY

[Under that headline the newspaper *Ya* published, on February 16, 1966, an "authentic extract" from a lecture delivered at Madrid's Higher Institute for Religious Culture by Don Amadeo Fuenmayor, professor at the University of Navarra, an Opus Dei center of higher learning.]

We are dealing with the theme in its juridico-social aspect, outside its pastoral implications. Withal, the Spanish case has been a polemical case and has given rise to an excess of speculation.

An analysis of history tells us that religion is a decisive element in the life of nations, as the mainstay of cultural forces and the creator of temporal ways of life. Secularization is a relatively modern phenomenon, anomalous in history. Only after the rise of Christianity can one talk of a distinction between the rigorously temporal and the strictly spiritual. Hence it is not surprising that until recently all political systems have maintained a certain degree of confessionality. At present there are non-Christian confessional systems such as the Islamic, which has lasted for thirteen centuries, or the Buddhist which obtains among the peoples of Asia. It can be said that two-thirds of humanity live under non-Christian confessional structures. The most advanced European States maintain non-Catholic confessional systems.

Catholic confessionality, as it is conceived in the contemporary world, is based on the doctrine of Leo XIII. [Under this doctrine] the attitude that the Church demands of Catholics is justified by two great ideals: the Religion of the Nation or the State, and the inspiration of [the nation's] social and political structures in the tenets of the Teaching Church. From this derives the fact that one can speak of confessionality in a double sense: "formal confessionality," which consists of the State's solemn acknowledgment of its official Catholicism; and "substantial confessionality," which is the actual inspiration of [the nation's] political and social institutions by the tenets of the Teaching Church. The State's acknowledgment of its official Catholicism—formal confessionality—necessarily demands substantial confessionality if "political pharisaism" is to be avoided. On the other hand, the inspiration of [the nation's] social and political institutions by the tenets of the Teaching Church—substantial confessionality—does not necessarily demand formal confessionality. The Council neither recommends nor rejects formal confessionality; but the Declaration on Religious Freedom consecrates [sic] substantial confessionality in its Paragraph 6, which, it will be noted, does not limit itself to Catholic confessionality.[2] The Church, which demands liberty everywhere, seeks above all to repulse laicism and atheism.

[2] Professor Fuenmayor's point should be measured against what is perhaps the most authoritative wording of the article in question, as well as a footnote appended thereto. I refer to the translation of the Declaration's text produced by Fr. John Courtney Murray, S.J., the principal architect of the Schema. It is contained in *The Documents of Vatican II, with Notes and*

II · ANTI-SPAIN

NOTES FOR A DICTIONARY OF "CHRISTIAN" MYTHOLOGY [Extracts]

[By Eduardo Obregón, a Santander educator; published in *Cuadernos para el diálogo*, September, 1964.]

Many myths owe their birth and longevity to the support which their idea of the established order offers to the interests of the privileged classes. . . .

These are the myths which are responsible for the fact that religion is so often presented as the *opium of the people*. One need only remember the unfortunate and ill-understood "Christian resignation" which has been preached to the low classes for so many centuries as "relief" from their oppression. . . .

Today, face to face with the new myths with which the upper classes seek to perpetuate the established order for their own profit, one could say that religion (if it were not actually a very different thing . . .) is the *opium of the bourgeoisie*. We find

---

Comments by Catholic, Protestant and Orthodox Authorities (New York: The American Press, 1966), a superb collection of all Council statements edited by Fr. Walter M. Abbott, S.J., of *America*. As stated therein (p. 685), the pertinent section of Article 6 reads: "If, in view of peculiar circumstances obtaining among certain peoples, special legal recognition is given in the constitutional order of society to one religious body, it is at the same time imperative that the right of all citizens and religious bodies to religious freedom should be recognized and made effective in practice." [17]

Note 17 states: "This paragraph is carefully phrased. The Council did not wish to condemn the institution of 'establishment,' the notion of a 'religion of the state.' A respectable opinion maintains that the institution is compatible with full religious freedom. On the other hand, the Council did not wish to canonize the institution. A respectable opinion holds that establishment is always a threat to religious freedom. Furthermore, the Council wished to insinuate that establishment, at least from the Catholic point of view, is a matter of historical circumstance, not of theological doctrine. For all these reasons the text deals with the issue in conditional terms."

ourselves, in effect, before one of the most curious myth-elaborating movements imaginable: the utilization of religion by the most pious sectors of the upper and middle bourgeoisie as an evasion from and antidote to the social demands of religion itself. . . . Such is, unfortunately, the hallmark of not a few "spiritual" and "apostolic" movements of our days, whose much-heralded mottoes of "sanctity," "witness," "sacrifice," etc. answer more to a selfishly individualistic concept of the demands of religion than to a search for the plenitude of truth and love which Christians must manifest in the world. . . .

ON SCHEMA XIII: REGARDING PROCREATION

[By José María de Llanos, S.J., from *El ciervo* for December, 1964.]

We have all read what the Fathers said at the Council, and added our two cents to the debate. Perhaps we lacked authority to do so; but we [spoke out] freely, as children of God. The theme is undoubtedly out in the open. And we of the clergy must acknowledge that on this subject we have to limit ourselves to theories. Married people are right; there is something fundamental lacking in our advice which makes it fall wide of the target—as I believe one of the Council Fathers pointed out. Conscious, then, of our most limited limitation, we are bold enough to say:

Two points were most discussed: one was the harmony between the two so-called ends of marriage; the other was procreation. Today we shall limit our remarks to the latter, although we recognize that the former is basic [to the issue] and cannot be casually dismissed by appealing to the distinctions between concupiscent love and friendship-love. What do married people, who experience this love, have to say on this fine distinction? Is their married love reduced to a wise dosage of each of these two distinct loves? Is that what sanctifies marriage and makes possible and defensible the indissolubility of the union?

But let us turn to the theme of procreation, omitting mention of the licit and illicit means of controlling it. Let us pause before the very fact of this control. The Schema presented to the Council admits [of this control], recognizing the right and even the duty of husband and wife to regulate the supreme end of their love relationship. It was on this point that the Council Fathers disagreed. Cardinal Alfrink, representing a good number of bishops, defended the contents of the Schema; Cardinal Ottaviani and some other Fathers attacked it. And Bishop Hervás, in the name of 120 Fathers, appended a *secundum modum* which stated that, instead of speaking of such control, it behooved [the Council] to praise, exult in, and bless Christian families with numerous children. And it is here, on this precise point, that I am bold enough to make the following observations:

Is the large family in itself, by virtue of abundant procreation, worthy of indiscriminate praise? Is the number of children itself a valid criterion for the praise and applause of the Church? I make bold to answer by pointing out the various motives for abundant procreation which I have witnessed during my pastoral life.

1. The truly Christian motive: parents have surrendered to each other in mutual love, through a mutual decision to obey the commandment "Increase and multiply" to the letter, without stopping to consider the sacrifices this implies.

2. The mysterious workings of female fecundity, which have triumphed over the parents' own will and resulted in an abundance [of children] which has in effect happened against their will and which, at best, they have borne as a trial. Rather than offering a motive for praising the parents, this case offers a motive for praising the Creator who acts against, or outside the margin of the couple's will.

3. A deliberate calculation on the part of parents planning for a secure old age through numerous children who will shelter them in turn, and save them from a sad end in a home for the aged. This motive is common enough among the lower classes, and in villages, where life is full of hardship. Many village couples have seen the happy results of abundant procreation in their parents and grandparents. And they have "made out their insurance" by having many children. This is not illicit, but neither does it offer us an inspiring portrait of generous parenthood.

4. Another deliberate calculation with a modern angle: a large family can obtain a series of economic benefits from the State and society. These [benefits] are not much; but they are something. When three children have been borne, the time comes to ask the question: "Why not one more? Then we shall obtain the benefits offered large families." [3] Again, this is not immoral, but we are still far from virtue and its due praise.

5. The profound desire of middle-aged women to show that they are still fecund. This is still a motive of great weight in some villages; [the particular woman's] fecundity is the subject of discussion, praise and envy among her friends; her pregnancy is a motive for [self-]satisfaction. And this is a very human, very feminine feeling (let us remember the case of the sterile Israelite woman and Anna's tears before Samuel). The childbearing championship will always be one of the favorites among women. I have seen this among the lower classes of our people. And we are not witnessing here anything that is gravely illicit, but rather the effects of a natural force which of course does not deserve a song of praise in the name of exemplary Christianity.

6. A sad and shameful motive which it is not seemly for us to analyze, but which all of us are aware of: the concupiscence of a husband who takes advantage of his wife—a concupiscence very typical of men who have no money to indulge it in the other, more expensive ways. Such a man even acknowledges [his conduct] without shame. In this case the hunger and wrath of the jobless worker will conspire with what, from the outside, appears to be a desire for procreation, but which is the result of nothing but great concupiscence. (Of course the concupiscence that ends in abortion—or the other one—is even worse; but this kind is not common among low-class couples, who prefer to face up to the consequences . . . and have the children.)

7. A last motive, which is more common than any of the others put together, and then some. This is the sum of the equivocal, most human cases where procreation is provoked by different factors—some good, some indifferent and others frankly immoral.

[3] The minimum number of children for qualifying as a *familia numerosa* is four.

Take a little of each and you will have the picture of the couple with seven, eight or twelve children. Indiscriminate applause, then? Censure?

The State can and should offer prizes in any case. The State—certain States—need men, and they pay bonuses for their production. That is all. No, perhaps there is more to it, since this production can also be put to use in war and for war. The State does well in offering prizes for demographic feats. But we do not believe this should be the case with the Church, which is more concerned with goodness and moral order than with the literal number of men produced, regardless of the motives for their production and their effect on salvation. The respective ends of Church and State are so different that it does not seem proper for the former to heap too much praise on the latter for its generosity towards large families.

Nevertheless, considering all motives in their just natural and supernatural order, we must say clearly and definitely that it will always be better to give God many, rather than few, children. But with the proviso that everything be in order, for disorder is inherent not only in birth control but, as we have said before, in indiscriminate procreation like rutting beasts. Man will never be a stud horse to be praised for his ability to sire offspring; man should look not only to the generation, but to the education, of his children. And before this problem of education, births may require control. A certain elementary logic must be granted those who say: the fewer the children to educate, the better their education will be. In support of this thesis we have every slum where gangs of children roam the streets; these children cannot stay at home, for there is no home to keep them and support them. On the other hand it is true—as was pointed out at the Council—that [parents of] large families usually bring up their sons and daughters better than those who have only one or two spoiled, indulged children. And I myself believe that this second premise is truer than the first. Hence the principle that judges the quality of the children inversely to their quantity is not in any sense clear. The quality of the children does not usually depend on their being few or many, but on the quality of their parents, and on [the

366

children's] having access to the proper social aids, especially schools.

The other reason adduced for [birth] control has to do with the husband and wife themselves, and it is not to be scorned. Does the mother benefit, or is she harmed, by abundant procreation? Let the doctors answer; for myself, I shall bring up the picture of so many women I have seen in the slums, loaded with children and prematurely aged at thirty-some. And this picture is not to be found among large families of the bourgeoisie. Why? Let us add, then, the effects of procreation on the father, on his character, on his anguish, on the social maladjustment he suffers because of the offspring who weigh so heavily on him. Some will say: he will work harder. And one can answer: he will work badly, and more bitterly. And then there is [the matter of] the home and its harmony or disharmony. Above all the Church wants marriage to be an institution which will sanctify parents and children. It is ingenuous to measure this capacity for sanctification by the number of children. There are so many factors involved! When all is said and done, the holiest family on earth wasn't exactly holy because it was large . . .

Last of all there is an elemental argument of great weight, which goes like this: if it would be absurd to tell a couple that they should dispense with reason in matters relating to their economic affairs, to the setting up of their home, and to each and every one of their secondary problems, then how can it be held that, before the first and holiest of their missions—the one which gives meaning to their unbreakable union—how can it be held that in this province only instinct should rule them? And I am speaking of that instinct which regulates the zoological aspects of sex; for if a superior [kind of] instinct is admitted, then we shall find ourselves in that area to which the Council addressed itself so wisely. Martín Descalzo [4] has expressed the Council's thinking in the following words: "As regards the number of children, Christian couples know that they should not abandon themselves to blind instinct, but that they will glorify God and perfect themselves in

[4] "The New Anticlericals" (see p. 372).

367

Christ if they carry out their procreational functions with full and conscious responsibility, according to the gifts of God and the true rules of love. Through prayer and dialogue they should come to a prudent agreement, not once and for all, but in each [particular] case, bearing in mind their economic conditions, their capacity to educate the children, their mental and bodily health, the good of the family and the Church, and the needs of society." These were the words which were discussed at the Council, and which caused widespread scandal. Let us applaud them.

A Protestant Cop

[By Ricardo Sanchis, S.J.; from *The Social Kingdom of the Sacred Heart,* a pious magazine published in Madrid. Year XLVIII, No. 435, March, 1965, p. 14.]

. . .

It was one of the rarities in the city, a Protestant cop. He was not a common officer; tall and corpulent, with his white helmet, he looked fit for a job among the London policemen. Besides, he was kind, cordial, smiling. Conscientious in the fulfillment of his duties, whenever he had to notify someone in an upper floor that the time set aside for shaking rugs was past, he did so with such politeness that people paid the fines with pleasure. . . . But he is a Protestant, don't you know?

And the truth is that the good cop had to suffer on account of that. Many years were to pass before that business of religious liberty would not be considered so monstrous. . . .

At the Jesuit school the boys used to list among the sacrifices offered to the Virgin that of exposing themselves to the Protestant policeman's fury. "I said 'Hail Mary Most Pure' to the Protestant policeman"; "I said 'Long live the Virgin and may Luther die' close to the Protestant policeman." And so it would go every day of the month of May, of the novena to the Immaculate [Conception], when the little ones would leave their slips in a small box at the feet of the Virgin in the study hall. On the Feast Day the slips were burned together with incense . . . the good children's virtuous deeds.

Poor cop! As if he didn't have enough troubles of his own to worry about one or two kids shouting, "Hail Mary Most Pure!" and then running for it. Though it seems likely that he did not pay much attention to the frightened boys. Much worse were the Catholic youths who thought of themselves as crusaders of the Catholic faith and stoned the windows of the [Protestant] chapel when services were in progress; and even worse were overly pious and influential men and women who waited in ambush for a too-energetic reaction on the part of the cop in order to denounce him. It was intolerable that in a city of Catholic Spain there should be a heretic, the worst kind of Red.

Of course nothing ever happened, because the Protestant cop had won the esteem of all for his honesty, his conscientiousness, his kindness.

The years go by for all of us—for those youngsters who have gray hair by now, and for the Protestant cop. Perhaps he has already retired. Surely he is no longer set upon by the boys of the Jesuit school, nor, fortunately, are there any more punks engaged in the defense of the Catholic faith. We Catholics have learned not to be cruel to our separated brethren, even if the heritage of the Inquisition has not disappeared completely.

Does it make sense to speak of ecumenism in Spain? The dissident minority is so small and is rooted in such low cultural strata, that we always think of ecumenism as something to be fostered abroad . . . in Great Britain, Germany, Switzerland and the United States of America.

Nevertheless, at the root of the ecumenical spirit is sincere charity, understanding and patience. And those few Protestants whose proselytism will perhaps make us indignant give us an excellent opportunity to behave as true disciples of Christ.

The Pope has stated many times that we have all sinned against unity. There are the old sins at the sad time of separation, the recent sins of keeping suspicion and prejudice alive, there are the anathemas hurled against persons, there are attitudes which differ radically from those we take today. And added to this is the cheap sin of mockery, of mistrust, of the pitying smiles turned on compatriots who, prompted mostly by the lack of Christian spirit among their very Catholic neighbors, thought they found a solution to their religious unquiet by embracing a different faith.

The road to unity is a long pilgrimage of patience, of consideration, of love and prayer. It is a path traced for the Universal Church, for contact between officials, for dialogue between leaders . . . and it is also the road each Christian must tread, a road of concrete charity and patience, of cordial relations with this or that person.

Children, please! The Virgin does not want you to shout "Hail Mary Most Pure" at the Protestant cop, but to pray for him, to say "Good morning" to him as to everyone else. All of that is past; you shouldn't harass Protestants any more.

THE MESSAGE OF THE COUNCIL [Extracts]

[From the book by Father Carlos Castro Cubells, a secular priest of the Diocese of Madrid.]

Before it became a complicated doctrine of the theologians, justification by faith (its sufficiency to save us) was—and here lies its true greatness—a religious intuition of irresistible power, produced by the pious reading of the Bible in Luther's tremulous, worshiping soul. . . . While reading the word of God, Luther —fearful for his salvation, counting so far only on his good will, his works, his merits, and despairing of success (isn't this, in fact, the situation of many Catholics?)—recognized in a flash that our salvation is not our own work but the work of God, the gift of his grace in Christ, who gave himself on the Cross for us. . . .

. . .

Luther himself, when he became the theologian of his own experience, elaborated—as did subsequent theologians—a unilateral and polemical doctrine. But Luther's religious intuition is basically the recognition of a fundamental Biblical truth, perhaps the central truth of the Bible: that we have not been the first to love God, but that God was the first to love us. . . .

That is why the Protestant is the man of the Bible. Protestantism is a religion, or a religious attitude, rather than a doctrine because it is the religion of a book in which all truth is contained. It is the religion of the Bible because the Protestants read the Bible in the light of a living, pivotal intuition of its contents. Only the decadence of religiosity could convert Protestantism into a lifeless creed.

. . .

. . . It was an afternoon during the last days of the [Civil] war. Like so many others [they] spent in the company of Professor Araujo, a group of students were discussing the latest events. . . . During a lull in the conversation we heard the Professor's voice ringing out in the tones of a paternal sermon, as it hadn't in a long time. . . .

As always, Araujo had closed a book he had been reading while holding it barely open, an attitude of his that used to strike our fancy. The kind of books he read also roused our curiosity. We used to say he read eighteenth-century mathematical treatises. . . . We used to imagine him poring over Leibniz and Luther, Calvin and Melanchthon. Probably none of it was true but we took pleasure in these hypotheses and their deliciously pedantic humanism. . . .

That afternoon Araujo spoke as never before: he spoke of the future of Spain. . . . He told us the war was over and that we could not stop to think of painful memories. We would have to work not only in the reconstruction of things, but of persons, of families. And, not looking at anyone in particular, but addressing those who could have had deeper sympathies with the defeated cause, as if speaking to someone in need of encouragement, he told us that it would be necessary to start from reality, from the new situation which was already imminent. . . .

I cannot remember his exact words, but they were transfixed with a spirit of kindness. Once we boys were alone, we said it openly: we have heard the first Christian sermon of this new era in which we will have open churches. I realize now what I didn't stop to consider then: that the first Christian sermon came from a Protestant. . . . I looked about for Professor Araujo on several occasions to give him, belatedly, my thanks.

THE THIRTY THOUSAND

THE NEW ANTICLERICALS [Extract]

[An article by Father José Luis Martín Descalzo, journalist, poet and novelist, which originally appeared in the religious magazine *Vida nueva* for July, 1965. It was the year that the Virgin "appeared" to four children near Santander with the message that the Church should beware of "perverted" priests; barely twelve months later the Establishment was openly vilifying the hundred Catalan clerics who massed together for a peaceful demonstration, on the charge that they had indulged in forbidden "politics."

Father Martín Descalzo's article was reproduced by *Pueblo* in its entirety on August 25, 1965. The following extract is taken from the *Pueblo* text.]

The hallmark of the new anticlericalism is its insistence on one theme: the clergy's involvement in social problems. Those who always found it natural for a military chaplain to wear an army uniform are now shocked if a priest wears a clergyman's suit or an overall. Those who thought it normal for a priest to devote his life to astronomy or mathematics now discover the notion that a priest's mission should be "strictly apostolic." Those who watched serenely while the clergy took part in parades or demonstrations for the Right now quake at the sight of a priest supporting workers' demands. Those who urged priests to speak out on politics from the pulpit around 1930 now want them to limit their sermons to the life of Christ. Those who never dreamed that a Marquis' chaplain could represent class distinctions now call a counselor for the Catholic Action Young Workers movement a radical. Those who always thought Radio Prague broadcast lies now attach great importance to its tactical praise of the Catholic labor initiatives.

The new anticlericals belabor priests for their involvement in secular issues and forget that silence and passivity are as much commitment to a cause as action itself. A priest who stirs himself on behalf of a social problem is no more partisan than another who, faced with the same problem, remains silent. He who tolerates injustice acts no less than he who takes a hand in fighting

372

it. He who supports a given policy is no more biased than he who condemns it.

The saddest part of this new anticlericalism is its uselessness. The traditional antagonism of the enemies of the Church used to be the cry which rallied priests to battle and which spurred them on, as a picador's hook spurs a fierce bull. The antagonism of the faithful, on the other hand, numbs, disconcerts and confuses the clergy.

It also confuses the simple people, who don't know which way to turn when they hear their priests are little less than Communists. It disconcerts the young, who are inhibited and robbed of their last vestige of confidence in the social efficacy of Christianity when they see individuals browbeaten and almost expelled from the Church for insisting on a few basic principles of social justice. "If what that priest wants is Communism," one teen-ager told me, "then Communism can't be as bad as they say."

It discourages us priests and makes us class-conscious. When someone who simply preaches the Gospel and its social message sees that an entire bourgeois bloc rises up against his preaching, it is not easy to persist in the belief that [they] are apt for Christianity.

Let us speak the truth: a calm dialogue will help young priests moderate their ardor and correct the failings which, like any other human beings, they do have. A campaign of defamation and alarmism will only rouse them, make heroes out of the handful of extremists among them, and embitter and sully the lives of the great number of moderates who walk in their midst, as they have in every generation.

CATHOLICS WHO ARE NOT CHRISTIANS

[By Enrique Miret Magdalena; from *Triunfo,* November 6, 1965.]

Revealed truths "vary in their importance and weight," has said the [Second Vatican] Council. And those who give a place of honor in their lives to such important affirmations will be better Catholics than those who do not love their brothers well (and all men are brothers, be they Jews, Mohammedans or Marxists), better than those who hide the figure of Christ behind a farrago of pious semisuperstitions or those who make God a tyrant and a spiritual miser.

Those who claim to hoist the flag of the most pure Catholicism but who do not want to center their lives in the love of men, of Christ and of God; those who love only people who think like themselves, who trust only the most wonder-working saint and believe only in a God who is the tyrannical master of all men—these are not true Catholics. . . .

Religion is a very serious thing which we must respect without taking any of those "anti" positions which are so opposed to our moral code as it is expressed in the Gospel. We Catholics are not anti-Protestant nor "anti" anything else; we are the friends and brothers of Protestants, and of all men.

More Papist Than the Pope—A Dissenting Letter

[Signed by F. Aguinagalde of Bilbao and published—along with many other letters for and against the article—in *SP*, December 19, 1965.]

It would be wonderful if we in our country could reach that spiritual maturity which permits social harmony without discrimination as to race, wealth or ideology. A maximum of spiritual liberty and a maximum of social discipline.

My convictions compel me to hold in profound respect all other opinions or beliefs on the origin, essence and ends of the Universe. That is why, though I might consider them dated, I regard all religious postures as sacred, since they spring from the human heart. . . .

For my part I understand the reasons why the Church in Spain, with its "official" majority, will not permit a free confrontation between the religious and mystical foundations of different religions and philosophical tenets, between different mystiques and ethics. . . . It is a phenomenon which is constant in history, analogous to the social conditions which brought on the drama of Socrates, of Jesus of Nazareth, and so many others. I think it is due to a species of historical inertia which prevents the instituted, official Church of any given civilization from accepting a change in the religious mentality brought about by the advances of real knowledge, by the feelings and the activity of the individual who is in the vanguard of progress, and who in most cases does not belong to the reigning official church. . . .

The Catholic theological scheme was outdated. The Council has made a praiseworthy effort to bring it up to date. Because, after all these years, the Bishops of the Church have done nothing but confirm the convictions that millions of human beings on earth already held. I remember how, when I was a child, my father, a humble laborer, defended ideas and rights which have now been approved by the Church. . . .

I am neither a businessman nor a man of violence.—F. Aguinagalde, Lic. Poza, num. 30, 6 derecha, Bilbao.

III · THE THIRTY THOUSAND: A FOREIGN REPORT

SPANISH PROTESTANTISM IN CONCLAVE

[From the German Catholic magazine, *Herder Correspondence* (Freiburg), Vol. 3, No. 1, January, 1966.]

A conference of Spanish Protestant pastors and fellow workers (Conferencia Nacional de Obreros Evangélicos) was held in Madrid on 6–8 October 1965. While it was emphasized by the organizers from the outset that this was neither a "council," a synod, nor an official church assembly, the president nevertheless declared at the end that the conference was "unique" in the history of Protestantism in Spain—for the numbers who took part, for the invitation extended to Catholic Christians, for the atmosphere of open discussion which prevailed, and for the echo roused abroad. The event was even announced in the Spanish press two months before, although the actual proceedings were not covered.

Regional "pastors' conferences" as well as one national conference (in 1961) had already been held, but these gatherings were isolated events of merely local interest. A closer study of Protestantism in Spain—to the extent that this was possible during the recent conference—reveals the incomplete and biased picture often given by foreign press reports, even by those originating from Protestant sources.

Various Denominations

In structure the Protestant minority in Spain corresponds more closely to the denominational situation in the United States than to that in Central Europe or the British Isles. It is made up of the following churches, religious communities and groups:

1. Iglesia Evangélica Española (union of Lutherans, Presbyterians and Methodists)   3,800
2. Iglesia Reformada Episcopal (though episcopal in constitution, this body corresponds rather to the English Low Church; it belongs to the Anglican Communion)   1,000
3. Union Evangélica Bautista (independent Baptist churches)   5,400
4. Federación de Iglesias Evangélicas (groups dependent upon foreign Baptist churches)   3,100
5. Asambleas de Hermanos (corresponds to the Plymouth Brethren, extremist wing of the Fundamentalists)   6,000
6. Iglesia Cristiana Adventista del Séptimo Día   5,200
7. Iglesias Pentecostales   3,500
8. Independent groups   2,000

There are also foreign groups of Lutherans, Anglicans and Waldensians, each a self-contained unit. The figures given above totaling some thirty thousand Spanish Protestants, cover members officially registered. Attendance at church services, including family members, is estimated at sixty to seventy thousand.

National and International Co-operation

There are 425 places of worship, 320 of which are churches and chapels and 105 private meeting rooms. Only 60 per cent of these are officially approved by the State, while a further 30 per cent are tolerated. There are some 300 pastors to serve the whole of Spain, approximately half of whom are ordained. Three training centers exist: one for each of the two Baptist unions and the Seminario Teológico Unido. All three seminaries, each with about ten students, are at present in Barcelona, but two are shortly to be transferred to Madrid. Most student pastors go abroad to finish their training, the Baptists to Zurich and members of the I.E.E. and the Episcopalian Church (churches 1 and 2) to Geneva, France or the Argentine.

Only these two churches belong to the World Council of Churches; for some time past they have begun to collaborate with Catholics, during the octave of prayer for Christian unity, for instance, and in the ecumenical centers (see *Herder Correspondence,* September–October, 1965, pp. 262–63). So far only groups 1–5 have shown any willingness to work together to further internal Protestant interests, establishing the "Spanish Evangelical Council" (Consejo Evangélico Español) as a meeting center. But this body has as yet no powers of any kind and cannot be compared either with the American National Council of Churches or with the British Council of Churches. The Comisión de Defensa Evangélica Española has long existed as a legal and administrative body; this institution—the name of which indicates the situation in Spain—protects the interests of all Protestant groups. The executive secretary is the Baptist lawyer and pastor José Cardona Gregori (C. Trafalgar 32, Madrid 10).

Restrictions Imposed by the State

Cardona Gregori was the first speaker at the conference. He made it clear that there was no question of "a new situation." In a survey of the present legal position he showed that although there were certain improvements, basically the legal situation remained unchanged. According to the Spanish Law of 1945 (*Fuero de los Españoles*), according to the law governing the National Movement of 1958 as well as the Concordat of 1953, the Catholic religion is "the one and only religion of the Spanish people." All other denominations are only allowed to worship in private. As a result:

1. Non-Catholic religious communities cannot be established as legal bodies.
2. Apart from religious services, any other activity is forbidden.
3. Propaganda of any kind is regarded as a threat to the spiritual unity of Spain.
4. Non-Catholic pastors are not recognized as ministers of religion.
5. Legally, training centers may not be opened.
6. Social and charitable bodies can only work in secret.
7. No official licenses have been granted for Protestant periodicals, though some such periodicals in fact exist and are distributed secretly.
8. Only buildings owned by foreigners may be used by Protestant groups.

Practical Difficulties

Non-Catholic marriages are still difficult. There are long delays before the requisite permission is received from the Catholic diocesan authorities and from the State; moreover, marriages thus contracted have no legal protection in Spain and can thus be dissolved quite easily upon application of either partner.

Non-Catholic children are exempt from religious instruction at their parents' request. On the other hand, Protestant schools are private and more or less secret; the legal establishment of non-Catholic schools will remain prohibited, according to declarations by the Minister of Education of 6 December 1964 and 8 July 1965.

Cemeteries are reserved for Catholics only. While in the larger towns there are separate graveyards for non-Catholics, the burial of Protestants in the smaller communities is often only possible under degrading conditions.

Pastor Cardona Gregori quoted from the speeches of eight Spanish cardinals and bishops who had spoken against religious liberty at the Council, or at least called for restrictions for Spain. At the same time he pointed out the far-reaching significance of the Council for Spanish Protestants. The attitude of the Spanish authorities would depend entirely upon the general atmosphere at the Council in regard to the declaration on religious freedom.

APPENDIX

When, he asked, would the long-awaited "Protestant Statute" at last be promulgated, the statute on which the evangelical Christians of Spain had pinned their hopes?

Distribution of Bibles

José Flores, director of the British and Foreign Bible Society in Madrid, gave a survey of the distribution of Bibles in Spain. He had also asked Catholic publishers for figures and had received the following information:

Editorial Católica: Nacar-Colunga and Bover-Cantera editions (whole Bible and New Testament, since 1948)	3,314,000
AFEBE (Bible, New Testament, and four Gospels, since 1952)	2,100,000
Centro Bíblico Hispano-Americano (New Testament and four Gospels)	770,000
Editorial Verbo Divino (New Testament and four Gospels)	572,000
Editorial Herder: Ausejo edition (New Testament and four Gospels, since 1963)	350,000
Apostolado de la Prensa, Petisco-Torres Amat edition (Bible and New Testament)	164,000
Ediciones Paulinas	37,000

To this list must be added other smaller editions, as well as scholarly Biblical works in several volumes. At least 7.4 million copies of the Bible have been distributed from Catholic sources over the past twenty years. Flores also reported on the activities of the Pia Union Bíblica which plans to issue a further million free copies of the Bible in the near future in connection with a radio program. Its members are bound to dedicate themselves to the Bible apostolate and to daily Biblical meditation.

Flores made no special comment on these Catholic activities, but stressed the difficulties encountered on the Protestant side. An agreement with the Spanish government permitted the Bible Society to import or print only 2,070 Bibles, 4,167 New Testaments and 18,000 extracts from the Bible each year. For the 10,378

379

Bibles and 9,169 New Testaments imported since May, 1963, 396,000 pesetas ($6,600) had had to be paid in duty. According to the Spanish pastors, the copies available are insufficient for the work of evangelization.

Participants and Guests at the Conference

The conference reflected the variety of Spanish Protestantism. The 130 participants included the Bishop of the Episcopalian Church, Santos Molina, presidents of churches, pastors, preachers, elders, as well as men and women evangelists. They met by turns in six different churches belonging to the denominations mentioned above, 1–5. The eight speakers as well as the preachers and precentors for the services with which the proceedings began and ended were recruited from these same communities. Four Spanish Catholics as well as several foreign observers were present as guests. Greetings were conveyed personally by Brother Robert Taizé, the director of the Preachers' Seminary of the Evangelical Church in the Rhineland, a delegate from Italy and one from Australia, a woman evangelist from the American Ashram movement, and Fray Diez Moreno, director of the Ecumenical Diocesan Center in Madrid. The assembly formally expressed its thanks at the end of the conference for the participation of the Catholic guests, asking them to convey the brotherly greetings of evangelical Christians to their fellow Catholics.

The whole atmosphere was gratifyingly positive. Only very rarely was a note of sectarian fanaticism to be heard. For the most part speakers refrained from bitterness or invective. "Evangelical Christianity must not be anti-Catholic"—"Let us beware of encouraging fanatics"—"The Catholics have launched an intense Bible campaign; it is for us Protestants to set an example by living according to the Bible."

Tension and Differences

Naturally the many differences within the Protestant body at once became evident, the tension between the two wings of the Episcopalians and the Fundamentalists, for instance, or between the supporters of a charismatic and a legal church. Speakers regretted that there was no proper definition of what in fact constituted an Evangelical Christian. One speaker called for closer collaboration and intercommunication ("We Protestants in Spain are all in the same boat in the eyes of the others; we ought to try to adapt ourselves to this fact"), but this view met with sharp protests from other delegates. The conference chairman, a Baptist pastor, reminded the assembly of the need for a proper ecclesiology and a common understanding of the sacraments. There was a characteristic lack of theological reasoning in the approach to the problem discussed, which struck the foreign observer particularly. The World Council of Churches met with certain criticism, likewise the brand of Protestantism which denied the divinity of Christ.

The most critical but also the most outstanding speaker was a young Madrid pastor of I.E.E., Alberto Araujo, known among his friends as "the Spanish Calvin." In his view the present situation of Protestants in his country was due to intolerance, a national characteristic of the Spanish. "Perhaps we would be even less tolerant than the Catholics in their place." He spoke of the Protestant ideology of a religious longing which could not be satisfied by the Catholic Church and of the self-assurance which was rooted in his conviction. Intellectually, he maintained, Spanish Protestantism left much to be desired, indeed it was in many ways illiterate. It lagged behind in the field of Biblical studies and lacked any real theology. "Bible texts and appeals to attend church services aren't theology." Naturally these views met with criticism in the discussion which followed.

Doubts about Catholic Reforms

Humberto Capó, pastor of the I.E.E. in Palma de Mallorca, spoke of the developments in the Catholic Church in Spain. He wondered whether the present development was not merely a new device for strengthening the old chain of monopoly. "Renewal within the Catholic Church can only begin with one fact: with the recognition on the part of our Catholic brothers that they and their Church can be criticized and must be reformed. . . . There can be no Christian faith without true freedom to accept and to practice this faith. . . . The belief that the State can proclaim and defend,

381

even enforce, religion, confused Christianity with a culture, with a system, with mass movement." And: "The developments within the Catholic Church are in God's hands. . . . If they seem problematic to us, they also call for our own development, for our own renewal."

During the survey of relations between Protestants and Catholics speakers feared that the present *aggiornamento* was merely a particularly subtle form of Counter Reformation, that the Council was content with general declarations while in reality the same restrictions still existed. Several speakers criticized the "intransigence" of the Spanish bishops and their attitude at the Council. Ecumenism was an illusion, a useless appeal to those who were themselves oppressed. Today the goal was to remove discrimination of conscience. Spanish Protestants did not wish to continue as aliens, as pariahs, they wanted to be accepted as full members of the Spanish nation, sharing equal rights with their Catholic brothers.

A Catholic Voice

A Spanish Catholic layman, E. Miret Magdalena, made a deep impression on the assembly when he attempted to correct the distorted picture of Catholicism which was sometimes presented. Miret is president of the graduates of Catholic Action and secretary-general of the National Union of the Lay Apostolate. He writes articles for the Spanish illustrated weekly *Triunfo,* and is recognized as one of the foremost champions of reform in the Church. In the issue dated 9 October Miret wrote: "If we content ourselves simply with proclaiming the Gospel in words without living it in our own lives, then the testimony of the Church is doomed. We have seen this during the last centuries with our pragmatic attitude directed first against Protestantism, then against the progress of the modern world, and now against atheism. We have forgotten that Protestantism is not to be fought with condemnations but rather met with understanding for the problems raised by the Reformation. . . . But if we simply oppose everything brought about by the Reformation without discriminating between good and bad, we will only further the dechristianization of the world which is so evident today."

Bibliography

Abbott, Walter M., S.J. (ed.). *The Documents of Vatican II, with Notes and Comments by Catholic, Protestant and Orthodox Authorities.* New York: The America Press, 1966.

Aguado Bleye, Pedro, and Alcázar Molina, Cayetano. *Manual de historia de España.* 3 vols. Madrid: Espasa-Calpe, 1964.

Anuario de la prensa española. Madrid: Dirección General de Prensa, 1965.

Aranguren, José L. *Catolicismo y protestantismo como formas de existencia.* Madrid: Revista de Occidente, 1952.

Aranzadi, Estanislao de (ed.). *Repertorio cronológico de legislación, 1938, 1944.* Pamplona: Editorial Aranzadi, n.d.

Araujo García, Carlos, and Grubb, Kenneth G. *Religion in the Republic of Spain.* London: World Dominion Press, 1933.

Bainton, Roland H. *Hunted Heretic: The Life and Death of Michael Servetus, 1511–1553.* Boston: Beacon Press, 1960.

Balmes, Jaime. *Obras completas.* 8 vols. Madrid: Biblioteca de Autores Cristianos, 1949.

Bataillon, Marcel. *Erasmo y España: estudios sobre la historia espiritual del siglo XVI.* Translated by Antonio Alatorre. Mexico City: Fondo de Cultura Económica, 1950.

Boehmer, Edward. *Spanish Reformers of Two Centuries: Their Lives and Writings, According to the Late Benjamin B. Wiffen's Plan and With the Use of His Materials.* 2 vols. Strassburg: Karl Trübner; London: Trübner & Co., 1874.

Borrow, George H. *The Bible in Spain.* New York: E. P. Dutton & Co., Inc., 1961; J. M. Dent & Sons, Ltd., 1961.

Calvo Sotelo, Joaquín. *El proceso del Arzobispo Carranza.* Madrid: Sociedad General de Autores de España, 1964.

Caro Baroja, Julio. *Los judíos en la España moderna y contemporánea.* 3 vols. Madrid: Ediciones Arion, 1961.

Carrillo de Albornoz, Angel F. *Religious Liberty: A General Review of the Present Situation in the World.* Geneva: World Council of Churches, 1964.

Carrillo de Albornoz, Angel F. *Roman Catholicism and Religious Liberty*. Geneva: World Council of Churches, 1959.

Castro, Américo. *La realidad histórica de España*. Edición renovada. Mexico: Editorial Porrua, S.A., 1962.

Castro Cubells, Carlos. *El mensaje del Concilio*. Madrid: Los libros del monograma (Ediciones Cristiandad), 1966.

de los Rios, Fernando. *Religión y Estado en la España del siglo XVI*. 1st. ed. Mexico City: Fondo de Cultura Económica, 1957.

Delpech, Jacques. *The Oppression of Protestants in Spain*. Translated from the French by Tom and Dolores Johnson. Boston: Beacon Press, 1955; London: Lutterworth Press, 1956.

Desumbila, José. *El ecumenismo en España*. Barcelona: Editorial Estela, 1964.

Discursos y mensajes del Jefe del Estado, 1960–1963. Madrid: Dirección General de Información, 1964.

El Concordato de 1953. Madrid: Facultad de Derecho de la Universidad de Madrid, 1956.

El pensamiento político de Franco. Selección y sistematización de textos por Agustín del Rio Cisneros. Madrid: Servicio Informativo Nacional, 1964.

Escrivá, José María. *Camino*. 22nd Castilian ed. Madrid: Ediciones Rialp, 1963.

Estruch, Juan. *Ecumenismo, actitud espiritual: aportación y testimonio de un protestante español*. Barcelona: Editorial Nova Terra, 1965.

Gutiérrez Marín, Manuel. *Fe y Acción: ética cristiana existencial*. Madrid: Editorial Irmayol, 1965.

La iglesia habla de España. Madrid: Servicio Informativo Español, 1964.

La Souchère, Elaine de. *An Explanation of Spain*. New York: Random House, 1964.

Ligorio, San Alfonso María de. *Obras ascéticas*. 2 vols. Madrid: Biblioteca de Autores Cristianos, 1954.

Madariaga, Salvador de. *Spain, A Modern History*. New York: Frederick A. Praeger, 1958; London: Jonathan Cape, 1942, 1946.

Marañón, Gregorio. *Españoles fuera de España*. 5th ed. Madrid: Espasa-Calpe, S.A. (Colección Austral, No. 710), 1961.

———— *Don Juan: ensayos sobre el origen de su leyenda*. 10th ed. Madrid: Espasa-Calpe, S.A. (Colección Austral, No. 129), 1964.

McCrie, Thomas. *Historia de la Reforma en España en el siglo XVI.* Translated by Adam F. Sosa. 2nd ed. Buenos Aires: Editorial La Aurora; Mexico City: Casa Unida de Publicaciones, 1950.

Medina, León, and Marañón, Manuel (eds.). *Leyes penales de España.* Madrid: Instituto Industrial Reus, 1947.

Menéndez Pelayo, Marcelino. *Historia de los heterodoxos españoles.* 2 vols. Madrid: Biblioteca de Autores Cristianos, 1956.

Ortega y Gasset, José. *Obras inéditas: Vives-Goethe.* Madrid: Revista de Occidente, 1961.

Pemán, José María. *La historia de España contada con sencillez.* 5th ed. Madrid: Escelicer, 1958.

Pérez-Embid, Florentino (ed.). *Forjadores del mundo contemporáneo.* 4 vols. Barcelona: Editorial Planeta, 1963.

Procesos inquisitoriales contra la familia judía de Juan Luis Vives. I. Proceso contra Blanquina March, madre del humanista. Introducción y transcripción de Miguel de la Pinta Llorente, O.S.A. y José María de Palacio y de Palacio, Marqués de Villareal de Alava. Madrid: Instituto Arias Montano, Consejo Superior de Investigaciones Científicas, 1964.

Quinlan, Maurice (ed.). *Guide for Living. An Approved Selection of Letters and Addresses of His Holiness Pope Pius XII.* London: Pan Books Ltd., 1958.

Suenens, León José, Cardenal. *Promoción apostólica de la religiosa en el mundo de hoy.* Bilbao: Desclée de Brouwer, 1965.

Valdés, Alfonso de. *Diálogo de las cosas ocurridas en Roma.* Madrid: Ediciones de "La Lectura," 1928.

Valdés, Juan de. *Alfabeto Christiano. A Faithful Reprint of the Italian of 1546: With Two Modern Translations in Spanish and in English.* London, 1861.

———— *Diálogo de la doctrina cristiana, nuevamente compuesto por un religioso.* Madrid: Librería Nacional y Extranjera, 1929.

———— *Diálogo de la lengua.* 4th ed. Madrid: Espasa-Calpe (Colección Austral, No. 216), 1964.

Index

387